COMING OF AGE IN THE OTHER AMERICA

Stefanie DeLuca,
Susan Clampet-Lundquist,
and Kathryn Edin

Russell Sage Foundation
New York

The Russell Sage Foundation

The Russell Sage Foundation, one of the oldest of America's general purpose foundations, was established in 1907 by Mrs. Margaret Olivia Sage for "the improvement of social and living conditions in the United States." The foundation seeks to fulfill this mandate by fostering the development and dissemination of knowledge about the country's political, social, and economic problems. While the foundation endeavors to assure the accuracy and objectivity of each book it publishes, the conclusions and interpretations in Russell Sage Foundation publications are those of the authors and not of the foundation, its trustees, or its staff. Publication by Russell Sage, therefore, does not imply foundation endorsement.

Library of Congress Cataloging-in-Publication Data

Names: DeLuca, Stefanie, author. | Clampet-Lundquist, Susan, author. | Edin, Kathryn, 1962– author.
Title: Coming of age in the other America / Stefanie DeLuca, Susan Clampet-Lundquist, and Kathryn Edin.
Description: New York : Russell Sage Foundation, [2016]
Identifiers: LCCN 2015048206 (print) | LCCN 2016004557 (ebook) | ISBN 9780871544650 (paperback) | ISBN 9781610448581 (ebook)
Subjects: LCSH: Urban youth—United States—Social conditions. | Poor youth—United States—Social conditions. | Youth development—United States. | Education, Urban—United States. | Inner cities—United States. | Social mobility—United States. | BISAC: SOCIAL SCIENCE / Sociology / Urban. | SOCIAL SCIENCE / Ethnic Studies / General. | SOCIAL SCIENCE / Poverty & Homelessness.
Classification: LCC HQ796 .D3937 2016 (print) | LCC HQ796 (ebook) | DDC 305.2350973/091732—dc23
LC record available at http://cp.mcafee.com/d/1jWVIe43qb3X5NP3XypKVJeVEV
vd7arPOpEVdFTd7bVEVjud7ab1JeVEVvd7arPPa9J56XxEVspouhdGX6TDR1kqqh
_w09Kdd8_M04Szrn26KfZvAkkkjhOqekneLsKCCYVOqqa8UQsCzAtR4kRHFGTd7b
DaxVZicHs3jq9J4TvAn3hOYyyODtUTsS03fJq77RJN6FD4XELToujKUrJiHoafHrydj9JBVB
wS91Emd426PQQgeRyq83hOeuKYehvoosvKrjsdNy7xXANd

The paper used in this publication meets the minimum requirements of American National Standard for Information Sciences—Permanence of Paper for Printed Library Materials. ANSI Z39.48-1992.

Text design by Suzanne Nichols.

RUSSELL SAGE FOUNDATION
112 East 64th Street, New York, New York 10065

10 9 8 7 6 5 4 3 2 1

We dedicate this book to the more than three hundred youth, parents, and teachers who participated in our research. Thank you for letting us into your lives. We hope that our rendering of your stories does justice to your remarkable journeys, and that you inspire our readers as much as you have inspired us.

Contents |

List of Illustrations |

About the Authors |

STEFANIE DELUCA is associate professor of sociology at Johns Hopkins University.

SUSAN CLAMPET-LUNDQUIST is associate professor of sociology at Saint Joseph's University.

KATHRYN EDIN is Bloomberg Distinguished Professor of Sociology and Public Health at Johns Hopkins University.

Preface | "Baltimore City, You're Breaking My Heart"

THE EVENTS OF April 2015 catapulted Baltimore onto the national (and international) stage. The story is now well known. On April 12, 2015, Freddie Gray, a young African American, was taken into police custody after making eye contact with officers patrolling near the Gilmor Homes. Gray died a week later from the injuries he sustained during his subsequent ride in a police transport van. In the days that followed, controversy over the cause of Gray's death reached a boiling point. On the afternoon of April 27, police clashed with black high school students at the Mondawmin Mall, setting off a chain reaction that spilled over into the surrounding neighborhood as some residents began looting, destroying property, and setting fire to cars. The media labeled these events a riot and blamed the youth at the mall for inciting the unrest. Yet the students had been doing what they do every day, trying to catch the bus after school—until they were greeted by a phalanx of police in riot gear and told to disperse. Then they learned that bus service had been suspended, leaving many with no way to get home.

There is no definitive account of how the confrontation at Mondawmin truly went down or who was to blame. What we do know is that the unrest prompted public officials to call in roughly five thousand National Guard troops, plus law enforcement officials from the surrounding area, who would occupy Baltimore for days. Police helicopters swarmed overhead as protesters marched, often ending their rallies at the intersection of Pennsylvania and North avenues (the heart of the unrest), the Western District Police Department, or City Hall. Each night as curfew approached area clergy held hands, creating a human wall between angry protesters and the police. With footage of these events in hand, reporters had no problem following a familiar script, painting Baltimore as burned out and hopeless. A pervasive narrative about Baltimore's youth was also stoked as an African American mayor, and even the nation's first black president, castigated at least a segment of them as "thugs."

Some journalists used the occasion to dig deeper into Baltimore's egregious past and explore the roots of the unrest—the city's ugly history of legalized racial segregation, the displacement of African American communities through urban renewal, and more recently, the destabilization of black communities by a wave of foreclosures driven by unscrupulous lending institutions that intentionally targeted African Americans for subprime loans.[1] But others invoked individual-level explanations for the deep poverty that held communities like Freddie Gray's Sandtown in a chokehold.[2] Just weeks after the unrest, David Brooks opined in the *New York Times* that "the real barriers to mobility are matters of social psychology,"[3] continuing a line of argument he'd begun a month earlier when he wrote that the suffering of poor communities is primarily due to deficient norms ("Do [people] have the freedom of self-control or are [they] in bondage to [their] desires?" he asked).[4]

News coverage of events following Freddie Gray's death only amplified the view that Baltimore's African American youth should be feared and controlled. One expression of this assessment, penned about a year before the unrest, went viral online. Following the murders of two neighborhood residents, Tracey Halvorsen, a white professional living in the Upper Fell's Point, raged in a blogpost entitled "Baltimore City, You're Breaking My Heart," that she was "tired of being looked at like prey" and "tired of looking at eleven-year-olds as potential thieves, muggers and murderers on my walk home from the office." She said she was "tired of reading about juveniles arrested for violent crimes who are let go because if it's not a 'murder' case, there's no time to worry about it."[5] Halverson's recommendation: more police.

The essay set off a citywide debate argued in the *City Paper, Baltimore Brew,* and online forums, with many of the critical posts pointing to the city's long-standing racial divide. One particularly pointed response read: "What breaks my heart is when someone says they are tired of looking at black youth in the city as potential predators, as if they are the ones at fault . . . when someone of seeming affluent white privilege seems so far removed from so much of the city and its residents, and can only seem concerned with how these problems are affecting her and those like her."[6]

At the time these events were unfolding, we had spent more than ten years conducting fieldwork with 150 black Baltimore youth who were born in the late 1980s and early 1990s to parents who lived in what had become the city's poorest and most violent environs: Baltimore public housing. Most hailed from high-rise developments, like those featured on David Simon's vivid HBO series *The Wire.* Yet the story that had unfolded over our decade of research was strikingly different from the "thug" narrative spun by politicians and news anchors alike. Despite childhoods of extreme disadvantage, our study of the unfolding lives of these youth offered a strong corrective to the popular perception of this group as being swept up in crime and delinquency and responsible for turning the city into a "complete shit-hole war zone," as Halvorsen characterized it.[7]

We followed these youth from childhood through adolescence and into young adulthood, talking to their parents, siblings, and teachers along the way. Contrary to the conventional wisdom, getting "caught up" in "the game" was far from the norm—by their own accounts, fewer than one in five had been "in the street" for even a brief time. Instead, the large majority were actively resisting the street, determined to be "about something else," and hungry for postsecondary education and careers. Most scorned the drug dealers and other hustlers who dominated the public space of their neighborhood and instead strove to model themselves after the nurses, forensic scientists, lawyers, bus drivers, dentists, carpenters, cosmetologists, social workers, chefs, police officers, or small business owners they hoped to become. The large majority finished high school and went on to college or trade school. Few got addicted to alcohol or drugs. Eighty percent found work in the formal sector after high school. And they did so while continuing to struggle against neighborhood risk and the trauma of coming of age in families often plagued by addiction, violence, and financial strife.

Such stories are rendered invisible in the glare of attention on the most sensational aspects of urban America. When covering an isolated incident of looting, it is easy for viewers to believe that the extreme is the norm. This is not to say that the city's youth do not face challenges. Poor children growing up in Baltimore are less likely to escape poverty than those growing up in any other city in the nation.[8] Paired with the strong mainstream aspirations of the large majority of the youth we studied, however, this finding suggests that the issue for youth in Baltimore is not a matter of "social psychology," to use David Brooks's words. Instead, it is further evidence of how much work there is to be done to keep structural barriers from neutralizing the ambitions of those raised in poverty.

Baltimore has changed in ways we never imagined since these young people were born. Baltimore's high-rise public housing has been torn down, and some of it has been replaced by mixed-income developments in neighborhoods that bring residents of varied incomes into close proximity. In the Inner Harbor, empty lots and rotting warehouses have been replaced by farm-to-table restaurants, coffee shops, galleries, and the like. Industrial areas that had been dormant for decades are now bustling with millennials and empty-nesters residing in new upscale condos and apartments. Baltimore's port, once on the edge of extinction, has seen a surge of containers moving into its channel.[9] Baltimore is not Brooklyn, by any means, but new life is being breathed into some blocks once previously lined with only vacant homes.

The unrest of April 2015 revealed in appalling clarity, however, that the benefits of this painstaking progress have not been equally shared. African American communities in particular have not reaped the dividends of the city's revitalization. Worse, in the wake of the April 2015 unrest, black neighborhoods saw a dramatic spike in homicide and violent crime, exacerbating residents' feelings of fragility and uncertainty about how to move forward and repair the damage and mistrust that had been building for generations.[10]

There is much work to be done in Baltimore, a city whose problems are a microcosm for much of what plagues cities across America. The roots and realities of these problems are invisible to most middle-class and upper-class Americans, who are largely unaware of the grinding routine of survival that more than forty-five million poor people in this country endure every day. This is the America that Michael Harrington powerfully wrote about in his classic book, *The Other America: Poverty in the United States*, over fifty years ago. Harrington brought to life the hidden suffering of the poor, and in doing so, galvanized a generation of policy-makers, social scientists, and activists.[11] Over a half-century later, we are living in times marked by even more economic inequality, and there still exists an "other" America—one where you can play by the rules and still not make it out of poverty. In the pages that follow, we describe what it's like to grow up in the "other" America.

Acknowledgments |

THIS BOOK IS the culmination of more than thirteen years of collaborative work, made possible by the generosity of the funders, colleagues, students, friends, and family we thank here. Our words only begin to capture our gratitude.

The first wave of the MTO Qualitative Study in Baltimore (MTOQ5) was generously funded by the Russell Sage Foundation, from 2003–2004, and administered through the National Bureau of Economic Research.[1] At Princeton, the Center for Research on Child Wellbeing provided two postdoctoral fellowships for the first year of the MTOQ5 study, and the Center for Health and Wellbeing provided one postdoctoral fellowship for the next two years of coding and analyzing the data from this first wave. Jeffrey Kling, then at the Center for Health and Wellbeing, secured funding for summer salaries for Princeton undergraduate students to transcribe and code interviews from MTOQ5, as well as funding for another full-time research assistant to code the youth and teacher interviews. We are also very grateful to the significant commitment that the William T. Grant Foundation made to our project. The foundation funded the MTOQ10 pilot study in 2006, and provided the primary support for the 2010–2012 MTOQ10 fieldwork, analysis, and writing through a major grant.[2] The William T. Grant Foundation also funded writing and analysis time for Stefanie DeLuca through a Faculty Scholars Award from 2008–2012.[3]

Ann Owens and Susan Clampet-Lundquist conducted their analysis of neighborhood poverty data and mobility patterns for Baltimore MTO households through a research grant from the Center for Poverty Research at the University of California, Davis. This analysis provided the measures that we used in this book for neighborhood poverty. Stefanie DeLuca received additional support for writing and analysis through fellowships from the Spencer Foundation and the Century Foundation.[4]

We have greatly appreciated the support of staff in the Office of Policy Development and Research at the Department of Housing and Urban Development, especially Todd Richardson, Mark Shroder, Ronald Hill, and Elizabeth Rudd. Over the last decade, we have benefitted from conversations and conferences with other social scientists involved in MTO research, including Xavier de Souza Briggs, Greg Duncan, John Goering, Jeff Kling, Jens Ludwig, and Susan Popkin. We also thank Alex Polikoff, Barbara Samuels, Philip Tegeler, Mike Daniel, Demetria McCain, and Betsy Julian for inspiring us through their fight to provide better neighborhoods and schools for our nation's most disadvantaged families and children.

The Department of Sociology at Johns Hopkins University provided administrative and grant support for DeLuca and Kathryn Edin. At Johns Hopkins, we received unparalleled administrative support from Megan Prior, Terri Thomas, Jean Free, Nancy Foltz, Jessie Albee, and Trinard Sharpe. Through the Summer Scholars program, Saint Joseph's University provided an undergraduate research assistant for Susan Clampet-Lundquist for two summers to work on coding and analyzing youth interviews across MTOQ5, the pilot study, and MTOQ10.

As we note in more detail in the Study History and Appendix, the work we conducted in Baltimore was a truly collaborative effort, a project we could not have done alone. First, we thank the other fieldworkers who conducted the interviews and ethnographic observations. For MTOQ5 (2003–2004), we thank Annette Waters, Alessandra Del Conte Dickovick, Rebecca Kissane, Anita Zuberi, and Jennifer Pashup. For MTOQ10 (2010–2012), we thank Melody Boyd, Barbara Condliffe, Siri Warkentien, Tracey Shollenberger, Peter Rosenblatt, Eva Rosen, Kathryn Mercogliano, Bridget Davis, Marisa Edin-Nelson, Kaitlin Edin-Nelson, Megan Holland, Queenie Zhu, Carly Knight, Jacqueline Hwang, Tanya Lukasik, and Anna Westin. For the ethnographic component (2012–2014), we thank Jennifer Darrah, Anna Rhodes, Elizabeth Talbert, Brielle Bryan, Peter Rosenblatt, Eva Rosen, and Phil Garboden. We especially thank Gretchen Wright and Melody Boyd for their assistance with grant support and coding. Jessica Wallace and Margaret Prisinzano, students from Saint Joseph's University, along with Melody Boyd and Peter Rosenblatt, diligently coded all the transcripts from MTOQ10.

Additional coding, reliability, and data analysis for the book was conducted by Holly Koogler, Robert Francis, Allison Young, Blythe George, Kevin Wells, Juliana Wittman, Jason Wright, and Olivia Long. Jeffrey Grigg and Curt Cronister at Johns Hopkins School of Education and the Baltimore Education Research Consortium generously provided data for our analyses of the Baltimore City Public Schools. Siri Warkentien conducted supplemental analyses from the NLSY97, and Erik Westlund provided additional feedback on national trends in college selectivity, affordability, and default rates. Erin Brereton copyedited the original draft of the manuscript.

A number of colleagues generously gave feedback on earlier versions of the manuscript. We are grateful to: Karl Alexander, Monica Bell, Nancy Deutsch, Eva Rosen, Jennifer Darrah, Andrew Cherlin, Tim Nelson, Keith Brown, Jill Amitrani Welsh, Anna Rhodes, Phil Garboden, Brian Adams, Jason Wright, Daniel Schlozman, Michael Oakes, Richard Settersten (and his students at Oregon State), Nicholas Papageorge, Elizabeth Talbert, Holly Koogler, Julia Burdick-Will, Meredith Greif, Robert Francis, and Allison Young. The book also benefitted from the sharp and thoughtful feedback of DeLuca's undergraduate students, including: Christian Cholish, Gillian Waldo, Matthew Nicola, Kennedy McDaniel, Camille Corbett, Charltien Long, Dana Schulman, Ritchie Assini, Rachel Becker, Hana Clemens, Jessica Cohen, Stephanie Irwin, Simon Marshall-Shah, Udy Obot, Ellie Park, Kathryn Rees, Jefferson Riera, Katherine Ross, Olivia Seideman, Natalie Soliozy, and Kevin Wells.

In addition to the intellectual energy and vitality of our colleagues, we could not have done this without the unwavering support of our closest friends and family members. Stefanie DeLuca thanks her research support team for providing the will to believe, and a steady supply of sushi, cycling, good wine, and dark humor. A million thanks to: Brian Adams, Rina Agarwala, Karl Alexander, Kathy Alexander, Jessica Ames, Deborah Berman, Keith Brennan, Erin Brereton, Jeff Brown, Grace Chan, Jessica Chen, Casey Cole, Regina Deil-Amen, Lynn DeLuca, Keith Demoura, Greg Duncan, Marisa Edin-Nelson, Kaitlin Edin-Nelson, Meredith Greif, Daniel Gubits, Sarah Gubits, Natalie Gubits, Virginia Jordan, Mike Jordan, Piper Jordan, Erik Meyers, Heather Moss, Michael Oakes, Kimberly Peck, Michael Resnick, Lisa Reynolds, Danielle Rockstad, Eva Rosen, Jim Rosenbaum (for taking a chance on a new graduate student in 1997), Dee Settar, Steve Siewerski, Mason Throneburg, Ben Timberlake, Dolores Walshe, Ed Walshe, Caroline Walshe, Sara Walters, Jason Wright, Twenty20 Cycling (Johnny, Michael, Ross, Tommy), and the staff at Minato Sushi. Stefanie gives special thanks to Salvatore DeLuca and Jennifer Walshe. Salvatore was there from the beginning and never wavered. Thank you for having faith in me, Dad—I would not be here without you. Jennifer Walshe has been a constant, from Englehart Hall at Northwestern to our careers and everything after. Jen, thank you for inspiring me, and keeping me full of wonder and hope.

Susan Clampet-Lundquist offers endless thanks to her family—Merrill, Magdalena and Sophia Clampet-Lundquist, as well as Mary and Jerry Clampet and Margaret Lundquist—who have patiently listened to story after story, supported me in countless ways, and have tiptoed around me

throughout the intense periods of writing. Thank you for graciously giving me the space and the motivation to continue digging.

Kathryn Edin thanks the Institute for Policy Research at Northwestern University (under the direction of Fay Lomax Cook) and the Malcolm Wiener Center for Social Policy (directed by Julie Wilson and then Bruce Western) for their excellent support in the implementation of this work.

Chapter 1 | "Different Privileges That Different People Inherit": Social Reproduction and the Transition to Adulthood

ONE IMPORTANT, LONG-HELD American belief is that the family a child is born into does not determine her destiny. Yet increasingly, social science has called that core belief into question. Economists show that the rate of intergenerational mobility in the United States is surprisingly low compared to other wealthy countries.[1] Parents' socioeconomic status is not the only thing holding children back—race matters too. If a child is born black and poor, for example, her chances of ending up in poverty as an adult are one and a half times higher than they are for her white counterpart from a poor family.[2] Figuring out why the American Dream is so far out of reach for some has been social science's focus for decades.

In 1982, Karl Alexander and Doris Entwisle set out to explore how children adjusted to their first years of schooling. What began as a modest study of early elementary school students ended up as a groundbreaking twenty-five-year look at the relative importance of family background and schooling in the lives of urban children. The Beginning School Study enrolled about eight hundred young black and white children and their parents from twenty elementary schools in Baltimore and followed them through age thirty, surveying them repeatedly and collecting data on their schools, teachers, test scores, and grades. Three decades later, their 2014 book (with Linda Olson), *The Long Shadow,* offered an answer to the question that scholars have long posed: who gets ahead?[3] Although variation in some aspects of their schooling did contribute to children's outcomes at age thirty, parents' income and race yielded a much more dramatic effect.

1

As Alexander put it, "The implication is where you start out in life is where you end up."[4]

The Long Shadow shows that while 45 percent of children with higher-income parents ended up with college degrees, only 4 percent of those with poor parents did. At age twenty-two, 89 percent of white high school dropouts were employed, compared to fewer than half that figure—40 percent—of blacks without a high school degree. White men from poor backgrounds had the lowest rate of college attendance and completion of any group, yet they fared better than their black counterparts because more had access to lucrative blue-collar jobs through their social networks. The industrial and construction sectors employed 45 percent of white men in the study, but only 15 percent of black males. Even among those in these working-class jobs, white men's earnings were nearly twice those of African American men.[5]

This isn't just a Baltimore story. Other scholars have shown that Alexander and Entwisle's results, while stark, have been reflected nationwide over the last thirty years. Family background and a history of racially discriminatory housing policies have continued to yield a strong influence on where children end up in life, and being born poor and black suppresses life chances to a frightening degree.[6]

Despite these sobering findings, we argue that social reproduction—children ending up "stuck" in the same place as their parents—is far from inevitable. We show that social policy has the power to interrupt the intergenerational transmission of disadvantage, and that when it does, children's trajectories can change dramatically. Young people's agency matters too. Even those coming from some of the most challenging situations can reach toward a brighter future if they manage to take hold of key resources that confer meaning and identity—a strong sense of what they are "about" and not about. Yet this book also shows that, despite their resilience and hard work, the strong undertow of the social origins of disadvantaged youth—the long shadow—can claw at their ambitions "like crabs in a bucket," as one youth said. When combined with the institutional traps that youth encounter in the pursuit of postsecondary education, these forces can shortchange the dreams of even the grittiest and most determined.

Twenty years after Alexander began enrolling first-graders in the Beginning School Study, we initiated a decade-long study of a cohort of Baltimore parents and youth who had hailed from public housing in the mid-1990s, most of them from four notorious high-rise developments in Baltimore City: Flag House Courts, Lexington Terrace, Lafayette Courts, and the Murphy Homes. Others came from highly distressed low-rises across the city. The study was an attempt to understand the transition to adulthood for poor minority young people, a group who had largely been left out of the literature on that topic. And while we did indeed accomplish that aim, our research also provided a unique opportunity to look under the hood of studies like *The Long Shadow* to understand, in rich detail, the processes and mechanisms underlying the disturbing immobility and high rate of social reproduction that Alexander and others have documented. Perhaps more importantly, we were also able to explore how to interrupt that cycle.

The youth in our study shared unique origins. As young children, all lived in highly distressed public housing projects that were some of the most physically and socially degraded spaces in our nation. Their parents' characteristics could hardly have been more disadvantaged. Only about one-quarter of these youth had a parent with a high school education, much less a college degree (only 13 percent ever attempted college).[7] Just under half had a parent who had been incarcerated while growing up, while just as many told us that their mother or father had struggled with alcohol or drugs. More than two-thirds had a parent or primary caregiver who was employed in 2010, but many of them worked at low-wage jobs and struggled to maintain steady work. As a consequence, nearly all of the youth in our study had spent the majority of their childhood years in poverty.

Yet in the mid-1990s, when these children were zero to ten, their parents had signed up for a program called Moving To Opportunity (MTO) that would enable them to escape the projects via a voucher with a special stipulation—they would have to find an apartment in a low-poverty neighborhood and remain there for at least a year. Because the program was part of a federal experiment, some of these parents won the coin flip and got the voucher while others—who landed in the control group—did not. Of the winners, roughly 60 percent managed to move with the program. Although our study sampled families across these groups, our book does not concentrate on MTO.[8] Instead, we consider more broadly how young people from deeply disadvantaged origins navigate the transition to adulthood.

This book centers mostly on the 2010 wave of our study. In that wave we focused on young people who were between fifteen and twenty-four, and because of our interest in observing youth in the transition to adulthood, we oversampled those who were nineteen or older. From a sample of 200 youth—stratified by gender, program group (experimental or control), and age—who had participated in a 2009 survey wave as part of the mobility experiment, we interviewed 150 young women and men between June and November 2010. We spent several hours with each of these young people—sitting at kitchen tables, on front stoops, at booths in

McDonald's, in basement bedrooms, in cars, or at the park. In 2012, we identified twenty youth who we felt represented the range of outcomes—positive and negative—that we had observed in 2010. After an initial lengthy conversation to catch up, we arranged an informal interaction with each youth at a place and time of his or her choosing. We hung out with these youth at home, at the mall, at a restaurant, or the park; on a drive around the neighborhood; during a trip to an ice cream shop; or, in one case, a visit to a doctor's office for a sonogram. We also accompanied these youth to important events in their lives: a child custody hearing, an eviction, a move into an apartment, and so on. The frequency and length of these interactions varied according to the willingness and availability of each young adult.

One particularly rich feature of the study is that there is significant overlap in the interviews and observations among family members. By luck of random draw, one-third (fifty-one) of the youth we interviewed in 2010 were children of parents we had interviewed in 2003–2004. Thirteen of the youth had also been interviewed in that round. Another fifteen had been observed in school, where we had also interviewed their teachers. And in eighteen cases we had conducted interviews with one of their siblings in the earlier wave. (We provide a more detailed description of our study in appendix A.)

How were these young people faring in early adulthood? At first glance, the experiences of these youth would seem to support the social reproduction narrative, much like that told by Alexander and his colleagues. After following these youth over a decade's time, we observed that around 20 percent had dropped out before completing high school. And while most graduates tried some form of postsecondary education, the rate of completion was abysmally low. Only fifteen of the eighty-six who had graduated from high school matriculated to a four-year college, and of those, two had already dropped out by the study's end. Most of the rest were attending community college or a for-profit trade school, often in fits and starts. By the end of our study, thirty-eight were still enrolled in some form of postsecondary education. Forty had gone directly into the labor market after graduation, but at the time of our last interview none had a job that could lift a family of four above the poverty line. Twenty-seven were neither in school nor employed when we last spoke with them. And nearly one in five, by their own admission, had gotten involved in the drug trade or committed a serious crime—crimes for which most of them could have been charged as felons—at some point during adolescence or early adulthood.

But that is only one way to tell the story. In-depth conversations and informal interactions with these youth and their parents over that decade revealed that at the cusp of adulthood they were not as different from their more affluent peers as one might expect. Most were, in fact, doing exactly what young people their age are supposed to be doing—discovering what they were "about," cultivating dreams, and engaging in a quest to "become somebody." Most—more than eight out of ten—had not become caught up in delinquent behavior or crime. Instead, the large majority had bought into the dream of college, a career, homeownership, marriage, and family.

Another way to understand the lives of these youth is in comparison to their parents' lives. Here we see that more than seven in ten of our youth completed high school (or a GED) compared to only about one-quarter in the parents' generation. Just over half of the youth not enrolled in high school had entered college or trade school, as compared to only 13 percent of their parents. More than 80 percent of the young people not in school either held a job when we last spoke with them or had done so recently. In contrast, only about one in four had parents who had been employed in the mid-1990s (when they were in their late twenties or early thirties on average). In sum, as shown in greater detail in chapter 2, we see large intergenerational gains in the domains of educational attainment, employment, and risk behavior.

At the heart of this book is the complex reality that both ways of reading these numbers are true. Our story is one of a glass half full and a glass half empty. These youth achieved far more than their parents. Most showed remarkable perseverance and optimism in reaching for mainstream goals while resisting the street as they moved through adolescence and into young adulthood. Many aspired to be nurses, electricians, police officers, social workers, restaurateurs, military officers, or teachers. Yet when we left them in 2012, too few had become all that they hoped to be—and were probably capable of becoming.

This book considers what inspired those intergenerational gains before going on to describe what made the gains possible—the rich and vital inner lives that sustained these young people as they fought against the riptide of family background and ongoing neighborhood risk while reaching for a better future. Finally, these youths' unfolding lives cast a bright light on the exploitative traps in the labor and postsecondary educational markets, often explicitly aimed at young people pushed by tough economic circumstances to take an expedited path to adulthood. We find that these traps cut dreams short and kept even some of the hardest-working, most ambitious youth from achieving their potential, relegating them instead to low-wage, unstable jobs at or near the bottom of the economy.

THE OUTLINE OF THE BOOK

Given that these young people were living in or near Baltimore—one of America's tougher cities by most measures—and they were reaching adulthood right as the Great Recession hit, how did so many complete high school, enroll in some kind of postsecondary training, stay clear of trouble, and find work? Our questions only grew when we contrasted what we gleaned from the youth with the narratives we had gathered from the cohort of 124 parents we interviewed in 2003–2004. These kids' lives were nothing like their parents' lives. As indicated earlier, when we talked with the parent cohort, many admitted that they had been or were currently addicted to alcohol or drugs, quite a few had been to prison and jail, few had finished high school, and only a handful had even tried college.

Looking deeper into these young people's residential trajectories, we noticed something we had not considered before. Granted, those who moved by using the special voucher from the housing mobility program saw a huge reduction in neighborhood poverty. *But virtually everyone else also ended up in less-poor neighborhoods over time.* How was this possible? As it turned out, a number of policy initiatives on the federal and state levels, such as HOPE VI, led to a huge drop in the supply of public housing units in the city of Baltimore, virtually all of which had been clustered within the city's highest-poverty neighborhoods. Nearly all of the complexes our families had been living in when the study began were either partially or totally destroyed, often within a few years after the housing mobility experiment began. So many of those who had been relegated to the control group moved too—usually with a voucher—and almost always to neighborhoods that were far less poor. Citywide, with that wave of demolition, the number of Baltimoreans living in areas of highly concentrated poverty fell dramatically, as did the number of neighborhoods that remained extremely poor. In a city where segregation runs deep, racial segregation measures hardly moved, but those for income segregation did.

We interviewed parents and youth for the first time in 2003–2004, and while some remained in public housing developments, many had left— through the MTO program, because their unit had been lost in the wave of demolition that swept the city in the 1990s and early 2000s, or for other reasons. By the time we returned in 2010, only 15 of the 150 youth we would interview that summer remained in public housing. As we discuss in chapter 2, MTO and HOPEVI were very distinct policy approaches. Each had considerable shortcomings, and neither policy helped many families enter what we would consider high opportunity neighborhoods with significantly higher performing schools. As a result, most still spent the majority of their childhoods in communities that contained considerable risk—the average rate of neighborhood poverty over the fifteen or so years since their parents had been randomly assigned through MTO was about 30 percent. Even so, this was a large improvement from where they had come from: in those neighborhoods poverty had averaged over 50 percent but could reach 60 or even 70 percent.

Thus, the question we consider in chapter 2 is whether there is at least speculative evidence for what the social science literature calls a "neighborhood effect." In short, we consider what happened to a group of children with highly disadvantaged origins who were offered access to a much broader range of imagined futures than had been available to their parents—many of whom had spent much of their lives in public housing or other very poor neighborhoods. Did these youth benefit not only from living in less-poor neighborhoods but also from a greater exposure to neighbors who worked, held college degrees, and lived in two-parent families? Were these young people's behaviors and aspirations in fact a profound testament to the power of neighborhoods to transform lives?

Despite the large intergenerational gains observed across a wide array of outcomes—from risky behavior to educational attainment to employment—we observed significant heterogeneity in the paths of these youth as they approached adulthood. We saw youth who enrolled in college and those who tried to find stability in the labor market, but we also saw disconnected youth—those who were floundering and a few who turned to the street, hustling drugs. What separates young people who stay on track from those who do not? For every two and a half young people in our study who were on track in 2010, there was one young adult who had fallen through the cracks. In chapter 3, we try to identify the key ingredient that distinguished who ended up where.

As we began to explore this question we looked at all of the usual suspects. Were the winners the kids who landed in the best neighborhoods? Did they have the least-troubled home lives or go to the best schools? Though we saw some associations when we considered these possibilities, particularly for the handful of youth who had been lucky enough to gain entrance to one of the top Baltimore magnet high schools (as we show in chapter 5), there was no clear story to be told. About as many kids in the experimental group succeeded in staying on track as the controls; even many with troubled home lives or parents addicted to drugs managed to stay away from trouble and adhere to mainstream norms and aspirations, while some kids from strong families strayed.

Another candidate from the literature on youth achievement remained to be explored. James Heckman, an economist from the University of Chicago, and Angela Duckworth, a psychologist from the University of Pennsylvania, along with others, have introduced pioneering new research showing the importance of personality traits like delayed gratification and self-control, which can be measured at an early age through novel experiments such as the famed marshmallow test (give a kid a marshmallow, tell her if she resists eating it that she will get two, and then see how long she holds out). Over time the most consequential of these personality traits—grit, the persistence toward long-term goals—proved to be a better predictor of adult outcomes than traditional indicators of cognitive ability, as measured by test scores. This research has encouraged a wave of efforts to boost noncognitive skills and character traits in young people.

Intrigued by these findings, we began to comb the narratives for instances where kids showed evidence of grit—which was where we ran into trouble. Given these young people's origins, examples of grit abounded. Almost all had had to endure—*and persist in the face of*—any number of almost unbelievable hardships: the death of multiple loved ones, sometimes as a result of violence; homelessness; hunger; older siblings in prison or jail; removal from the parental home on allegations of child abuse and neglect; spells in foster care; and directly witnessing murder or coming across a dead body in an alley. More generally, even given the high prevalence of on-track behaviors and goals, the street was a force that many of them had to reckon with each and every day. It pulled at them, tempted them, and polluted public spaces in such a way that a simple trip home from school could be an exercise in deft navigation that bore some semblance to a military operation.[9] In short, it required remarkable grit just to get through the day—the kind of grit that most people from middle-class origins cannot even imagine being able to muster as a child.

Over time, among the families we were lucky enough to follow, we began to see a wearing down of sorts during adolescence. Despite the decrease in neighborhood poverty and the increase in exposure to neighbors with characteristics that reflected mainstream norms, many of the youth still had to deal with more than their share of crime, low-performing schools, and family trauma. A pall often set in. Some youth were becoming listless, sleeping long hours, failing to turn in homework assignments, procrastinating about college or trade school applications. It seemed as if some were beginning to lose hope. In the face of these challenges, youth needed not only aspiration but inspiration—something to keep them motivated enough to do the gritty things it took to achieve dreams. And during this time about half of our youth did in fact discover a "life raft," an "outlet," a "passion in life" that seemed to spark renewed effort. Adolescents who found a consuming, defining passion—what we call an "identity project"—were much more likely to remain on track than those who did not. In telling their stories, young people often explicitly credited their passion as the source of the fortitude they needed to beat the streets and work toward a brighter future. Therefore, one question this book addresses is whether these narratives do indeed provide evidence that grit, which is thought to be a skill carefully cultivated through years of socialization and possibly a feature of inborn temperament, can also be inspired by acquiring a passion during adolescence.

In keeping with this notion, we show that the youth who best managed to perservere found a passion through an identity project, which can serve as a virtual bridge between challenging present circumstances and an uncertain, but hoped-for, future. Through identity projects, youth often distanced themselves from family and neighborhood influences that threatened to bring them down, while connecting with others, like teachers, programs, clergy, and coaches, who helped them thrive. Identity projects could spring from activities at places like school, work, or other institutional sites, or interests picked up from friends or family. Some youth were set apart from the pack by a unique interest—such as writing poetry, listening to punk rock or country music (these interests traditionally seen as the choice of white youth are seen as unique when chosen by a black youth), customizing cars, building pigeon coops, attending anime festivals, pursuing modern dance, or writing "beats" and selling them online. These activities protected and distinguished these youth, providing them with a sense of pride and accomplishment instead of the "drama" they saw around them. Others adopted identity projects that were more directly tied to school and a career. These aspirations transformed everyday activities into kindling for careers and sparked the grit that helped them beat the streets and persevere in school.

While these outlets helped some complete a training program or pursue a four-year degree, for others, identity projects helped them remain hopeful even in the face of a dead-end job—for instance, reconceptualizing a job at Chick-fil-A as an entrée into a career in the hospitality industry (Jackson told us, "It's in hospitality, but it's not the part of hospitality that I [ultimately] wanna do") or envisioning a CNA degree as the first critical step on the road to becoming a doctor. Still others hung on by creating a potent sense of identity—a rapper, an author, a committed father—that had little to do with a career. These self-conceptions and the concrete day-to-day activities they entailed kept these young people going and gave them dignity when they had little else to prop them up.

Not all youth in our study found an outlet that allowed them to beat the street, as we show in chapter 4. For a few, the street itself created a sense of meaning and identity. But most youth lacking an identity project were just stuck. They had no map, no foothold on their future. Often, they could not shake loose the dark and traumatic experiences of their childhood and fell through the cracks when schools and other institutions did not catch them. Some ended up homeless, alcoholic, socially isolated, suicidal, or completely disconnected from school and work. In many ways, it was the experiences of these youth that highlighted the importance of following a passion.

We don't argue that the search for meaning or identity is unique to these disadvantaged African American youth. Erik Erikson noted more than half a century ago that the adolescent and early adult years are a time of independence and identity formation, a period when youth explore the boundaries and possibilities of who they might be.[10] But we contend that the stakes are arguably much higher during the transition to adulthood for youth such as ours: their identity work was not just about discovery, it was about survival. They had to move emotional and psychological mountains not often encountered by their middle-class peers. As Antonio, twenty-three, put it, "This city can kill you . . . but if you can survive it, you can survive anywhere. . . . If you can weather the storm, and make it through that, and not get into any trouble, it's a blessing."[11]

In chapter 5, we begin to consider what happened as these youth transitioned to adulthood and why their launches, despite such promising prospects, did not yield bigger payoffs. This research was originally conceived with the goal of incorporating the experiences of a cohort of disadvantaged youth into the scholarly narrative surrounding the transition to adulthood. Drawing on mostly middle-class youth—or at least those who were more advantaged than the youth we followed—a number of scholars, including the psychologist Jeffrey Arnett, author of *Emerging Adulthood,* have produced a portrait of America's young adults that, in its popularized form, looks a lot like Peter Pan and the Lost Boys in Never-Never Land: twentysomethings transitioning at such a glacial pace that it seems that they might never grow up.[12] Arnett coined the term "emerging adulthood" to describe this new reality in which, rather than moving in a relatively quick and orderly fashion through life stages—high school, college, career, marriage, children—middle-class young adults are stretching the process out (as indicated by the subtitle: *The Winding Road from the Late Teens Through the Twenties*). This body of literature has proved useful for understanding this critical life stage—at least for the middle class.

But our question was whether this characterization fit the young adults in our story, and if not, whether we could draw on the life experiences of our youth to describe how their pathway from adolescence to adulthood was different, and why. Our 2003–2004 study had included several dozen high school students when they were not quite old enough to be fully engaged in that transition but were moving along the path. If anything, these youth seemed to be in a hurry to transition into adult roles. Thus, we had strong reasons to suspect that the story of the young adults we were set to interview in 2010 would diverge from Arnett's account. And it did: unlike their middle-class peers, most were on an expedited path to adulthood.

Yet we saw something else as well. One after another, those who had been the most promising as children—those we had seen as having the greatest potential when we interviewed them, their parents, their siblings, and their teachers in 2003–2004—seemed to be falling short of what they could have achieved, at least in our view.[13] For many of these youth, there had been clear validation of their academic skills beyond their own self-report: parents' and teachers' reports of aptitude, top grades, admission to highly competitive magnet schools, or high scores on achievement tests or the Preliminary Scholastic Aptitude Test (PSAT). Yet kids who had aspired to be nurses were ending up as nurse's aides. Bridget, a girl of exceptional promise who had aspired to attend an Ivy League school and pursue a career in law or medicine, ended up enlisting in the U.S. Army at eighteen and abandoning plans for her higher education. Bob, who had dreamed of attending Johns Hopkins University and becoming an engineer, ended up working three low-wage jobs so that he could move out of a West Baltimore rooming house and into a two-bedroom apartment with his fiancée. Most of these young people still merited the designation "on track"—they were still working or in school, and they remained committed to mainstream goals. Yet certainly there was a profound degree of what the economists Caroline Hoxby and Christopher Avery have termed "under matching."[14] And it seemed to us that even that term—which has often been used to characterize youth who could get into Ivies but end up at nonselective schools—could not begin to describe what we saw.

Thus, perhaps the most critical theme this volume explores is how the process occurred. In chapter 5, we find that the legacy of deep racial subjugation, intergenerational poverty, and resource-depleted neighborhoods often pulled these youth down, as one said, like "crabs in a bucket." And these struggles within family and neighborhood echoed throughout their launch to adulthood, even after they were well on their way to finishing high school or entering college and work.

As we have said, few of our youth seemed to fit the pattern of "emerging adulthood." Rather, they were in a hurry to travel what we call an "expedited" path to adulthood, with little scaffolding from parents or school counselors and plenty of financial struggles. The urgency of their desire to launch led to real consequences in the schools they attended and the occupations they ended up holding. This book explores in depth the factors that put youth on an expedited path to adulthood and why it is so problematic.

In chapter 6, we turn away from our analysis at the individual, family, and neighborhood levels and consider the institutional level, following the sociologist Mario Small, who has redirected the attention of poverty scholars to the role played by institutions in the perpetuation of disadvantage. In this chapter, we pose our final question in this volume: do the institutional structures that envelope these young people—namely, the postsecondary educational institutions that serve many black youth and a stunted labor market—serve as traps or as on-ramps? Here we consider the unique needs and vulnerabilities of African American young adults who were on an expedited path to adulthood. These youth launched with fewer resources and encountered blind alleys and traps in the higher education marketplace that prevented their efforts from *adding up*. We found considerable evidence that these vulnerabilities provided an unusually ripe opportunity for exploitation, particularly on the part of the for-profit trade schools. These schools, which paired poor graduation prospects with large student loan debts, provided especially egregious examples of exploitation. But other nonselective postsecondary schools in which our young people enrolled performed poorly as well: among these community and four-year colleges, the percentage who graduated within six years sank as low as 4 percent. Their experiences in these institutions often quashed the hopes and dreams of even the most able and ambitious young adults we studied.

In exploring this theme, we focus on the following questions: How did a group of highly disadvantaged African American young people on an expedited path to adulthood engage with these institutions? Why did they choose them over other options of higher quality? We also consider the experiences of young adults who decided to go directly into the labor market, hoping to craft what one called "a real working man's career." How did they look for a career while lacking a postsecondary degree? How did they traverse a world of low-wage, often part-time work as they attempted to navigate other key stages in the transition to adulthood, particularly as they began to form families of their own?

Given these young adults' perception that they had limited time to launch, we show that they did so haphazardly. The institutions they encountered often exploited their need to launch quickly, and their dreams were downsized in the process. Some community and four-year colleges they attended were underresourced and sometimes woefully inadequate, trade schools often promised much but delivered little, and employers in the low-wage sector seldom showed loyalty to their workers or offered chances for advancement. Any real social safety net for them was all but missing during this period. Meanwhile, many recreation centers and local library branches remained closed or offered limited hours as city funding was scarce. Perhaps as a result, few of our youth aspired to raise their children in Baltimore. As twenty-two-year-old Rhiannon said, "We see ourselves outside of the city."

SOCIAL REPRODUCTION INTERRUPTED

The mechanisms underlying social reproduction have been largely a black box for studies like *The Long Shadow*. Yet there has been no shortage of theoretical or empirically informed ideas about how the process works. Generally, explanations invoke economic resources or educational institutions and culture, while much recent work in urban sociology has centered on the role of neighborhood effects in reproducing inequality.

Resource theory (originally formulated by Gary Becker) holds that if parents have fewer resources, they have less to invest in things that bolster child development, such as books, cognitively stimulating toys, high-quality preschool, good after-school care, and the like.[15] Although the correlation between parental income and educational attainment is high, scholars have long debated whether money matters more than other aspects of parenting. For example, Susan Mayer finds that money alone does not buy the material or psychological resources that ensure a child's success.[16] On the other hand, recent work by Sean Reardon and others has shown that increasing income inequality has large effects on educational inequality, and some scholars attribute these effects to wealthier parents' increased spending on items for their children's educational enrichment.[17]

Parental resources also get translated into neighborhood location, and poor families rarely end up living in middle- and high-income neighborhoods. The neighborhood itself can be a site of social reproduction, not only because of its physical and social conditions (crime, housing quality, job growth) but also because in most places around the country schools are linked to residential addresses. Countless studies have shown stark disparities in school quality by neighborhood income and racial composition, as well as the implications of these disparities for children's learning.[18] Poor children growing up in contexts of concentrated poverty suffer not only because they are poor and their schools are lower quality, but also because their neighborhoods offer them fewer adult role models who work and have successful careers, fewer institutional resources, and greater exposure to deviant peers. The landmark work of William Julius Wilson is the best-known explication of this view.[19] Recently the work of Raj Chetty, Nathaniel Hendren, and their colleagues has lent powerful evidence to support this argument.[20]

Neighborhood effects, in Wilson's formulation, have both structural and cultural components, but some sociologists and linguistic anthropologists have made more distinctively cultural arguments that are either purely theoretical (like Pierre Bourdieu) or drawn from in-depth field work like ours.[21]

For Bourdieu, cultural capital—knowledge, disposition and skills passed on from one generation to the next—is the vehicle through which social reproduction occurs.[22] Upper-class children imbibe significantly different cultural capital from their parents than working-class or lower-income children do. Basil Bernstein and Shirley Brice-Heath expand on this theme, highlighting the importance of linguistic patterns passed on from one generation to the next.[23] Each of these scholars argues that the school sets up working-class children for academic failure by valorizing one set of skills (those of the upper class) and not others, thus relegating them to a lower position in the economic hierarchy while hiding the process of social reproduction under the guise of meritocracy.

For Paul Willis, up-close field work among working-class youth in a British secondary school reveals a somewhat different mechanism. Though most youth in the school conform, the "lads" adopt a counter-school culture out of an unconscious realization that there is little ahead but menial, meaningless work. In addition, they adopt a narrow outlook on their aspirations, where manual labor is equated with masculinity while mental labor is equated with femininity. Thus, the lads often freely elect to follow their fathers onto the shop floor.[24]

Annette Lareau draws on intensive observations of the parenting practices of poor, working-class, and middle-class black and white parents to argue for yet another mechanism: deep cultural logics that guide parenting. While working-class parents adopt a hands-off parenting style, following the logic of "the accomplishment of natural growth," middle-class parents are guided by "concerted cultivation," a logic that compels them to foster their children's interests and talents in ways that promote high school and college success.[25]

All of these arguments have merit, and we see hints of each in our data—resource constraints hindering parental investments in children, poor-performing schools, limited mainstream (or "dominant") cultural capital,[26] and some live-and-let-live parenting.[27] Yet one of these explanations—neighborhood effects—seems to capture the story our decade of research has revealed better than the others. For these youth, something seems to have propelled them far beyond what their parents have achieved (the glass half full). Many of these youth not only have remained "on track" for most of their young lives but have high aspirations and optimism.

We find that transforming a youth's neighborhood context can interrupt the intergenerational transmission of neighborhood disadvantage. As several decades of social science research have shown, neighborhood context has a profound influence on children's unfolding lives. One especially deleterious neighborhood characteristic—concentrated poverty—is too often passed on from one generation to the next, particularly among black children. As the sociologist Patrick Sharkey points out, "The unique ecological location of African Americans in the most disadvantaged urban neighborhoods, over long periods of time, has played a central role in re-producing racial inequality across multiple dimensions."[28]

Whether examining the generation born between 1955 and 1970 or the one born between 1985 and 2000, Sharkey finds that the average African American experiences levels of neighborhood poverty unheard of among whites. A tiny 1 percent of whites in both cohorts were raised in neighbor-hoods where at least 30 percent of their neighbors were poor, compared to almost one-third of blacks. The few white families who do spend any time in such a neighborhood usually do so just for a generation, yet the experi-ence is typically a multigenerational one for black families: two-thirds of black families who start off in the poorest-quartile neighborhoods remain in such a neighborhood a generation later, compared to only 40 percent of whites, according to Sharkey. Sharkey and his colleagues also show that this legacy of neighborhood disadvantage has both direct and indirect ef-fects on these youths' educational prospects, including measures of their academic ability and chances of dropping out of high school.[29]

The surprise here (which will come as no surprise to students of neigh-borhood effects) is that a set of social policies—in our case, a mobility program, plus the large-scale demolition of mostly high-rise and highly distressed public housing in Baltimore—managed to disrupt the intergen-erational transmission of *neighborhood* disadvantage. We see a correspond-ing disruption in the intergenerational transmission of *social* disadvan-tage. Along with the changes in the physical and social conditions of the neighborhoods themselves—felt keenly by parents and children alike—another mechanism we identify is changes in parenting behavior, as we show in chapter 2. This suggests that social reproduction is far from cer-tain, but rather is a legacy of policies and practices that have mired poor and minority children in highly segregated contexts where their life chances are badly diminished. When their contexts improve—even if only modestly—their trajectories can be transformed.

In addition to understanding how changing neighborhood contexts disrupts the process of social reproduction, we explored the heterogeneity we observed in outcomes *among* these youth. We did not find strong dif-ferences in parents' economic status (most were poor and had little discre-tionary income to invest), in cultural outlook, or in cultural capital. In-stead, what emerged from inductive examination of youths' narratives was a key social-psychological resource that helped many young people mitigate against the intergenerational transmission of disadvantage—the aforementioned identity project. Importantly, as chapter 3 shows, identity projects that are sparked by or linked to institutions offered the strongest bridges to later success.

But even youth with strong identity projects struggled to launch. Per-sistent poverty, the ongoing undertow of their neighborhoods (which did not improve nearly as much as they might have), and their families (through the intergenerational transmission of trauma) still exacted a price from our young people (the glass half empty part of the story). We argue that these factors steered them away from the leisurely emergent path of their middle-class peers and put them on an expedited path to adulthood. This led many youth to downshift their dreams—to aim, for example, for a trade that was more tractable and, importantly, attainable sooner instead of a four-year degree and a professional career. Thus, the majority ended up trading college dreams for the shorter programs at trade schools, a corner of the educational marketplace rife with exploitation. When expedited adulthood meets institutional traps such as these, potential is stunted via the very pathway that is supposed to build the vital human capital that is needed for youth to achieve their full potential.

WHAT CAN WE DO BETTER?

The cracks in these young people's stories show us where the light can come in, what we can do better, and how we can leverage the grit these youth already possess so that they can become the adults they strive to be, and maybe more. The book concludes by addressing the question that each chapter in this volume introduces: how can we do better? Most of these youth are not future "murderers, thieves, and muggers," as Baltimore resident Tracy Halvorsen wrote in her incendiary blogpost "Baltimore City, You're Breaking My Heart." Rather, they are hopeful, ambitious, resilient kids, and as such, our stance toward them must be vastly different than the containment strategies, such as zero-tolerance policing and strict youth curfews, that have dominated the approach to black youth in Baltimore in recent years. Instead, we must capitalize on the goodwill and high hopes of a generation of young African Americans who are trying so hard to follow their dreams.

These youth include seventeen-year-old Mia. Neither of her parents graduated from high school, but she has set her sights higher. "I want to become something that nobody in their family, let alone mine, has ever thought about doing," she says. "Like [becoming a] management accountant." To Mia, success is "finishing college and reaching that goal that you have been itching for since day one." We must undergird such aspirations with opportunities based on the American ethos that one can get ahead by playing by the rules. Right now, we are failing to do so, at a huge cost of human potential.

Chapter 2 | "More People That Have Stuff to Live For Here": Neighborhood Change and Intergenerational Attainment

AT TEN YEARS old, Dana Jenkins had a lot of things on her mind. In search of an outlet, *Dana's TV Show* was born, shot in her bedroom using an old video camera of her dad's. On that VHS cassette, Dana recorded her innermost thoughts, read new poems she had written, and talked freely about her up-and-down relationship with her father, an addict who was in and out of jail. Often she added an element of show-and-tell, featuring favorite toys. Sometimes she talked about boys—mostly how she found them disgusting. She added new episodes to the tape throughout middle school. Even now, when Dana and her mom, Lisa, need a laugh, they pop that tape into their old VCR, exclaiming, "Remember when . . .?"

In the eighth grade, the budding poet's classmates chose her to represent the school in a citywide dramatic poetry contest. She competed, but could not find the courage to be as open and expressive as she was in the privacy of her bedroom filming *Dana's TV Show.* Self-conscious about the baby fat she still carried, it took all of middle school for Dana to come out of her shell. Her English teacher, Ms. Austin, celebrated Dana as "an excellent writer" who was extremely motivated and "an important part of the learning process of the classroom." Despite Dana's shyness and "laid-back manner"—or maybe because of it—Ms. Austin was overjoyed to see Dana blossom into a social "go-between," ably straddling the dividing line between the "rambunctious" troublemakers and the more mild-mannered "nerds," while maintaining friendships with kids from both groups.

Dana's literary promise and "mathematical brain," as her mom liked to call it, earned Dana entrance into one of the best high schools in Baltimore

17

City, where she took up the saxophone and argued for the school debate team. For her, Claremont High was a place where you could "express yourself [and] find out who you really are." She even joined the marching band, until taunts from peers, who thought band members were losers, pushed her to quit. Like many American teens, Dana worked to juggle her burgeoning popularity alongside her academic goals.

Then, at fourteen, Dana found herself helping to care for a half-sister who was dying of AIDS. The experience proved to be both devastating and inspiring, prompting Dana to realize one day, midvisit, "Wow, I actually think this is something that I could do." The tragedy of her sister's death sparked the motivation for Dana's life's work: to be a registered nurse. Her teachers and parents—and even Dana—expected her to go on to a four-year college after graduation. But when the time came to apply, the prospect of investing four more years of her time in school seemed less appealing than the chance to put her skills to use sooner and gain practical experience in the work world. Dana reasoned that training as a certified nursing assistant (CNA) was a first step toward her dream. With the support of her mom, who paid the $700 tuition, Dana completed her training through a program offered by the American Red Cross. Right away, she got a job and began caring for patients, just as she'd hoped.

Two years later, however, the shortcomings of her approach had become apparent. "[I'm tired of] wiping butts all day," Dana said. "I can't do this for the rest of my life!" Perhaps the way forward, she thought, was to diversify her professional skills. So, at twenty, she enrolled in a program that would certify her to draw blood—a trade called phlebotomy. Halfway into the program she learned she was pregnant. Nauseated much of the time, drawing blood day in and day out didn't seem so appealing to Dana anymore. While plotting her next move, Dana worked retail— Lowe's, TJ Maxx, The Gap—and even did a stint as a field interviewer for the U.S. Census Bureau.

In 2010, Dana and interviewer Eva Rosen talked for more than three hours; her toddler intermittently sat on her lap, fidgeted, pulled at her hair, climbed all over her, then fell fast asleep in her arms before waking up and playing some more. All the while Dana barely moved, patiently telling the story of her circuitous path through school and the impact of her sister's death on her future goals. Now twenty-three, Dana still clung to her dream of becoming an RN—but was back to CNA work. She told Rosen that she was running low on sleep, working full-time hours, plus as much overtime as she could, for a company that helped people with learning disabilities accomplish everyday tasks, ranging from mastering the alphabet to tying their shoes and eating with utensils. While long stretches of her day were slow-moving, Dana believed that the work was helping her cultivate communication skills and tolerance. "[It's] teaching me how to be patient and to basically find ways to get into their world," she said. The job had also sparked an interest in psychology—Dana now wanted to "learn about people, and how they feel, and what they think." She was still searching for a way to pursue her RN dream; she did not want to be a nursing assistant forever. Yet, between keeping up with the rent on her apartment and raising her daughter, she was even more reluctant to invest the time to get a four-year degree than she had been at eighteen. To beef up her medical credentials, she had recently enrolled in an emergency medical technician training program, which would start in a few weeks. As she thought about her future, she saw herself "working on trying to get it better"—because, she said, "I can't just give up."

Twenty-two-year-old Erica, a striking young woman whose long red wig and jewelry had been carefully chosen to match her dress, talked excitedly about her passions: school, the medical field, and her two-year-old son, Khalif. Erica was now a junior at Morgan State University, one of fifteen youth in the study currently enrolled in a four-year college; she was majoring in family and consumer sciences. Along with attending classes, she held down a work-study position at the student health center, staffing the reception desk. Of all the jobs Erica had worked over the years, it was her favorite. But ultimately, she felt, she was meant for more. "I'm not into [just] copying paper, answering the phone," she said. "I need to be part of something [bigger]."

Erica's confident, up-beat persona belied the tough years that came before. During elementary school, she struggled. "My mother put me in [special education] when I was in the fourth grade," she said. "I don't know, I just [wasn't into school]. And [eventually] something just told me, 'Erica, wake up!'" In middle school, she realized that she had a talent for writing, a gift nurtured by several of her teachers. Writing proved to be the key to unlocking Erica's academic potential. By high school, she had left special education behind. Erica told the story of her metamorphosis with pride: "I was progressing, progressing . . . yeah. I came a long way. I showed those people!"

Show them she did—Erica graduated in the top 10 percent of her high school class. She was also elected class vice president and helped plan the school's prom. While popular with most students, she was sometimes gently teased by her peers for her academic focus and myriad of extracurricular activities, which took up her free periods and after-school time. "We never see you in the cafeteria anymore!" they would complain. Erica did not mind these taunts; she had gotten "really into school." Her love of learning would stay with her. "I love learning because it's something that nobody can take away from you," she said. "I love college . . . I'm being fed with new information every day. Like, I can't imagine not being in school."

Erica yearned to have a job where she would be "the one in charge, the one that has my name on the plate." Her passion to pursue a health-related occupation was so strong that she seemed ready to burst at times. "I really do see myself being a doctor or being a nurse," she said. "When I say I'm into that, I'm really into it. Like, I'm *really* into the medical field."

Outside of classes and her work-study job, Erica fed her interest in health by volunteering with an on-campus student group that promoted HIV and STD awareness. She considered herself an "advocate on health" and loved drawing on the latest medical research to hone her message. "I love research," she said. "I'm really into promoting STD awareness. . . . I know *all* about it." In this regard, Erica's older sister had been a motivating force: she held a bachelor's degree in biology. Erica said that her sister was her "champion of courage," the person who helped keep her motivated to "not mess up."

"I'm ready to go forward," Erica said. "I'm ready to graduate, and I'm ready to say, 'Hello, world, here I am!'"

In high school, Antonio was intensely curious, a voracious reader who loved to learn about history and current events. His mother maintained a subscription to the *Baltimore Sun* just for him, and each day after school he would sprawl on the floor, soaking up all the news. Antonio was a uniquely empathetic teenager too. In tenth grade, his English teacher burst into tears in front of the class after a tough day of students being disrespectful. Moved by her despair—she was the rare teacher he felt really tried—Antonio called her at school when he got home later that day. "I told her I appreciated it and all that," he said. "And ever since then, we got real cool. . . . She wrote me a letter saying thank you and all that."

Antonio obsessed about his appearance, since arriving at school well dressed each day was a key ingredient in gaining respect from his peers. Students paid attention to others' attire, and he felt that teachers did too, noting that, "if you [don't] dress a certain way, the [teachers] ignore you [in class]." Antonio needed a job to have enough money to purchase the kind of wardrobe that he thought would earn him that respect. In middle school, he felt like a social pariah because he "wore the same two shirts for, like, almost a whole year." Once, during that year, his mother bought him a new shirt. "Everybody was looking at me like, '[Wow!] he has on a different shirt today,'" Antonio recalled.

His mother's finances continued to fray, however, and his attempts to look "fresh" became ever more desperate. When Antonio's jeans or jacket began to show wear, he tried to cover up the light spots with pens and markers. When that strategy stopped working, he started squeegeeing car windows for money around Baltimore's Inner Harbor. Eventually, he found an after-school job at Kentucky Fried Chicken and could finally show up at school with pride. "When I got my job at [KFC], that's what changed my life," Antonio said. But his newfound financial independence—at only fifteen—was a double-edged sword. "I'm on my own, even though I'm living with my mom. . . . I'm feeling that pressure of 'you've got to take care of yourself,'" he said somberly. Antonio sold marijuana for a brief period while he was working at KFC but quit because he was worried about being caught; he also did not like the way it made him feel. "I felt more better walking to work with the KFC uniform on, [as] opposed to selling some weed," he said.

Now twenty-three, Antonio worked as a security guard at Johns Hopkins Hospital, a job he secured right after high school graduation. Dressed in the requisite white dress shirt and black trousers, he proudly pointed to his uniform and badge ("[I'm] a working man . . . as you can see!"), Antonio had angled hard to get that job. He'd grown up near the hospital, where campus security was a palpable presence, and he'd been impressed with the neat, professional way the security guards looked. He had come to know some of the guards, as his daily routine often took him along the perimeter of campus, and had asked if they would serve as references when it came time for him to apply. It took nine interviews to finally land the job.

Antonio aspired to become a police officer one day—but not the kind who makes drug arrests, because, he said, "I couldn't get up and have a passion for waking up at six o'clock in the morning, going to work, chasing drug dealers. I wouldn't get anything out of that." Instead, Antonio wanted to fight for the innocent. He believed that as an officer of the law, he "would have that ambition for, that drive for, [arresting] child molesters, people who abuse little kids, touch innocent people. I don't like innocent people to get hurt." Antonio had applied for a job as a police officer, and he was busy studying for the written exam, in addition to working out regularly so he could pass the required physical.

Over the years Antonio had had his share of challenges and at times had felt like he should just give up. But he identified himself as a survivor—and as someone who "was never attracted to negativity." Antonio believed that he was in a good place right now. He had gotten his own car and his own apartment. But when he thought about the future, he was starting to feel the need to move on from a job to a career. "[The] pressure that I got to take another step forward, I got to take that next step and become a police officer, solidifying myself as a man," he said.

When Jackson entered middle school, he was already attempting to fight the skepticism that accompanied the "behavioral problem" label he had earned in elementary school, when he had burned through a number of alternative schools because of incessant fighting. Determined to defy expectations, Jackson began to excel. By the ninth grade, this former delinquent had been dubbed a "computer whiz" by his mother, Candy, who noted the intensity with which he attended to his homework from computer science class. His teachers saw his transformation too, especially once he developed a trusting relationship with Miss Roberta, a school counselor. "Once I started talking to her, I just changed a lot of stuff, [started] maturing a lot, and I just calmed down," he said. Miss Roberta kept him on the straight and narrow, focused on academics even when his older brothers mocked him, calling him "gay" or a "clown" when he completed homework assignments and handed them in on time. Even now Jackson communicated regularly with Miss Roberta on Facebook.

We caught up with twenty-two-year-old Jackson in 2010, and again in 2012. Gone was the shy fifteen-year-old we first interviewed in 2004, a kid who spent his hours tinkering with his computer or watching *Fox Kids* online. Well dressed in a clean white T-shirt and faded red chino pants, Jackson greeted us with a handshake and a smile before catching us up on the last few years. For a while, he had left Baltimore for an apartment on a quiet, tree-lined block in Washington, D.C., where he, his girlfriend, and their two young children lived for several years. While his older brothers had predicted he "was going to be bad," Jackson was actually the first in his family to graduate from high school. He won an academic scholarship to use toward his tuition at Baltimore City Community College (BCCC). He started BCCC with a desire to be a computer engineer, but after struggling the first semester, he decided that pursuing a four-year degree was too long, and too uncertain, of a haul.

Jackson dropped out and began working as a barber's apprentice but did not find the trade fulfilling. A customer at the barber shop suggested that he try TESST, a for-profit trade school that offered a number of accelerated degrees. TESST could help him finish faster and get into the work world more quickly, he was told. Jackson jumped at the suggestion and enrolled at TESST, starting but not finishing programs in computer technology and medical assistant training. Jackson put a positive spin on this trail of incompletes. He thought that it might have had "something to do with talent," explaining that, "once I accomplish one, then I want to do something else," he said. "Instead of fully accomplishing, I accomplish it my own way, which is knowing what you doing and getting it done, and then move on to something else."

As a result, Jackson was not exactly where he wanted to be. (We explore his rocky educational trajectory in more detail in chapter 6.) Between stints in various training programs, he had found part-time employment as a security guard. For a time, in between jobs, he had become a "house dad," caring for his son and his girlfriend's daughter—she was making more money as a medical assistant than he was as a part-time security guard. He did not mind being the family caretaker because he did not like the idea of leaving the kids in the care of strangers.

Jackson's struggles to find his place in the world had served as the inspiration for three unpublished manuscripts. "I just have so much that I wanted to vent out about, so I just put it all into books," he said. He had crafted each volume so that the narrative resembled his life and his peers' lives. The first, *The Truth Behind Love*, was about male-female relationships. In it, he described the highly abusive relationship suffered by a female friend. The second, *Acquired Skill*, centered on the struggles of a "young man . . . and his obstacles," an autobiographical tale describing the pain of parental substance use. The third remained untitled, since Jackson had just started on it—he was still working on the introductory chapter. He hoped to publish the books on Amazon Kindle or on iBooks, an avenue he learned about from hours scouring the Internet. He had considered launching the first book alongside some do-it-yourself promotional modeling—Jackson got the idea from some modest success he had had posting his pictures on a site for amateur models.

Writing gave Jackson a chance to process his inner thoughts and search for the answers to his most vexing questions. He was still finding his place in the world, "still in the mixture of trying to figure out what I want to do." Most recently, he had started working at Chick-fil-A. Always entrepreneurial, he put a positive spin on the job, saying that he considered it his entrée into the hospitality industry, although "not the part of the hospitality industry I wanna do." Looking ahead, he thought he might want "to do real estate" or own his own business. In the past year, he had also made a major transition in his personal life, severing his relationship with his son's mother, coming out to family and friends, and beginning a new relationship with a man. When he reflected on his life, he saw the silver lining in his many struggles—"'cause I like how strong I became," he said. "Everything was a learning experience, so there's nothing that I want to change, 'cause it's never too late to finish school or go back. It's never too late to accomplish things that I want to accomplish."

Dana, Erica, Antonio, and Jackson had much in common. They shared a passion for their creative outlets—whether it was producing a pseudo TV show, penning poems or novels, or cataloging each day's events by devouring the *Baltimore Sun*. They held mainstream aspirations—two wanted to work in the health field, one in law enforcement, and one in the hospitality industry. They viewed their challenges not as obstacles but as assets that had made them stronger. They had also demonstrated a persistence in seeing their dreams through, in at least modest ways. Like most young adults, they felt the pressure to accomplish. They seemed like ordinary kids—like "our kids," to use Robert Putnam's terminology.[1] And in these ways and more, they were.

However, their origins were not ordinary at all, nor were the struggles they had had to endure as a consequence. Each had spent early childhood in some of the poorest and most violent places in the nation—public housing projects bearing names that dominated the city's crime reports for decades: the Flag House Courts, Lexington Terrace, Lafayette Courts, Murphy Homes, Latrobes and the Somerset Homes. These projects were not just poor, they were pernicious. By the time these young people were born, law enforcement had all but ceded control of these addresses to the mayhem. They were places where drugs and gunfire were prevalent unless you hid inside of your home. Journalists noted the "unrelenting procession" of people who came from across the city to purchase drugs there, wandering in past children and useless security booths, twenty-four hours a day.[2] What was worse, the drug trade incubated drug abuse and addiction among the families who lived there. The buildings themselves, long neglected by the local housing authority, bred danger too. Residents burned themselves on malfunctioning heating pipes, and children who got stuck in the elevators were sometimes forced to climb through the shafts to get out.[3] No wonder these projects were the backdrop for the television miniseries *The Corner* and the HBO television series *The Wire*, dramas written and produced by David Simon, who learned about Baltimore's housing projects while working for roughly a decade between the early 1980s and 1990s as a police reporter for the *Baltimore Sun*. These series shocked the nation with their portrayals of a dystopian world where children were inexorably sucked into a vortex of delinquency and crime.

Erica spent the first five years of her life in one of these environments, Somerset Homes, located east of downtown Baltimore. Somerset was one of the oldest public housing developments in the city; originally built to house African American war workers, it opened as a "Negro only" complex in November 1943.[4] Demolished in 2009, Somerset was a 276-unit, low-rise red-brick development spread across eleven three-story buildings. Each home faced a common courtyard where children could play, but by the time Erica was old enough to play outdoors plots that should have held grass were mere parcels of hard-packed dirt, all signs of vegetation worn away.[5] That was the least of the complex's problems. Erica said that she was "glad to move away from there" because at Somerset, she recalled, "people were different. It was all, like, addicts there." As a result of the Moving To Opportunity housing mobility experiment, her family moved to a peaceful, lower-middle-class enclave of the city called Ednor Gardens—where, Erica said, there were "more friendly people, more people that have stuff to live for . . . aspirations to do something with themselves." She continued: "[In Ednor Gardens,] people have mothers and fathers, you know?" she said. "What do they say? It's a nuclear family?"

Jackson's early childhood was spent on the 21.5-acre campus of Lafayette Courts, a cluster of six high-rise buildings and seventeen low-rise structures located just south of Somerset Homes, encompassing 807 units.[6] Opened in 1956, Lafayette Courts was the city's first high-rise public housing complex, and one of the largest in the nation. Jackson's mother, Candy, and her seven siblings had moved to Lafayette with their mother when she was ten, in 1971. Candy secured a unit in her own name when she turned nineteen and had her first child. Just over a decade later, when Jackson, her third son, was about to turn five, the Baltimore Sun proclaimed that this "high-rise dream of the '50s" had become "a nightmare of the '90s."[7] By that time, 30 percent of its units stood vacant, at least in part because families were afraid to live there because of the complex's drug-related crime and violence. The Baltimore Sun called Lafayette "a stark symbol of the country's failed attempt to 'warehouse' the poor."[8] Like Erica's family, Candy and her sons got a voucher through MTO. Candy used that voucher to rent a row house in a mixed-race East Baltimore neighborhood called Bel Air-Edison that would become more socioeconomically fragile over time but that in the 1990s had a much lower poverty rate than Lafayette.

Dana had spent her earliest years in Flag House Courts, another of the city's four high-rise public housing complexes, located just south of Lafayette Courts alongside Baltimore's Little Italy neighborhood. Comprising three twelve-story towers and multiple low-rise buildings totaling 487 apartments, Flag House, which also opened in 1956, had been a disaster almost from the beginning. Elevators broke down often, trapping riders for hours. Residents were forced to run fans even during the winter because a faulty heating system made the buildings unbearably hot. The stairwells reeked of urine and were hotspots for crime. Vacant apartments within the development had become hangouts for junkies and dealers.[9] "You could look out the window and see somebody get shot . . . in daylight," Dana recalled.

In contrast, Antonio, who prized family above all else, loved Flag, where he lived until he was seven years old, because Flag was more "family-oriented" than the neighborhood became later. Antonio now lived near the newly renovated, low-rise, mixed-income community that took

Flag's place in the same footprint after the high-rise was demolished. His godmother, plus a myriad of aunts, uncles, and cousins, had lived there too, offering a rich web of support, particularly when his mother was repeatedly hospitalized for mental illness. Yet, he said, "it was, like, scary sometimes. . . . A lot of people die, killing, robbery, all that. Your friends get killed . . . [and there was] a lot of rape."

Antonio's mother, Tammy, saw no redeeming aspect to their time at Flag, which she called "the worst nine years of my life"—a significant judgment considering the chilling account she offered of the extreme abuse and material want she experienced as a child, which included being locked in a closet for days and fed only bread and water. For her, Flag was "an environment which made you feel trapped, caged, and worthless, just stuck into the atmosphere of absolutely no progress. . . . No one encouraged no one."

Violence was a normal occurrence at Flag. "I've seen people lying on the steps with bullet wounds in their chest," she said. "I've seen people jump out of cars and get beat. . . . The place was just not fit for children to grow up to see, [or] to play." Even the project's architecture seemed to broadcast the city's contempt for the residents, Tammy felt. "It was two bedrooms, but these rooms were cells," she said. "They looked like a prison cell. The whole house looked like a cell. Concrete walls, concrete floors."

To Tammy, perhaps the worst aspect of living and raising kids in the projects was the direct exposure to violence and death. She once had to lug groceries up eleven stories in Flag—because of a broken elevator—only to be greeted at the top of the stairs by the body of a man with a gunshot wound. She had no appetite for weeks afterwards and later became bulimic, a condition she blamed on the incident and the mental link she made between death and food. Another parent recalled her three years in these projects as "pure unadulterated hell. . . . It was right in the heart of drug territory, and I mean just, oh, it was bad. It was bad. . . . In order for you to survive . . . you had to know somebody, or you have to be brought up down [there] or born down there or had a family member down there. And you also had to know how to fight because if you didn't, you wasn't going to make it."

According to the mothers, the impact on the kids was the worst. "It was real bad," one told us. "I mean, it was bad for [my daughter] because anytime you go in the playground and you see dead bodies and you keep playing, you know, or you just see death, you see people get shot in the head, knife wounds and stuff. . . . It toughened her up [in a bad way]." In response, many lived in fear, keeping their kids inside, isolated from the violence, as much as they could. Another related, "I was afraid to let [my children] out much when we lived [in the projects]. You never know when somebody [would] start shooting. The guys were shooting crack, [you] found [evidence] all in the hallway. You just never knew when something was going to happen."

Antonio, Erica, Dana, and Jackson would leave public housing when they were relatively young, along with many of the other youth whose families left owing to MTO, because of the wave of public housing demolition that swept Baltimore in the late 1990s, or for other reasons. Each experienced a remarkable improvement in neighborhood quality as a result. As we argue later in this chapter, it is plausible that these improvements in their social environments yielded powerful intergenerational dividends as these children began their journeys into adolescence, when they would accomplish far more than their parents had.

MOVING TO OPPORTUNITY, HOPE VI, AND THE FALL OF PUBLIC HOUSING IN BALTIMORE

By the late 1970s, Baltimore's public housing and the crime and violence it spawned held the heart of the city in a two-fisted grip. In East Baltimore, just across the Jones Falls Expressway from downtown, Flag, Lafayette, Somerset, plus Perkins, Douglass, and Latrobe Homes formed a tight constellation. This area was possibly one of the largest concentrations of public housing in the nation after Chicago's highest-density pocket of public housing, which once ran for miles along the Dan Ryan Expressway in that city. In West Baltimore the story was much the same, with Poe Homes, McCullough, and Lexington Terrace lying cheek-to-jowl with the Murphy and Gilmor Homes just to the west. Further south, in an isolated section of South Baltimore, one neighborhood alone—Cherry Hill—boasted four projects, more than any other in the city.

Several of these complexes began to fare badly during the late 1960s and '70s, as white flight intensified after the 1968 race riots in the wake of the assassination of Dr. Martin Luther King Jr. The physical buildings themselves were falling apart, having been built with corner-cutting budgets and maintained with scarce funds.[10] Then, in 1981, Congress began to make a series of decisions that served to concentrate poverty in public housing at levels not seen before. It amended the U.S. Housing Act of 1937 such that those families whose income was below 50 percent of the area median were given priority for public housing, effectively blocking families with slightly higher incomes from living there.[11] In this way, housing policy became an even more active force adding to the segregation of the poor.[12]

By the mid-1980s, many policymakers on the city, state, and federal levels had concluded that a sizable portion of the nation's public housing projects were a clear liability to not only the cities but also their residents. If these critics needed any scholarly ammunition for their views, it came from William Julius Wilson. A leading sociologist then at the University of Chicago, Wilson famously blamed the failure of Lyndon Johnson's "war on poverty" to fully achieve its aims on the sharp increase in concentrated poverty that occurred in the 1970s, especially among African Americans.[13] Wilson argued that despite the civil rights gains of the 1960s and '70s, one countervailing trend—the increasing likelihood that a poor child, particularly a poor black child, would grow up around poor, not mixed-income, neighbors—was what had crippled the progress of the low-income black community. He, in turn, linked the astonishing growth of concentrated poverty in the '70s to a whole host of deleterious social trends—the breakdown of the traditional nuclear family, the growth in male joblessness, welfare dependency, and crime.

In 1992 a major national commission on public housing bolstered Wilson's claims and the accounts that journalists had been putting forward for years. Housing projects in many large cities—which were by then contexts of concentrated poverty by design—were indeed rife with drugs and violent crime, and the primary victims were the disproportionately black families trapped inside their crumbling walls.[14] In these and other high-poverty areas, Wilson would go on to write in 1996, work had virtually disappeared—while dependency on government transfers was rampant—and the next generation had few visible options for a way out.[15]

In the wake of the emerging research and Wilson's bold claims, two federal interventions were launched that would profoundly shape the young lives and early adult trajectories of Dana, Erica, Antonio, Jackson, and their contemporaries—kids who were experiencing early childhood in some of the most disadvantaged, socially isolated, and crime-ridden addresses in the nation. First, the U.S. Department of Housing and Urban Development (HUD) launched its MTO demonstration in the mid-1990s to test the premise that improving the neighborhood environment of parents and children trapped in the nation's most distressed public housing by offering them special vouchers to move to a low-poverty neighborhood could dramatically improve their well-being. Specifically designed as a randomized control trial, MTO's architects hoped that the demonstration would provide a definitive answer to the question of whether the destinies of a generation of very poor, and mostly minority, young people could be altered by breaking through the barriers of racial and economic housing segregation. The plan's sponsors reasoned that if growing rates of concentrated poverty were responsible for the many social ills that Wilson attributed to them, reducing exposure to such poverty—and increasing time spent in low-poverty neighborhoods—ought to lead to the reverse: greater human capital attainment and labor force attachment for the parents, plus less crime, fewer teen pregnancies, and enhanced academic achievement for their children.[16]

The MTO interim survey fielded four to seven years later showed that the girls and their mothers in the experimental group saw a marked gain in their mental health and significant decreases in obesity. But the verdict on the experiment was weighted more heavily by what did not change rather than by what did: the impact on parental employment rates and earnings was null; children's test scores and graduation rates did not differ between experimentals and controls; and boys in the experimental group were not less but in fact somewhat more prone to engaging in delinquency and crime than members of the control group.[17] This disappointment deepened with the (mostly) unremarkable findings from the final evaluation, conducted ten to twelve years after random assignment. Receiving an MTO voucher was related to a reduction in morbid obesity and diabetes, as well as less psychological distress among adults. But there were no significant gains in other domains, like economic self-sufficiency or educational attainment.[18] Many policymakers and journalists, as well as some social scientists, concluded that if even an intervention like MTO—which had moved parents and their children from some of the nation's worst addresses to better locales, at least in terms of their poverty rates—could not move the needle for these families, then it was not clear what could.[19]

In the wake of these less than hoped-for results, scholars began to question the quality of MTO's implementation.[20] They argued that the "treatment" that families in the experimental group received was far less dramatic than had been promised. Most MTO families never made it into the resource-rich suburbs, as people had imagined that they would. Instead, most landed in neighborhoods that, while meeting the threshold of less than 10 percent poor in 1990, were on a downward trajectory. Fewer left the low-performing Baltimore City school district than were expected to.[21] Others ended up leaving the neighborhood they had first moved to with the MTO voucher after just a year or two.[22] Since their MTO voucher could be used to rent a unit in any community after a year and not just in a low-poverty neighborhood, most families ended up moving to poorer neighborhoods over time.[23] Thus, families in the experimental group spent only two and a half years—thirty months—on average in a neighborhood that was actually less than 10 percent poor, weakening the contrast between the two groups considerably.[24]

But even these critiques failed to tell the full story behind why there was not a sharper contrast in adult human capital development and child educational achievement between the experimental and control groups. Arguably as important as the so-called failure of the experiment was what was happening to the control group over time, particularly in Baltimore.[25] As previously mentioned, MTO was only one of several federal interventions launched in the 1990s aimed at improving residents' lives in our nation's distressed urban housing projects.

In 1993, backed by the findings of the National Commission on Severely Distressed Public Housing and unprecedented support from Congress, HUD launched a major urban redevelopment intervention—the Housing Opportunities for People Everywhere (HOPE VI) program. HOPE VI provided funding for housing authorities across the country to tear down deteriorating housing projects.[26] In Baltimore, roughly a dozen complexes were partially or fully demolished, some funded by HOPE VI and some through other sources. Although low-density, sometimes mixed-income developments would eventually rise in their place, the new construction would replace only a fraction of the public housing units that had been lost.[27]

In Baltimore, Lafayette Courts fell first, in 1995, followed by Lexington Terrace in 1996, Fairfield Homes in 1997, Murphy Homes in 1999, and the Flag House Courts, Hollander Ridge, and the Broadway Homes developments in 2000. By the spring of 2007, the stock of public housing units had fallen from a high of 18,393 in 1992 to 10,748 available units in its inventory—1,123 of them vacant, according to one analysis.[28] Furthermore, the housing authority announced that it planned further demolition, including Somerset Courts (257 units), Westport Extension (242 homes), more than half of O'Donnell Heights (about 600 units), and most of the scattered-site program (out of 2,872 scattered-site public housing units, 1,707 were slated for demolition).[29] By 2010 many of these demolitions had occurred, and the stock of public housing dedicated to families with children dropped by 70 percent compared to its height in the 1980s.[30]

Peter Rosenblatt has shown that in Baltimore these demolitions were often positively correlated with improved safety and economic conditions in neighborhoods immediately surrounding the former complexes. Scholars have found this effect in other cities too.[31] In addition, the dispersal of such a large percentage of the neighborhood's residents, often into the private rental market via a Section 8 voucher, almost certainly contributed to the sharp decline in Baltimore's rate of concentrated poverty (defined as tracts where at least 40 percent of the residents are poor). A decline was evident both in the 1990s, when most cities were showing a decline, as well as in the 2000s, when concentrated poverty was on the rise in most other cities. In fact, as table 2.1 shows, after somewhat modest decreases in

Table 2.1   Poverty in Baltimore City, 1990–2012

	1990	2000	2005–2009	2008–2012
Percentage of poor people	21.9%	22.9%	20.1%	23.4%
Number of poor people	156,284	143,514	123,956	139,915
Number of extreme-poverty census tracts	35	30	16	25
Number of poor people living in extreme-poverty tracts	52,480	32,563	19,512	31,241

Source: U.S. Census 1990, 2000; American Community Survey (ACS), 2005–2009, 2008–2012.

the 1990s, concentrated poverty in the Baltimore metropolitan area fell fairly markedly—more than in almost any large metro area—during the early to mid-2000s, though there has been an uptick since from the economic fallout of the recession.[32] Even taking this spike into account, Baltimore City contained just under 140,000 poor individuals by the period 2008–2012, but only 31,241 of them remained in tracts with concentrated poverty—21,239 fewer than in 1990, right before the wave of demolition began, an overall decline of 41 percent.[33]

Furthermore, as maps 2.1, 2.2, and 2.3 show, the number of city neighborhoods (tracts) that were 40 percent or more poor declined dramatically, from 35 of the city's 215 census tracts in 1990 to only 16 in 2005–2009, just when our youth were coming of age. Though high-poverty tracts increased during the recent recession to a worrying degree, overall there was still a decline by 29 percent over two decades.[34] These maps illustrate not only the changing landscape of poverty but also the central role that public housing played in anchoring Baltimore's poor neighborhoods.[35] Each map also reveals the transformation of public housing and the corresponding reduction of concentrated poverty in the city's neighborhoods over the last two decades.

Nowhere was the impact of these declines felt more sharply than among the young adults in this study, virtually all of whom had lived in these very housing projects as young children. Map 2.4 displays the location of their baseline residences. (Note that each dot represents one individual living in the tract, not the actual street address, and the dot is placed at a random coordinate in the tract.)

Owing to the wave of demolition—which affected all of the public housing developments where our youth had resided—even control group members experienced improvement in neighborhood poverty rates, resulting in smaller-than-anticipated differences between experimentals and controls by 2010. (Note that more experimental youth lived in neigh-

(*text continues on page 36*)

Map 2.1   Public Housing Developments and Poverty Rates in Baltimore,
1990

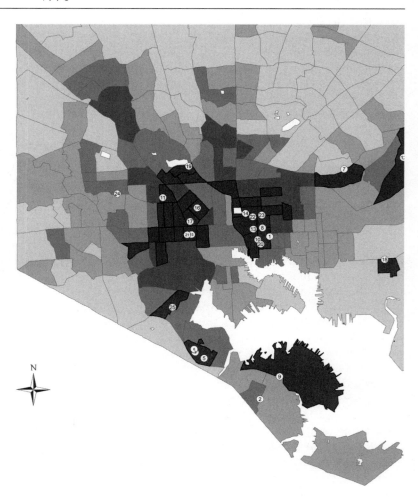

Percentage Poor

- ░ Less than 10%
- ▒ 10 to 19%
- ▓ 20 to 29%
- ▓ 30 to 39%
- █ 40% or more

1 Broadway Homes	10 Flag House Courts	18 O'Donnell Heights
2 Brooklyn Homes	11 Gilmor Homes	19 Oswego Mall
3 Charles K. Anderson	12 Hollander Ridge	20 Perkins Homes
4 Cherry Hill	13 Lafayette Courts	21 Poe Homes
5 Cherry Hill 12	14 Latrobe Homes	22 Somerset Courts
6 Cherry Hill 17	15 Lexington Terrace	23 Somerset Extension
7 Claremont Homes	16 McCulloh Homes	24 The Dukeland
8 Douglas Homes	17 Murphy Homes	25 Westport
9 Fairfield Homes		

Source: Authors' compilations using data from the 1990 Census, Housing Authority of Baltimore City.

Map 2.2   Public Housing Developments and Poverty Rates in Baltimore,
           2000

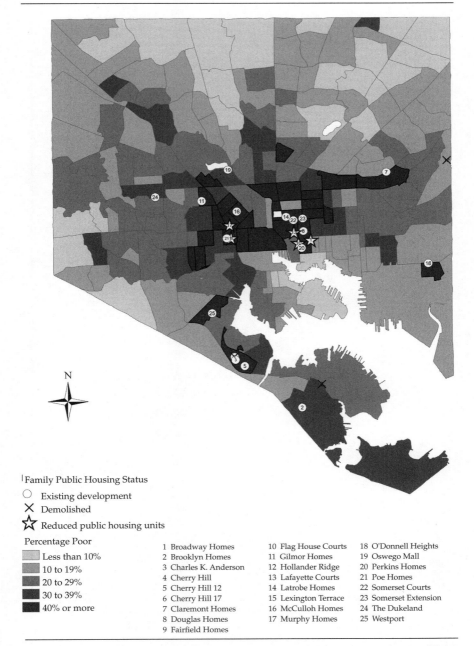

Family Public Housing Status

○   Existing development
✕   Demolished
☆   Reduced public housing units

Percentage Poor

Less than 10%	
10 to 19%	
20 to 29%	
30 to 39%	
40% or more	

1 Broadway Homes
2 Brooklyn Homes
3 Charles K. Anderson
4 Cherry Hill
5 Cherry Hill 12
6 Cherry Hill 17
7 Claremont Homes
8 Douglas Homes
9 Fairfield Homes

10 Flag House Courts
11 Gilmor Homes
12 Hollander Ridge
13 Lafayette Courts
14 Latrobe Homes
15 Lexington Terrace
16 McCulloh Homes
17 Murphy Homes

18 O'Donnell Heights
19 Oswego Mall
20 Perkins Homes
21 Poe Homes
22 Somerset Courts
23 Somerset Extension
24 The Dukeland
25 Westport

Source: Authors' compilations using data from the 2000 Census, Housing Authority of Baltimore City.

Map 2.3   Public Housing Developments and Poverty Rates in Baltimore, 2010

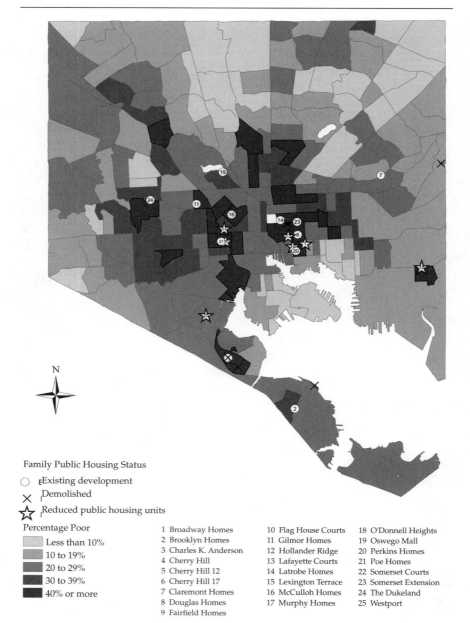

N

Family Public Housing Status

○   Existing development

✕   Demolished

☆   Reduced public housing units

Percentage Poor

Less than 10%

10 to 19%

20 to 29%

30 to 39%

40% or more

1 Broadway Homes	10 Flag House Courts	18 O'Donnell Heights
2 Brooklyn Homes	11 Gilmor Homes	19 Oswego Mall
3 Charles K. Anderson	12 Hollander Ridge	20 Perkins Homes
4 Cherry Hill	13 Lafayette Courts	21 Poe Homes
5 Cherry Hill 12	14 Latrobe Homes	22 Somerset Courts
6 Cherry Hill 17	15 Lexington Terrace	23 Somerset Extension
7 Claremont Homes	16 McCulloh Homes	24 The Dukeland
8 Douglas Homes	17 Murphy Homes	25 Westport
9 Fairfield Homes		

Source: Authors' compilations using data from the ACS, 2008–2012, Housing Authority of Baltimore City.

Map 2.4   Poverty Rates and Baltimore Neighborhoods Where Youth Lived at
            Baseline

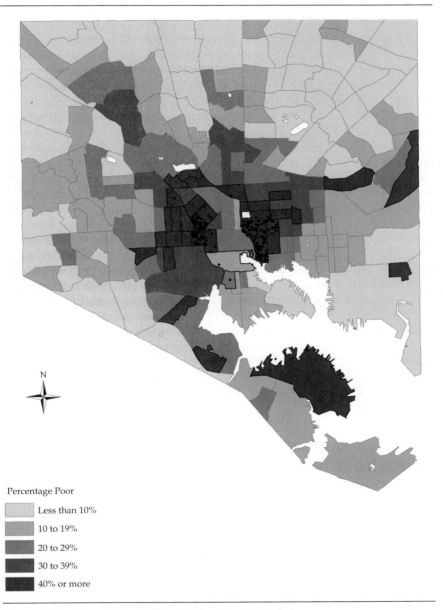

Percentage Poor

Less than 10%

10 to 19%

20 to 29%

30 to 39%

40% or more

Source: Authors' compilations using data from the 1990 U.S. Census.

borhoods where the poverty rates were under 20 percent.)[36] Table 2.2 shows that for the sample as a whole the declines in their neighborhood poverty rate were dramatic. Nearly three in four participants (73 percent) experienced neighborhood poverty drops of at least 30 percent relative to where they and their parents had been living when the experiment began, and 30 percent of the total saw declines of 50 percent or more. Only 5 percent—seven youth—experienced increases in their neighborhood poverty rate over that time. Just over one in four youth remained in a neighborhood that was more than 30 percent poor.

Map 2.5 shows the corresponding geographic distribution of youth addresses in 2010.[37] When compared to map 2.4, it is clear that youth were now living in a much wider array of neighborhoods than they were at baseline. Instead of residing in the thirteen highest-poverty tracts in the city, youth were now living in more than sixty tracts across the city and another twenty tracts in four counties outside of the city.

To confirm that these drops in neighborhood poverty, especially among the controls, were not unique to the youth in our subsample, we looked to data from the baseline MTO surveys, both interim and final, for all Baltimore households (a group from which the parents and youth for our qualitative study were drawn).[38] Table 2.3 shows that controls in the full sample saw a large drop in poverty—from 53 percent at baseline to 27 percent, only five percentage points less than the experimental group.[39] In short, both groups began in extreme poverty, but moved over time to neighborhoods that were moderate to high in poverty. (Note that these were far from the gains that were hoped for—the program's architects intended that those in the experimental group would remain in lower-poverty and better-resourced neighborhoods and schools. We can only imagine what these youth might have accomplished if they had done so, a topic we return to in chapter 7.)

A PROFOUND, INTERGENERATIONAL LEAP FORWARD?

Did these sharp drops in neighborhood-level disadvantage make a difference? Three decades of research would suggest that these changes should have had a meaningful impact on the lives of the young people we studied, for both those who moved through MTO and those who moved out through the HOPE VI program (and for other reasons.)[40] Bolstering this body of research is the recent work of Raj Chetty, Nathaniel Hendren, and their colleagues, who found substantial evidence for the impact of living in a low-poverty area on later-life gains (including large gains in earnings and large reductions in single-parenthood for the youngest of the MTO

Table 2.2 Neighborhood Poverty Rates for MTO Baltimore Youth, from Baseline to 2010 (N = 150)

	2010 Neighborhood Poverty					
Neighborhood poverty rate	0 to 10%	10.1 to 20%	20.1 to 30%	30.1 to 40%	Higher than 40%	Total
Percentage of youth	13.3%	28.7%	31.3%	12.7%	14.0%	100.0%

	Change in Poverty Rate from Baseline to 2010					
	Decrease of 50% or more	Decrease of 30 to 50%	Decrease of 20 to 30%	Decrease of 0 to 20%	Increase in Poverty Rate	Total
Percentage of youth	30.0%	42.7%	12.7%	10.0%	4.7%	100.0%

Source: U.S. Census, 1990; ACS, 2008–2012.

Map 2.5   Poverty Rates and Neighborhoods Where Youth Lived in 2010 in the Baltimore Metropolitan Area

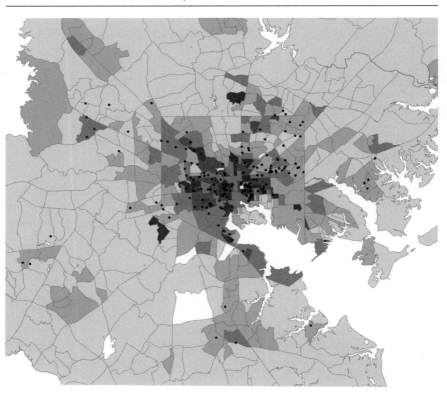

Percentage Poor

Less than 10%
10 to 19%
20 to 29%
30 to 39%
40% or more

N

Source: Authors' compilations using data from the ACS, 2008–2012.

Table 2.3   Neighborhood Poverty Rates for Baltimore MTO Households, from Baseline to Final Evaluation

	Experimental	Control
Baseline	53%	53%
Interim	26	37
Final	23	27

Source: U.S. Department of Housing and Urban Development (HUD), Office of Policy Development and Research (PDR), Moving to Opportunity Final Evaluation Impacts Survey.
Notes: Baseline addresses are interpolated from the 1990 and 2000 censuses. Interim addresses are four to seven years post–random assignment, using the 2000 census. Final addresses were recorded in 2008 using the 2005–2009 American Community Survey.

youth once they reached their mid to late twenties).[41] Because we limited our sample to only those youth who were zero to ten at the time of random assignment, and because most of the demolition occurred before the youth in our study entered their adolescence, those in both groups had limited exposure to the kinds of neighborhood environments to which their parents, often for much of their lives, had been exposed.

One test to determine if there is at least prima facie evidence to back up our claim of a strong neighborhood effect for both experimental and control youth is to compare the educational and behavioral outcomes of the affected youth relative to their parents. To our knowledge, these analyses have not been done before—researchers have focused almost exclusively on the differences between the experimentals and controls, not the differences between generations. If youth benefited as we are suggesting, then we should see meaningful contrasts across the generations in key outcomes, particularly high school graduation and college attendance. In line with these expectations, the intergenerational gains among youth are quite substantial.[42]

As table 2.4 shows, only 27 percent of these young people's primary caregivers (usually mothers) had a high school diploma by 2010, and only 13 percent had tried college or trade school.[43] For youth not still in high school, the figures were 72 and 51 percent, respectively—gains of between roughly 300 and 400 percent over the parents' generation. By either measure, this is a substantial increase. To be sure, over this time period there was also an upward trend in high school graduation and college enrollment in Baltimore (as we'll discuss in chapter 6), plus a reduction in violence and crime.[44] However, these gains exceed what one would predict by an order of magnitude, especially for children who had some of the most-disadvantaged social origins of any in the city.[45] Despite their backgrounds, their graduation and college-going rates matched those for the city more generally by 2010.

Table 2.4   Intergenerational Change in Educational Outcomes

	High School Graduate	GED	Entry into College or Trade School
Parents	27%	5%	13%
Youth[a]	72	5	51

Source: Authors' compilations.
[a]Denominator includes only those not still in high school.

In addition to educational progress, we attempted to compare youth and their parents on other indicators, like risk behavior. We were not able to interview parents when they were the same age as the youth in our study, so we cannot directly compare rates of employment, drug use, and criminal activity across the generations. Nonetheless, we find that few of these youth fit the stereotype of the delinquent troublemaker that has dominated the accounts of Baltimore in the media. Only 14 percent of the youth we spoke with reported struggling with alcohol or drug abuse, only 29 percent had ever been arrested, and even fewer—18 percent—said that they had ever been "in the street"—their shorthand for involvement in criminal activities.[46] As we show later, struggles of this kind in the parents' generation were rife.

One might ask whether these findings are the result of a biased sample—perhaps the youth whose parents signed up for MTO were somehow more advantaged than other youth living in the projects as children or poor youth more generally. John Goering and his colleagues tried to address this concern by comparing MTO households with public housing residents in four of the five MTO cities. (Chicago's data were too incomplete to include.) MTO families were headed by adults who were younger on average (thirty-five versus forty-one), more likely to be female-headed (93 versus 78 percent), more likely to be receiving welfare (75 versus 51 percent), and less likely to be employed (22 versus 30 percent). If anything, the MTO households in our Baltimore study were *more* disadvantaged, not less, than other, similarly eligible public housing residents.[47]

As the stories of Antonio and Dana indicate, most youth in the study had family members who had experienced trauma or they had been traumatized themselves. Nearly half of the youth—47 percent—had a parent who had struggled with alcohol or drug addiction. Roughly one-third had a primary caregiver (usually a mother) who had done so. Half the youth had a primary caregiver who had been involved in illegal activities or incarcerated. Taken together, two-thirds of our youth had experienced one of these forms of trauma in their family of origin. One-third had both one parent behind bars and one suffering from drug addiction in 2010.

In sum, significant neighborhood gains for both those in the experimental group (through MTO) and the control group (through HOPE VI and other programs) may have yielded a powerful enough effect to at least partially account for the intergenerational gains observed. It is plausible that these youth watched their worlds open up, began to aspire to a brighter future, and, for many, started down the road to get there. This is consistent with the narratives of Erica and many of her peers. As we show in chapter 3, nearly three-quarters of the sample as a whole was on track—in school or at work—in 2010, when they had reached ages fifteen to twenty-four. This is not to say that they were significantly closing the gap with their more affluent peers in the Baltimore suburbs. Nonetheless, few fit the stereotype of delinquent or idle youth, and most were surviving difficult childhoods and growing up aspiring to the American Dream.

HOW DO NEIGHBORHOOD GAINS YIELD IMPROVEMENTS IN EDUCATIONAL AND RISK-TAKING BEHAVIOR?

James Coleman argued in 1990 that linking cause and effect at the macro level—in this case, neighborhood change and youth outcomes—must be complemented by an examination of the mechanisms at work at the micro level.[48] Following Coleman's prescription, we first considered whether positive changes to parental well-being and behavior after the moves may have been passed on to their children through enhanced parenting (what social scientists call "indirect effects"). To do so, we drew on the 139 parent and primary caregiver interviews we conducted in 2003–2004.[49]

Second, we examined census data, both from the youths' neighborhood addresses when the MTO experiment began in the mid-1990s and from their 2010 addresses, to examine the differences between their exposure to what we call—for lack of a better term—"mainstream influences" (the number of adults who reported having a high school or higher degree or holding down a job; the number of households led by a married couple; and so on), and their exposure to what we call "nonmainstream influences" (the number of adults who were unemployed or recipients of public assistance).[50] The latter approach is inspired by the work of William Julius Wilson, who lamented the departure of jobs due to deindustrialization, the resulting flight of the black middle class from inner cities, and the concurrent loss of mainstream influences in these areas; Wilson cites the resulting social isolation as among the causes of persistent poverty.[51] We also examined exposure to violence and victimization over time, for both parents and youth, using data from the MTO survey at interim and baseline.

Third, we examined the narratives of the youth themselves—at least those of the ones who were old enough to recall what it was like to live in housing projects like Flag, Somerset, Lafayette, Lexington, and Murphy. While we cannot expect the youth to do our analysis for us, those who did remember could point quite clearly to the large differences they perceived in their neighborhood context before and after they moved. Some even directly connected the moves to changes in their aspirations.

Indirect Effects: Parenting

We begin with an analysis of the 2003–2004 parent interviews. Here we find numerous accounts where parents explicitly linked neighborhood change with improved mental health and behavioral improvements, particularly with regard to substance abuse and parenting.[52] This is fully in line with the MTO interim and final evaluations, in which mothers in the experimental group were still experiencing significant mental health gains, relative to control group mothers, five, seven, and even ten or more years after random assignment.[53] Elsewhere our colleagues Kristin Turney and Rebecca Kissane, along with Kathryn Edin, have examined the means by which MTO might have improved the mental health of mothers in the experimental group, drawing from the same data we do here.[54] But it is likely that the controls also experienced some improvement upon moving from the projects, even if they did not relocate to neighborhoods that were quite as low-poverty as the ones where the experimentals lived.

Our analysis clearly shows a strong association between leaving the projects and mothers' accounts of quitting drugs and alcohol, a story that is told by both experimental and controls. Of the forty-four mothers who admitted to ever using drugs, twenty-seven claimed that they were no longer using in 2003–2004, a change many credited directly to their move from public housing into new, lower-poverty neighborhoods. One described her transformation:

> I'm more settled. I'm not as wild and wide-open as I was when I was in the [projects]. In the [projects], I stayed in the streets more. I did work—that's one thing. [But] it was basically all about drinking and hanging out. Out here, you gonna be responsible because everyone I'm surrounded [with] works and is responsible, you know? And it's not a bunch of sitting around and gossiping about negative stuff.

This account contrasts sharply with descriptions of life in the projects, which parents sometimes pointed to as having the opposite effect. One recounted, "I really didn't socialize with anybody down there [in the projects]. [But] that's one of the things that allowed me to continue to use drugs, 'cause I was always looking at people that was worse than me, instead of looking at people that were better, that were doing better than me." Notably, this mother subsequently managed to move to a much-lower-poverty neighborhood, albeit not through MTO, and had managed to leave drugs behind, a success she attributed to the change in her neighborhood environment.

Accounts of parents explicitly linking the change in their neighborhood environment to their parenting are common too. When we spoke with Antonio's mother, Tammy, in 2004, she reflected on how living at Flag House Courts had profoundly limited her ability to be an effective parent:

> When I was down in [the] project . . . I wouldn't even deal with my children. I couldn't provide well for them, so I was detached from them. I didn't know what to teach them, living in a place where I couldn't point out this and I couldn't point out that [to illustrate a good role model]. I was very unhappy. There was never a punishment because I always felt like being there was their punishment.

For Tammy, every aspect of trying to parent in Flag was all wrong. "You could not raise a child [well] in the projects," she said. "What could you teach them? Don't kill, when there's killing going on . . .? Eat well; eat well, why? When all that's being sold in the area is chicken boxes and fried foods, and you know, nobody else is eating well?" Once out of Flag and relocated to the Frankford neighborhood on the city's northeast side, Tammy claimed, her parenting was transformed. Suddenly, she told us, it seemed worthwhile to strive for discipline in the home, consistent bedtimes, and healthy meals.

Peaches, whose daughter, Keala, we would meet in 2010, also attributed her improved parenting ability to leaving the Murphy Homes for the working-class neighborhood of Evesham in Northeast Baltimore. Peaches told us,

> When I first moved [here], I just cried. . . . I was like, "Oh my God, a house. Now I can raise my family in the way I want to raise them. . . ." If I had not had that opportunity to go into the MTO program, I would not have known what it would have been like to live in a house in a positive environment. . . . It just gave me the opportunity to see how the average American who is just working and living middle-class [lives]. It just made me want that.[55]

In 2003, Annette Lareau drew data from twelve families across the spectrum of race and class to offer a fresh answer to a question that had plagued researchers for decades: how is social inequality passed down between generations?[56] Based on careful in-depth observations with these families of varied class backgrounds, she shows that middle-class parents practice "concerted cultivation"—they make sure that their children's schedules are chock-full of sports, music lessons, and tutoring, carefully managing the dizzying schedules these activities require. They also have rich linguistic interactions with their children, which help the children sharpen their reasoning skills. According to Lareau, the socialization that children receive through these activities and exchanges helps groom them to fulfill teachers' expectations and live middle- and upper-class professional lives. In contrast, she finds, parents from lower-income and working-class backgrounds are more hands-off in their parenting. While no less loving, these parents allow their children to spend their out-of-school time in unstructured play, typically issuing directives rather than reasoning with children about their requests. These less-advantaged parents are more likely to cede control over educational decisions to those in authority at their children's schools instead of intervening on equal footing.

Lareau argues that these class differences in parenting flow from deep cultural logics embedded in one's class position in the capitalist economy. And they may make a crucial contribution to reproducing inequality from one generation to the next. However, based on our data, our view is that these cultural logics are not immutably anchored in one's class position but instead may shift with a change in context. We were struck by how frequently the parents of the youth in our sample ascribed changes in their parenting behavior to a change in neighborhood conditions, even with no corresponding improvements in parental education or earnings (that is, no change in social class). Tammy's case, cited earlier, is only one example. Further, some parents associated neighborhood change with the adoption of parenting behaviors that looked much like what Lareau calls concerted cultivation. These data suggest, though do not prove, that gains in neighborhood quality may yield a parenting dividend, one that might help set children on a better course.

One mother's story provides a particularly powerful example. Sheila, now a carefully coiffed mother of four whose short hair artfully framed her face in finger waves, was raised in a strict home. "My mother raised me up in church," Sheila said. "She taught me morals, and principles, and values." Yet Sheila had started drinking by ten and smoking pot by twelve, and she had "tried everything there was to try" by eighteen. She spent her early years in East Baltimore, in a neighborhood not far from Lafayette Courts. As middle school ended, Sheila's mother moved the family to the West Baltimore neighborhood of Edmonson Village, then a stable, working-class African American enclave that has since seen harder times. Sheila graduated from high school, got a job, and soon earned enough to move out of her mother's apartment.

After that, Sheila went from job to job, curbing her drug use during the workweek. At nineteen, she got pregnant and married the father of her child, a man who shared her taste for alcohol, pot, and, eventually, heroin and cocaine. Then, at twenty-two, a serious leg injury stemming from a bus accident kept Sheila from working. She landed on welfare, and with nothing to do except mind Clarice, her baby daughter, her drug use—and her husband's—spiraled out of control. In her words, "From welfare, I got caught up, and I became an addict. I got caught up on drugs." Sheila lost the apartment and ended up homeless, squatting in a vacant property with other hard-core addicts and sleeping on a mattress on the floor. As she put it, "At one point, I was living in a home where I had to get Clarice out of the home 'cause it was not a safe environment." Consequently, Sheila gave Clarice to her husband's family for a few months.

Alarmed at her daughter's situation, Sheila's mother intervened, called the housing authority, and somehow managed to secure Sheila and her daughter a unit in Lafayette Courts. But there Sheila's drug use continued unabated. "I [became] an IV user at [that] time," she said. "Smoked, drank, you name it, I did it. And then I stayed caught up for a long time." Sheila remained in Lafayette, where she had two more children, until 1996, when an MTO voucher allowed her to move to Waverly, a mixed-race neighborhood that was solidly working-class. "Work, work, retired, work, work, welfare, on drugs, work, retired, retired, work . . . own their own business, own their own business," she said, listing the occupations of her immediate neighbors. "Right here [next door], she works up at Morgan State University. [The neighbor on the other side] works at a bank. . . . The older lady all the way up on the end, she does nursing assistance too [as Sheila did]. Everybody does something."

It took her a year to get clean. Sheila recounted her story of transformation to Susan Clampet-Lundquist, sitting at her kitchen table one Saturday morning. She told Susan that she quit heroin and cocaine cold turkey, but let go of alcohol and weed more gradually. After years of using, what pushed her to make the change?

> When I first moved around here, it was a different environment, and it was clean. . . . It looked like the people that lived in here were homeowners, and they were working and . . . I didn't want to look like or act like I was on welfare, [and] I wanted to do right by my children. So, um, I just basically felt like it, it needed to stop.

Sheila not only got sober after the move but became a different parent. She regretted deeply that she had used drugs while pregnant with her younger son Tristan and was determined to make sure that he would not suffer because of it. Around the time Clarice entered kindergarten—just a few years after the move—Sheila noticed that Tristan, now two, "wasn't really talking," so she arranged to have him assessed by the state. This entitled him to daily sessions with a speech pathologist. Upon entering kindergarten, she insisted on an individualized education plan (IEP), and her son started receiving special education services. Tristan continued to attend speech therapy through middle school, and Sheila said that she regularly discussed his quarterly report with his therapist and school officials.

Clarice, older by three years, moved without incident through the K–5 neighborhood school, but Sheila was less happy about Tristan's experience there. After he finished first grade, she arranged to transfer him to another school several miles away that had become an Edison School, a model that emphasizes extended school days, lots of homework, and uniforms. She had heard through the grapevine that it was a good place, and she would be pleased by his experience there. "I love it," she said.

> It's a good school. Lots of people have problems with it 'cause they feel like it's too much for them because school starts at seven-thirty in the morning. It gets out at three-thirty, [but] I love it, the reason being is because you have to teach your children there are going to be responsibilities, especially in the work world. Most workplaces start [at] seven in the morning—sometimes six, maybe five, it all depends. And it's a lot of work.

Then Clarice started showing evidence of trouble in middle school. Sensing something was wrong, Sheila took action and ensured that after eighth-grade graduation Clarice would not follow her peers to George Washington High, which Sheila described as "terrible." Instead, Sheila used her mother's address across town and enrolled Clarice in West Glen High. She knew little about the school beyond the fact that it required uniforms, which she favored because she believed that they tended to stave off fights over clothes. The choice also made logistical sense; the school was near her grandmother's home, where the family often spent time, and Clarice could spend a few safe hours with her peers hanging out at the Mondawmin Mall before taking the bus home.

Still, Clarice's turmoil continued. She began cutting class and earned a D in one of her courses. By then, Tristan was thriving and Cindy, her youngest—born just as the family was about to leave Lafayette Courts— had scored "high among the nation in scores." Sheila knew that her kids were smart and believed that each of them would thrive in the right environment, so she decided that stronger medicine was required. Over time the area where the family had moved with their MTO voucher had seen big increases in disorder and crime. Though her mother did not know the whole story, Clarice was running the streets, dealing drugs, and courting trouble by driving stolen cars. She had also acquired a gun. Later, Clarice described that time: "We was hanging out around there. I think if my mother wouldn't have moved us from around there, I would probably be one of those statistics, locked up. I mean, that's just how the neighborhood was, and if she wouldn't have moved us from out of there, who knows what would happen." Sheila moved the family to Waltherson, a neighborhood close to the far eastern boundary of Baltimore, and geographically as far away from the trouble Clarice was getting into as the city limits would allow.

In a new high school, and in an area far removed from the public transportation routes that could have taken her back to her old neighborhood, Clarice found herself hanging around the house, not running the streets all the time. She described the change as follows: "When I was [in my old neighborhood], I was stressing, seeing how much money I'm a get tonight [dealing]. Being outside over there, something would be going on. I'm here [now], I'm just chill, 'cause I be home, so laid-back, [I] watch TV, talk on the phone. . . . I'm pretty sure if I was to move back over there I'd be back at it again. . . . I'd give myself a week."

After the move, Sheila pushed Clarice relentlessly to graduate from high school. Clarice recalled: "I was just giving up. I wasn't even gonna go back to school in my senior year, and what made me go back was my mother. I was not gonna let my mother down, 'cause all she was asking for is just [that I] graduate." When we last spoke with her, Clarice had earned her degree and was about to enter a program that would train and certify her as an electrician.

Meanwhile, Tristan had turned out to be "a real sweet boy," Sheila said. "He's not rough-and-tough like most nine-year-olds. He's timid, you know, soft." In his mother's estimation, Tristan had flourished under the guidance of the speech pathologist in particular, though she also pointed to the special education services he had received during his early school years. When he got beat up twice in fifth grade, Sheila enrolled him in karate, not just for the protection but "for the discipline part." Then she insisted that Tristan and his sisters enroll in the Baltimore Police Athletic League so that they could be under the careful eye of police officers during the summer and in the hours after school while she slept off the night shift she worked as a nurse's aide in a local psychiatric facility.

Three years later, when he failed to gain entrance into one of the city's high-performance magnet schools because of some C grades in middle

school, Sheila stepped in to broker a spot for Tristan at a college preparatory charter school. Though they had moved even closer to the city line—
to the Armistead Gardens neighborhood—neither Tristan nor Sheila was
convinced that the neighborhood school would be sufficient to prepare
him for college. The charter school chose its students by lottery, but Sheila
took matters into her own hands. With Tristan and his middle school transcripts in tow, she arrived at the school without an appointment, demanding an interview. Her assertiveness won the day, and Tristan was admitted. He had just completed his junior year in high school when we
interviewed him in 2010. His early academic delays seemed to have disappeared, and he proudly showed us a trophy he had received for having
one of the top ten grade point averages in his school. He played flag football and ran track, and he also had a trophy for debate—a program that
ended when its funding was cut after he finished tenth grade. With all the
activities he was involved in, Tristan did not usually leave school until
seven o'clock at night. He was taking Chinese and advanced placement
and honors classes and had his eyes set on college.

To that end, he had joined other honors students in organizing a young
scholars program, which involved college visits. His school offered SAT
prep instruction, worked with students on their college essay, and invited
college recruiters to visit the school. When we spoke with him, Tristan
exhibited a wide range of knowledge about the college application process, gleaned partly from his school but also from his mother, who had
convinced him that he had to work extra hard to perform well in high
school so that colleges would take a second look at him. "[Colleges] don't
actually think that a city student will do more better than a student who
go to a county high school," he said. "All I know is that I try to prove them
wrong every time."

About to enter his senior year, Tristan hoped to attend college at the
University of Maryland, a goal inspired by a visit to the campus that summer. His mother, now remarried to a coworker at the psychiatric facility,
had left her job and was pursuing a registered nursing degree full-time.
Tristan credited her with providing inspiration. He wanted to study criminal justice, become a Baltimore police officer, and move up the ranks to the
SWAT team. "I want to be a police officer because . . . I would make sure I
get the job done. And I always want to be there and help." Though he believed that police "abuse their power a lot . . . for me, it would be a different story." Tristan's outlook on life was profoundly different from the outlook of his older sister and older males in our sample who spent more
time in high-poverty and high-crime neighborhoods. In these less distressed neighborhood environments, Sheila no longer had to focus on survival or her own depression and instead could start thinking ahead about
educational options for her children.

Europe

MEDITERRANEAN SEA

SPAIN

TOLEDO

PORTUGAL

BARCELONA

FRANCE

SWITZERLAND

TOUR DE FRANCE

PARIS

BELGIUM

BAY OF BISCAY

ATLANTIC OCEAN

IRELAND

ENGLAND

LONDON

START

NETHERLAND

① ② ③ ④

Direct Effects: Neighborhood Influences

Parents' improved mental health, behavior, and parenting are what so-cial scientists call indirect effects—improvements in the lives of those in one generation yielding benefits in the lives of the next generation. But there is ample evidence that the change in neighborhood environment could have had direct effects on youth as well.[57] We can compare census data on both their original and 2010 addresses, documenting exposure to both mainstream and nonmainstream influences at the neighborhood level during the two time periods. We find that, compared to where they and their parents were living when they were zero to ten years old, our youth experienced a dramatic increase in their exposure to mainstream influences.

We display some of these indicators in table 2.5, which shows that the number of high school graduates in their neighborhood (defined as a cen-sus tract) was 62 percent higher than in their earlier neighborhoods. Youth were exposed to almost double the number of neighbors holding bache-lor's degrees and a 120 percent increase in the number of married couples than had been present in their earlier neighborhood. Along with these gains, youths' exposure to nonmainstream influences fell sharply. These young people experienced neighborhoods with significantly fewer high school dropouts (a decline of 55 percent), a falloff of 27 percent in the number of neighbors who were unemployed, about one-third (32 percent) fewer single-parent homes, and an 83 percent drop in individuals report-ing public assistance receipt than would have been the case if their neigh-borhood had remained the same as at baseline. This is in addition to the 62 percent decrease in the poverty rate experienced by the sample as a whole, experimental and control groups combined.

Patrick Sharkey and others have argued that much of what makes poor neighborhoods detrimental to child development is exposure to violence.[58] Ideally, in addition to the social and economic indicators in table 2.5, we would have liked to compare tract-level violence over time. Unfortu-nately, the data are not available before 2000, and according to many, they are unreliable for the years since.[59] So we take another approach and use parents' and youths' reports of safety and victimization for the Baltimore MTO survey sample over the same time period. All the measures reported in table 2.6 are taken from the adults, for the sake of comparison to the baseline survey, except the measure of neighborhood safety at the final survey.

The changes in parent and youth reports of safety over time are strik-ing. Parents reported large drops in perceived neighborhood danger and personal experiences of victimization. Although the experimental group shows the largest drop in the percent of household heads reporting vic-

Table 2.5 Socioeconomic Change in Baseline and Current Neighborhoods of MTO Baltimore Youth, 1990–2010

	Married Couple Households	Single-Mother Households	High School or GED	Bachelor's Degree	Unemployed	Households Receiving Public Assistance
Baseline address (census 1990)	16.88%	77.70%	46.85%	7.84%	24.04%	46.57%
Current address (ACS, 2008–2012)	37.13	53.25	75.92	15.85	17.54	7.95
Percentage change between baseline and current neighborhood	120.0	–31.5	62.1	102.2	–27.0	–82.9

Source: U.S. Census, 1990; ACS, 2008–2012.

Table 2.6   Safety and Victimization in Baseline and Final Neighborhoods

	Experimental Group[a]	Control Group
Baseline—member of household victimized in last six months	48%	39%
Final—member of household victimized in last six months	20	25
Baseline—streets near home felt safe at night[b]	42	45
Final—streets near home felt safe or very safe at night	68	69
Final—streets near home felt safe or very safe at night (youth)	63	64

Source: HUD, PDR, Moving to Opportunity Study Final Evaluation Impacts Survey.
[a]For the baseline survey, $N = 631$; for the final adult survey, $N = 451$; for the final youth survey, $N = 610$.
[b]The survey questions at baseline and at final survey were slightly different. The baseline variable calculated those who felt very unsafe in their neighborhood at night, and we flipped the percentage around. Since this percentage now includes even those who felt unsafe in their neighborhoods, the difference in safety between baseline and final is even more profound than noted here.

timization, both groups show drops of more than 30 percent. Around 40 percent more family members and youth also reported very large gains in perceived safety. These numbers lend strong support to our claim that our youth spent their formative years in much safer neighborhoods, neighborhoods that they felt they could more comfortably explore, with more neighbors who were working and more educated and two-parent households.

Youth Perspectives on Neighborhood Change

These numbers tell a powerful story, but the interviews with the youth themselves drive the point home. Some youth could clearly remember the violence, the idleness of their neighbors, and the physical deterioration of their buildings, often drawing sharp distinctions between the housing project neighborhoods where they spent their early childhoods and the ones they grew up in after they left.

For example, after Erica's family left the Somerset Homes, they moved to Ednor Gardens, a place with "more people with stuff to live for." Sarah, nineteen, recalled her time in the Murphy Homes: "I remember the little playground that they had in front of it, and I remember the little nastiest stinking elevator that I ever rode in. . . . And they used to have some of the biggest rats. I remember one Christmas I fed it cheese." Annmarie, twenty-two, felt a sharp sense of relief when her family left the Lafayette Homes, where, she said, the hallways were full of people "standing around, like, distributing drugs and playing loud music and drinking and all that. It was terrible." She recalled a time when one of the young addicts in the complex came to the door to ask her mother for help with child care: "This woman, like, she don't even know my mother, she ask her could she hold her child while she high. . . . I'm glad we don't live in the projects [any-more]." Twenty-one-year-old Sierra remembered that leaving the projects meant she could ride her bike outside safely. "We felt uncomfortable, so [my mother] took us away from there. And from there, we went to this nice house on Loch Raven, a nice quiet block. . . . I felt real comfortable. I could trust that neighborhood. I felt safe . . . we could ride our bikes and we won't [be hearing] the gun shooting."

Tyler, twenty-one, believed that if he had remained in the O'Donnell Heights project, he almost surely would have turned to hustling. "So I felt like if I was still livin' out there, I woulda probably got caught up in it. I think my chances would have been probably, like, 97 percent of getting caught in that. 'Cause that was the only thing to do out there." Christopher, twenty-one, directly linked leaving the violent Murphy Homes and moving to the working-class neighborhood of Highlandtown with staying on track and finishing high school. He described his former neighborhood as a "very violent" place where you had to "show some type of tough-ness" and be ready to fight just to protect yourself and your family:

> Every day you would hear a gunshot, or every day you would see some-body fighting, and you never know, like, when is that going to happen to you, or when, you know, it was gonna be your family member, or when you was gonna have to bear it all, just go out there and just fight a war or what-ever. Um, Highlandtown, not really, 'cause it was most likely a quiet neigh-borhood, like I said, I lived around a bunch of older people, you know . . . so, it was really like, *safer,* but Murphy Homes, you really had to have a mind-set, like, can you really take this, can you really stand hearing the gun-shots every night, or every morning?

Christopher had discovered his passion for cooking even before he started high school. After graduating from Digital Harbor High School, he took classes at the Baltimore International College Culinary School, hop-ing to eventually open his own restaurant. He reflected on how important for his future it had been to leave Murphy: "I think if I wouldn't've left

Murphy Homes, I probably woulda been a disruptive kid . . . out running with people who had a record, or, maybe selling drugs, because that's the lifestyle I was around. So I think it was a better purpose for me to move. . . . So I believe that my move, or my schools actually helped my life."

In making these claims, our data suffer from two primary limitations. We did not observe these children while they were still living at their public housing addresses, so we have to rely on their retrospective accounts. A similar limitation holds for the intergenerational comparisons. Ideally, we would have been able to compare the narratives of our youth to those of their parents when they were also in early adulthood. But the parents did not usually sign up for MTO (and thus enter our study) until around age thirty. The survey did not ask whether they had lived in public housing as children, but when we collected the life histories of parents in 2003 and 2004, many said that they too had grown up in the projects or in the low-income neighborhoods around public housing. It would also have been useful to compare our youths' narratives to those of their significantly older siblings who had had greater exposure to the projects. We do have a few of these comparisons: Tristan and his older sister Clarice, for instance, and other sibling pairs, including Bridget and her brother, featured in chapter 5. These cases, while few in number, certainly conform to the argument.[60]

Regardless, our data document a profound intergenerational leap forward that affected both the experimental and control group youth. The possible mechanisms we point to include: improved parental mental health; dramatic drops in parents'—and especially primary caregivers'—drug use; more focused parenting; dramatic increases in exposure to mainstream influences at the neighborhood level; and declines in exposure to violence. These changes provide at least circumstantial evidence that, together, MTO, HOPE VI, and other demolition efforts in the city of Baltimore—however imperfectly implemented—changed the neighborhood contexts in which low-income young people were raised and are currently coming of age, and that these differences, in turn, may have a dramatic impact on key young adult outcomes such as schooling, risk behavior, and employment.

As succeeding chapters show, these accomplishments were forged against long odds stemming from our youths' families of origin and the ongoing challenges faced by those living in even moderately poor neighborhoods. After all, Baltimore continues to rank among the country's poorer cities, and even after violent crime allegedly fell by 40 percent in the wake of then-mayor Martin O'Malley's "get tough on crime" policies of the early 2000s, the city still ranks among the most violent in the nation.[61]

We can see the undertow from the family of origin (as we refer to it in chapter 5) in the intergenerational comparisons as well. For example, in terms of exposure to trauma, the intergenerational differences, while meaningful, are not as dramatic as the improvements noted earlier. For example, while nearly six in ten (58 percent) of those in the parents' generation had experienced victimization, trauma, abuse, or domestic violence in their lives—a high rate by any yardstick—23 percent of the next generation had already had a family member die from addiction, overdose, or homicide. Thirty-five percent had seen someone shot, stabbed, severely beaten, or killed, either at home or in the neighborhood. Fifteen percent had been the victim of rape, child sexual abuse, or severe emotional or physical abuse at the hands of a caregiver. And almost one-third (30 percent) had had to live apart from their family of origin for a period of time.

The young people profiled at the beginning of this chapter were no exception. The father of Dana, the producer and star of *Dana's TV Show*, who was inspired to become a nurse while caring for an older sister who eventually died of AIDS, was an addict and had been in and out of jail for drug possession and check fraud. These traumas mimicked those experienced by her mother, who saw three of her siblings die by the age of fourteen, one from AIDS and two as a result of street violence between rival drug dealers. Yet by the time Dana had left high school, her mother had defied the odds, holding down a steady job as a midlevel civil servant for more than a decade and becoming the homeowner she had always aspired to be. Though a big improvement over the Flag Homes, the Northwest Baltimore neighborhood she and her mother now shared still had its problems. Dana noted that it was easy to see the drug activity in the townhomes behind her house.

Erica, once a special education student and now nearly ready to graduate from Morgan State University with a four-year degree, lost her father before she was two, and the uncle who took his place as a father figure died from cancer while she was in high school. Her mother battled alcoholism for years, perhaps as a way to cope with the early deaths of all seven of her siblings, Erica's aunts and uncles. "She watched everybody go," Erica said. "I wanna say everybody pretty much died as a result of drug use, some type of, if it was alcohol or narcotics or something like that, and eventually they got sick. My uncle, my last uncle on this side, he died in April. He had some type of rare cancer that was smooshing his heart and his lungs."

In the face of these challenges, Erica's older sister had been a guiding force, a source of support and connection. Erica's sister had a bachelor's degree in biology from Morgan State and a master's degree in human resources management from an Ivy League school. "My sister, oh, my sister, we're really close," Erica said. "She's twelve years older than me. I'm twenty-two, she's thirty-four. She was more like a mother to me." Erica also derived inspiration from an older brother who had a bachelor's degree from the University of Connecticut and was a lieutenant colonel in the army, working at the Pentagon. Like her sister, her brother was much older (forty years old). She described him as one of the most successful people she knew.

Antonio, the boy who loved to come home from school each day and sprawl on the carpet with the day's *Baltimore Sun*, had experienced perhaps more trauma than any of the others. While she was alive, his mother Tammy was often severely depressed, a victim of childhood abuse herself—which made it hard for her to parent Antonio, who often went hungry. Once, he witnessed her stab an abusive boyfriend in the kitchen, only to go on cooking afterwards.

Just as he entered young adulthood, Tammy was driving through Perkins Homes projects on a Sunday afternoon with her youngest son and daughter when she was shot in the head, seemingly at random. Antonio's sister jumped out of the car, and his younger brother leapt into the front seat to stop the vehicle from moving. Not surprisingly, the shocking, sudden death of their mother took an enormous psychological toll on all of her children. Antonio's older brother moved to Philadelphia, and his sister had what he referred to as a "mental stress breakdown," which landed her in the hospital for two weeks. Antonio went through a severe depression that made him unable leave the house. No one was arrested for the shooting. Antonio could not make sense of the situation. "Like a lot of people say, God has his time for everybody, or when it's your time to go, it's your time to go," he said. "I just don't feel like that. I feel like she was taken from me."

Antonio's father, the man who fathered Tammy's three youngest children, was little help. While he was young, the man had spent time in jail for domestic violence and other offenses. By the time Antonio was in middle school, his father had married, had a daughter, and virtually cut off contact with Antonio and the two other children he'd had with Tammy. In 2004, Tammy had told us that Antonio took his father's absence especially hard. "[Antonio] wants his father to be in his life so much, you know," she said.

During that time, Antonio began cutting school because there was so much fighting—with knives—going on. "I was scared for my life," he recalled. "People were getting killed." The first week of his ninth-grade year, a boy was beaten up in front of the school so badly that his skull was fractured. In response, Antonio adopted the following strategy: "If you go to school and you talk too much or you try to be out there and, you know, you not a certain way, it's either you going to be this kind of person, you better be ready to kill somebody . . . that's the kind of attention that you going to bring to yourself." By twenty-three, Antonio could tick off the list of middle school and high school peers who had been killed or put in prison.

Jackson, the budding author who graduated from high school and went on to enroll in—but not complete—several postsecondary degrees, was one of five siblings with three different fathers. Jackson's father was an addict whom he rarely saw. His youngest brother's father, who helped raise him, was also an addict and was presently incarcerated. An older brother was incarcerated again after getting into fights while on probation.

Now enjoying a rare bout of sobriety, Jackson's father worked in a hotel downtown as a prep cook. One of Jackson's novels was inspired by his travails over his father's drug use. He spoke poignantly about how his father's addiction, and his frequent absences, had affected him: "He was getting high and stuff, and then I didn't understand it or know what was going on," Jackson said. "I just always knew he was in my life for, like, a couple of months, and then he'd be doing good, he'd be working, have an apartment and stuff. And then the next, I just don't know where he at. It's like he disappeared." The last straw for Jackson was when his father failed to show up for his high school graduation, despite the fact that Jackson had reserved a ticket for him. "I'll never forget," he said. "I went to his house, and the reason for him not coming to the graduation was because his head was itching. . . .[62] That was the petty excuse he gave me."

CONCLUSION

In the 1950s and '60s, when most of the nation's public housing complexes were constructed, the narrative around public housing—and perhaps the reality as well—was entirely different from what we describe in this chapter. During those years, reformers concerned about the social and health conditions in the nation's overcrowded urban neighborhoods were pushing for slum clearance. Behemoth housing complexes, first low- and then high-rise, were constructed in many major cities, often on the footprint of segregated black belts, and in high-poverty enclaves of other ethnic groups as well. Heralded as great advances, these projects offered a key asset: safe, clean places to live. Racial segregation was quite literally the rule, not the exception: initially, they served only those whose race or ethnicity matched the complexion of the surrounding area.[63]

Although racial segregation was the norm, the income of residents in the projects was somewhat mixed during this time. In fact, when Lee Rainwater and his students studied the Pruitt-Igoe housing project in St.

Louis in the 1960s—the largest in the world at the time—he found plenty of blue-collar workers, maids, and married couples among the African American residents there. However, for reasons we detailed in this chapter, this golden era of mixed-income inhabitants was short-lived. By 1983, the historian Arnold Hirsch had charged, federal housing policy had merely remade the ghetto and nearly everyone concurred with Hirsch that many of these housing projects were incubators for the social ills they had sought to alleviate.[64]

Yet, through the federal housing policies of the 1990s—namely HOPE VI—federally constructed ghettos disappeared by the hundreds. And in Baltimore at least, the number of high-poverty tracts and the percentage of the poor population living within them contracted quite dramatically, allowing most of these youth to grow up exposed to far less neighborhood-level disadvantage than they would have otherwise. We argue that these changes, and the moves afforded by MTO, were an important part of why they experienced such large intergenerational gains. These gains, arguably a result of a reversal in federal and local housing policy, support our argument that social reproduction and inequality are not inevitable: this chapter provides at least circumstantial evidence that, by dramatically improving the social settings to which children are exposed, especially neighborhoods, we can interrupt the intergenerational transmission of disadvantage.

Our results also concur with powerful new research on MTO, alluded to earlier in the chapter. In 2015, Raj Chetty, Nathaniel Hendren, and Lawrence F. Katz took a fresh look at the long-term effects of MTO—drawing on IRS records—once the children from the study had all reached adulthood. Their study revealed substantial gains roughly two decades later in earnings and other indicators among those who were younger than thirteen when their parents enrolled in the program.[65] Children who had moved before the age of thirteen showed earnings that were nearly one-third higher than earnings for those in the control group. They were also about one-quarter less likely to become single parents, and more enrolled in college and lived in lower-poverty neighborhoods as adults.

The fact that all but fifteen of the youth in our study (both those in the experimental and control groups) also moved from public housing before the age of thirteen may partly explain their relative success compared to their parents. Chetty, Hendren, and Katz document a far bleaker portrait for children who moved at older ages, suggesting that there is a distinct developmental window during which children can benefit from such a move. We did not follow our youth as long as Chetty, Hendren, and Katz were able to through IRS records. Our shorter period of follow-up, along with our smaller sample size, did not allow us to detect degrees of difference between experimentals and controls. We think it is plausible that the mechanisms we have documented in this chapter—decreases in parental drug use, a parenting dividend, lower rates of victimization, and greater feelings of safety, as well as exposure to more neighbors who worked, had college degrees, and were raising their children within two-parent families—could help explain the gains that Chetty, Hendren, and Katz document among younger youth.

However, as chapter 5 shows, revamped housing policies did not go nearly far enough—youth were still relegated to neighborhoods with considerable risks for much of their childhoods. Not only did the youth in our study have to navigate dangerous neighborhoods and underperforming schools, but many also had to contend with ongoing trauma stemming from their family of origin. While each of the youth featured in chapter 5 had managed to graduate from high school, enroll in some type of post-college training or education, or find formal-sector employment, about one-third of our youth were neither working nor in school, sometimes because they felt that the street had more to offer. So a question remains: what separates those who manage to stay on track from those who do not?

In the next chapter, we show that what often distinguished youth like Antonio, Erica, and their similar peers from other, less successful youth was their discovery of something meaningful and inspiring that they could "be about" while in high school—an identity-defining outlet. These identity projects provided a powerful antidote to the street and the drama many saw around them, as well as another way to be. As we show, it was typically an identity project that helped these youth avoid risk in their families, neighborhoods, and schools. Often, identity projects forged a bridge between their challenging present and their uncertain—but fervently hoped for—future.

Chapter 3 | "Following My Passion": How Identity Projects Help Youth Beat the Street and Stay on Track

Children cannot be fooled by empty praise and condescending encouragement . . . their identity gains real strength only from wholehearted and consistent recognition of real accomplishment, that is, achievement that has meaning in their culture.
—Erik Erikson, *Identity and the Life Cycle* (1959/1980)

So the seeker of his truest, strongest, deepest self must review the list [of possible selves] carefully and pick out the one on which to stake his salvation.
—William James, *Principles of Psychology* (1890)

TERRY BEGAN LIFE in the Cherry Hill projects, part of a dense constellation of public housing in an isolated section of South Baltimore. "The things that are worth having seem like they be so far away from you when you come from where I come from," he said. His home life was no haven from the violence and crime outside of the apartment's walls. From the age of eight, Terry ran away repeatedly to escape a physically abusive, drug-addicted mother who singled him out from among her nine children as the focus of her rage. After fleeing the house in the wake of one of her tantrums, he would wander the streets; sometimes he would be found by a police officer or a pastor when he inevitably fell asleep on a bench, exhausted from walking. In a cruel twist of fate, Terry was removed from his mother's care and made a ward of the state the same year she received an MTO voucher, in 1996. She used the voucher to move with Terry's siblings to the mostly white, affluent suburb of Columbia, only twenty miles south

59

of the city but a world away. Meanwhile, Terry moved through a succession of group homes in West Baltimore. Back then he wondered, "Out of nine kids, what the hell was wrong with me?"

Terry rejoined his family in Columbia at fifteen, when his mother regained custody. But his return was not the warm reunion he was hoping for. There was no celebration, "not even, like, a welcome-home gathering," he said. It was a difficult transition because he had to "relearn who my family was." By this time, he was fully grown and too big for his mother to pose a physical threat. Yet she "still had this power over me, it was like mind control." To deal with this tension, Terry started binge-drinking so heavily that he sometimes blacked out. After a year, he left home to live with an older brother in West Baltimore. When the brother married a year later and no longer had room for him, Terry opted to sleep in Leakin Park, a heavily wooded area in Northwest Baltimore notorious for the number of dead bodies that the police had discovered there. For Terry, this was better than returning to his mother's home and facing her anger. "I threw my bags in the woods, and I registered myself [for school] to finish my senior year."[1]

Although sleeping outdoors had been a coping mechanism Terry used during those early episodes of running away, he now fell deeply into depression. To survive emotionally, he reached out to God, weed, and booze, all at once. "I prayed, and I smoked a lot of weed. It made emotions easier to deal with at the time—at least it seemed that way. I prayed a lot because it was important for me to graduate." At one point Terry contemplated suicide and prayed that God would "miraculously just stop me from breathing. I didn't wanna be here." Instead, he found an alternative family in the form of the other homeless or near-homeless youth in the area, who also congregated in the park. Now, several years later, Terry had the space to reflect on what had felt so compelling about that community of cast-asides, the sense of false camaraderie that shared desperation inspired:

> People—out of a desperation—they cling to each other, complete strangers. . . . But they were never really friends. Kids, they drink together, they smoke together, because they don't have anybody. . . . It's a culture in urban life, man. It's like this depression thing in the air, man, pain in people's eyes and everything. . . . Nobody knows what to do, so they just party and [do] drugs.[2]

In the midst of this turmoil, Terry found structure and purpose in the routine of going to school. He became a "perfect attendance kid," showing up on time every day of his senior year. After school and on weekends, he worked a succession of jobs to feed and clothe himself—as a pizza delivery boy, a fast-food cook, even a salesman at an expensive handbag store at the high-end Galleria Mall in Baltimore's Inner Harbor. He would do what he could to establish rapport with his managers, and then ask them to recommend him for other, better positions. Meanwhile, he kept himself afloat by listening to Tupac, "my sanctuary." During the year he had spent in Columbia with his mother, he had started performing at open mic nights, which had sparked an interest in the arts. "I wanted to go where artists were, people doing visual, art, music," he said. While living in the woods, he began reading poetry and eventually writing his own songs— many focusing on his growing relationship with God. At school, he forged familylike bonds. Teachers reached out to him. There were "a couple of counselors who just wouldn't let me drop out, they just wouldn't. . . . They just loved me, and they showed me a lot of support and just—I don't know if I would have made it through there without them."[3]

It was during that difficult senior year that it all changed for Terry. When he was offered a chance to work with some of the students with special needs at his school, he became attached to one particular student and spent time with him even on the days he was not scheduled to work with him. Terry also sat next to the children with disabilities—whom the school called the "life skills kids"—during lunch, much to the confusion of his more popular classmates. But Terry was struck by the resilience in his new charges, something that resonated with him on a deep level. "I [had] felt like I had the right to be angry at life and this and that," he said. "But these kids, man . . . some of them couldn't change their own clothes, you know, and they were happy . . . so I stayed around them. And after high school I knew—that's what I wanted to do. I wanted to help people."

After graduating from high school, Terry continued to live on the streets for another two years. He worked nonstop at entry-level jobs, yet "always" stayed involved with community service, which he saw as the link to what he hoped would be his future career. His heart had been captured by helping those life-skills kids, and he was determined to stay the course of pursuing a career in human services. When he was about to turn twenty, he discovered a shelter in downtown Baltimore where he could secure a bed and some support. He took full advantage of what was offered: "I started [learning how to take] advantage of the different resources in the area—how to get bus fare, how to apply for housing, different stuff," he said. "I was trying to get on my feet." While living at the shelter, Terry had a chance to participate in the organization's outreach work. He loved going out in the community because it gave him a chance to keep that spark of generativity alive. "I just did that from following my heart, following my passion, which is like doing something for people, you know, always wanting to reach out," he said.

Terry carefully put together a résumé, built on his volunteer experiences in high school and subsequent community service. He landed a job as a youth leader for A Place to Call Home, a program that helps homeless young adults find independent living—a position he still held in 2010. The tall twenty-three-year-old now wore his hair in short twists, with a carefully manicured mustache and sideburns and a pair of silver framed glasses that he frequently took off and cleaned while he talked. A few months earlier, he had moved out of the shelter and in with a friend. As to next steps, he expected to be placed in a low-income apartment complex for single adults by fall. The latest news was that the staff at the homeless initiative had recommended him for a job through AmeriCorps, which was launching a new youth outreach program in the Irvington neighborhood of West Baltimore, close to where Terry spent so many years homeless. "I'll be designing a program that can get kids off the street!" he exclaimed. Terry believed that this position would "open a lot of doors . . . to meet people, different nonprofits in the city." He acknowledged that while he was embarrassed not to have a job that paid more, he felt like he was on "a mission" and this was his chance to "start focusing on what I'm really interested in." Plus, he wanted to "start going back to church and trying to break some of the old habits that I've picked up, as far as being around the wrong people." For Terry, it was not about the money. It was about "peace of mind," which he had been searching for his whole life. "I've found it in working with youth," he said.[4]

As Terry embarked on this next phase, he reflected on what he had already accomplished. The miracle of his remarkable tenacity and resilience was not lost on him. He proudly assessed where he stood: "You know, I just be tryin' to ride this thing out the best way I could since I've been born, and I think I'm doin' a pretty damn good job."

Chantal spent her middle school and high school years living with her grandmother in the beleaguered Sandtown-Winchester neighborhood, a tract that could serve as a poster child for "the vacants"—Baltimore's shorthand for the blight that consumes so much of the city. At the time of our interview, however, one could hardly see any evidence of the troubles she had faced early in life. At twenty-three, she was articulate, friendly, and outgoing, her slicked-back ponytail bobbing as she energetically shared her story. Chantal and her partner Lisa were raising Chantal's six-year-old son in a beautiful three-bedroom apartment in suburban Columbia on a tree-lined street. There was a large park so close to her house that when she was not walking their Chihuahua with her son, she could watch the boy play there from her balcony.

Now a college junior, Chantal deftly juggled her studies as a sociology major at Morgan State University with a full-time job as a receptionist at an insurance company. On Saturdays she volunteered for a program housed at a health center near her West Baltimore childhood home, an organization she founded to help other young women avoid some of the pitfalls of growing up in that community.

These accomplishments were hard-won. Chantal spent her early years living with her parents in Lexington Terrace, where both her mother and father became addicted to heroin and were in and out of jail. With the support of her grandmother and a caring middle school counselor, she made her way to one of Baltimore's most selective magnet high schools, Shadyside High, located in the leafy Roland Park neighborhood. Shadyside regularly sends its top students to selective schools, including the Ivies. "I've always been into school, and my grades was pretty much always there," she explained.

During her high school years, Chantal dodged risk at every turn. Despite her grandmother's best efforts to serve as a substitute parent, one of Chantal's three brothers started selling drugs and ended up in prison. Several close friends from the neighborhood resorted to selling sex for money. At fourteen, she became involved with a boy who was in a gang and dealt drugs. They were an odd couple, she said: "[I was] the girl who went to school and went to work and kind-of-sort-of did what she had to do, and then him kind-of-sort-of ripping and running the streets." She believed that the relationship was "serious," and while she did not plan on getting pregnant, her vigilance about contraception lapsed as the relationship progressed.[5] Chantal learned that she was expecting during her sophomore year. After the baby was born, she was shocked that her boyfriend did not seem willing even to help watch his son for a few hours. Once his infidelity was revealed, she cut him off for good.

Shadyside High required students who became mothers to sign an "attendance pledge." Insulted by the implication that she would let a baby stand in the way of her education, Chantal left Shadyside and opted for Garrison, the high school close to her grandmother's Sandtown-Winchester home. Soon she discovered that this school was a huge step down from the academic rigors of Shadyside, which "prepared you more-so for that college environment." Chantal described Garrison, which had long ago nurtured several African American luminaries, as a place with "wild and tacky" people, where "all you had to do was show up." Eager to maintain that edge she had gained at Shadyside, she took advantage of Garrison's Upward Bound program. She gave birth to her son over winter break her junior year, relieved that the timing of the birth made it possible not to "miss so much work" at school. Eventually, the Upward Bound staff would help Chantal with everything from SAT prep to her financial aid application.

Rather than a distraction or a burden, Chantal saw her son as a motivator. "I can't give him what I want to give him [if I'm] unemployed . . . and I want him to know you can be above this," she explained six years later. In recounting her story, she said that the strong sense of generativity that her baby sparked gave her a new focus and resolve, which began to extend far beyond ensuring that her son would rise above their circumstances. She was also inspired to help other young women like herself avoid the traps of the neighborhood she was raised in, a cause to which she hoped to devote her life.

Shortly after high school graduation, she founded an organization that reached out to young women in some of the city's toughest neighborhoods to help them weather the storms of their childhoods and launch their adult lives. Housed in a community health center, My Best Self encourages young women to be proactive about everything from "personal development to career achievements . . . [and] set their standards [high] so they are not just [taking the first thing they see]." The mantra of Chantal's organization is, "If you don't stand for something, you'll fall for anything." She hoped the program would eventually help outsiders see the girls in these neighborhoods "for more than what a lot of people see them [as] being, growing up in [this kind of] community." Eventually, she hoped to expand the program's offerings to include a group home for girls "with addictions or [other] problems." She believed that she was particularly well suited for this work because she could say, "Hey, I've also been in your shoes. I've walked through these streets as well, but you too can get out of it."

THE POWER OF AN IDENTITY PROJECT

Despite deeply troubled childhoods and challenging neighborhood environments, Terry and Chantal both managed to "beat the streets" and in fact find ways of giving back to their communities. Are they the exception or the rule? We believe that there are two reasons why many ethnographies of youth from disadvantaged origins portray lives awash in serious delinquency and crime. First, some researchers set out to study youth involved in delinquent activities, thus "sampling on the dependent variable," or choosing the outcome they intend to portray. (There is nothing wrong with this approach; indeed, it is one that we have practiced ourselves in many studies. But like any approach, it has its pros and cons.) Second, other researchers advocate for naturalistic observation over interviews, which they view as less reliable. And there is often good reason to be skeptical—interviews privilege young people's own understandings of their lives, not necessarily objective reality, and social desirability bias may cause them to underreport deviant or delinquent activity and over-report conforming behavior. For example, in the interim survey, adminis-trative records revealed somewhat more arrests than the male youth re-ported to survey researchers from MTO, though the discrepancy was not large.[6] But observational studies run the risk of giving disproportionate voice to those few who dominate public space ("the corner") rather than those youth who withdraw to their bedrooms to play video games, who head to the library to read books after school, or who spend their after-school time working.

We were fortunate to be able to identify our sample in early childhood from a population of children whose parents' characteristics, collected in a baseline survey, were largely representative of those raising their chil-dren in public housing in the mid-1990s (albeit somewhat more disadvan-taged), as we noted in chapter 2. Their shared origins, not their outcomes, were what got them into our study. This allows us to observe diverse pathways and gives equal voice to those youth who are seldom, if ever, to be found on the corner, who spend their time elsewhere—in their home, at the library, or at a job. For example, we find that among these youth—a group of young people who had been born into the poorest communities in the nation's third-most-violent city—82 percent claimed that they had never been "in the street," at least not up to the point of our last interview. The term "in the street" is drawn from their own accounts; our young people generally used the term to denote drug dealing, car theft, robbery, and other seriously delinquent activity, not to what they viewed as petty crimes, such as smoking weed or riding in a stolen car.[7] And "being in the street" was typically a short-lived stage; at our last contact, only six youth, or 4 percent, were currently engaged in such activities.

We have little doubt that this is an underestimate, but even if we dou-bled the number, the vast majority in our sample would still be found re-sisting the streets. By the end of our study, 82 percent of the young adults were either working or in school—what we call being "on track," again drawing on the language these youth themselves used. The remaining 18 percent of the young adults were what we call "disconnected"—either they had dropped out of high school and not found work or they had graduated from high school and were neither working nor attending col-lege or trade school. As a testament to their attachment to mainstream as-pirations and values, only about half of these disconnected youths were ever "in the street," as we discuss in the next chapter. Rather, they were just struggling to find some kind of foothold in the world—sometimes as they battled mental health and substance use problems.

The terms "street" and "on track" bring to mind the language that appears in two well-known ethnographies of low-income communities, one in Washington, D.C. (Ulf Hannerz's *Soulside*) and the other in Philadelphia (Elijah Anderson's *Code of the Street*). These authors use the terms "mainstream," "decent," and "street" to describe similarly divergent pathways among the people in their communities. In the neighborhoods they studied, such terms appeared to connote (according to residents, not necessarily to the authors) moral evaluations about individual character. Although we do not doubt that community members sometimes drew distinctions of these kinds, the way our youth generally deployed the terms "in the street" and its opposite, "on track," was to describe behaviors that one was engaged in at present. Indeed, one could be "in the street" and "on track" at the same time, as we see in the story of Ron in the next chapter. One can also switch designations over time, as Antonio, featured in chapter 2, did when he left drug dealing in favor of legal employment.[8]

But what determined whether youth would be "on track" or disconnected? As we combed through the narratives to try to understand the divergent pathways among the youth in the study, we explored a variety of possibilities from the literature, such as childhood trauma in the family of origin, direct exposure to violence, the presence of adult role models, and whether a parent or primary caregiver was employed, struggled with a substance abuse problem, or was in jail.

Each of these factors turned out to be important, as revealed by a number of simple statistical tests that we ran (especially when predicting whether a youth was ever in the street, as we discuss in chapter 4).[9] None of these factors was as powerful, however, as what we call an identity project.

Our definition of an "identity project" emerged inductively from youths' own narratives.[10] An identity project is a source of meaning that provides a strong sense of self and is linked to concrete activities to which youth commit themselves.[11] They were often forged in direct opposition to the street, to demonstrate that a young person was "not about that life," but had bigger dreams and goals: to "be about something."[12] We also find that identity projects helped some youth avoid associations with delinquent peers and instead forge connections with teachers and mentors. Identity projects came in several forms. At their weakest, they were activities that youth pursued in private. Identity projects were more protective when they linked youth to like-minded peers through shared interests in the arts or music. In their most robust form, they connected young people with institutions that had a ready-made set of concrete activities and supports. And it was when youth formed identity projects in the context of institutions that we saw the strongest link with future vocational goals.

Table 3.1   Identity Projects and Trajectories After High School (N = 116)

	On Track	Neither Working nor in School	Total
Youth had an identity project	94%	6%	100%
Youth did not have an identity project	65	35	100

Source: Authors' compilations.

One recurring theme was that many institutionally linked identity projects were motivated by a strong desire to give back to their communities, with the aim of helping others who might be struggling as they had done, as is evident in Terry's and Chantal's stories.[13]

We find a striking connection between whether youth had adopted an identity project in middle or high school and the paths they took later, particularly the educational and vocational pathways they pursued (see table 3.1). Ninety-four percent of those who met the criteria of being on track after high school had an identity project. In contrast, just under one in fifteen (6 percent) of those who were neither working nor in school had embraced one.

Terry had found several sources of support along the way—especially a few caring school personnel and a program for homeless youth with encouraging staff. But for Terry it was working with the "life skills kids" that ultimately provided the inspiration he needed to persevere and forge a career helping others. For Chantal, adult relationships and institutional supports were vital too—particularly her grandmother's guidance, the middle school counselor's help in paving the way for her admission to Shadyside, and her participation in Upward Bound. Yet Chantal said that the birth of her son was like flipping a switch. It changed her entire self-identity, gave each aspect of her daily routine new meaning, and motivated her to found an organization that would raise her to a position of prominence in the Sandtown-Winchester community in her early twenties. Despite extraordinarily tough childhoods, Terry and Chantal each found a passion that provided a bridge between the challenges of their youth and the conventional adult pathways they ended up pursuing.[14]

As we have indicated, the identity project is both internal—what an adolescent is "about"—and external—a concrete set of activities he or she commits to doing.[15] Perhaps the core function of the identity project is to preserve psychic wholeness in the face of very challenging conditions.[16] Sometimes these projects eventually lead to a specific vocation, or life calling (such as "helping people"), but not always. For the youth in our study, identity projects were virtually always cast in sharp opposition to the street—they informed the young person's sense of self and the course to follow, as well as those to avoid.[17] These projects provided inner sustenance, meaning and purpose, and sometimes a deep connection to like-minded others. As we will see in chapter 4, the street itself can offer an alternative sense of identity, but in our data at least, it does not accomplish what an identity project does—preserving these adolescents while preparing them to launch into adulthood at a time when there is a real risk that they will not make it past the dangers in their families and neighborhoods. We also argue that identity projects work because they inspire grit, which is then deployed to pursue a brighter future.[18]

In looking across the 150 youth as a whole, just under half (45 percent) had adopted an identity project in adolescence or very early adulthood.[19] For these youth, it was not enough to hold mainstream aspirations or to define themselves in opposition to the street. They also had to actively resist a strong pull, a toxic undertow that threatened to suck them into self-destructive or delinquent behavior at many turns. Tony, twenty-one and in college, had vowed never to let his family down through his actions or those of people with whom he associated. His strategy was clear: "I don't want anyone to throw me off, so I'm like, 'If you talkin' negativity about doin' something, I don't even wanna hang around you. You can do that by yourself,'" he said. Others echoed his resolve. Eighteen-year-old Tyleah, a community college student who worked at the Baltimore Ravens stadium, believed that "you gotta distance yourself away from things that's not helping you," while Georgia, a high school senior who aspired to be a radiology technician, chose not to "hang out with people who are troublemakers." For his part, George, nineteen, who worked as a cook at a seafood carryout restaurant, felt that, while it was sad to part ways with some high school friends, he "just stopped hanging out with a lot of people because they . . . doing things that [they] shouldn't be doing."

These youth often proudly scorned the "knuckleheads" in their communities, especially drug dealers, whom they saw as being "about nothing." The last thing they wanted was to "become a statistic" or to feed into what they perceived as the stereotype of a young African American from Baltimore. Chantal spent her high school years living in the same neighborhood as Freddie Gray, whose death sparked the 2015 Baltimore unrest. Sandtown-Winchester is a community with such a long history of violence and drugs that it inspired the 1990s television miniseries *The Corner.* Yet she bristled at the idea that youth from her neighborhood were like those portrayed on TV. "I think [the show] presented a really poor image of the neighborhood and what's really expected," Chantal said. "Yes, some of the things happen, but that's not what you see *every day* . . . [most people] just kind-of-sort-of try to rise above it and not become a part of it."

Even though it was rarely taken by our youth, the street was the pathway most clearly on display, with entry points most easily recognized; its strategies and stages were largely familiar to them.[20] As twenty-three-year-old Ray put it, "You see there's an opportunity . . . it's something you know you can be." Other, more conventional paths were also present, but good information about college and career training was scarce, while misinformation abounded.[21] Thus, these young people had to contend continually—and consciously—with the street in a way that their middle-class peers did not. With the street adding a weighty additional task as they navigated the transition to adulthood, accomplishing their goals required extraordinary perseverance. However, at least for our youth, the perseverance required to accomplish this task seemed to require inspiration. The force of this undertow needed an opposing and even more powerful force to counteract it—which was why identity projects played such a critical role.

GRIT AND INSPIRATION

Grit has been defined by the concept's leading proponent, the psychologist Angela Duckworth, as "perseverance and passion for long term goals."[22] There are countless examples in our narratives of identity projects sparking grit in kids whose pathways had been unsure. Take Tony, the twenty-one-year-old college student from Edmondson Village. It was an internship with the Maryland Poison Control Center one summer during high school, via the city's YouthWorks summer employment program, that sparked his identity project—a fascination with the medical professions that had since morphed into his goal to become a pharmacist. "I would just deliver mail from the Center to the School of Pharmacy," he said. "So I would walk around on the campus, and I'd see what's going on. [The medical professionals] would basically talk to me, tell me how things worked and how things were going there. So that's what kind of sparked my interest to become a pharmacist." After high school, Tony applied to a selective four-year college's pharmacy program and was admitted, but he could not afford the tuition and did not get enough financial aid to make up the difference. He decided to complete the prerequisites at Baltimore City Community College and transfer after his sophomore year. To keep his eye on the prize, he had carefully made a list of all the prerequisites required and taped it to the refrigerator at home. At the end of each semester, he delighted in taking that list down, marking off completed requirements, and smoothing the document's many wrinkles and folds before re-adhering it with a clean strip of tape. The inspiration afforded by that internship, where the sight of medical professionals bustling between labs proved so compelling, was what helped Tony accomplish the gritty work of staying in college—completing a major he could pursue only a course or two at a time while holding down a full-time job.

A school field trip to the morgue was enough to ignite nineteen-year-old Jasmine's interest in a science career. "We seen real dead bodies, got to touch them and stuff," she said. "And I was all into it. [I said to myself,] 'I like this life.'" Others found a way to escape and create through hands-on hobbies. Jamal became absorbed in caring for pigeons when he was younger—he excitedly recounted that at one point he had over thirty birds, kept in separate sections for the "breeding, mating, flying, and show birds." Building pigeon coops inspired him to consider a career in carpentry. Raising pigeons, it turns out, is not just for boys—as Vicky's story, told later in this chapter, will show.

The concept of grit has received considerable public attention in the last few years. The author Paul Tough has written compellingly about the power of "character" and "grit" in shaping the life chances of disadvantaged youth.[23] Angela Duckworth, who is among the cadre of researchers who inspired Tough's book, *How Children Succeed*, won a MacArthur "genius award" for research showing that grit is a more powerful explanation for achievement than other measures of talent or intelligence. According to Duckworth and her colleagues, people with grit continue to push toward their goals even in the face of significant adversity, and even if they receive little to no positive reinforcement. Grit has been linked to performing well in the National Spelling Bee, completing West Point's rigorous summer training program, and attaining high grades in college.[24]

Tough's book, along with the body of research it summarizes, has been widely praised, and Duckworth's ideas have prompted entire school districts to consider new curricula designed to teach grit.[25] The concept of grit is optimistic and compelling, as it suggests that youth are neither doomed by their cognitive ability (something educators find hard to change) nor implicitly limited by their social backgrounds. In our review of the psychological literature on grit, social structural factors—such as economic inequality, inadequate schools, institutional racism, and labor markets—are conspicuously absent. In this way, the notion of grit is a perfect cultural fit with American individualism. People in the United States are more likely than their European counterparts to believe that a person's success or failure is tied to personal effort rather than social background or level of state support.[26] With few exceptions, these Baltimore youth ad-

hered to this ideology, even though the contexts in which they were supposed to exhibit grit were dramatically different from those of a typical
middle-class teen. In fact, aspects of their environments might have actively worked against their ability to cultivate grit. Recent findings by
neuroscientists indicate that the stress and lack of resources from growing
up in poverty may impair the development of the prefrontal function of
children's brains—the executive control panel that is supposed to help
them resist marshmallows in the famed delayed gratification test.[27]

In media interviews, Duckworth has reported that her family has a
"hard thing rule": each family member identifies one thing that challenges
him or her and sticks with it.[28] The youth in our sample had to deal with
multiple hard things, sometimes on a daily basis; many would have wel-
comed just one. We situate our discussion of grit within the particular
contexts that our youth were growing up in. Some of the questions we
consider are: In what circumstances, and from what sources, does grit
emerge? Is it an attribute one is born with, like red hair or brown eyes? Or
is it a skill cultivated by a particular kind of parenting? (This seems to be
a takeaway from Duckworth's research.) Or is it grit like a switch that is
flipped on when a young person suddenly begins to ascribe a special
meaning to her life, after having adopted a powerful new self-narrative—
an identity project—and acting on it in concrete ways? The literature dis-
cusses grit as a trait—perhaps shaped by poverty, but inculcated early on
and not easily changed—but we find that expressions of grit often require
inspiration.

For example, at many points in Terry's school career he was on the
verge of dropping out. But a chance to help a child with special needs
translated for him into a "hard thing rule" that he believed gave him the
motivation to graduate from high school. The same can be said for Chantal. Some individuals no doubt possess more perseverance than others or
were parented in ways that are more conducive to the formation of perseverance, but grit can also be sparked by the meaning that young people
ascribe to their everyday actions and routines through an identity project.

On a concrete level, identity projects offer an organizing principle for
daily life that dictates how a given young person will invest her energy
and time. Alex, sixteen, said that the key was to keep himself "occupied."
He credited his dedication to football—which occupied much of his spare
time, even during the off-season—with motivating him to stay the course
in school and hold college as a goal, since the "University of Maryland has
football and my trade, [pharmacy]." He was grateful for his current situation. "I was one of the people that could make positive changes in my life
and not be a person doing drugs—on drugs or dealing drugs or in jail or

dead or any of that negative stuff," he said. "I'm happy that I'm keeping my life positive." It is diversions like this one—passionately pursued— that seem key to helping adolescents resist the street and deploy the grit they need to continue along a conventional pathway.

DIY IDENTITY PROJECTS

At their most basic level, identity projects, as we have defined them, are conceptions of the self that confer a powerful sense of identity, involve a concrete set of activities, and provide an alternative to the street. Identity projects that rise only to this basic level are generally "do-it-yourself"— they are highly individualized, functioning more as a means of escape than engagement. DIY identity projects are like life preservers. They keep young people psychologically afloat while they resist the pull of the streets.

One example of someone who had fashioned a DIY identity project, twenty-year-old Vicky, was unusual in that she hailed from a neighborhood so poor that it was little different than the project she came from. Vicky was quick with a gesture to emphasize certain points in her story. But about an hour into our conversation it became clear that we had not quite hit the topic she wanted to talk about most. Finally, she could not contain herself anymore and in her husky voice blurted out, "Y'all wanna see my birds? I got pigeons!" She gestured to the backyard, saying that she went out there "a lot. I go out there and feed 'em, throw 'em up, let 'em out—walk around on the ground. They're in a coop me and my father built."

Vicky told us that she was spellbound the first time she saw her father handling the birds. "He was doin' it outside one day, and I started goin' out there. 'Let me hold the bird, Daddy, let me hold the bird!'" she said. Vicky had always had a soft spot for animals. She ticked off the pets she had cared for over the years on her fingers: a turtle, a baby alligator, several dogs, and now, the fourteen pigeons who lived in the coop out back. Vicky had always been emotional and easily moved. In some ways, her sensitivity was an asset: it had made her good at taking care of animals— and people, for that matter. She practically raised her cousin's daughter (she called her a "niece") for two years when her cousin got a full-time job at a university downtown. Vicky had also been a draw for the neighborhood kids, who often flocked to her, begging her to take them to the park.

However, there was a downside to how easily Vicky's emotional strings could get played, and rage could spill out when her feelings were hurt. Her pets had been more than just a hobby: they were her friends, and they had provided an escape when she felt like she might lose control.

Vicky was born in Lexington Terrace, a public housing complex so infamous that it drew a crowd of 20,000 onlookers—many former residents—as its five eleven-story towers were imploded with dynamite in July 1996.[29] Vicky was four when she left Lexington Terrace, so she did not remember much about the towers, only that she and her first pet, a dog, would walk the halls and climb up and down the stairs between the many floors, exploring. Vicky's mother was one of the lucky ones who won the MTO lottery, but the family never managed to find an address that qualified before the voucher expired.[30] Instead, the complex's closure entitled them to a regular housing choice voucher (colloquially known as "Section 8"), which could be used to rent any affordable unit that passed inspection. They did not move far—in fact, they settled about a mile away, in a narrow whitewashed brick row house. Vicky and her family still lived in that unit fifteen years later.

The block Vicky lived on was very much like the one Chantal grew up on: some of the brick row houses leaned precariously, and every third address or so had a piece of plywood where the front door used to be. Many young men were riding bicycles up and down Vicky's street when we visited her there, and we saw two young teen boys walking a pit bull on a belt used as a leash, plus several extremely thin, disheveled white men wandering around. Just two blocks away was a bustling West Baltimore Street, which boasted a chicken shack, several check-cashing joints, and a pawn shop. A corner store with a red exterior sat at the end of Vicky's block, and a coterie of folks were propped up against the building while they snacked or had a cigarette.

Since she was very young, Vicky had been prone to bouts of explosive, sometimes violent, behavior. We did not interview her mother or teacher back in 2003, so we had few clues as to the source of that violence, and neither did she. Vicky said that she first started getting into big trouble in middle school, after "zapping out" (her word for the blackouts that occurred when her anger got out of control) when she learned that her new puppy had been found dead in their basement. She had another episode a few years later, while attending Oaklawn High, on the day a beloved aunt died. This time she struck a teacher who was trying to rein her in, and she was expelled. She was sent to an alternative high school for a year. At the school she transferred to after that, West Glen, Vicky started to do a little better academically—she "liked it" because she found the teachers and the activities engaging, and she made a few friends. "I played basketball, I did a lot of activities with the little group I was in, and we went places. They was the best years," she said.

While at West Glen, she began to see a counselor about her anger issues. Vicky credited this counselor with helping her "with all my troubles I be havin' in school." The fall of her senior year Vicky participated in several school-sponsored college tours in the surrounding area and became enamored with the University of Delaware. She applied there and to a few other schools, including Salisbury University on Maryland's Eastern Shore. In the end, she did not attend because "I ain't have the money. . . . The colleges sent me papers [saying I got in], but [with the cost of] transportation—and how was I gonna pay for the school and all that? I couldn't do it. So I had to choose a better thing for me."

Initially, the "better thing" was the local community college, but she quit after attending only a few classes because it became clear to her that the other students were not as serious as she was about school. "Everybody was in the hallways, [when] you supposed to be in the class, like [I'm] tryin' to learn!" she said. She then enrolled in a for-profit trade school, TESST; she was now completing a one-year program that would prepare her to take the certification exam to be a certified clinical medical assistant (CCMA). Vicky really liked the courses so far, especially the hands-on clinical work. "We learned blood pressures, how many bones in the body . . . how to do CPR . . . I'll be doin' good in school, I ain't miss a day yet!" she said. Her eventual goal was to become a pediatrician because "[I've always wanted to] work with kids." Vicky saw the CCMA certification as a first step. "I'll take whatever I can get in for that field right now, until I get more experience in the doctor field, like, go back to school for surgeries on people and all that stuff," she said.

Meanwhile, she often felt that she was the only grown-up at home. "In this house, I gotta be the responsible one," she said. The house was "a party house," where family on both her father's and mother's sides came to drink. Sometimes they brought out the karaoke machine. "They get to bein' loud, I gotta go upstairs, lock my door," she said. The noise, which could go on until all hours, was taking a toll. "I'll be like, 'Oh man, I'm tired!'" Vicki said. "And I gotta do this, I gotta do that, run [to school, run to work]. Oh man, that's just makin' me even tireder."

The neighborhood was often a source of stress too. Ten years earlier, Vicky's brother was murdered right on their block. And just weeks before we met her, two teens were killed at a cookout down the street. One of the victims was her pregnant cousin's boyfriend. When Vicky heard the shooting, she was terrified and ran screaming toward the scene. "I was crying, *Who is it!?*" she said—terrified that it might be her remaining brother, her boyfriend, or one of her cousins. In the days since, she said, she had felt lost. "I don't know what's going on. . . . Some nights I go to sleep wondering what's goin' on, what's gonna happen the next day," she said. Outside her apartment we saw a handmade sign with the letters RIP on the telephone pole at the corner, along with remains of torn blue balloons, a memorial to the shooting victims.

Now that she had embarked on her medical career, Vicky had had to cut herself off from several of the friends she made in high school, a choice that had left her isolated and lonely. But she felt that their paths were no longer compatible with hers, because they were about "nothing" and she wanted to "live my life." In her words, "I used to go out a lot of places . . . but I don't do it no more. I got school to do." She said, "I got tired of hangin' with the crew. They was just not doing nothing for theirself, so I left 'em and I was like, 'I gotta go . . . 'cause I ain't wanna sit out here, I wanna live my life how I'm supposed to live my life—right?" Ideally, she would have liked to separate herself from the neighborhood too. "I wanna just go somewhere else. I wanna just get away for some years, like, come back and see people, stay with people for, like, a week or two, then go back. I'm tryin' to make it big . . . with my work, what I'm gonna learn in school, and the rest of my careers I'm gonna go get. I'm gonna get me a car, be successful. I'm gonna get there one day."

In the meantime, when she felt tired or angry or just needed some time to think and be alone in the overcrowded house, she escaped out back to the birds. "I separate myself from everybody . . . sometimes [when] I don't wanna be bothered," Vicky said. "I go out there and mess with my birds. We just train 'em to fly in the area and see if they come home. We got to Payson Street, we got Frederick Avenue, and we took 'em up to Baltimore Street. That's the farthest we got. [Soon,] we take 'em down to Carroll Park. We ain't get that far yet." Vicky's dream was that her birds would become familiar with the whole city someday. "We gonna get there, the birds, you gonna see how the birds fly," she said. "You're all gonna see the bird land in [your] yard area with the gray band on their arm. You're gonna be like, 'Oh, that's Vicky and them birds!'" The connection between Vicky and her birds was powerful. Partly, the birds were a special bond that she and her father shared. Partly, it was that she played with the birds in the backyard, generally the only place that was quiet around her home. And partly, it was that she had always been an animal person—animals of any kind were easy for her to feel affection for.[31]

Many of the DIY identity projects that we observed—held by about one-fifth of the youth with identity projects—had an entrepreneurial quality to them, and we saw a wide array of activities to which youth committed themselves. Some of these included writing poetry, recording rap songs, or making "beats" online and selling them for a few dollars. Nineteen-year-old William proudly showed Stefanie DeLuca the computer and speakers he had set up in the corner of his small bedroom—he had learned how to create and edit music online, mostly by himself.

IDENTITY PROJECTS LINKING YOUTH TO SUBCULTURES

Identity projects have greater force if linked to a subculture, which can connect youth with others like themselves and offer a sense of belonging. Youth encounter these subcultures in various ways—in the mall, on TV, on the Internet, or at places such as an after-school program.[32] All of these venues had served as avenues for Bob's identity project.

Bob was born in Somerset Homes, where "I used to hear gunshots a lot." He never lingered long outside while living in Somerset, or in any place he had lived since, preferring to "keep to himself" at home. When we spoke with her in 2004, Bob's mother, Teresa, described him as a "good reader" with a big imagination. She recalled that the stories he conjured up in grade school were often full of vivid scenes. He illustrated his stories too. Once, "he drew the train track [and all that], [and then] the little, the train crashing—you know how a train look when it crash," his mother said. "He had with the little fire, and he had, like, the little fire coming out of the front of it, and it was smushed up."

Bob was a visual kid, so when he first came across the Japanese cartoon Pokémon, he was enthralled. "I mean, it was so fast-paced and high-octane, the colors were awesome!" he said. The show's brilliant graphics were compelling, and so was the world the cartoon and games created: in the Pokémon world, hundreds of unique creatures were trained for battle and had sophisticated skills and powers. Bob also relished books that were offbeat and unusual. If he was not poring over graphic novels in the anime genre, he was "reading something weird like witchcraft or wizardry . . . I'm into the weird, weird stuff, you know, like witches, wizards, vampires, werewolves."

Bob's interests had always ensured that he would be "a loner," in his mother's words. In middle school, he had a penchant for reading Shakespeare sonnets and considered the poet Paul Laurence Dunbar a personal hero. He joined the chess team, spending weekends at tournaments and forming a strong bond with the coach, one of his teachers, who often invited Bob and his classmates to his home for pizza. At Somerset, "everyone my age was dealing drugs," Bob said. "[There was] nobody to relate to—everyone was literally out to get money. I wasn't. I was trying to get my schoolwork done and make sure that I had a good high school career." Bob's isolation was usually relieved only when he went to church with his stepfather, a preacher, and acted in a number of Afrocentric plays that his youth pastor's theater troupe would adapt from the original. "If he hangs with anyone, it's a few kids from the church," Teresa told us in 2004.

Bob continued to try to find ways to be "a black kid, growing up in the city, and not liking what everybody else liked." Soon after getting hooked on the edgy anime cartoons and books, he caught a glimpse of another way to express himself. One day at the White Marsh Mall, in Baltimore's northeast suburbs, Bob explained:

> I saw this guy, a black guy, he had on this black trench coat and these really puffy black pants. They had spikes, they had chains, the whole nine yards. He had a shirt of a band that I had never seen before, but the shirt was so awesome, it just stayed in my mind and it was etched there. . . . And I was like, "Dude, I want a piece of that!" He showed me that you can be black, but you don't have to be like these guys out on the street.

The African American man with spikes and an "awesome" concert shirt— sporting the name of a band Bob had never heard of before—made a strong impression. Nothing could have been further from the "blue jeans and long white T-shirts" that Bob's Somerset peers wore each day, like a uniform.

Throughout middle school, Bob continued to excel, racking up science trophies and discovering a love for math. When we first spoke with Bob in 2004, he lit up when he talked about the subject. "There's so many different ways to get to a solution!" he said. At the end of eighth grade, Bob's grades and teacher recommendations had gained him admission to the prestigious Claremont High, a highly selective magnet school in a wealthy, white enclave of the city, near Chantal's Shadyside High. Bob had felt an immediate connection to the social world of Claremont. At freshman orientation, he had confided in his mother and stepfather, "I finally feel like I belong." Bob saw Claremont as the beginning of his path to college, where he hoped to study engineering. During his freshman year, he and Teresa were already scanning college brochures together.

Just as Bob's world seemed to be coming together at Claremont, however, life at home had started falling apart. When Bob was a freshman, Teresa and Bob's stepfather—who served as a confidant and role model for Bob—divorced. The split was devastating for the entire family. Financial pressure intensified too; although Teresa held a full-time job at the Social Security Administration, which she had gotten through a welfare-to-work program years before, the rent now took up "half my check," she told us. Technically, her rent should have been adjusted downward by the housing authority, but that did not happen. And since her ex was not the father of any of her children, she had no right to child support from him.

Somerset seemed to be falling apart too. Maintenance no longer came to fix anything, according to Teresa, probably because a demolition plan for Somerset was in the works. During that time, there were "lots of bad days," Teresa admitted. "I'm not even gonna sit here and lie to you. We were miserable. I just was in this rut, in this routine of just going to work, taking care of the bills, trying to keep us as stable as I could, even though we was going through a lot of stuff. But the depression was so thick in the house, and the memories was all thick in the house, and [it was so hard] to keep coming through that door."

When Somerset closed, Teresa and the kids moved a few miles east to a modest, working-class area, Highlandtown, a mixed-income neighborhood that was a huge step up, at least in relative terms. Their new block consisted mostly of blue-collar workers, civil servants, and retirees. (However, while the block itself seemed safe, drug dealers operated during broad daylight from a corner just one block over, which we witnessed.) Still, it was as if there was a "cloud over the family," Teresa said. They stopped eating meals together. Bob and his brother began to withdraw more often to their bedrooms. Bob's brother starting acting out. His mother reached a breaking point when she learned that her wages were going to be garnished to recoup a long-overdue student loan for a training program she had never completed. "I wanted to run screaming out of the house and say, 'Forget it all,'" she told us. She felt "like I was a worm that came up out the hole, and the bird spotted me from the tree, and he swooped down and sucked me up."

Then things really fell apart. Bob watched helplessly as his mother struggled to get out of bed on workdays. Eventually, he started noticing evidence that she was using cocaine. "[I saw] half-cut-up straws around. I kind of figured that something was going on. . . . She'd get sloppy, and sometimes she would still be a little high when we were home." Bob felt that his mother's stumble was understandable given her stress, so he took "everybody's burdens" and put them on himself. Teresa confirmed that it was "Bob to the rescue . . . the boy was just so grounded. . . . Throughout all this, Bob's been my rock, he really has."

However, the drama at home took a toll on what mattered most to Bob—school. Both he and his brother failed a grade that year. Claremont expelled Bob, and he was forced to transfer to Hamilton High, a school reputed to be a dropout factory. It was a place where, he said, "a lot of those troubled kids like to pick on the smarter kids."

"I had no outlets, I had no one," he said. To make matters worse, Bob had just been dumped by his first serious girlfriend and was heartbroken. His struggle was painfully clear to us when we talked with Bob during his junior year in 2004. While he was charming, obviously bright, and articulate, there also was a palpable sadness and anguish about him. That year we wrote in our field notes, "This is a kid who is in trouble emotionally, he is just emotionally a wreck. . . . He shows many, many signs of depression. . . . [But] he's a fighter, he wants to make it, he wants to believe in the future . . . but without any kind of support from somebody . . . he could easily lapse back into a . . . depressive state." Seven years later, when we spoke with Bob a second time, he noted, "I'm surprised [I made it through that time]. I relied heavily on my poetry to help me vent some of my feelings."

At Hamilton, Bob was disheartened by the lack of intellectual challenge but determined to excel, so he asked the principal if he could take extra classes. He gave up his lunch hour to take a creative writing course. "So for the entire eight hours, I was just school," he later recalled. Bob made up his tenth-grade credits and took all his eleventh-grade classes in one year. And at Hamilton, Bob found something else that deeply resonated with him. "I found an outlet . . . they had an after-school program that a lot of kids liked to go to, and I started playin' card games [there]," he recalled, games like "Magic the Gathering" and "Dungeons and Dragons." His favorite was YuGiOh!, based on the anime comic books and movies. Other kids ridiculed Bob and the other "outcasts" who played cards—all of them students, Bob said, who "liked being different, who didn't want to fit in."

Then he encountered something else that struck a chord. One day after school he went home with one of his new friends, and "I got to see him out . . . of our uniform. What he wore, he dressed just like that guy!" he said, referring to the black man he had seen wearing spikes and chains at the mall. Thus began Bob's initiation into Goth culture and, in particular, a white hip-hop and rap duo with a devoted underground following called the Insane Clown Posse. Bob was thrilled. He said that his new friend was "[just] like me, alienated from everybody." Showing off his colorful skull rings to us as proof of his new interests, Bob proudly declared, at seventeen, "as you can see, I am different—I am not like the other guys in Baltimore. As a matter of fact, I don't think I belong here." He had found his niche, a group of kids who were "alienated" but academically oriented.

Along with others in his group, Bob came to revel in wearing dark makeup, chains, and skull T-shirts. Dressing that way provided a shield and served as a source of intimidation while in the neighborhood. "I used to wear tripp pants, which were pants with chains . . . black clothing, black makeup," Bob recalled. The clothing and makeup marked him as different from the kids around the corner who were dealing drugs. Bob believed that the way he dressed made it clear to his peers that he was "about something." He and his friends were not out to pick fights or hurt anyone, but they looked the part, which was enough. The delight of watching the looks on people's faces as they moved through the neighborhood was worth it—they saw that people could tell that they were not to be messed with. The whole thing was "exhilarating . . . we were all so different, and that got me through those last two years of high school."[33] Note that, for white youth, listening to Goth music and wearing the requisite clothing and makeup is considered anti-establishment, a sign of rebellion against the mainstream.[34] But for Bob, a black youth, immersion in Goth denoted the opposite—that he was different from the deviant peers who dominated the public spaces of the neighborhoods he often had to traverse as he moved about the city. The tripp pants, makeup, and chains were a way for Bob to confront the street, not defy society.

Finding a community of like-minded peers was the key discovery that helped Bob persevere. Other supports mattered too.[35] He credited his stepfather, the preacher, with keeping him in church and teaching him "to be a gentleman." Another mentor, his youth pastor, got him involved in Afrocentric theater. Besides the fantasy card games he played with his Goth friends after school, play rehearsals also kept him busy until at least seven o'clock most nights. Bob relished the challenge of playing lead roles, memorizing dozens of pages of lines. He played the lead in an adaptation of Hamlet and noted that "it was very interesting to see how we integrated Shakespeare into modern times." Being connected to mentors at church also provided Bob with a window onto the world of work in a field one is passionate about. He explained how he gained this insight: "[My youth pastor] majored in theater, and he's been doing theater ever since, and he just loves it. I was like, 'How can this be? You go to work to work, you're not supposed to like it!' And he showed me, yeah, you can definitely like what you do." All of these factors provided a sense of community, belonging, and fuel for Bob's academic interests, as well as a powerful alternative to "the corner." But it was the hobbies he stumbled on to in particular—all linked to avid subcultures that connected him with like-minded peers—that gave Bob the perseverance to stay the course.

Over an eleven-year period, we spent time with Bob on nine separate occasions, talking with him at length in 2004, 2006, and 2010, with follow-up visits through 2012. Since graduating from high school, Bob had remained closely connected with the anime subculture, regularly attending Otakon, the anime convention held annually in Baltimore's Inner Harbor. Most recently, he had gone dressed as a ninja fox. Now, at twenty-five, he worked as an assistant manager at a coffee shop in the bustling BWI airport.

Just a few months earlier he had left the West Baltimore rooming house where he had been living for a small two-bedroom apartment that he now shared with his fiancée, a fellow anime fan who worked as a cook at the popular Bo Brooks Crab House, also at the BWI airport. Bob envisioned a future raising children together in a modest house in Northeast Baltimore, where the streets are quiet and the schools are decent, in his view. The pall of depression was gone, and the bright and handsome young man with short, neatly groomed dreads had a ready smile and carried himself with confidence. Summing up his experiences so far, he said, "When I started your study [I was seventeen], I was a depressed little kid back then. I made it. I'm happy."

IDENTITY PROJECTS THAT CONNECT YOUTH TO INSTITUTIONS

Bob's identity project took him further than Vicky's, in that it connected him to established subcultures and offered opportunities for connections with others who shared his passions and were, like him, decidedly not "street." Unlike Vicky's interests, Bob's projects were publicly performed: he and his friends would walk through the neighborhood and attend conventions, decked out in Goth gear. For Bob, the clothing was a particularly salient element, a theme we see reflected in Cody's story as well. It called attention to the fact that he and his peers were "about something else."

Yet Bob's passions did not take him as far as some others' do, because anime, Goth, and a devotion to the Insane Clown Posse failed to connect him to institutions. As Cody's story shows, the advantage of pursuing an identity project within the context of an institution is that once the connection is made, the institution has a momentum of its own.[36] Such identity projects are like getting aboard a moving train that takes you in a clear direction—a far cry from the DIY projects pursued by young people like Vicky. In Cody's story, the clear career focus of the activities he chose added structure and connectedness to his life.

When Cody's mother signed up for MTO, the family was living in the Latrobe Homes in East Baltimore, tucked into the shadow of the Baltimore jail which was wreathed in barbed wire. His mother "abused me mentally and physically . . . until I was seven," he said. His grandmother took custody of Cody and his youngest sister at that point, and they moved in with her in the nearby Milton-Montford neighborhood for the next twelve years. The neighborhood, while still around 30 percent poor, registered less than half of the poverty rate of Latrobe. With his grandmother's support, Cody excelled in middle school, and when it came time to choose a high school, he picked a small comprehensive school, one of several that had been carved out of a large high school in Northeast Baltimore that had become notorious for fighting and disorder. Cody's school, Chesapeake Academy, marketed its focus on law and leadership, which piqued Cody's interest.

Cody started high school strong, but ran into some trouble his freshman year. He recalled that because he was "the shortest kid in school," he was picked on by the other students; he fought back, calling his especially tall peers "Amazons." By tenth grade, he had been suspended many times for fighting—the only way he knew to make the teasing stop so that he could go back "to doing my work." Cody channeled his frustration into athletic pursuits to gain strength so that he could defend himself. Soon he started to "take my sports very seriously." Cody threw himself into football, baseball, indoor track, and wrestling. He kept busy, juggling the after-school practices with his jobs at places like Chuck E. Cheese's and the Food Depot grocery store.

But Chesapeake Academy offered more than just sports. Ever since he had enrolled, Cody had been entranced by the JROTC students marching outside. His initial interest in the military was sparked, much like Bob's fascination with Goth, by the striking clothing he saw—the "navy blue pants with yellow stripes, white shirts, it looks nice, it looks great," he said. "I wanted to be one of them, and I started doing the law program [at school], and then I did the JROTC [too]."

A counselor at school who knew about Cody's interest in law enforcement told him about the city's Police Explorer program, which provided another way to fill his weekends; they even traveled to national conferences. When we first met Cody at nineteen, he had been participating in the Police Explorer program for five years and wore the badge proudly around his neck. Much like Antonio's hard-earned Johns Hopkins security guard badge, he saw it as a mark of distinction. It helped keep him safe in the neighborhood: "people look at that," he said, "and are like, 'Oh, he a police.'"[37] The badge even warded off police harassment. When Cody had been stopped by police—which happened "all the time," he said—he would pull out his badge and they would respond: "Oh, you're a Police Explorer! Sorry, keep going."

Hands-on "scenarios" and trainings—like K-9, white-collar crime, and crash instruction—were Cody's favorite activities. He eagerly described how "the Explorers actually do what police do every day, and see if we can fix a scenario in the right way." When we spoke with him for the first time, he had just come back from Atlanta, where the Explorers had held their annual convention at the University of Georgia. He vividly recounted a simulation exercise that his group had engaged in for a domestic violence call.

Cody found even more fulfillment in the JROTC program, where he trained and competed in drill exercises and agility tests. Both programs helped him live up to the claim that he was a "disciplined, motivated type of personality." But the programs had another strong draw. The live-action training sequences, competitions, and uniforms gave Cody a concrete sense of what life might be like as a police officer or as an officer in the military. Suddenly the path ahead seemed clear.

Once armed with a clear sense of his future, the fights stopped and Cody's grades improved—markedly. The positive source of inspiration was paired with the push provided by his negative experiences in the past. Watching his parents' drug use "really motivated me *not* to [do drugs]," he said. "It motivated me to do right." He saw the future he wanted to avoid—his father was still in rehab, all these years later, and while his mom had held some jobs in security, "now she ain't workin' at all. She living off an SSI check." He knew he had to do better. "My mom, my father, my grandmother, my oldest cousin didn't graduate from school, and it couldn't be me," he said. "I couldn't see myself like that." The hard work paid off. Cody was the first in his family to complete high school, with a 3.0 grade point average to boot.

Cody was pursuing the army—he had an interview scheduled with a military recruiter—because he was intrigued by the promise of working with "a whole bunch of machineries." After a stint in the army, he wanted to leverage his training and return to Baltimore to become a police officer. He wanted to be different from some of the officers he had encountered, whom he described as "lying, sticky, [and] conniving." But he also saw police work as a way to change not only what was happening in the city but what people *think* about his hometown. "I wanted to become a police officer just from . . . seeing what people think about Baltimore out of the state," he said. "They think badly about Baltimore. So, me looking at that and me living in Baltimore for nineteen years, I want to change that."

WHEN IDENTITY PROJECTS SPARK GRIT

In this chapter, we have argued that, at least for a group of young people with very disadvantaged origins, the grit required to "make it"—to resist the streets and not become disconnected—must often be inspired.[38] In this regard, adopting an identity project was instrumental for our youth. Bob was brimming with grit as he distanced himself from the "baggy T-shirt" guys in the projects. His grit had been essential in helping him cope with his mother's depression and addiction. He had drawn strength from his church too—in particular, a youth pastor who helped the church youth plot, produce, and perform Afrocentric plays. But mainly he credited his ability to persevere to anime, fantasy card games, and the Goth culture he shared with his friends.

Consider the following facts about our youth (see figure 3.1): 93 percent of those with an identity project were able to beat the streets, while only 73

Figure 3.1   Identity Projects and Postsecondary Outcomes

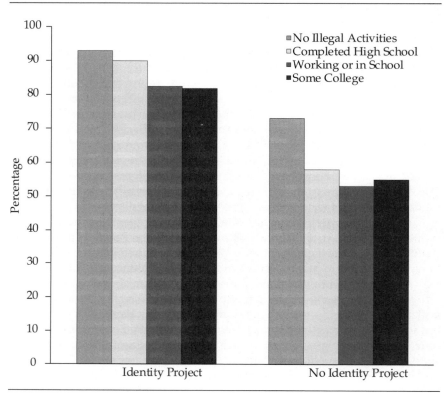

Source: Authors' compilations.

percent of those who lacked one managed to do so.[39] For the 116 youth not still in high school, 90 percent of those with an identity project graduated, compared to only 58 percent of those who did not. And of these 116, 82 percent with an identity project were either in school or working at the time of their last interview, compared with 53 percent of those without an identity project. For the subsample of our youth who had, by 2010, earned either a high school diploma or GED (86), fully 82 percent who had an identity project had entered college or trade school, compared to only 55 percent of those lacking one.

But as we suggested earlier, we also found that not all identity projects work the same way or have the same impact. In the absence of a way to link up with an established subculture, as Bob did, or the strong institutional supports that Cody found in the Police Explorer program and

JROTC, others created their own identity project.[40] Youth like Vicky seized on an outlet, such as tending to pigeons, to find meaning and add structure to their days. The youth who constructed DIY projects often did remain on track, pursuing school and work and avoiding the street after high school. But without strong community or institutional supports, they were not on such solid ground as they moved into college or the labor market. While youth with any identity project were more likely to be "on track" than those without identity projects, we found that youth with an institutionally supported identity project were twice as likely as youth with a DIY or peer-subculture project to be "on track" after high school, holding constant gender and age.[41]

We note that outward markers, such as Cody's Police Explorer badge and his JROTC uniform, send a strong message to others in your neighborhood that you are about something.[42] Antonio's KFC uniform fulfilled that function when he was in his teens. An added benefit is that these markers can render a youth less vulnerable to police attention, since a youth in a uniform is less likely to be mistaken for the "suspect," who wears a baggy white T-shirt and jeans, a number of male youth claimed.[43] When Antonio was stopped on the street and questioned in conjunction with a recent robbery or another crime, he would be dismissed when the officer saw his work ID. Gary was often pulled over when he ventured into the suburbs in his vintage Cadillac (which he restored himself—his identity project) on his way to work, but he had learned to hand over his work ID along with his license. Wearing his scrubs to and from work was another strategy he deployed. In addition to their protective power, these visible markers of employment also have an incorporating effect, communicating to the rest of the world that you are a "working" person, a member of mainstream society.[44]

CONCLUSION

We have found evidence that identity projects can play a crucial role in the lives of disadvantaged youth. Yet it is still an emergent concept, one that merits more investigation. We did not go into the field anticipating that this theme would arise; instead, it emerged inductively from the interviews.[45] More research is needed to explore the facets and functions of identity projects in the transition to adulthood, particularly for disadvantaged youth. For example, we cannot always tell from our interview data when "the switch flipped" or what flipped it. However, identity projects seem critical at a particular developmental stage—adolescence. Of those with an identity project, nearly all (88 percent) found it before the end of high school, and the rest discovered it shortly thereafter, usually while still in their teens.[46] Therefore, for the large majority of the youth in our study, adoption of the identity project preceded our measure of being on track.

It is not clear from our data why some youth develop identity projects while others do not. From what we can tell, it is often the luck of the draw—being in a high school that happens to have a JROTC program and finding that it clicks with your interests; running into someone at the mall who is dressed in a way that happens to captivate you; a summer job at YouthWorks that involves delivering blood samples to a pharmacy school; or even a chance field trip to the morgue. In addition, we cannot say for sure exactly why some youth "take up" opportunities in their schools while some of their classmates do not.[47] Yet, as we discuss in chapter 7, as a society, we should be able to do better than "luck" in providing these youth with opportunities to find their passions, perhaps because there was so little variation in our sample.

As we established earlier in this chapter, we cannot nail down what differentiates those who adopt an identity project from those who do not. At least in our small sample, there is no clear link to the level of family adversity or neighborhood disadvantage. Family adversity and neighborhood disadvantage seem to compel some youth to lay hold of an identity project, but leave others adrift.

We also observe that identity projects serve a number of functions. Sometimes they are a life raft during a dark time, sometimes they spark grit when adversity seems likely to derail a youth's trajectory, and sometimes they serve to amplify inner resources and motivation that are already there. For some, finding their passion comes in an instant. For others, adopting an identity project is a process. Identity projects can either have a singular focus—like Vicky's pigeons or, as we show in chapter 5, Bridget's commitment to dance—or encompass a set of activities that morph over time, like Bob's many interests. Most readers can remember what it was like to be an adolescent, trying on identities and seeing which ones fit. The youth in our sample were open to the possibilities they encountered, hungry for identities to rub up against—like social flypaper—to see which ones would stick.

It may be that some identity projects get in the way of achieving more. Recording your own "beats" and being engrossed in a rap group—William's identity project—might keep you off the street, but it could also distract you from studying or making college plans. Similarly, identity projects born from emotional distress, such as finding one's life calling in the nursing field in eighth grade stemming from caring for a sister dying of AIDS, may forestall further career exploration.[48] On balance, however, the correlational evidence suggests that identity projects play a strong protective role.

Across our nation, the civic fabric of poor and working-class neighborhoods has atrophied. Communities used to be full of opportunities for kids to connect to institutions. The work of Robert Putnam, for example, has shown that among whites (the corresponding data are not available for other groups) there is a growing class divide in civic engagement, which he argues is highly consequential for the degree to which Americans are willing to view kids at the bottom of the ladder as "our kids."[49] Melody Boyd and her coauthors have written about two communities in Philadelphia where they conducted interviews with both adolescents and their parents; they found a sharp falloff in participation in—and availability of—key institutions offering opportunities for civic engagement among youth, particularly church activities, summer employment, and clubs, such as the Police Athletic League.[50]

Facing tight budgets, many cities have cut back on city-organized sports leagues, arts and after-school programming at neighborhood recreation centers, and libraries. For example, in Philadelphia, Mayor Michael Nutter infamously advocated for deep cuts in library hours and staffing at the height of the recession. Philadelphians fought back with an outrage that surprised the mayor, who perhaps forgot that libraries in low-income neighborhoods do more than loan books: they also host award-winning chess clubs and science programs for teens and provide access to the Internet and, through that, to the wider world.

Over the last decade, trends in public education have resulted in a reduction of funds for the very activities—art, music, and sports—that can spark identity projects.[51] Bob's enthusiasm for debate, for example, was quashed when the school decided that it was no longer going to fund the program. As public school systems have rushed to boost students' scores in math and reading, arts education and extracurricular activities have withered.[52] This is particularly the case in schools and school districts with higher proportions of low-income students.[53] In New York City's public schools, spending on art supplies dropped from $10 million in 2007 to just over $2 million three years later.[54] Middle-class parents can find ways to fill in the gap when public funding for arts education or extracurricular activities is reduced.[55] But children and adolescents from economically disadvantaged backgrounds do not have the private resources to compensate for cutbacks in public funding for schools, libraries, and after-school activities.

Yet some shining examples remain. The vehicle for Cody was the JROTC. Career academies are another example. These small learning communities, sited within larger school buildings, are organized around an occupational theme. Representing one of the more successful evidence-based interventions for improving life outcomes, especially among boys, these academies synthesize training in technical skills with regular academics. And similar to the internship that sparked Tony's interest in a pharmaceutical career, the academies partner with local employers to provide students with concrete learning opportunities in the field. Other promising programs include one that is now undergoing rigorous evaluation: YouthBuild is a "second chance" program for disconnected youth that offers construction training and a wide range of other services.[56]

Although only some identity projects have an obvious connection to school or a career, they may serve other, equally important purposes for youth, such as providing a respite from home life and the neighborhood.[57] These projects also provide a sense of dignity, something to escape to, a place to find a sense of efficacy, and sometimes a way to demonstrate it to the world. As twenty-year-old Kareem explained: "I like to draw. . . . Da Vinci [is] my favorite artist and his paintings are exquisite . . . so if I could paint, that would be even better—it's basically my freedom from being around here." After leaving public housing at the Flag House Courts, he and his family moved to the newly remodeled Townes at the Terrace, the West Baltimore HOPE VI development where the Lexington Terrace once stood. Kareem dropped out of high school and was making a little money sketching out tattoo designs for people who were considering the permanent version. He also did odd jobs in the neighborhood, like mowing lawns or patching walls. But he was in a precarious position. When asked how he made ends meet, he said, "Well . . . technically I don't. Like, in the sense of if my mother and father were both to be gone today, I would have to [be in the street] 'cause I don't have nothing else." At twenty, Kareem was not on track, and although his interest in drawing and painting was strong, he never had the chance to really cultivate these skills as an identity project. We would argue that if Kareem had found institutional support for his interests in painting and drawing, he could have achieved more.

One purpose of this chapter has been to suggest that even among our nation's most disadvantaged youth, the will to play by the rules, pursue mainstream goals, and actively resist the pull of delinquent behavior is present. Yet we also observed that it was much easier for these young people to demonstrate the grit needed to persevere when they found something to be about, especially if they could share that passion with their peers or find it within an established institutional context. Just holding on to what Jay MacLeod calls "the achievement ideology"—as almost all of our youth did, on track or not—was not enough.[58] Key public investments in adolescents of just the right kind can be transformative. As we discuss in chapter 7, the policy tide in recent years has turned away from adolescents in favor of early childhood education, swayed by research showing large gains for interventions conducted in the preschool years. But it is hard to look at any of these stories and not think that we could do more to support these seekers who find ways to persevere with so much stacked against them.

Terry felt like he deserved more, given the effort he had devoted to staying on track and out of trouble:

All [society] see[s] is you're twenty-three and you should damn well have it together by now, you know what I'm sayin? "What the hell is wrong with him?" "This kid is angry," or "I don't wanna deal with him, he's got too much shit goin on." . . . They think less of you, but they don't realize, man, what I've been through. So I have to deal with that. I have to learn how to play the game, so to speak . . . how to "yes, sir, abso-fricking-lutely," like, all of that shit, and I hide the fact that I'm fuckin-like—I've really gone through some shit, you know? Like, where am I gonna sleep tonight, and I'm sittin' here in a suit, and I'm in a job interview, like, fuck, where am I gonna put my clothes . . .? Can I call anybody [back or tell them how to reach me by phone]? Damn, I didn't have a phone . . . I had to ask strangers on the street can I use their cell phone.

Though Terry was certainly still struggling economically, his identity project helped keep him hopeful and motivated. Not every adolescent is able to find salvation in an identity project. The next chapter considers the vulnerability and fragility of youth who do not find an identity project and the consequences for the few who turn to the street to find meaning instead.

Chapter 4 | "You Never Know What's Happening—This is Baltimore": The Vulnerability of Youth Without an Identity Project

Despite the gains that young people like Vicky, Bob, and Cody have made—achieving far more than their parents ever did—there is no denying that the disadvantages they continued to face were often enormous, for three primary reasons. First, leaving the projects did not always erase the trauma stemming from their earlier childhood experiences. Second, even given the large decreases in neighborhood poverty they experienced, about half of these young people had still lived in neighborhoods where the poverty rate was "moderately high"—over 30 percent—for at least six years. Third, many received most or all of their education in the Baltimore City Schools.[1]

Early trauma and ongoing risk are precisely why identity projects were so critical for many of the youth in this study: identity projects provided the emotional sustenance that helped them survive. To review, there is at least prima facie evidence for the protective role of identity projects in our data. Nearly all—94 percent—of those with an identity project were "on track" (working or in school) at the last interview, versus 65 percent of those without one. Equally importantly, those who had an identity project were significantly less likely to get involved in illegal activities (see table A4.1).[2] Furthermore, those over age nineteen who had formed an identity project in adolescence were more likely to have earned a high school credential than those without one (89 versus 59 percent), more likely to have enrolled in postsecondary education of some kind (71 versus 37 percent), and more likely to have pursued a four-year college degree (25 versus 3 percent).

90

Those who had not managed to find their passion through an identity project in adolescence were far more likely to end up disconnected—neither working nor in school—at the time of our last interaction than those who did. Some were also struggling with mental health and substance abuse problems. These youth were more vulnerable to the forces that acted as an undertow on their trajectories, like ongoing neighborhood risk, inadequate schooling, and family trauma (forces we discuss in more detail in chapter 5).

Here we offer brief vignettes of two of these youth, Emily and Joseph, who fit this description at present. Their stories demonstrate that while most youth without an identity project manage to avoid getting caught up in the street, they are still often adrift and at risk. Others try on a street identity but only for a brief period of time, as Ella's story shows.

A few, like Whitney and Ron (profiled later in this chapter), drew a strong sense of identity from the street.[3] Yet their narratives illustrate why street identities are so fundamentally different from identity projects: while the street can provide an alternative sense of identity, rather than being protective, it literally invites risk, and rather than forging a bridge between the present and one's future goals, street identities seem to lead almost exclusively to dead ends or to a significant delay in achieving young adult milestones.Although youth who were ever in the street were the exception—even among those without an identity project—they are a significant focus in this chapter. We show that street activities seriously compromised their transition to adulthood.[4] For these youth—who also referred to themselves as being "caught up" or "in the game"— we found strong associations between family trauma and significant exposure to neighborhoods with concentrated poverty. Just under half of those who were ever involved in the street ended up "disconnected," neither working nor in school, by the end of the study, a stark contrast to the figure for those who lacked an identity project but continued to resist the street—only 16 percent of this group was disconnected by the study's end.

DISCONNECTED AND ADRIFT

Emily ticked off the long list of difficult things she had been through in life, her chin-length bob swinging back and forth as she talked. She was still living in the same house in suburban Columbia that she moved to when she was five. Her younger sister Michelle lived there too, along with her two children. But the clean and orderly home we had observed back in 2003, when we talked with Emily's mother, Mariah, for the first time, had been overtaken by the stench of ripe garbage and urine-soaked diapers. Every available surface seemed to be covered with crumpled paper napkins, half-empty food containers, diapers, and toys. Though Mariah's name remained on the lease (to retain the voucher that paid most of the rent on the home), she had moved out three years before, after marrying her longtime boyfriend.

The story of Emily's traumatic childhood unfolded as follows. Both of Emily's parents were heavy drinkers and drug users when they were young. Mariah continued using while pregnant with each of her three children. Back then, they had lived in the "drug-infested" Poe Homes, as Mariah described them. Mariah was, by her own admission, part of the problem. Hers was an address you could come to "every day, all hours of the night," to "smoke drugs, whatever you have to do with the drugs." Adding to the chaos for her children, Mariah had the habit of getting involved with abusive men who shared her drug habit. At one point, she and the kids had to flee from one paramour to a domestic violence shelter. When Emily was five, Mariah found a drug rehabilitation program and got sober. A year later, she used her MTO voucher to move the family out to suburban Columbia, hoping the dramatic change could lead to a new life.

From first grade on, Emily attended public schools that were vastly better than the schools she would have attended had they remained in the Poe Homes. Plus, she was no longer living in an apartment that doubled as a shooting gallery. But the weight of those first five traumatic years and the ongoing drama of abuse and serious substance use in her extended family seemed to stall her progress. Emily's visits to her grandmother's home terrified her. Having witnessed her grandmother beat her cousins, "I [would] literally pee on myself coming through the door. That's how scared I was." Amid these difficulties, Emily never found the inspiration for an identity project or the supportive relationships that could have helped her craft a path forward. After graduating from high school, she hopscotched through community college, a trade school, and then Job Corps, never completing any certification. Her time at Job Corps in West Virginia was cut short because an untreated case of chlamydia turned into pelvic inflammatory disease, so she was sent home. She had worked a series of jobs since: as a cashier at Walmart, at the day care center where her mother worked, and as an attendant at a nursing home. It was by taking the drug test for the nursing home job that Emily found out, at the age of twenty, that she was pregnant; that news derailed the plan she had begun to form—to enlist in the navy.

For some of the youth we met, becoming a parent had a transformative impact on their lives.[5] Unfortunately, this did not happen for Emily. A month after she gave birth to Lamont, she was admitted to a psychiatric hospital for three weeks because of depression. Typically, her depressive episodes—three or four in the past year—lasted for about a month. Sometimes during these episodes she locked herself and Lamont in her bedroom for up to a week at a time. She said she did that to isolate herself from her sister and her sister's children.

Joseph did not experience the depth of family trauma that Emily did. But at nineteen years old, he was struggling to find out where he fit in the world. After being a target of bullies in middle school, it just seemed easier to him to skip school rather than risk the taunts and threats from his peers. He continued to skip classes in high school, but this time skipping school was an effort to impress girls with his toughness. He missed so many classes in ninth grade that the principal told him he would have to repeat the year. Instead, he decided to leave school for good.

Looking back, Joseph regretted his behavior and recognized how a lack of a high school diploma limited his employment prospects. He had managed to find work at the Coca-Cola bottling company just south of town, at a pizza shop, and at a company that did mass mailings, but none of these jobs lasted for more than a year. His sister received Social Security disability, which paid the rent on the apartment where he and his girlfriend (who was pregnant) were staying at the time. His mother and two other two siblings, none of them with a permanent place to live, were staying there too.

Despite his precarious housing—and the added stress of a baby on the way—so far, Joseph had resisted selling drugs to bring in cash. He wanted to improve his chances of landing a better job by completing a GED, but could not muster the $45 fee for the program. Beyond that, he did not have much of a plan. Like Emily, Joseph struggled with depression and suicidal thoughts. Heartsick with the thought that he would not be able to provide for his baby, he confided that he recently told his mom that he was going to "cut myself." He said that she responded, "I ain't raise no quitters. . . . I raised you [to be] the man. . . . Are you a little boy?" But finger-wagging did not make up for the confidence he lacked or the bleak opportunities in the labor market. In reference to his unborn daughter, Joseph asked, "You're supposed to make it better, easier for them, right?"

In his current South Baltimore neighborhood of Westport, Joseph estimated that perhaps two people on his block had jobs: "It ain't enough motivation over here." Crime was endemic—he was worried about people robbing him as he walked home from the bus stop in broad daylight. Although he had moved several times since leaving the Somerset Homes when he was eleven, he had spent most of his life in neighborhoods where at least 30 percent of the population was below the poverty line.

Emily's and Joseph's stories illustrate what it is like for young adults who have grown up in disadvantaged circumstances and lack an identity project. As noted earlier, a good number—35 percent—are disconnected, like Emily and Joseph, from work and school. Many in this group said that they struggled with anxiety and depression.[6] Some self-soothed with weed, like Emily, or excessive amounts of alcohol. But their risk behaviors usually stopped there—just under one-third of the youth without identity projects were "ever in the street," and of those, few remained caught up for long, as we show in the rest of the chapter.

Like Emily and Joseph, Ella never managed to find her passion during adolescence. She was also one of the twenty-seven youth who spent some time "caught up" in the street, though in her case it was just for "a minute." Her story illustrates many of the risk factors that are shared by others who get caught up, but also how fleeting street involvement can be. She spent her earliest years at Lafayette Courts, on Baltimore's east side, where her mother moved just after she was born. At that time an astounding eight in ten people living in her census tract—which included the Courts plus the surrounding neighborhood—were poor. Four years later, the family was given a chance to move through the MTO program. Ella's mother, Renee, used the voucher to relocate to a predominantly white, middle-class, inner-ring suburb, Catonsville, where fewer than one in ten residents lived below the poverty line. But the respite lasted just a year. One ugly aspect of their lives in Lafayette Courts—Renee's abusive husband—followed them to Catonsville. After he kicked down the apartment's front door, the landlord refused to renew the lease, and the family had to move again.

Bouncing back to East Baltimore, Renee and her children moved from apartment to apartment, always trying to find a unit on a block that was a little better than the last. These neighborhoods were all more than 30 percent poor. Navigating the neighborhood, however, was not as difficult as avoiding the land mines at home. While Renee had divorced her husband by then, she continued to form relationships with abusive men. After Renee had evicted one such man after a fight, a frightened young Ella saw him sneaking back in through a window and called the police, who arrested him for breaking and entering.

We talked with Ella's mother for several hours in the summer of 2003, when Ella was in seventh grade. By then, the family had moved into the Pleasant View Gardens HOPE VI development, which had replaced the Lafayette Courts housing project. While the new development offered housing that was designed to facilitate interaction between people with a variety of incomes, it was still a pocket of concentrated poverty where nearly six in ten people were poor.

We also spent a day at Ella's school, where we interviewed one of her teachers and observed both her English and math classes. Sitting in the back of the classroom, we were witnesses to the chaos within these classes, even with visitors in attendance. In English, Ella and her fellow students settled into their seats and got ready to take a test—one of their last before the Christmas break. Their teacher, Mrs. Bowden, started reading the test directions out loud, but students almost immediately volleyed back questions about things she had just explained, and she became visibly irritated. Twenty minutes in, the loud buzz of the school office intercom interrupted. Soon after, noise erupted from the hallway outside and an adult voice screamed, *"I'm not taking any mess from y'all today!"* A few minutes later, Mrs. Bowden took out her cell phone, dialed a number, and entered into a lengthy conversation about her car insurance plan at full volume. Despite these disruptions, twelve-year-old Ella kept her head down, assiduously applying pencil to paper. By the end of the period, several textbooks had fallen to the floor and students walked over their open pages as they left. No one bothered to pick them up.

Later that day, during math class, several students were openly disrespectful to the teacher, Mrs. Hill. One shouted, *"Move, teacher!"* when unable to see the blackboard behind her. Mrs. Hill finally lost her cool and shouted at one of the girls, "You can go to the bathroom or just run the halls. Just leave my classroom!" One of just a few students who were even attempting to stay on task, Ella seemed to be trying to block out the commotion as she struggled with the assignment that Mrs. Hill had written on the board. Eventually, frustrated that she did not know how to solve the problem—the teacher was too busy trying to keep order to offer one-on-one instruction—Ella gave up and began talking with friends instead. By the end of the period, Mrs. Hill had completely lost control of the class.

Ella's story illustrates how significant exposure to poor-performing schools can lead to squandered opportunities.[7] In the course of observing the schools that Ella and thirty-nine other youth in our study were attending in 2003–2004, we noted buildings that were crumbling, curricular material that was out-of-date, and playgrounds that were little more than compounds of broken asphalt. Visiting these schools also revealed the implicit messages that these students were receiving from the physical environment about their value and potential. The water fountains in many of the schools were cordoned off, with signs citing lead poisoning concerns.[8] Several of the buildings were built like fortresses reminiscent of prisons, with thick metal grates covering the small windows. During the winter, some classrooms were so cold that students had to wear hats and coats, while others were so overheated that windows had to be opened. One student described her school as a "slave ship" to a reporter at the *Baltimore Sun*.[9]

Almost as soon as she arrived, Ella wanted out of Bainbridge Middle School and begged her mother to transfer her elsewhere. She was an honor roll student, and the school counselor was urging Renee to transfer her daughter to a better school. Mrs. Bowden, Ella's English teacher, told us that she had recommended the same, noting that Ella had "this really great innocent, care-free smile. She's not hardened. . . . I don't know how that didn't happen. In order for her [Ella] to blossom, she needs to leave this environment," Mrs. Bowden emphasized when we spoke with her after class. Somehow the transfer never materialized.

For Ella, the bright spot at Bainbridge was a special program for particularly talented students, which included advice on how to apply for the more selective magnet schools in the city. With the support she received there, she was able to matriculate to the best high school in Baltimore, Central High. But at Central she just couldn't keep up. Looking back, Ella reflected that Bainbridge Middle was a "terrible" school and that it didn't "build me up enough to go to [Central]." She also had a hard time fitting in socially, as many of her peers were from more affluent backgrounds. Ella coped by skipping school a couple of times a week. Not surprisingly, she was expelled from Central High at the end of ninth grade owing to poor attendance. Over the next three years, she would transfer three more times, trying to find a good fit, each time to a high school that ranked among the city's lowest performers—Marsh Run, Hamilton, and then Bayside, a school that ranked in the bottom fifth of the state distribution and twenty-fourth among the twenty-eight high schools in Baltimore City.[10] Shortly after she graduated, the school board closed two of these three high schools owing to their abysmal performance.[11]

After earning her diploma from Bayside, Ella enrolled in Job Corps, hoping to be trained as a heating, ventilation, air conditioning, and refrigeration (HVAC) technician. She did not complete the program. Without a job or sense of direction, she considered her options. For a brief time during high school, she had sold weed—she had a connection to a supplier through her cousin. But she was not willing to return to that now. "[It was just] not my thing; I don't like having to keep looking over my shoulder," she explained, describing the nearly constant fear that dogged her during that period. But her current job—she had been flipping burgers and grilling hot dogs at the Ravens football stadium for the last few months—was hardly her life's dream either, especially since she had burned herself on the stove several times.

Ella's free time was spent with her boyfriend, Mark, who was on house arrest when she first met him, after serving time for assault. He had beaten his mother's brutally abusive boyfriend severely enough to be charged with a felony and was sent to prison for a year. Shortly after they met, he was incarcerated for another year owing to a parole violation—he had cut the "box"—the homing device police sometimes use to detect the movements of those on house arrest or parole—off his ankle. When we spoke with Ella in 2010, Mark had been home for a couple of weeks and was trying to find work. But neither he nor Ella was optimistic about his prospects, given his felony record. For her part, she toyed with the idea of attending community college and then the police academy, with the goal of becoming a detective. Yet she had made no moves to enroll. At nineteen, she was floundering—still lacking that tailwind to move her forward.

Meanwhile, the family trauma continued. Recently, Renee had kicked Ella out of the house after accusing her of sleeping with Renee's new boyfriend, a charge Ella denied. Ella's grandmother's home in East Baltimore's Milton-Montford neighborhood, shared with her aunt and several cousins, had offered respite, but the move had put her in a neighborhood that, while only one-third poor, was "terrible," according to Ella. She described the drug trafficking she observed each day, plus the seemingly unrelenting background noise of police helicopters cruising overhead. Several of Ella's friends had been shot and killed around there, often over small beefs. Sometimes she carried a pocketknife for protection.

THE ROLE OF STRUCTURAL FACTORS IN GETTING "CAUGHT UP"

Because of her brief stint selling drugs, Ella was among the twenty-seven youth we defined as "ever in the street."[12] We adopted the term from the youth themselves (as in, "the streets still call you back") to describe those who at one time engaged in activities such as selling drugs or stealing cars.[13] Of the youth who fit this designation, twenty-four sold drugs, three had stolen cars, two reported robbing homes, one reported carjacking, and one spent a year as a prostitute after she became homeless.[14] Like Ella, some of those who got involved in illegal activities only dabbled in them for a few months' time. But nineteen youth coded as "ever in the street" were engaged in street activities for at least a year, eight of them persisting past the age of eighteen.

What distinguishes the youth who get caught up in the street from those who do not? To answer this question, we looked to the role of family trauma, neighborhood poverty, and schools in predicting who would be involved in illegal activities. Even given her brief time in the street, Ella's story shows that she had been exposed to each of the risk factors usually associated with street activity. First, Ella had had significant exposure to neighborhoods that were at least moderately poor (30 percent or more). Second, there was trauma in her family of origin. Third, she had spent most of her time in low-performing schools, defined here as schools that score in the bottom quartile of the state of Maryland's standardized test scores.[15]

For all but two of our 150 youth, Susan Clampet-Lundquist and one of our other collaborators, Ann Owens, were able to draw on data collected as part of the MTO final evaluation survey to construct neighborhood trajectories, estimate how long youth had lived at each of their addresses from 1994 to 2008, and calculate their tract's poverty rate. We analyzed the data in two ways. First, we looked at length of exposure to a neighborhood that was more than 40 percent poor, which is consistent with the threshold used in much of the literature on neighborhood poverty. As one might expect, given the data on neighborhood change we presented in chapter 2, after MTO began, the median amount of time that our youth spent in a neighborhood that was more than 40 percent poor was just a year and a half. However, even neighborhoods scoring lower—we use 30 percent as a threshold—contain serious risk.[16] When deploying this alternative threshold, we see that fully half of our youth, about even numbers of girls and boys, had been exposed to such environments for six years or more. Ella, for example, had spent over half her life in a neighborhood that was over 30 percent poor by 2008. Thus, even with the overall decrease in concentrated poverty that we noted in chapter 2, driven in large part by the changes to public housing, many youth still churned through at least moderately poor neighborhoods or settled in neighborhoods that became poorer over time.

We looked to see how closely length of exposure to poverty was related to the likelihood of ever engaging in illegal activities. To do so, we divided the youth into three groups of exposure—more than six years, one to six years, and less than a year.[17] We found that among those who were "ever in the street," two-thirds had lived in a neighborhood that exceeded the 30 percent threshold for more than six years (see table 4.1). On the other end of the continuum, only 11 percent of youth ever involved in illegal activities had spent less than a year in neighborhoods over 30 percent poor.

Other things mattered too. Research has long showed that the strongest correlates of crime are age and sex. Men commit far more crime than women do, and both genders' criminal activity tends to desist as they age, particularly in the late teens and early twenties.[18] Explanations for these patterns range from simple biology (testosterone levels and delayed fron-

Table 4.1   Percent of Youth Who Were "Ever in the Street" by Duration in
             Neighborhoods More Than 30 Percent Poor ($N = 27$)

Less Than One Year	One to Six Years	More Than Six Years	Total
11%	22%	67%	100%

Source: Authors' compilations.

tal lobe development for adolescents)[19] to more sociological explanations
that focus on gender socialization and peer influences.[20] Other explanations for the age-crime correlation center on the important role that life-
course transitions, such as marriage, parenthood, and career entry, play in
increasing one's "stake in conformity," thus leading to desistance as young
people move from adolescence into adulthood.[21]

Consistent with these findings, males in our study were far more likely
to have ever been in the street (twenty-three boys versus only four female
youth). Fully one-third of boys who had spent at least six years in neighborhoods that were at least 30 percent poor engaged in such behavior,
while only about one in ten (11 percent) of their female counterparts living
in such neighborhoods did. Matthew had been involved in a variety of
criminal activities during his teen years. He had spent most of his life in
neighborhoods that were over the 30 percent threshold. Evicted from Flag
Homes for owing back rent, his family had cycled from apartment to
apartment and through homeless spells in neighborhoods with rampant
drug trafficking, in which both of his parents were involved. By twenty-
one, the risk endemic to these neighborhoods had profoundly shaped
Matthew's outlook on life: "Anything could happen anywhere. . . . I might
not even make it to the future . . . you never know what['s] happening.
This is Baltimore, so. . . ."

Because we had followed more than one-third of the youth over time
and collected detailed life histories from every young person in the study,
we also observed desistance. While 18 percent had said they were "ever in
the street," only 4 percent of the youth (six young adults) were still involved in illegal activities when we conducted our last wave of fieldwork
in 2012. But our youth varied in age, thus adding the complication that
those who were older had had more chance to engage in and exit from
street activity. Not surprisingly, youth over eighteen were four times more
likely to say that they had been caught up in crime than those eighteen
and younger.

To test the proposition that neighborhood exposure continues to matter
after taking gender and age into consideration, we ran a logistic regres-

sion to predict the likelihood that a young person in our study would be coded as "ever in the street" and found that, while gender mattered most, age and neighborhood were close behind (see table A4.2). Importantly, holding gender and age constant, youth with less exposure to high poverty contexts (those who had spent less than six years in a neighborhood that was at least 30 percent poor) were only 45 percent as likely to engage in illegal behavior as youth who had been exposed for a longer period of time (see table A4.2).

We added trauma in family of origin (we did not have consistent data on domestic violence, but did know whether each youth had a caretaker who had a substance abuse problem or had been incarcerated) to predict the probability of ever engaging in illegal activities (see tables A4.3 and A4.4).[22] We found that, even taking into account age, sex, and neighborhood residence, youth whose parents had substance abuse problems were nearly three times as likely to have engaged in illegal behavior.

Originally, we had hoped to explore the relationship with school quality and involvement in criminal activities. However, as we suspected from our time spent observing the schools, school quality varied so little that the element was rendered useless in a statistical exercise such as this. Drawing from data on our youth from the final impact survey, conducted in 2009, we find that the median ranking of school quality was at the fourteenth percentile of Maryland schools.[23] Eighty percent of the young people in this study attended schools throughout their childhood and adolescence that ranked in the lowest quartile of Maryland schools. When we looked at the school quality to which our young people had been exposed, only six had an average school experience that exceeded the fiftieth percentile, based on test scores on Maryland standardized exams.

For the remainder of this chapter, we focus on two youth who were caught up in illegal activities for a significant period of time and who drew identity from the street itself. Our first question is: what draws youth in? Then we consider how their participation in illegal activities, combined with other factors, can hinder them from reaching the conventional goals they adopt as they grow older, even for those without the formal barrier of a felony record.

We begin with Whitney, who commanded her own corner by the time she was in middle school. In some ways, hers is a classic teen thrill-seeking narrative,[24] though a deeper look also reveals the strong appeal of the intellectual challenge—a chance to put her considerable intelligence to use, yet with tragic long-term consequences. When we left Whitney in 2012, she was a twenty-three-year-old mother of three who seemed broken by the trauma she had experienced while "running the streets" and plying her trade.

We then turn to Ron, who was tutored in "the game" from a young age and sought to cultivate a street identity as early as he can remember. Until 2011, we had counted Ron as among the toughest and most "in the street" youth in the study. But the birth of his daughter had transformative power. Now, he said, he wanted to "go straight" and "take care of my family." When we left him in 2012, he was still dealing drugs, yet also struggling toward a more conventional path and striving to be a model to the baby daughter he found endlessly fascinating.

"THAT'S THE WAY I HAD TO LEARN"

Whitney leaned over the railing of her mother's porch in Belair-Edison, keeping an eye on her two young sons, Andre, age eight, and Brison, age nine, as they played with two neighbor boys on the edge of the large park that sat at the end of her row of tiny "two-by-two" row houses—two stories high, two windows across. It was a block where stoops and porch roofs were mostly off-kilter. The porches and stoops were active with both adults and children. The adults sat, talked, and watched the traffic or shouted greetings to passersby, while children ran in and out of the houses, screen doors banging, and then hopped onto scooters or bikes, creating sidewalk traffic that mimicked the busy road beyond the parked cars.

Whitney, who was currently unemployed, did hair on the side. Her own hairstyle was constantly in flux—sometimes she wore it in long extensions, and other times it was carefully shaped into a bob that framed her pretty face. She was tall, model thin, with white teeth contrasting against dark skin. When Susan Clampet-Lundquist and Megan Holland first met Whitney at this address, she was twenty-one and living with her boys there—along with her mother, stepfather, little sister, and two of her three brothers (the other was in prison). The home, with three small bedrooms upstairs and three in the finished basement, was crowded, to say the least, and tensions were running high. Despite this, Whitney was warm and gracious to us, and we sat around the dining room table while her mother, Neena, tried to keep the boys quiet and occupied upstairs.

Whitney had held the same job as a food runner in a nearby military base cafeteria since she was sixteen. The job was full-time—a rare perk in the Baltimore low-skilled economy—but just a month or two prior to our interview, she was forced to quit because her informal day care arrangement had fallen through. Without a high school diploma or even a GED, she was struggling to find another job.

From time to time, Whitney had contemplated trying for her GED, but even though she scored high on intelligence tests as a child, she and school never saw eye to eye; middle school was as far as she had gotten, and it had taken her three tries—three middle schools—to accomplish that. It was not that she disliked the work; she just could not seem to keep from being expelled for fighting. She had gotten pregnant in the eighth grade, so the school district assigned her to an alternative high school, but she seldom attended. She withdrew two years later without earning any credits toward a high school degree.

Born in Murphy Homes, Whitney and her family had moved from the high-rise towers just before they were demolished, when she was five years old. The family relocated to Shipley Hill, a Southwest Baltimore neighborhood where her grandmother and grandfather had lived for decades as homeowners. Once a solid working-class area, it had become one of the city's most disadvantaged by that time, boasting a poverty rate of over 40 percent, a figure that jumped to 70 percent when considering only households with children under eighteen.[25] "Everybody killing each other, everybody down and stuff . . . over people hating, over people just getting more money than other people, and it's just a lot of hate and stuff going on over there," Whitney later said of the neighborhood.

Neena was a nurse's aide who worked long hours. To make ends meet, she took on double shifts, which made supervising her four children difficult. Whitney's grandmother, who was "old school," stepped in to provide some supervision, and she and Whitney grew close. However, when she died suddenly, any structure in the household routine went with her. Soon Whitney and her brothers were soaking up the street life of the neighborhood like sponges.

Because Neena worked an afternoon and an evening shift, Whitney and her brothers could run the streets unsupervised after school, only returning home to feign sleep when their mother stopped home around 8:00 to 9:00 PM to check in on them between shifts. After she left again, they were out of bed in a flash, playing tag and hide-and-seek in the neighborhood's alleys and backyards with other unsupervised kids. Whitney especially loved the times they would break into the old Eigenbrot Factory; long since shut down, it was a four-story, red brick structure that had once housed one of the city's leading breweries. Its unused rooms were a children's wonderland where Whitney, her siblings, and the neighborhood kids performed impromptu plays, creating a fantasy world. When those thrills began to pale, Whitney and a friend began breaking into homes just for fun, stealing whatever struck their fancy. Guns were one of the best spoils. They used them only one time, to intimidate a boarder who lived with her aunt and was trying to bully her cousin: "The girl kept on messing with [my cousin], so [my cousin] wanted her out of there. So me and my best friend, we went up there, and we had guns on us. So [we] went in there, took the door down . . . made her get out. Made her strip, made her walk down the steps, get out of the house and all that, right? She wouldn't come back in there."

Then, at age twelve, Whitney started selling drugs, including heroin and crack. She would set her alarm for 5:30 AM and be at work by six, rain or shine. She was proud to have earned the distinction of being the only girl in the neighborhood with her own corner, on a bleak stretch of Pulaski Avenue just a half-dozen blocks away from the busy Westside Mall, a low-rent strip mall that anchors the southwest side. In 2012, Whitney took Kathryn Edin and Jennifer Darrah on a tour of Shipley Hill by car, pointing out the vacant storefront with a side door that had a small awning (handy in case of snow or rain). There she would wait until she received a call. Then she would pop into the alley, pick up the product, and deliver it to the waiting customer. She claimed that she could bring in $1,300 on a good day. With the exception of the time she was in school, she spent 6:00 AM to midnight on that corner. When Whitney thought back to that time, she recalled both the intense thrill and the gnawing fear.

> It was fun. I ain't gonna lie, it was fun running back and forth. [But] when I was hustling at night [once,] I got robbed. So . . . the only thing I was scared about was, is they just gonna take the stuff and go ahead and leave, or [was they] gonna hurt me and still take the stuff? So other than that . . . other than getting robbed and the guns in your face, [it was great].

What Whitney loved most was the mental challenge—the need to be on the alert, assessing risk from every angle, evaluating others' motivations, anticipating their actions, and adapting accordingly.

> You can't just trust everybody. . . . Most of the people just be looking at one street, one street, they looking at this side, and they're looking at this side. Well, you gotta look at this side, [and] that side, all these sides. . . . You can't just think for one person—just yourself—you gotta think for a lot of other people, what this person was threatening in their mind or how this can go down or stuff like that.

She still valued the practical skills she gained, which she felt outweighed the costs of the choices she made:

> When I sit here and think about it—by me being older and grown up—you [would think I'd be] wishing that, "Oh man, I wish I would have stayed in school. I wish I would have stayed with that program and did this and did that. . . ." But I don't regret nothing I did. . . . And I ain't ashamed of none of

my mistakes. That's the way I had to learn. By me being in the street, by me selling drugs and hanging with this people . . . it helped me to learn [how] I cope with life and know all different types of people.

Two years after we first met Whitney at the Belair-Edison row house, we were able to reconnect and follow her over the next year for the ethnographic portion of our study. Several months earlier, after a fight with her younger sister, she had left the boys at Neena's and was couch-surfing between the nearby homes of several people: her best friend, who lived next door in a home she had inherited from her mother (she had a child by Whitney's brother); a middle-aged woman a few houses down (whose incarcerated son was Brison's father); and an older lady across the street whose son was Whitney's on-again, off-again boyfriend and the father of her third child.

Things were tense, as Whitney was in the midst of a battle with the child welfare authorities over custody of that child, a four-month-old boy who had been removed from her care when he was two months old. At first Whitney had told us that the infant rolled over and fell off the bed onto the floor and that after she rushed the baby to the hospital to ensure that he was not injured, the doctor was concerned enough to call child welfare. But the next time we got together and Whitney took us on a tour of her old haunts in Southwest Baltimore, she told us a different story. During a smoke break outside of the Wendy's at the Westside Mall, she explained that when she became angry, she would black out. That day she had been frustrated with the baby, who would not stop crying. She blacked out, and when she came to, the baby was on the floor. She had no memory of what had happened. She confided that she had been asked to attend anger management classes as a condition of regaining custody. When asked whether they were helping, she shrugged, shook her head from side to side, indicating she did not think so.

Child welfare required Whitney to attend a number of court hearings in the months that followed, and Jennifer Darrah accompanied her to one of these. Whitney knew that her family was on the line. Eager to come across as her best self, Whitney had dressed carefully for the occasion, spending hours the night before doing her hair and planning her outfit; she showed up a half-hour late owing to her last-minute indecision over the color of her nails. She rushed into the courthouse on four-inch-high platform heels, wearing a tight beige dress ending just below her hips. She had fresh extensions, dyed blue, and brightly painted nails with glittering sequins. She looked stunning—but her elaborate preparations may have had the opposite effect on the judge from what she had intended.[26] In any case, the hearing was postponed.[27]

At twenty-three, Whitney did not have a clear direction, or even any ideas of what to do next. Though she had a roof over her head—she was now mostly living with the baby's father and the baby in his mother's home, while the two older boys remained with Neena across the way—she had no job and no credentials. One could speculate that her time on the street—from about age twelve until fifteen—had affected her in many ways. She was pretty sure that she first got pregnant in that old brewery up the hill from the Westside Mall, for example, and it is possible that the stress of those years contributed to her pattern of "zapping out"—her term for the blackouts—when she was angry, a possible cause of her infant's injury. Her entry into the drug trade coincided with the onset of behavioral problems so severe that she was expelled from two middle schools.

There had been other sources of trauma in Whitney's life as well. She was thirteen when she saw her father, on her birthday, for the last time. Apparently, he thought that Whitney would be an easy mark for getting money to fuel his drug habit:

> Yeah, on my birthday, he want my money. . . . And he hit me and . . . I was gonna beat him . . . with a chain 'cause he hit me, [but] I just gave him some money. . . . He came back a hour and a half later talking about couldn't he have some more money. "No, you ain't getting no more money, I don't got no money to give you." [He said,] "Yes, you do," and tried to go in my pockets, so I pushed him, and he slapped me. And I was about to kill him.

In addition, her son Andre's father died of a brain aneurysm when she was only fifteen. She says they were deeply in love. Pregnant again at seventeen, she and Brison's father ended up on the lam for several weeks—fleeing police—after he failed to appear in court on a probation violation. Ironically, their spell in the Eastside Motel in Essex, about ten miles east of Baltimore, was the only time Whitney got a taste of suburban living. Eventually, he was apprehended and sent back to prison, so she had to go through the last stages of her pregnancy by herself. Five years later, when we spoke with Whitney for the last time, he was still incarcerated.

All of these factors had probably contributed to where Whitney found herself at present. Yet it was almost certainly the case that investing her considerable talents in the street rather than in more conventional pursuits also played a role. In sharp contrast to the identity projects described in chapter 3, Whitney's time in the street did not ultimately build a bridge toward a viable future.

Ron was a slender young man with smooth, light brown skin and braided hair. He was personable and smiled easily, especially when talking about his baby daughter. His arms were covered in tattoos, acquired in a friend's basement. He felt that the tattoos were a way to express his values. Although he had nothing but adoration and respect for his mother, one of his tattoos—MOB (Money Over Bitches)—reflected his mistrust of women, which he said he learned from his father. A set of numbers representing the range of addresses on his block adorned the same arm, indicating a territorial loyalty that one might fight for. Theater masks—comedy and tragedy—were also inked there, with the words LAUGH NOW, CRY LATER. The tattoo F.O.E. (Family Over Everything) adorned his other arm. When he became a father at eighteen, he had his daughter's name tattooed across his chest in large letters: DESTINY.

Ron said that, growing up, he always aspired to be "street," given the role models around him—especially his dad, who tutored him in how to navigate the streets and carry himself "like a man." Joyce, his mother, was determined to save him from the influences of the Murphy Homes when she used her MTO voucher to move to Woodlawn, one of the city's northwest suburbs. During this time, Joyce worked long hours for a telecommunications company in sales. She also fell in love and got married to someone with a steady job. Then Kevin, Ron's younger half-brother, was born. When Ron talked about his little brother, his voice became tender and a smile spread across his face. Ron was thrilled: "I was happy because I wanted a little brother, I wanted somebody younger than me to be around . . . that I could teach stuff," he said.

Two years later, Joyce qualified for a first-time home buyer's program and dutifully saved for a down payment. Thus, when Ron was seven, they moved to a neighborhood that was affordable and close to Joyce's mother—her top criteria. Their new neighborhood was the West Baltimore community of Walbrook, which had once been a solid working-class enclave but had recently fallen on hard times, as several vacant row houses on her street bore witness to. Their block consisted of two-story row houses and larger detached homes with wide porches. Joyce, her husband John, and the two boys moved into one of the latter. We visited the home three times over the years we were watching Ron's life unfold. Each time the Victorian structure—complete with a striking leaded glass window in the foyer—was extraordinarily well appointed with tasteful furnishings and impeccably kept.

In contrast to Joyce's efforts to attain mainstream success—by working steadily, getting married, purchasing a home, and keeping it neat as a pin—Ron was determined to brand himself a "city boy." His father, Terrence, was a powerful guide, schooling him in how useless it was to be faithful to one woman, how to avoid trouble when dealing drugs, and how to be tough. Ron spent time with his father at his paternal grandmother's home whenever his father was not in prison.

When Ron had been very young, Terrence and Joyce had been fellow addicts. Joyce had managed to kick her addiction just before Ron was born and broke off the relationship, but Terrence continued to use and deal drugs to finance his habit. Terrence never helped financially with child support. Yet Ron adored him—calling him "the best man in the world"—and spent time with him during rare moments when he was out of prison. Ron said that it was mostly his father, not his hardworking mother or stepfather, who shaped his ideas about what it was to be a man. Yet John, Ron's stepfather, earned his respect as well—not because he held down a job, but because he too had come "out of the streets. . . . Nobody play with him. He carry himself like a man carry himself. They respect him." Ron said that his stepfather taught him "street smarts," including how to discern who to trust and who not to trust, and advised him that it was best to stay close to family. He also taught Ron to exit a situation if it seemed "shaky" and could lead to him being locked up or killed.[28] All of these lessons were to serve Ron well once he followed in Terrence's footsteps and entered the game.

Like so many of the youth who participated in the MTO experiment, Ron did not move to a suburban school after his family moved to the suburbs. Instead, he remained in a city school using his grandmother's address—a high-crime West Baltimore neighborhood—so that his grandmother or aunt could pick him up at the end of the day and watch him while Joyce was working. In middle school, Ron was branded a behavioral problem and assigned to a special program whose classrooms were physically separate from the rest of the school. His teachers recommended that Joyce consider getting him on medication for his behavior—he had trouble paying attention and sitting still—but she resisted, worried that taking a drug of any kind might increase his chances of becoming an addict. She had good reason to believe that a propensity toward addiction ran in the family. In fact, all six of her siblings had become addicts, as she had herself, despite a middle-class upbringing in a stable, two-parent home.

Ron's narrative suggests that his teacher's request may have been prompted by more than just his failure to sit still. As he explained, "I used to be bad when I was younger. I have cooled off now." Ron described frequent fights with teachers during his middle school years and "messing with girls." Once, Ron was suspended for bringing a pair of brass knuckles to school. He said that the source of his unruly behavior was the despair he had experienced when his father was convicted of murder and went away for seven years. This event "crushed" Ron. But his behavior was also calculated, a way to project a certain image to his peers. "If you carry yourself like you are a punk or a swine, they going to treat you like swine," he said. "[You're going to] keep getting punked by everybody . . .

like anybody treat [you] any type of way. I ain't going to let nobody treat me any type of way."

Though middle school was rough, the school Ron ended up attending in ninth grade—Rockville—was a disaster. His description: "Fighting in the bathroom every day . . . teachers were scared of the students." Joyce took him out midyear, a prudent move since in the months that followed Rockville was deemed so unsafe and so low-performing that the school district shut it down.[29] Somehow, despite his behavioral problems, his mother managed to get him into a high-performing charter school. Charter Oaks was a "shirt-and-tie" kind of place with a radically different social world than Rockville, which Ron said was more "like a battlefield." However, the Charter Oaks principal sent him home almost every day for misconduct. Ron's personal charisma was so strong that other students started mimicking his behavior, much to the school administration's consternation. They asked him to leave at the end of the year. Ron's third try was at a school housed in the location of his former middle school, which had been closed as well. He was at the Economics Leadership Academy for just half a year; he was constantly getting in trouble for fighting and skipping school. Ron began eleventh grade at Garrison High but dropped out at the end of the year. "I ain't really a school type of person," he said.

What was happening in school was mild, however, compared to what was going on when Ron was not in the classroom. When he was only nine, older peers taught him how to smoke pot and, later, how to steal cars. "That's what messed me up . . . learning stuff before I was supposed to, learning it at a young age," he told us in 2010. Part of Ron's trouble was that he seldom spent time in his own neighborhood, a relatively "quiet" area. He was instead drawn to the rougher neighborhoods to the south— especially Brooklyn and Cherry Hill. There he took sides with boys from one housing project in their "beef" against another. He was drawn to neighborhoods like these because there were "more opportunities for stuff to happen." For the most part, Ron moved through these neighborhoods without much fear. His secret: "It's just how you carry yourself. Like, I carry myself like a man. That's how my father raised me."

Throughout adolescence, Ron sold marijuana, crack, and heroin, doing a brisk business in school as well as on the streets of those neighborhoods. He was particularly proud of one arrest: he had twenty-five bags of weed on him that the police never found—he had hidden them in a packet in the front panel of his briefs. In fact, that was precisely why he made sure he wore briefs each day. Ron was arrested multiple times during these years, yet his longest spell in lockup was only two days in "baby booking," the slang term for juvenile detention. The experience just seemed to stoke his confidence. "I been down there [baby booking] chillin' . . . I don't even pay them no mind," he said. "People go down there all scared. They really—all they thinking, 'I am going to get killed or something.' I just go in and put my feet up and go to sleep. I don't think none of that." Ron was sixteen when we spoke with him the first time. One of his statements stood out: "I ain't trying to do no bus stop until I get older." Doing a "bus stop"—commuting to work on the bus—was not in his plans in the near term. He wanted something more exciting, something that would make him feel more like a man.[30]

Two years later, when we reconnected with Ron, things had changed rather significantly. The birth of his daughter had seemed to transform him. During our last conversation—he was nineteen at the time—he could not stop talking about his ten-month-old baby. She lived with her mother nearby during the week, but she was all Ron's on weekends. He went on and on about teaching her how to walk, getting down on the floor to join her as she played with her toys, and the fun of watching TV together. Ron was fascinated with everything about the toddler. He told us that the best thing about being a father was "watching your kid grow up, for real. . . . They start out so small, and then they get bigger and bigger!"

For Ron, becoming a parent triggered two key shifts. First, probably to the surprise of the administrators at Garrison High, he returned to school, eager to get his high school diploma. He was actually showing up and doing the homework this time around, because, he said, "I don't want to be no deadbeat father." He described his new approach to life: "I look at it different now, I'm more focused on work and stuff. Like, back then, I didn't do no work, but now . . . I do what I gotta do so I can get out of there for real." Older than most of his classmates, Ron felt the contrast between himself and the younger students, who were not serious about working hard, in his estimation. His goal was to graduate from high school in a year and attend trade school to become a mechanic.

Second, Ron had cut himself off from most of his previous West Baltimore companions and was staying to himself, inside the house, focusing on schoolwork and being the "man of the house" for his daughter and his younger brother Kevin. That so many of his old friends were by now incarcerated made this challenge easier. But Ron was also consciously distancing himself from activities that could get him into trouble:

> I think about my actions more now, like, every little thing. Like, when I was younger I used to do petty stuff, and I just didn't think that stuff would always come back, but now I'm thinking about the future for real, and I think before I act. . . . Like, if my friend ask me to do something, I'm like no, if it's something I know they going to get in trouble for.

Ron still earned his living selling drugs, but he was trying to do it in a less risky way. He estimated that he netted about $1,000 a week selling marijuana. (He no longer sold heroin and crack.) And now he made his transactions over the phone, rather than out on the corner, so that he would be less vulnerable to being robbed or arrested. Being a father, he said, had made him "more cautious about my moves and my actions." Yet parenthood also pressured him to be a provider, the reason he still sold drugs. Ron explained: "I'm a man now, so I do stuff like I was taught to do, as a man, for real, like taking care of my daughter . . . taking responsibility like a man is supposed to do." With only a long-ago summer job through YouthWorks, the city's summer youth employment program, in his job history, Ron had not had any luck applying for a legitimate position, especially now that he had to juggle school, so hustling was his default.

Ron's years in the streets were all-consuming and about more than the thrill and the money—being engaged in the street was an attempt to live out his ethos of manhood, first instilled by his father Terrence, but then inadvertently nurtured at the knee of his stepfather John, a man who had come from the streets and still lived according to the tenets that had preserved him during those years. Ron idolized his father, an addict and dealer who had been in and out of prison ever since Ron could remember. He never questioned his father's lessons and eagerly followed the path that his father had set for him—until he had a child of his own. Now he had less of a sense of what he had gained from the streets than of what he had lost—time. Nearly twenty, he was just finishing his junior year of high school. He would be twenty-one before he would be "out there for real." By that time, his daughter would be three years old and the pressure to be a provider would be even more real. How would he take the time that he needed to invest in a credential that could lead to a living-wage job? Would he keep selling weed and risk being injured or physically separated from his daughter if he was incarcerated? Would he be forced to substitute a job that would pay just above the legal minimum wage for his desired trade? The answers were unclear. What we do know is that, because of the time he lost and the adult responsibilities he gained, Ron's launch would be far more difficult than it would have been if he had found his passion in more conventional pursuits.

Neighborhoods provide opportunities and avenues for young residents to find meaning to different degrees. We have seen how Whitney's Shipley Hill neighborhood was a stage for her, her friends, and her brothers. Act I, scene II: inside the abandoned brewery, fooling around out of adults' eyesight. Act II, scene III: pulling drugs out of a hidden crevice in an alley and passing them through the open window of a car. The landscape of the neighborhood, complete with vacant buildings and well-known places to hide, provided the perfect setting for Whitney and her friends to live out their adolescent thrills.

Ron's quiet Walbrook neighborhood was not his main stage for delinquency—Brooklyn and Cherry Hill served that purpose. The opportunity
to dip in and out of the drug game in so many of the neighborhoods where
our youth spent their formative years was there for the taking. But as Ron
was attempting to shift to a new chapter, Walbrook had become his stage
for withdrawing from the game to spend time with his daughter in safety.

Justin, who remained in Murphy Homes until they were torn down
when he was eleven, initially moved on to an apartment on North Avenue, in Sandtown-Winchester. There would be six more addresses after
that, all in West Baltimore. Most of his life was spent in neighborhoods
more than 30 percent poor. Justin was probably the toughest, most at-risk
young person in our study, by our estimation. He explained: "When you
put us in this environment, it's not nothing else to do. . . . If you born
around a bunch of drug dealers, like, come on, as soon as you short a dol-
lar, you taking the pack to the block, you know? I've been holding my
own since I was nine. Shit, sold my first pack when I was nine . . . everybody was doing it."

To be sure, limited opportunities in the neighborhood make the situation harder. We heard from a number of young men about the lack of jobs,
vocational training opportunities, and recreational centers—the very
things that provide a viable alternative to the street.[31] As Kareem, twenty,
put it bluntly:

> I know a million people who if I needed to sell drugs or rob houses or stuff
> like that, that I could have the job at any time and be making enough money
> to support myself, but it's—I'm not, I guess, not ready to sell out yet. [Em-
> ployers say] they'll call you back . . . and you can tell [they're] lying by what
> they sayin'. And *those* type of things that make me mad ['cause] all you goin'
> think about is the fact that I didn't get that job and the fact that it's as if—it's
> as if I was destined to be a criminal.

Family trauma and dysfunctional schools also make youth vulnerable
to the streets. Whitney suffered from the death of her grandmother and
the neglect of a mother who had to work too many shifts. Ron followed in
the footsteps of the father he never quite had, only to come to the realization of what a dead end it was when his own child was born. Schools that
are "underperforming"—a mild word for the utter chaos that envelopes
so many in the city of Baltimore—often stifle rather than stoke potential
and frequently fail utterly to meet the deeper needs of those who have
chronic behavioral problems. Occasionally, a teacher or a counselor shines
through—think back to Vicky from chapter 3—but these stories are the
exceptions, not the rule.

For these youth, the street was often where their intellects found stimu-

lation. In this world, street smarts—the ability to read people and antici-
pate their moves—were far more vital than book smarts.[32] The ability to
navigate the street could literally be the difference between life and
death.[33] But all of these gains were fleeting because they were profoundly
out of step with the conventional world. And in the end it is the conventional world, with its conventional rules, that offers the safety and stability that so many of our youth engaged in the street ended up seeking.

In chapter 3, we described how a different group of young people
grabbed hold of something with which they could forge an identity project. As we conducted the analysis for this chapter, we expected that the
ability to "follow my passion"—in Terry's words—would be hampered by
the same forces that were so strongly correlated with the probability that
a young person would fail to resist the streets: the threat of neighborhood,
family, and school without better options. Yet we found no significant association. Vicky—with her pigeons, featured in chapter 3—and Whitney
both came of age in similar neighborhoods adjacent to one another. Both
experienced significant trauma as a result of growing up there. Possibly as
a result, Vicky also blacked out when she got angry. In fact, both women
used the same phrase to describe the episodes—"zapping out." But following her father's lead, Vicky found an outlet in caring for and training
her birds. When life became overwhelming, she could retreat with the
birds to the backyard. When we last spoke with both of them, Vicky had a
high school diploma and was in community college, but Whitney seemed
utterly lost.

Both Cody and Ron attended schools that were shut down for poor
performance shortly after they left them. Both had parents whose lives
had brought trauma to their children: Cody's mother's abuse led child
welfare to remove him from her home at age seven, and because of Ron's
dad's life path as a drug addict and dealer, Ron said, he was "taken from"
his dad at the age of eight when his dad was convicted of murder. Being
perceived as strong was important to both. Cody's motivation to join
sports teams in high school was spurred by a desire to defend himself
against others who "punked" him for being short. Participating in the Police Explorer program and JROTC further defined Cody as a strong person
who knew how to handle difficult situations, a message that was rein-
forced through the scenarios his Police Explorer team had to confront in
local, state, and national competitions. Ron's route to manhood bypassed
these institutional contexts, with the exception of his brief spell in "baby
booking," which only served to reinforce his street identity. Cody's identity project earned a badge that he wore around his neck at all times. It
served as a shield against "negativity"—quite literally for the police, who
stopped "messing" with him as soon as they saw the symbol and realized
that Cody was a Police Explorer cadet.

In short, adversity can both propel young people toward an identity project as a way to survive and inhibit them from doing so. Identity projects can be powerful tools with which to surmount adversity in one's neighborhood, family, and school. The street usually provides some semblance of meaning only for a "minute"—even for those who are several years deep into the business.

CONCLUSION

Young people get drawn into the street for many reasons. Some in our study did so out of a desire for material things. Ray, who started life in Lexington Terrace, moved briefly to suburban Rosedale through MTO but spent his adolescence in Belair-Edison, where the local high school was so low-performing that it was later broken up into a number of smaller schools. It was a neighborhood on the decline, the same community from which Whitney also now hailed. Ray began selling drugs after the move to Belair-Edison. He told us, "You see an opportunity where there's money to be made, so I took the opportunity."

Jayden and his family escaped Murphy Homes through an MTO voucher, moving to a suburban apartment complex near Towson University, where the young man next door happened to be dealing drugs. "And I seen the money, the money was coming so fast, and I was like, 'I want it,'" Jayden said. "Yeah, I kept seeing him buying what he want, he got his own car, his own clothes; I got tired of asking my mother for help, so I decided to get them on my own."[34]

Others had more philanthropic motives. Jaquan's brother sold drugs and contributed some of his profit to sustain his family. After his brother was arrested, Jaquan temporarily stepped into his business, motivated by a desire to help shoulder his mother's economic burden. "My brother had got arrested, and my mother, she was working," he said. "I wasn't working, and I just felt like she needed some help in the house. And I was still filling out applications and stuff like that, but it wasn't moving quick enough, so that's why I started doing that."[35] However, like others in our study, Jaquan knew deep down that being "in the streets . . . wasn't me." Instead, he said, he "was always into books and doing school."

Marcus had spent most of his life in Cherry Hill and Park Heights, neighborhoods that were notable for their poverty and blight. He quit school in the ninth grade to pursue drug dealing full-time out of a deep sense of anomie—an utter loss of faith in conventional society and its rules—that enveloped him after his cousin, a college student, was confronted by police in the Cherry Hill projects as he was leaving his mother's home, told to kneel with his hands over his head, and then shot five times in the back, for no apparent reason.[36] For Marcus, selling drugs was the only way he knew to indicate his contempt for a society that offered such uncertain rewards for those who play by the rules, as his cousin had. But as was true for Jaquan, drug selling was also a way for Marcus to help out his mom financially—a reformed drug addict turned missionary for her local church, she spent her days hauling other dealers off the streets, preaching the hope of salvation in contrast to the wages of sin. "For once, the bills got paid," he said, with some satisfaction, recalling that time.

In addition, these narratives offer ample evidence of a claim we made in chapter 3—that in many communities where these young people spent their formative years the street can be perceived as the default, especially for boys. This was the path whose contours were most familiar to them. Recall that Ray explained, "It's [something] you know you can be. [Something where you] know what you can accomplish. So you get it and do it. Keep doin' it." Similarly, James, who spent most of his twenty years in neighborhoods that were at least 30 percent poor (with only a brief spell in suburban Owings Mills, via MTO), said that he got involved in selling drugs because "I just knew what to do, I did. So ain't worry about have to ask anybody."[37] The ease with which young people can access criminal activity, the low barriers to entry, and their familiarity with its requirements and routines make it all the more remarkable that of the 150 youth in our study, only 27 were "ever in the street" and only 19 got "caught up" for any significant period of time.

However, as the stories of both Whitney and Ron show, for the youth who get caught up "for real," the street is more than a paycheck, a way to help shoulder the burden at home, or the path of least resistance for those who grow up in "a certain type of environment." It is also a vehicle to formulate an identity; it is something to "be about," a way to be "known." Whitney and Ron were trying to resolve the same developmental dilemma that Vicky, Bob, and Cody were, but in a different way, with vastly different results. This suggests that broadening access to identity projects tied to the conventional world, especially those within an institutional context— to help young people get on a moving train (to refer to the metaphor we used in chapter 3)—could be a way to turn the lives of even the most delinquent around.

The other remarkable feature of the narratives we analyzed is that so many of these youth desisted from crime—all but six during the course of our study. They moved away from the street for a variety of reasons. Whitney slowed down or quit dealing entirely when she had her first child. Becoming a dad had slowed even Ron down. Other relational ties mattered too. For example, Michael stopped selling drugs when his mother started using again and he realized that, with his grandmother becoming increasingly frail, he would have to take responsibility for his younger brother. Jay decided to quit dealing when he aspired to date a young woman who was attending Goucher College, a small liberal arts school in suburban Towson, just north of the city line. As proof of his determination to quit, he convinced his mother to move away from the Brooklyn neighborhood, a moderately poor, mixed-race area in the far south section of the city, where he'd become known for being a dealer, to a street near Clifton Park, on the other side of the city. Jay was proud of his choice. "If you decide not to hustle no more, and you put your mind to it, you can do anything," he said. These stories are in line with the argument of some scholars that life-course transitions can alter trajectories, "knife off" delinquent behaviors, and reorient youth on a more conventional path.[38]

Like Ella, more than one-quarter of our youth said that they stopped dealing drugs or stealing cars because of fear—either fear of the police or fear of getting robbed (or worse) by their compatriots. This fear became especially salient when youth turned eighteen and could be charged as an adult. Cole, nineteen, told us, "You can't hustle all your life. You hustle all your life, and you gonna get in jail. Or dead." Most often, however those who got caught up for a time simply tired of the game, claiming, like James, that they had lost the desire once they understood the "bigger picture." Many, like Antonio, found that they simply preferred earning money the "slower" way at a legal job because "it's too much you have to worry about when doing it the wrong way. . . . Even though it's slower money, working harder, you don't have to worry about going to jail. You don't have to worry about being sneaky. You don't feel good about [fast money]." Similarly, Marco said, "I'd rather babysit or something; like, then, at least I'll know I am guaranteed to get the money and guaranteed to be free, at least."

Though he sold drugs throughout his adolescence, Michael, now eighteen, had come to believe that drug dealing was the antithesis of manhood. He sat across from Susan Clampet-Lundquist and Siri Warkentien in his grandmother's clean but worn dining room, explaining, "That's not the way I wanted to live. These people in the street, that ain't being a man, selling drugs . . . being popular, havin' all them ladies and stuff like that, that's being a man to them. To me, that's not being a man. To me, being a man is doing what you gotta do for your family and you, and [to] have a future and stuff like that."

In sum, even among the minority of youth who get "caught up" for more than just a short period of time, "street" is fleeting, and "decent"—to use the ethnographer Elijah Anderson's terms—retains power.[39] For all but a very few, the hunger to be part of the "bigger picture," to earn their money the "slow" way, was strong. A few, like Whitney, seemed so damaged by the street and the other trauma they had experienced that they could not see a future, at least at present. More often, like Ron, they were attempting to reform.

Yet, as we have argued in this chapter, time for these youth was both precious and in short supply. In the years they had lost to the streets, others had moved quickly through postsecondary schooling and into careers, as chapter 6 shows. These young adults emerged from the streets ready to reengage in the conventional world, but there was little to scaffold them. Their stories were far from over—we do not know how their lives will unfold. But as they transitioned to other adult roles, roles that intensified their desire to "go straight" (as was true for Ron), their burden was greater because they were at an age when the push to establish a separate residence, become a parent, and establish a serious romantic relationship is strong.

Yet, just as important, like Emily and Joseph, most of the youth without identity projects either had not made a detour through the streets or had done so only for a very brief period of time (like Ella). Nevertheless, they were far more likely than those with identity projects to be neither working nor in school during young adulthood. Disconnected from social institutions of any kind, they were casting around, without a path forward. Depression and anxiety, as Emily and Joseph experienced, might complicate their ability to figure out their next step. For low-income youth who have grown up in moderate- to high-poverty neighborhoods, graduating from high school is a well-known rite of passage into adulthood, one not to be taken for granted. But even for those who finished high school, the institutional support needed to get them to the next stage of young adulthood—especially vital for youth whose parents have little education and have only worked at menial jobs—was missing. For the 28 percent of our youth who, like Joseph, did not manage to finish high school, job prospects were clearly worse. Though GED programs may abound, even minimal informational and cost barriers may be difficult to surmount.

Unlike their middle-class counterparts, many youth in our study were on a hurried, "expedited" path to adulthood, the subject of chapter 5. Even for the youth with identity projects, the disadvantage they had grown up around held them back, despite their best attempts to move forward into adulthood. As they struggled to obtain their own apartments and begin work or college in the face of these challenges, the ambitions of their younger years began to fade. Some began to perceive that the short-term price for those long-term human capital investments—the efforts that would produce the biggest payoffs, such as a bachelor's degree or a remunerative trade—might be too high.

Table A4.1   Logistic Regression Predicting Whether Youth Were "Ever in the Street" with Identity Project

	β	Exp(β)	Standard Error
Female[a]	−1.900**	0.150	0.607
Age	0.212*	1.236	0.118
Lived less than six years in a neighborhood more than 30 percent poor	−1.064**	0.345	0.527
Had an identity project	−1.914**	0.148	0.617

Source: Authors' compilations.
[a]Whether youth were male and spent more than six years in a high-poverty neighborhood are the omitted variables.
*$p < 0.10$; **$p < 0.01$

Table A4.2   Logistic Regression Predicting Whether Youth Were "Ever in the Street" with Duration in Neighborhoods More Than 30 Percent Poor

	β	Exp(β)	Standard Error
Female[a]	−1.977**	.138	.582
Age	.220*	1.246	.112
Less than six years in a neighborhood more than 30 percent poor	−.810*	.445	.481

Source: Authors' compilations.
[a]Whether youth were male and spent more than six years in a high-poverty neighborhood are the omitted variables.
*$p < 0.10$; **$p < 0.01$

Table A4.3   Logistic Regression Model Predicting Whether Youth Were "Ever in the Street" with Parental Substance Use

	β	Exp(β)	Standard Error
Female[a]	−2.137**	.118	.599
Age	.217*	1.242	.113
Less than six years in a neighborhood more than 30 percent poor	−.798	.450	.492
Parental drug and alcohol problems	.992*	2.696	.490

Source: Authors' compilations.
[a]Whether youth were male, spent more than six years in a high-poverty neighborhood, and no parental substance use are the omitted variables.
*$p < 0.10$; **$p < 0.01$

Table A4.4   Logistic Regression Model Predicting Whether Youth Were "Ever in the Street" with Parental Variables

	β	Exp(β)	Standard Error
Female[a]	−2.139**	.118	.599
Age	.216*	1.241	.113
Less than six years in a neighborhood more than 30 percent poor	−.805	.447	.496
Parental drug and alcohol problems	1.010*	2.746	.524
Parental incarceration	−.053	.949	.516

Source: Authors' compilations.
[a]Whether youth were male, spent more than six years in a high-poverty neighborhood, no parental substance use, and no parental incarceration are the omitted variables.
*$p < 0.10$; **$p < 0.01$

Chapter 5 | "It's Kind of Like Crabs in a Bucket": How Family and Neighborhood Disadvantage Hinder the Transition to Adulthood

What happens to a dream deferred?
—Langston Hughes, "Harlem" (1951)

WHITNEY AND RON, from chapter 4, turned to the streets instead of finding an identity project. For them, the streets filled a similar need but produced far different results. Whether because of fear of repercussions, the transition to parenthood, or simply the sense that they were not "about" the streets—that, as they said, "it wasn't me"—most youth eventually left criminal behavior behind. Some, like Ron, still hustled on the side, but also got on track and began working to earn a degree. Others, like Whitney, remained disconnected and adrift, perhaps damaged by the years of living a high-risk lifestyle.

These youth stood in stark contrast to the young adults in chapter 3, such as Bob, the expressive and creative Japanese anime fan who grew up in Somerset Homes. His passion for theater, poetry, anime, and Goth style made him stand out from the other young men in the projects. When we first met Bob in 2004, his deep intellectual curiosity, strong performance in both English and math, and unwavering work ethic made him one of the strongest college prospects in the study. Equally stunning was Bridget, a bright young woman who, in 2010, was trying to keep the perils of her neighborhood and home life at bay by committing deeply to dance. Her exceptionally high scores on her ninth-grade PSAT had instilled an ambition to attend an Ivy League college, and she had taken it upon herself to audition at a competitive performing arts magnet school. Getting into the magnet school would enable her to avoid the local high school, where she felt that most kids were not serious about their studies.

If we had been asked to predict which of the young adults we met during our Baltimore fieldwork were most likely to complete a four-year college degree, we would have chosen Bridget and Bob. But even for some of these most promising youth in our study—including those who found a strong sense of purpose through an identity project—family, school, and neighborhood could still act as an "undertow"—a drag on their momentum as they attempted to launch. This compelled them to take shortcuts to fulfill their ambitions, propelled by the need to make an expedited leap into adulthood.

"I'M TRYING TO GO ALL FOUR YEARS!"

When we spoke with Bob's mother Teresa in 2004, she proudly listed his many academic achievements, alongside extensive activities at church and in an Afrocentric theater troupe led by his youth pastor. When he was in seventh grade, Bob submitted an entry to the "Champions of Courage" essay contest—sponsored by a local news affiliate in Baltimore—and won first prize for a story he had written about how much his stepfather meant to him. By eighth grade, he had earned a place on the best chess team in the city. Teresa recalled the evening she turned on the television to relax with her husband. Just at that moment, to their surprise, the local news anchor was handing her son the microphone as he proudly claimed victory on behalf of his team. Teresa extolled Bob for always being the "top person in his class" and never missing a single day of school that could not be accounted for by a high fever or a doctor's visit. Although it was no surprise to her that he ended up gaining admission to the competitive academic magnet school Claremont High, he was the only one from his eighth-grade class to do so, and only three of his middle school peers got into any of the selective schools in the city.

Once at Claremont, Bob flourished. It was the place where he felt he finally fit in, where his enthusiasm for literature and math was the norm and did not attract the cruel teasing he had endured in middle school when he showed a penchant for reading Shakespeare sonnets for fun. At Claremont, he said, "I knew I had come for business. . . . I wasn't there to play around, I was there for school." In 2004, Teresa described how he came home each day, bursting to tell her about everything he had learned. "'Ma, oh we did this, we did that [at school]!'" she said. Bob became engrossed in Claremont's world, both during and after classroom hours. At seventeen, Bob called Claremont a school where, "if you wasn't doing your academics, then you were doing sports; if you wasn't going to do sports, you had the band, if you didn't have the band, then you had other little things to get into."

Once at Claremont, Bob quickly became consumed with college plans. He remembered thinking, "I definitely want to go to college. I want to move away from Baltimore. I cannot wait to leave here because there's nothing—there's no opportunity for me here at all because I am so different." He predicted that by twenty-two he would be "out of college, preferably [living] in New York." He planned to double-major in engineering and acting, unable to choose between his love for math and the theater. He and Teresa would talk often about his college plans. From among the brochures that began to arrive in the mailbox, they each picked their favorite prospects. Teresa favored a religiously affiliated school, given Bob's deep involvement in the church; Bob thought any school located in New York City sounded good.

When we interviewed her in 2004, Teresa was committed to supporting her son's college plans. "He deserves it," she said. "He has put in all the work, and he really wants to further his education, he wants a career." While she worried that the family's financial situation would prevent him from going, she said that she was willing to "go in debt for him to go . . . whatever I gotta do to get him in there." With academic accolades already under his belt from his middle school years, deep engagement in after-school activities like band, ongoing involvement with the theater, plus honors courses in math and English locked into his freshman schedule, Bob might well have been as strong a contender for America's best universities as many of his high-performing, suburban peers.

Martha Graham, the renowned founder of modern dance, is one of the psychologist Angela Duckworth's go-to examples of "grit."[1] One of Graham's most celebrated quotes speaks to the power of finding something that inspires a will to achieve: "Some men have thousands of reasons why they cannot do what they want to, when all they need is one reason why they can." For fifteen-year-old Bridget, dancing was her reason to say "I can." Ask Bridget who she was and she would tell you, "I'm kind, courteous, and bold . . . and I love to dance."

Bridget was born in the Flag House Courts in 1994. Her parents, Naomi and Paul, had moved there four years earlier to escape a dilapidated apartment in West Baltimore after her older brother, Carl, tested positive for severe lead paint poisoning—the doctors told Naomi that it had left Carl with mild brain damage. But Flag proved to be unsafe in another way—two years after moving in, Bridget's father was shot in the court-yard three times by drunk young men showing off their guns on New Year's Eve. Although he survived, Naomi packed up and moved the family to Paul's Oklahoma hometown to prevent him from seeking retribution in Baltimore. Life there was quiet for a few years, until Carl started to draw attention from the local police when he began acting up, possibly a result of the lead poisoning. After hitting another boy in the head with a brick, Carl was sent to a juvenile facility for several months. Once released, his parents decided it was time to move back to Baltimore, since Carl was clearly on law enforcement's radar in Oklahoma. When they returned, they settled in suburban Dundalk.

It was abundantly clear that Bridget, by age fifteen, had become the rising star of the family. Paul, a former DJ and singer in an R&B band, had nurtured her interest in the arts. She loved when they sang "back in the day songs" together. But Bridget's thing was dance. With sheer drive and family support as raw materials, Bridget made up her own routine and won admission to the competitive Academy for the Arts, despite a lack of any formal training. Her Dundalk peers called the arts school a "wack school" because it did not have enough "drama" for their taste. To them, lack of action equaled boredom. Not so for Bridget; she said at the time, "I'm here to get an education." Some of her middle school friends had already started to become "kinda bad . . . they get high, sell drugs, skip school, get in trouble with their parents, sexually interactive and stuff like that." Bridget began drawing a clear line between herself and these friends, even telling several of them, "You're cut!" when they failed to meet her standards. She chose her circle of friends carefully, preferring to spend time with fellow students who were "not easily influenced. . . . They're trying to actually get an education and graduate, unlike *other* kids." Bridget credited her parents, with whom she was close, with encouraging her to go down a more positive path. "My parents be like, 'Don't ever be a follower,'" she said.

During ninth grade, dancing became Bridget's all-consuming passion, and she would often spend up to six hours at a time in the studio. Dancing gave her the opportunity to commit wholeheartedly to something of her own and pursue the precision she strove for. She was thriving. Naomi noted that Bridget had always been a perfectionist, recalling that in fourth grade she had refused to settle into her work until she had her pencils and papers "just so." Bridget especially liked the physical demands of dance. "They be like, 'I'm gonna do two hundred sit-ups over here,'" she said. "'[Well,] I'm about to join you.' That's what most dancers do. . . . It be tiring, especially when we have ballet, [which] is helpful . . . especially for the calf muscles."

Academic accomplishments complemented her new "four-pack" abs. In fact, Bridget's ninth-grade PSAT scores earned her a National Achievement Award—a program sponsored by the College Board that recognizes the highest-scoring African American students on the PSAT in their home state.[2] Only ten students in the whole school had scores that equaled or exceeded hers. Afterwards, college brochures started pouring in. Like Bob and his mother, Bridget and Naomi eagerly scanned the mailings when Bridget arrived home from school. Her grades were good too. Though not originally placed in the honors track, her freshman-year grades earned her a spot in honors English and math, and she was placed in an AP biology class her sophomore year. She was conscious of how taking honors and AP classes could help her, and she planned to add more AP classes in her last two years "because it looks good on your college résumé."

When we spoke with Bridget in 2010, it seemed as if college was all she and her mother could talk about. She dreamed of going to Harvard or another highly selective four-year school. "Oh, I hope I get into college," she said. "And not a community one! . . . I want to get into a university. [I'm] trying to go all four years, and plus some. I was picturing that, you know? Having a dorm. My roommate better be clean!" She aspired to a career as a doctor or lawyer but also dreamed of running a dance studio for inner-city kids. Bridget recognized what an important role dance had played in her life and hoped to provide that opportunity for others. "I'm a take kids who do things that they're not supposed to and give them something to do," she said. "'Cause that's what they be looking for. Like, I be hearing kids all the time, 'I want something to *do*. I wanna dance.'"

When we asked Bridget to name her biggest fear, she was quick to say, "Not going to college." This goal provided a compelling reason to avoid following in the footsteps of her older sister, who had become a teenage mom. Bridget reasoned, "How you gonna take care of a baby if you're still paying tuition?" Naomi was happy to help to reinforce this idea, and the two had even dreamed up what they called the "chastity belt" dance. Naomi would say, "Remember what I told you, [if] you turn around and [boys] trying to get in y'all panties, what are you supposed to do?" In response, Bridget would shake her hips side to side and sing, "*Clink, clink!*" while mimicking the motion of clipping a seat belt across her body. Then they would both laugh and give each other high-fives. Naomi proudly related that dance had helped Bridget get rid of a "disrespectful" boyfriend, saying that it did not work out with him "'cause she had the *clink, clink!*"

Bridget concluded our 2010 interview sharing the following philosophy: "Success is when you go through with the goal and not—you know—just cut that off and say you can't, 'cause you can!"

By ninth grade, Bob and Bridget seem to be on a path to college. For both, it involved hard choices. Both had to draw a bright line between themselves and their peers. Both took academics seriously and started high school determined to be "about school," and both found a supportive peer culture there. Bob was consumed with his passion for anime by that time, and Bridget was buoyed by the identity project she had found through dance. It is worth mentioning that both had exceptionally supportive parents at the outset, though Teresa's ability to parent would soon be compromised by a divorce and a mushrooming addiction to cocaine.

Bob's and Bridget's stories are similar to those of a number of other youth in our study who, with high hopes for a four-year college degree, were separating from delinquent peers and putting in the work at school. For many, identity projects played a critical role in motivating these trajectories. For several young adults, aspiration for college *was* their identity project. Their ambitions and concrete efforts to achieve them—inspired by a strong sense of what they were about—were helping them to the starting gate of adulthood. But were ambition and effort enough to help them stay the course?

As we noted in the introduction, Karl Alexander, Doris Entwisle, and Linda Olson conducted a twenty-five-year longitudinal study of Baltimore youth just a half-generation older than our youth, and their findings suggested that Bridget and Bob would have trouble attaining their dreams. Their book, *The Long Shadow,* tells a story of young people whose destinies seem inevitably anchored to their family of origin despite their best efforts to escape its reach. And they show that the chances of completing a bachelor's degree are much lower for disadvantaged youth relative to their better-off peers, even holding constant test scores and grades.[3]

Why should this be? We argue that the problem is not necessarily a lack of effort or ambition, but the way those qualities are swamped by a persistent undertow that weighs them down. The forces that pull at youth include the trauma of early years spent in some of the toughest neighborhood environments in the nation and the inadequacy of so many of their schools, as prior chapters have shown. But there are also ongoing struggles in their families of origin and continued neighborhood risk, the factors that loomed largest in Bob's and Bridget's accounts. As we will show, this undertow can even affect those who hold on tightly to their identity projects. As a result, many young people end up "downshifting"—trading in big ambitions for modest substitutes they believe will allow them to make an expedited leap into adulthood.[4]

EXPEDITED, NOT EMERGING ADULTS

About twenty years ago, something interesting started happening among American youth: they seemed to be taking much longer to grow up. Even by their late twenties, some had yet to complete school, find a career, gain residential independence, or settle down with families. As rosters of college students grew, young adults seemed to enter more slowly into other adult roles, like marriage, parenthood, and homeownership. The median age of first marriage for women went from twenty in 1960 to twenty-five in 2000 and rose to twenty-seven by 2014. In each of these time periods, men made these transitions, on average, two years later than women did.[5] The same trend holds for parenthood. The average young woman in 1970 had her first child at about twenty-one, but by 2013 that number had increased to twenty-six.[6] The psychologist Jeffrey Arnett coined a new term for these trends: "emerging" adulthood.[7] He argues that the traditional life-course markers of adulthood have been replaced with a prolonged process of self-discovery during which many "revisions to the plan" are made. The key attribute of emerging adulthood, according to Arnett, is its independence from age-specific expectations and its emphasis on exploration.

Gone are the days of the orderly and predictable life course, when education and career entry were quickly followed by marriage and children.[8] Perhaps the key indication for middle-class parents that something had changed was the rise in the number of college graduates returning home to live.[9] In the wake of the Great Recession, the "returning to the nest" phenomenon seemed to push the panic button for the middle class. Debates about whether millennials were slackers garnered significant media attention.[10] While Richard Settersten and Barbara Ray find some upsides to the "later launch," some of the more colorful pundits worried publicly that the current generation of twentysomethings seemed destined, like Peter Pan, to never grow up.[11]

One of the primary questions that drove our research was whether this model of the emerging adult, drawn primarily from research on the middle class, fit a cohort of disadvantaged youth.[12] Certainly, one way to read our data is that our youth were simply putting off the mainstream trappings of adulthood—the college degree, the career—until they had figured out what they really wanted. But, we argue, their reality was very nearly the opposite. These youth told us that they were under great pressure—both from within and without—to become independent and assume the status of adult, and to do so as quickly as possible. Similar to working-class youth, few of our youth had the luxury of "emerging" into adulthood. Instead, they were often compelled to seek an *expedited* route to adulthood. What was distinctive for the young adults in our study, however, were the trauma they had been exposed to or experienced firsthand and the sheer number of other obstacles they had to surmount in the process; these obstacles made their path to adulthood less linear than it is even for their working-class counterparts.[13]

As Bob pointed out, after high school, "nobody's going to give you a handout; nobody's going to help you. You have to make it on your own." Most youth in our study absorbed virtually all of the risk and responsibility for their launch.[14] Twenty-four-year-old Rhiannon told us: "It's kind of like crabs in a bucket, where I'm from, you don't really have people supporting you, it's kind of, like, bringing you down."[15] In many ways, Rhiannon was the exception to the rule in this study—the single graduate from a selective four-year institution, at least so far—yet even for her, upward mobility was a particularly onerous struggle with so many forces exerting downward pressure, as we show later in the chapter.

Meanwhile, a close look at the next phase of Bridget's and Bob's lives—the period when each chose to downshift—can tell us much about the forces that swamped the ambitions of so many others. It was the undertow of chaotic households and risky neighborhoods in particular that posed the strongest threat to Bridget's and Bob's ability to launch.[16]

"ALL OF THE EMOTIONS WERE GETTING ME DOWN"

When Bridget was fifteen, she shone, but at eighteen, the time we last spoke with her, she was six months out of high school and unemployed. She did not apply to any colleges. She had tried to enlist in the U.S. Army but had been sent home a few weeks into basic training in South Carolina because a blood test revealed that she had been pregnant recently, though she had the abortion before she left Baltimore. How does a National Achievement Award winner, a dancer who worked to hone her craft up to six hours a day and a Harvard aspirant, fail to even apply to college? To understand the undertow in Bridget's life, we must explore the conditions in the neighborhoods where she lived between the end of her sophomore year and the end of her senior year.

Bridget's parents had moved their children to Dundalk in 2004—when Bridget was nine—after Oklahoma became too risky for her older brother Carl. A few months after their return, we interviewed both Naomi and Carl. Dundalk at the time was a mostly white, working-class, inner-industrial suburb. The apartment subdivision they lived in was surrounded by small single-family homes in various states of disrepair. Their address was home to a swirling cast of characters—an older sister with kids who moved back in when the going got tough, an out-of-work friend and her three children, plus other relatives. Up to ten people could be found crowded into the small apartment. During those years, Naomi held a series of jobs: she cashiered at TJ Maxx, cleaned rooms in a hotel, and inspected bottles of detergent on an assembly line. It was hard for her to keep any one job for very long as Carl's behavior often required her to appear in the principal's office or in front of a juvenile court judge. Naomi and Paul tried everything—discipline, prayer, Ritalin. Carl, they felt, was "a zombie" on Ritalin, but off the medication he was often violent. As Bridget completed middle school, Carl circulated through three juvenile facilities—two in Maryland and one in Pennsylvania. Eighth grade was the last he completed; his reading skills were barely at the fourth-grade level.

When we interviewed Bridget in 2010, the family was still living in Dundalk. Paul was now the maintenance supervisor for their complex, so they had moved to a larger unit, boasting four bedrooms and two bathrooms. It was a moment of optimism for the family, and it was at that point that Bridget's parents decided to make it official: four children and twenty years into their relationship, they finally got married. Bridget and her younger sister were bridesmaids, and every detail was attended to— the peach, purple, and white colors of the dresses were beautifully coordinated with the flowers, and a quote from *The Color Purple* was read before the first dance. Unfortunately, the family's celebratory mood could not last long. Bridget's uncle was found murdered in Baltimore's Patterson Park within days of the wedding.

Then turbulence at home and in the neighborhood began to take its toll. Dundalk had deteriorated in the years since Bridget's family moved there; the family's complex in particular had declined. Her younger sister, Melissa, whose academic potential was perhaps equal to Bridget's—at least according to Naomi—had started hanging with the wrong crowd. By seventh grade, she was out of control, fighting regularly at school. She had even been part of a burglary gone wrong, according to rumors her mother had heard. After being sent to juvenile detention several times, she had been assigned to Futures Forward, an alternative middle and high school for youth with serious behavioral problems. And Carl, who had returned home about a year earlier, had found trouble once again; this time it was something that would deal a blow to Bridget's optimism from which she would never quite recover.

The incident happened during the spring of Bridget's sophomore year, during a cookout to celebrate Mother's Day. Just playing around, Bridget's young cousin Dominique fell down and had to be taken to the hospital for a broken tooth and a gash on her head. Several family members accompanied the child to the hospital, including Carl. Bridget, who had gone upstairs to do homework, glanced out of the window every now and then. She noticed one of Carl's friends and his girlfriend heading toward their apartment. What unfolded next seemed like a bad dream: Bridget watched in horror as the young man and woman were shot by two males on foot, right in front of her eyes. The girlfriend would survive, but suffered a gunshot wound to the face. (Bridget saw the men circle back toward Carl's friend, "just to make sure he was dead.") It was, she said, "like my brother lost a friend and I witnessed the whole thing. It was crazy. From my window. I wish I could have called his name . . . it happened so quickly. . . . I never seen nobody die in my life, especially a friend."

Later, Carl told her that if it had not been for his niece's accident, he would have been there to meet his friend and, he believed, would have been a victim too. When the police came later to question Carl, they found that he was in possession of his friend's vest, which was chock-full of drugs. Carl was initially arrested as a murder suspect, but when his hospital alibi was substantiated, he was sent to jail on drug charges instead. Bridget was badly shaken by these events. "It was overwhelming," she said. "You wish you could help that person, but you know there's nothing you can do. It was, like, so far away but so close."

Bridget came to hate the neighborhood. It was one thing to be disgusted by the other kids "having sex . . . in [empty] sheds." It was another to watch helplessly as two people were shot within a few feet of her bedroom, knowing one of them could have been her brother. Bridget began to have nightmares that her siblings would meet similar fates. "[What if] my sister, if she follow the path my brother did?" she said. "I used to have nightmares about her, like, dying in the streets or something like that. Or like my brother, fearing him—[that] I'll get in a car with him, being shot or something."

Soon after the murder, Paul's position was abruptly cut at the rental complex—a new supervisor was firing existing staff so as to bring in his own crew—and the family was forced to move. Although it was stressful for the family, Bridget saw the move as an opportunity to escape. "Anything to get out of the neighborhood, for real, it's like a dread every time we're outside," she said at the time. "Oh gosh, I hate this place. It's like, as soon as I know I'm leaving this area, I feel uplifted, happy." Yet the transition was tougher than she had anticipated. Ultimately, the only affordable place Naomi and Paul could find was in East Baltimore, a long walk and two bus rides away from her school. The unit was about half the size of their Dundalk apartment, yet soon after the move Bridget's aunt and her four children became homeless and moved into the basement. The three-bedroom, one-bathroom house then held thirteen people. "It's hard," Bridget said, "to keep track of who is in the house."

And the new neighborhood was dicey. The family's block in East Baltimore's Milton-Montford was mostly occupied, with many front stoops decorated with colorful plastic flowers provided by a landlord who wanted to attract tenants to the less-than-desirable area. But many of the surrounding blocks were ghost towns with nothing but vacant, boarded-up homes. When we spent time with Bridget again in 2012, she claimed she heard gunshots frequently. The violence really started to escalate once the place next door became a "trap house" for crack deals. "One corner over here, one around the corner, somebody in the alley across the street— somebody over there," she said, pointing to each place from the front stoop of the apartment where a shooting had occurred. "It's a lot. . . . I don't know what to expect sometimes. It's just crazy . . . most of that stuff happens [when] nobody is outside, except for that one shooting in the alley. That was during the daytime."

Soon after they moved from Dundalk, Bridget was sitting on the secluded back porch talking on the phone with her boyfriend Damon at about ten o'clock at night and watched as a man stumbled down the street clutching his stomach, blood spurting all over the sidewalk. Luckily, the police came within minutes, and she watched as the ambulance followed shortly after, hauling the victim away. In late October 2012, while Bridget was preparing to leave for basic training, we visited her again, and she and her mother were eager to relate a fact about the neighborhood they had just learned—that it was dangerous for young girls there to venture outside during the month of October because gangs killed young girls in the weeks leading up to Halloween as part of an initiation rite. We were not able to confirm the story and did not hear it from any other youth in our study, including others who lived in the area, but the family believed that the risk was real.

Witnessing death firsthand and hearing rumors of violence in the neighborhood added an emotional weight to Bridget's shoulders. She summed up her views of her community as a place that "can get you down . . . all the girls want to get pregnant . . . all the guys think it's fun to sell drugs. They're just clowns." The enthusiasm Bridget had shown about high school and college in the summer after her sophomore year diminished in the wake of these events. Logistical problems also dampened her enthusiasm about finishing high school. Her school was now two bus rides away, and it took her an hour and a half to get there—if the notoriously unreliable buses were on time. Bridget set her alarm for five o'clock in the morning to avoid being tardy, but that was not always early enough. At times she felt like dropping out. She believed that she would have, if not for her mother, who, she said, "just kept me going, like, 'You should get up.' Because some days I just didn't even feel like going to school. I just felt like there was no point. She just was like, 'It's your last [two] year[s]. It's no point in staying home now. You can't give up now just 'cause you think something is going wrong.' So I'd go to school."

Then another family tragedy struck. A younger cousin died, which Bridget found devastating. Dancing reminded her to "take three deep breaths . . . this could always be worse." But she became, she said, "really depressed" during her senior year. The weight of the violence she had witnessed, the stress of being packed into the house like sardines, the constant feeling that death was near, all became too much. In an uncharacteristic move, Bridget and some friends shoplifted some clothes from H&M. As she fled the scene her conscience got the better of her and she "stopped running" and returned the merchandise, apologizing to the clerk. She knew this was not who she was, but she was starting to fray. "Everything in my life was getting to me. . . . I just let it get me down, all the emotions I held in over the years were getting me down. . . . I needed a source to let it go." While her plans for college had seemed so certain at fifteen, her hold on that dream had started to weaken. During the summer between her junior and senior years, a cousin visited. He was in the marines, and his choice "inspired me," Bridget said. "He kept me going." Bridget started thinking that she would enlist in the army, so she skipped the SAT and missed the college application and financial aid sessions, figuring they were unnecessary if she was going into the military.

When she told teachers and friends from the Academy for the Arts about her plans to enlist, she could see their disappointment. She was mystified by this response and thought perhaps "they think I'm going to get killed in a war . . . but obviously not everyone gets killed or there would be no more military!" She told us that joining the army "wasn't something I was looking forward to [initially], but my cousin inspired me, and my mother gave me the push. I just did it." Her dance training enabled her to pass the physical with ease. She had heard that some people cracked under the pressure—but the demands of the army strongly appealed to the part of her that sought a challenge and a chance to display commitment. Her recruiter pointed out another advantage: the military could provide a route into the medical field, which was attractive because she had started to worry that the usual path to becoming a physician was going to take "too long" and had wondered whether she should consider nursing school instead. Ultimately, with its lure of a signing bonus and eventual free college tuition, Bridget decided that the army was the best way forward.

Her desperate desire to escape from her overcrowded home and move on with her life pushed her forward. Although she loved her parents, things at home had only become more complicated. One day that spring, after Naomi began bleeding severely at work, she had to undergo an emergency hysterectomy. Naomi subsequently announced that she was "done working," though she was only forty-five. Most days she hardly got off the couch, presenting a subdued version of herself with hair unkempt and added weight. Melissa had been allowed to return to the local high school but was again running wild and getting arrested regularly. Even worse, the whole family watched in agony as Carl ignored his beautiful infant child and instead sat for much of the day, with an aimless stare, on the futon stuffed into the corner of the living room where he slept. Once, while Kathryn Edin and Jennifer Darrah were visiting, the baby was passed around a circle of women—Edin and Darrah, Melissa, Naomi, Bridget's aunt—but when it was Bridget's turn, she refused to touch the baby. "I'm not about that," she said. Yet Bridget had also met someone special, Damon, who had just bought her a promise ring to complement the bracelet he had already given her, engraved with the word "Legit." Damon, whom Bridget described as "a gentleman," supported her plans and hoped to join the military himself or become a police officer. Although they tried to be careful, Bridget ended up getting pregnant the summer before basic training. She got an abortion, with her parents' encouragement, but the blood test at the camp revealed lingering hormones from the pregnancy, so Bridget was sent home to wait several months before the next round of basic training. With Damon in her life, she started thinking that local schools sounded attractive—Coppin State or perhaps Loyola might be better than going farther away. She and Damon would "probably get a one-bedroom" apartment when she completed her military service, she reasoned, and return to Baltimore to attend college.

Despite numerous setbacks, Bridget still clung to the image she had honed in high school—the confident dancer who knew how to express herself. Right before she was to leave for boot camp, Bridget took Jennifer Darrah on a tour of her former high school. As she walked around the school, students shrieked with delight upon seeing Bridget and ran over to give her hugs. Her "strict" dance teachers lit up and opened their arms to embrace her. Standing at the edge of the dance studio and watching a class in progress, Bridget said, "This is a place I could always feel calm, no matter what else was going on." In the midst of the practice, Bridget ran to a side room, changed into dancing gear, and helped the teacher guide the students through a rigorous routine. As she stretched her long legs and leapt into the air, one could see the mastery she had achieved from many hours of practice. No one could miss it: she was the best performer in the room.

"GETTING OUT OF THIS HOUSE"

There was hardly a young man more prepared for college in our study than Bob. But as we explained in chapter 3, his success at Claremont was short-lived in the wake of his mother and stepfather's divorce. After the divorce, "a whole lot of things started coming down on me at once, so it started affecting my grades," he said. "And unfortunately, [the] tenth-grade year is really important [for college], but I didn't make it." Although he was successful at Hamilton—the high school he transferred to after Claremont expelled him—his early difficulties set off a chain reaction that led Bob to downshift his dreams.

Between ninth and tenth grade, Bob saw his stepfather, the man he had written the award-winning essay about, less regularly. His own father was in and out of jail on drug charges. "My father was never there for me and my mom, not during my childhood, not during my teen years, and he won't be there during my adulthood," he said. Around that time Teresa's cocaine abuse also became obvious. (Bob later learned that it was the reason his stepfather left his mother.) Pushed out of Somerset owing to its impending demolition, they moved into Teresa's mother's house in Highlandtown, near a notorious drug corner just east of Hamilton High. Yet, even while Bob's grades suffered and his depression set in, he never missed a single day at school at Hamilton. "Maybe school was his escape," Teresa told us.

Getting expelled from Claremont was "devastating," but Bob turned disappointment into motivation. "I took that [expulsion] letter, and I tacked it on my wall, and every day before I walked out to my summer job, I looked at that letter," he told us. "I was like, 'I'm not gonna do this anymore.'" Fortunately, Teresa met with a counselor at Hamilton and persuaded her to give Bob credit for the courses he'd completed at Claremont so he could make up some of his tenth-grade credits and complete eleventh grade in the same year. Nonetheless, Bob felt that there was no challenge. "I am bored all the time," he said. Counselors tried to fill the rest of his schedule with non-academic courses, such as electives and gym class; he "had to fight," he said, for the more demanding classes he took, like principles of engineering and advanced calculus, "so I can have, like, you know, credits to go to college."

Even with college preparatory classes added to his schedule, Bob found few other students who were as capable and motivated as he was. "In my principles of engineering class, it's about four kids that's passing, out of like twelve, and my English class—it's like eight people passing out of twenty five," he said. Then there were the fights and arrests at Hamilton, a more than weekly occurrence. "They got police officers that's there every other day, people getting suspended, people getting expelled, it's just ridiculous. . . . I only seen one fight while I was at Claremont [for two years]," he said. As we detailed in chapter 3, Bob survived this tough time at Hamilton by finding his own crowd, his "specific groups"—card players and anime fans. To him, these friends proved critical. They too "wanted more than what we had and what we grew up around . . . and we all pushed ourselves to get that far."

Even with the support of his friends, Bob felt as though the best Hamilton had to offer was not enough to ready him for college. "[They are] not preparing us for the SAT, ACT . . . things like that. . . . I knew if you wanted to get into college, you have to take the SATs." At Hamilton, he was not encouraged to take the test, and the school had no SAT prep program. Bob tried to prepare for the test by himself. His view was that, "for the most part, Hamilton focused on most of the troubled students. . . . They figured that most of the smarter kids, they pretty much had themselves figured out, they already knew what they wanted to be." The climate was far from the college-for-all focus that he had experienced at Claremont, or that Bridget had experienced at the Academy for the Arts. "If anything, [they push you] to a community college, if that at all," he said.

Bob was frustrated because he had to track down the school's guidance counselor for college advice, practically engaging in a sit-in at least twice a month. "He wouldn't call people in and say, 'Hey, what are you doing for college?' No, I had to go to *him*, say I wanted to do this," Bob said. Bob took the SATs for the first time while at Claremont, but his scores got lost in the transfer between schools. Eventually, Bob did apply, but the applications were received after the deadline. Without the SAT scores attached, he never heard back from any of the four schools he applied to.[17]

Bob went on to graduate from Hamilton with honors. Immediately afterwards, he began to apply for jobs, submitting, he said, "fifty-plus" applications before getting a call back at the Wendy's in the BWI airport. He started there at $7.75 an hour, working the early morning shift. Bob got up at midnight and took two buses to arrive by 3:30 AM for his 4:00 AM start. He did not mind the commute because it was "getting away from here, you know" (by which he meant his grandmother's house). By the time we spoke with him in 2006, nineteen-year-old Bob was driven by one pressing need: to earn enough money to get out of his grandmother's crowded home. The aunts and uncles who intermittently lived there just did not understand Bob's unique style of Goth clothing and music. "I would always get into fights with my aunt and uncle," he said. "They didn't understand what I was going through, and they just wanted to make things worse." Things got particularly tense one night when Bob had friends over for some games of YuGiOh! and family members were upstairs yelling and cursing. He had "had it," he said, and went upstairs to tell them so. The night ended with Bob's friends having to leave, Bob in tow behind them.

Bob despised the neighborhood as well. "This is one of the worst neighborhoods I've actually lived at, and the worst thing about it is that my family is actually a part of it," he said. "It is hard to see people that I supposedly love out there just corrupting theirselves." We saw this for ourselves when we visited. The home was filthy and roaches crawled the walls. In the middle of the day, a young woman we were not introduced to drank beer on the couch, and Bob's brother smoked weed on the porch with a friend as we left. Bob said he felt unsafe there. Money he left in the basement, where he stayed, would go missing, as would some of his video games. His family would party and socialize loudly, waking him up at night. A few times a month his younger brother would come into the house drunk, "acting a fool," Bob said, and wave his gun around angrily. Once, he even "pulled one on me," Bob said. He was anxious and frustrated and desperate to escape. "My main concern is getting out of this house as fast as possible. . . . I would really like to go to a place where I have my own lock and key," he said.

The final straw came about a year later, after another sleepless night. Bob was working more than forty hours a week at that point and needed the rest. He had saved up enough money for a used car by then, and with the time he saved on the commute, he was able to increase his work hours. "At that time, I was still working at the airport, I had the super-early morning shift, but everybody in the house wanted to . . . stay up, drink, be loud and things like that," he said. "So it got so bad, until the point I was actually sleeping in my car and then going to work from there. So it got to the point where I was like, 'You know, I can't take this.'" Bob had a friend who was living in a rooming house in West Baltimore—a single-family home with separate tenants renting each of the bedrooms, plus the living room, dining room, and the basement. It was the perfect solution: at $400 a month, it was much cheaper than any apartment Bob could get on his own. His youth pastor, the one who had sparked his love for theater, still pushed him to consider college. But Bob could not see himself making the trade-off between the urgent need for money now and the long-term investment college would require. "I got into the working world early, and it was really, really hard for me to say, 'Okay, I'm gonna stop making money, and I'm gonna go back to school,' especially when I wanted to be out on my own so badly," he said.

Three years later, when we talked to him in 2010, Bob, at twenty-three, was still living in the rooming house in Westmont. The house was a two-story brick row house with a small, fenced-in front yard and a bay window on the second floor. There were six rented rooms, including a space in the gloomy unfinished basement, and a shared kitchen. The house had fallen victim to a heavy snowstorm the winter before and now had a large hole in one corner above the kitchen sink, exposing the lathing strips of the ceiling. The front room of the house had been turned into a bedroom, so there was no common space other than the kitchen. Another tenant who came up from the basement during the interview brought with him a Coke bottle full of urine, which he left on top of the refrigerator because the single bathroom was in use.

By this point, Bob had met his girlfriend, Cassie, through MySpace, after discovering a shared love of anime and Otakon, Baltimore's anime festival held each July. Eventually, Cassie moved into the rooming house with Bob, and the two subsisted on takeout because there was no secure place in the kitchen to keep food (and no pots, pans, or cooking utensils). She was in the final stages of her medical tech program, living off of student loans.

Between the two of them, they were "just scraping by." He had worked the early morning shift at Wendy's in the BWI airport for about three years, taking every chance to show his skills. Many of his regular customers owned or operated other businesses within the airport, and when he saw them coming, he would have their order ready and waiting and would greet them by name as they stepped up to the counter. He caught the eye of one such customer who managed a high-end coffee shop one concourse down, and the man offered him a management position and a raise—to $10 an hour. Two years later, Bob had worked his way up to $11 in hourly pay, or about $22,000 a year. Even on this modest amount, Bob felt hopeful. By combining his wages with what they hoped Cassie would earn as a medical tech, they could begin to save for a modest home in Northeast Baltimore and raise their children there. Unfortunately, the shop did not make it through the recession, and Bob had to start over again as a barista in a coffee shop downtown, where he took a "very heavy pay cut"—back down to $7.25 an hour.

It was around this time that he pondered college again. "Every day I think about going back to school or at least taking some kind of certification," he said. "It would be nice if I could save up . . . but for the most part, my checks always go to rent." Plus, the one-hour commute and eight hours on his feet each day sapped his energy, so the thought of taking night classes exhausted him. He became frustrated that no matter how good an employee he strove to be, he could not seem to earn enough to get ahead. "I have a plan, I know what I wanna do in life . . . but I can't get there . . . because the only thing that's stopping me is, you know, this economy and the competition that I have for such limited jobs. It's ridiculous . . . I haven't had a job yet where I've had benefits," he said.

When we met up with Bob again two years later in 2012, he and Cassie were still living in the rooming house. He had remained at the downtown coffee shop until it burned down. He became depressed after losing that job and had collected unemployment while he looked for another position. Eventually, after "filling out applications like crazy," he got called back for an interview at a job at Johnny Rockets in the Inner Harbor, Baltimore's main tourist area. It was not the move he had in mind. Not only was the job another entry-level position in the food industry, but management made the employees sing and dance for the customers, an aspect of the job that Bob found particularly humiliating. But "when bills need to be paid," he said, "you can't be picky. So I just went on with that and made sure I put my all into it." Eventually, he picked up a second job in the suburbs as a cashier at an office supply store and even took on a third job for a few months, training as a bank teller in East Baltimore. Bob had lost his beloved car in an accident the year before, so the commute, which took him from downtown to the city's western suburbs and all the way over to Baltimore's east side, was daunting. In addition to working sixty to eighty hours per week, each leg of his journey took up to an hour. As he juggled all three jobs Bob was careful to include an iron in his backpack so he could freshen up each of his uniforms as he changed from one to another. "I iron on the go!" he proudly exclaimed.

Eventually, Bob left the two minimum-wage jobs in favor of the bank position, which paid more and allowed him to wear a suit. He saw the job as his ticket to getting ahead, though he was just shy of full-time hours and did not qualify for benefits. Seven months into the job, however, his ledger came up short. Although the branch manager eventually ruled it a computer error, the bank's rules were strict, and Bob was let go. That same day he was back on Craigslist, sending off his résumé to another coffee shop at the BWI airport. His previous experience in the industry served him well: he landed the job quickly. Five months in, his work ethic and punctuality—he again had to be at the coffee shop by 3:30 AM—seemed to be paying off. Bob had already earned five raises and a promotion to assistant manager. He said that it felt thrilling to be rewarded for his effort. "I try to put 110 percent into whatever I do, so that everybody can see that I'm not just a fair-weather worker, I'm not just here for the check, I do it because I want to take pride in what I do, I want everybody to see me shine when I'm working," he said.

Cassie had left school by that time, and Bob was vague as to why, merely saying that the medical tech program "didn't really work out for her." She was working at the airport too, cooking at Bo Brooks Crab House, where she made $10.50 an hour. By pooling their income, Bob and Cassie managed to get out of the stuffy room in the West Baltimore rooming house. On a rainy day in October 2012, Anna Rhodes, one of our ethnographic fieldworkers, drove the U-Haul truck to move them from this cramped room into a spacious two-bedroom apartment in Waverly, a neighborhood on the edge of Johns Hopkins University, where Bob once dreamed of going to college. The proximity had prompted him to think about going back to school. "It always crosses my mind . . . my whole thing with college, it's always been the cost," he said. "I really don't like the idea of being in debt in order to further my education. . . . I hear about people having problems getting cars, getting jobs, getting houses because they still owe the school." Bob had witnessed this up close— both his mother and Cassie failed to finish certification programs and were seeing their wages garnished and tax returns seized to pay back their student loans.

Bob felt "content" with the job at BWI, he said, especially because he was earning "good money" and had a set schedule. Yet his sights were still set on something bigger. "For the most part, I'm looking at where I am right now as a job," he said. "I mean, I don't see myself at this place in the next few years. This is going to be a stepping-stone to something else. I would really, really like to find one of those career-type jobs, but what they're asking for, as far as qualifications, I really don't have yet, whether it's the X amount of years as a supervisor or the X amount of years of college and things like that. So I'm going to say I'll get there when I get there, for the most part." Despite his setbacks, he remained confident that the "money is everywhere; you've just got to go get it."

When we last saw them, Bob and Cassie were putting the finishing touches on their new apartment. Cassie was still glowing with the excitement of having their own place, a big step for both of them. They had scrounged a used sofa and love seat from a friend, and Teresa bought them a glass coffee table as a housewarming present. A short and wide set of wooden shelves housed their precious video game systems and a DVD player. Typical of Bob's usual flare, they had placed a combination lamp and fan in each corner and attached strips of orange crepe paper streamers to the rim of the lamp's glass shade, so that when the lamp/fan unit was turned on, the flapping streamers caught in the light looked like fire.

Bob still pursued fantasy card games with old friends and wrote poetry. Cassie had joined his church, and they went as regularly as they could. Although they could not afford to attend the previous year, he and Cassie had saved up enough to attend the Otakon anime convention at the Baltimore Convention Center that summer; they were calling it their "vacation." Bob was looking forward to seeing the colorful costumes, meeting people from Russia and China, and donning his tripp pants and graphic T-shirts. Bob and Cassie were hoping to indulge in some of the many imported products from Japan too, the special soaps and candies, sushi, and new video games.

And now that they had been together for four years, Bob was planning to propose. It was going to be a surprise—he had bought the ring already, but was waiting for "the conditions to be right." He wondered out loud, "[Should I] do it in a crowd, or do I want to do it by ourselves? Do I want to do it at dinner? I am one of those romantic types, so I'm pretty sure I'll come up with something."

THE EXPEDITED PATH TO ADULTHOOD

When we left them in 2012, there was no doubt that Bob and Bridget had earned their share of accomplishments. Bridget managed to graduate from high school and was set to return to army basic training after the waiting period had elapsed. Bob had landed a management position at a coffee shop and felt content for the moment, even if it was not exactly a career in his eyes. Bob and Cassie had managed to secure the clearest marker of achieving adult status that one sees in this cohort of youth—an apartment of their own. And Bob was set to propose, another step toward his dream of owning that home with a white picket fence, with children in the yard, in the quiet northeast section of the city.

At the end of their freshman year of high school, each had been on track to enroll in a four-year college, perhaps even a selective university. Bob had already completed AP calculus and engineering classes, and Bridget had won the National Achievement Award and earned good enough grades to be moved up to AP chemistry and honors English and math the following year. But as their young lives unfolded, they were still held back by families and neighborhoods that pulled at them, like "crabs in a bucket," as Rhiannon put it—a metaphor immediately familiar to a Marylander.[18] Both had lived in overcrowded homes where family members used drugs (Bob's mother and younger brother) or sold them (Bridget's brother Carl). Both had experienced family instability and suffered because of it. Bob lost his place at Claremont due to divorce and his mother's accelerating drug use, while Bridget's household was like an accordion, expanding to provide a place for literally dozens of kin when they needed a place to stay. She watched as her mother's body broke down at only age forty five, possibly because of the emotional duress from years of worrying about her son Carl's whereabouts, plus years of standing on her feet performing rote manual labor. Neither Bob or Bridget had family who could provide the financial assistance or know-how that would have been necessary for them to attend a four-year school.

Other things got in the way too. The drug-infested Somerset Homes had claimed Bob's father. The specter of the addict he had become was the cautionary tale that both propelled Bob forward and haunted him, especially when it looked for a while as if his mother was heading in the same direction. The little section of Highlandtown where the family had landed after the divorce felt like a hellhole to Bob as he watched his mother and brother get caught up in the "neighborhood drama." For Bridget, witnessing the murder of Carl's closest friend and compadre in the drug trade—knowing it could have been Carl if not for his need to accompany his niece to the hospital—was only one in a series of traumas that exposed her, again and again, to early death and violent assault, including incidents involving her beloved uncle and cousin.

Amid all this turmoil, college plans got lost as these young people tried to take an expedited path to adulthood. Both needed something now, in the near term, to give them some stability and move them toward independence. For Bridget it was the military, and for Bob it was a low-wage job. By no means is working in the military or as a certified nursing assistant an unfortunate route to take. Our point here is that when those who aspire to career options that require more education (and thus more time and money) instead feel compelled to take a quicker route, they may very well be closing the door on these other careers.

We saw this downshift happen among many of the youth we spoke with. Their narratives implicated family and neighborhood conditions again and again in dictating their choice of strategies in the quest to achieve adulthood. These young people's stories show how adolescents who were at the top of their game at an earlier point could not fully escape the "bucket," in part, because their family and neighborhood contexts clawed at them. "Cooling out" is a classic phrase that the sociologist Erving Goffman used to describe how people adapt to the loss of a once-desired goal.[19] Similarly, we saw a sort of "cooling out" among our youth, as they substituted more quickly attainable, but lesser versions of the careers and educational plans they once held. They were in too much of a hurry, for many very good reasons, to take the slower, lengthier path that could have yielded middle-class rewards.

Take Sherika, a seventeen-year-old girl from Franklin Square who "always wanted to go to college" and was ranked at the top of her class. By tenth grade, she started skipping school to protect a younger sister who was being abused. She had started to consider Job Corps instead of college, just to get away from the neighborhood faster. By twelfth grade, she still aspired to go to college—but was almost a year behind in credits. Or consider the case of Chanel, twenty-one, who dropped out of Towson University halfway through her four-year degree program and enrolled in a training program that would certify her as a CNA in just a few months' time. She explained: "It's so much, and I was just like, 'Look, you know, I need to get a job, I need to help my mother out with the house and the bills and stuff,' 'cause things got a little overwhelming."

Unpacking these stories, we find four common mechanisms at work that combined to pull these youth down. First, at the most basic level, ongoing poverty and financial strife in the family of origin made it difficult for families to scaffold young adults in ways that supported their pursuit of a four-year degree. They often simply could not afford it.[20] Second, many youth expressed intense pressure, both externally and from within, to get out of the house at eighteen. Part of that pressure may have derived from expectations in low-income families about earlier adult role transitions, brought about by economic necessity.[21] More often, however, the pressure seemed to stem from the overcrowded conditions of so many of the homes. No doubt, these conditions were fed by the housing affordability crisis. Consider the fact that across the United States, 7.7 million very-low-income households now pay over 50 percent of their income for rental housing.[22] The need to make money quickly so that they can get out puts youth on an expedited path, yet the cost of securing an apartment of their own is so great that they often have difficulty doing so. More affordable options—even low-end options like the rooming house Bob lived in—are not plentiful in most housing markets. When they can be found, they are often in the most derelict and dangerous parts of a city.

Third, repeated experiences of early death led to a sense that life is short. As we indicated in chapter 2, nearly one in four of our youth told us that they already had a relative die of an overdose, drug addiction, or homicide, and over one-third had directly witnessed a serious assault or death by a violent act.[23] Nineteen-year-old Tiara told us, "I actually dropped my classes because I kept having a death in family . . . since 2010 started, every month I done had somebody in my family that died or somebody that was real close . . . [with funerals] and stuff, so it's no way I could have been going to school." In general, this burden is disproportionately borne by the most disadvantaged of Baltimore's residents. Health statistics tell us that life expectancy in Baltimore's poorest neighborhoods may be fifteen years lower than in tree-lined Roland Park, one of the best-off neighborhoods in the city, and twenty years lower than in suburban Severna Park.[24] But youth who live in these environs often peg their estimates of life expectancy even lower than is actually the case. Twenty-year-old Jay, who sold drugs on and off when he was younger, believed that if he had not turned away from the street, he would be dead. He did not take the beginning of his third decade for granted. "I feel happy that I made [it] to see the age of twenty," he said. "I really am. The reason why: most people don't get to see the age of twenty nowadays."

Our best guess is that it is the unpredictability of violence and the sense that life could be snuffed out at any time—driven by traumatic direct exposure to early death—that drives this disproportionate sense of risk. As twenty-one-year-old Crystal said, "It could be a person you don't know, they could be thinking, 'I'm gonna kill her,' like, for nothing. . . . That's just how fast life go sometimes." All of these factors work together to put youth from disadvantaged origins on an expedited path. As we describe in the next chapter, youth like Crystal reasoned, "So why wait for, like, years to become something, when you can become something in like the course of a year [at a trade school]?"

In so many ways, Crystal's choice makes abundant sense once we learn about her life experiences. Violence was an everyday experience in Somerset Homes, where she grew up. Just before she moved away at age twelve, she was sitting on her porch in a plastic chair outside of her unit waiting for her sixteen-year-old cousin when she saw him get shot in the head by a stranger—who then fled and was never apprehended. Crystal ran to the scene, watching the blood flow from her cousin's head, while a neighbor called 911. The house was just blocks from the emergency room of the Johns Hopkins Hospital, yet the ambulance took a full fifteen minutes to arrive. "He could have been saved, because it took them fifteen minutes [to get there]." She remembered hearing him whisper the Serenity Prayer as he lay dying.

Years later, just after she had related that story during her 2010 interview, Kathryn Edin asked her how she had gotten through that time. Crystal shrugged and said, "It was his time." She then elaborated: "I don't cry anymore, like, 'cause it's, like, [I'm] so used to it, and I know he in a better place. 'Cause the way the world is today, he probably would have ended up dead anyway, or in jail." She admitted that the experience had made her hypervigilant with regard to her surroundings. While sitting with friends on the porch at night in the moderately poor neighborhood she lived in now, she took on the role of a sentinel. "I gotta watch [while] you all into the conversation . . . 'cause you never know what could happen to you," she said. Still, she believed that there was no real way to protect the ones you love. Similarly, after Veronica, fifteen, recounted the fatal shooting of her cousin at a basketball court just down the street, she shrugged and said, "As soon as you get to know a person, they are gone. Life is too short; he was only nineteen."[25]

Finally, a young person who comes from disadvantaged origins has friends, family, and neighbors who vary considerably in terms of their educational and work achievements.[26] Some disadvantaged youth have college graduates and career professionals in their family, but instances of either were still rare for the youth in our study. It is more often the case that most of the family members of these young adults have not finished high school, and many have seen a parent suffer from addiction or become incarcerated, and they may have lost other family members to early death. Given these realities, beating the streets, graduating from high school, and surviving past age twenty is indeed something to feel proud of.[27] In this context, going to college is a luxury—a goal that young adults may aspire to, but that is unnecessary for them to feel like they have succeeded. These youth often adopt a remarkable attitude of gratitude, noting frequently that no matter how discouraging their circumstances, "it could always be worse." Bob's response to multiple setbacks was emblematic of this attitude, and it was easy to see how it aided in his perseverance.[28] But we wonder whether there is a darker side to this highly adaptive mind-set. Does setting the bar for what counts as success fairly low perhaps make it more tempting to downshift?[29]

Bella had made it to a four-year college in western Maryland, yet still exemplified a similar way of thinking as she voiced a stereotype adopted from wider society. "[You know] the typical black family, as far as the mother not workin' or unemployment, Social Services, that type of thing?" she said. "I just pretty much didn't see myself stooping to *that* type of a level." Though Bob was not where he hoped to be back when we first met him in 2004, in comparison to those who were "in and out of jail or . . . unemployed or . . . uneducated," he could feel that he had achieved something, and in fact he had. He continued to strive to "be in the percentile of, you know, young men who actually grow up to be something," he said. Jessica, twenty-three, left Frostburg University when money got too tight living away from home. But she was proud of herself and her friends, whom she called "the circle of success" because they were all working. She contrasted their position with the "knuckleheads . . . with no goals," the unemployed men and women loitering on her block. Terry, the homeless poet who found his vocation in helping other disadvantaged youth, put his struggles in context by saying he's glad not to be, "a frickin' addict." Antonio had survived incredible trauma, and when the young security guard assessed where things stood for him at present, he said, "[At least] I'm not in the hospital with crazy mental problems."

As we noted earlier, twenty-four-year-old Rhiannon, who described the downward pull of her family and community as "crabs in a bucket," stood as the rare exception. She was the only young person to have earned a bachelor's degree by the time the study ended. She was the only one in her family to even try going to a university, community college, or trade school; few of her neighborhood peers had graduated from college, as far as she knew. However, as the metaphor she used to describe her social context implies, her path too had been fraught with tragedy and risk. She had "made it"—but she was paying another price now as she straddled two worlds, not quite feeling like she fit into either one.

When Rhiannon was five, her mother, Linda, used her MTO voucher to move to the affluent suburb of Owings Mills. During their eight years there, Rhiannon attended a high-performing public school. She also experienced a more diverse social world than she would have had they remained at Murphy Homes. When she was thirteen, the landlord refused to renew their lease because he did not want to continue dealing with the voucher program, so they bounced back to the city, eventually landing in the Alameda neighborhood, an area that was about 15 percent poor, for most of Rhiannon's teen years. Not long after their return to the city, Rhiannon's sixteen-year-old brother was killed in a random shooting while hanging out with friends in another neighborhood. In the aftermath, her mother began to experience post-traumatic stress, which changed her, Rhiannon said.

Rhiannon attended one of the top magnet high schools in the city. There she excelled academically and, with the support of school counselors, won a full ride to Frostburg State University. Still, she had to work full-time to cover her living costs. Graduating in the midst of the Great Recession of 2007–2008, it took her a year to find a job. Her financially strapped family found that hard to understand, and her mother, who expected her to contribute to the household bills, was constantly complaining, "Okay, well, where's the money? You have to get a job!"

"I've been feeling a lot of pressure from her, and, like, she's adding up how much I owe on everything since I've graduated," Rhiannon said. Contributing to the household expenses was nothing new for Rhiannon. Since she was fourteen, she had been working various jobs and giving her mother money. Not feeling respected for the hard work she had put in for years to support her family, not to mention funding her college education on her own, Rhiannon grew increasingly bitter toward her mother, who did not seem to understand what it meant to look for a job that would serve as an entry to a career. To Rhiannon, Linda seemed intent on making her daughter's life miserable. She stole Rhiannon's identity, running up her credit cards and transferring household bills into her name, including the cable bill. Linda incurred $35,000 in debt in just a short time, which Rhiannon was then responsible for.

To counter this stress and find support, Rhiannon spent time with her friends from college, most of whom did not live in Baltimore City, and several friends from her magnet high school who had also graduated from college. They hung out together in their free time, often in the Fell's Point neighborhood, with its many down-market restaurants and bars. She told us, "None of them are, like, mothers or have kids, so we're kind of in the same place. Not completely alike, but we complement each other. We're all doing something and trying to get ahead—[we] *see ourselves outside of the city.*" When we last spoke with Rhiannon, she had landed a job as a milieu therapist at a mental health facility, a job she enjoyed, and she was living in her own apartment in a quiet neighborhood in Northeast Baltimore.

CONCLUSION

Certainly, Jeffrey Arnett was on to something when he developed the notion of "emerging adulthood." The demography does not lie—many twentysomethings are spending more time in school, delaying career entry, and putting off marriage and parenthood until they feel they have really "found themselves" and are established in a career. But what the public conversation about the issue has missed is the fact that emerging adulthood is often a luxury reserved for better-off young adults. If anything, young adults in Baltimore's poorest families are in a *hurry* to launch and find the shortest possible route to independence. We have labeled this transition "expedited adulthood."

The four-year college experience plays perfectly to the emerging adult, but for most of the youth in our study the model is out of sync with expedited adulthood. Monique, fifteen, told us, "Like, I know what middle school, elementary school, and high school is for. But that's when I thought, like, what's college, what is it for? We don't need it." When Stefanie DeLuca asked twenty-year-old Cassidy how he saw the value of a four-year college degree versus one from a community college or trade school, Cassidy said, "It ain't nothing important. It's just explore, living on campus or something like that."

Family finances impinge on those who aspire to college, and the pressures of their home and neighborhood environments compel a speedier launch. As we show in chapter 6, poor information and institutional traps exacerbate these problems. Even for those who do enroll in a four-year institution, the four-year window leaves time for a lot of "drama" to happen. For Chanel, who started at Towson University, family demands got in the way, so she dropped out to bolster the family budget. Family difficulties can happen even within the short window of an associate's degree—twenty-three-year-old Isaac was mere credits away from finishing when his twin sister became fatally ill. He left school to live with her until she died.

Others falter because they are juggling the demands of raising their children. Their families of origin may be far from perfect, but they nonetheless lead lives tightly linked with those of their loved ones—Teresa, for example, now lived right across the courtyard from her son Bob and his girlfriend Cassie—and that tight link can keep them in a risky orbit. The economists Chris Avery and Caroline Hoxby have documented that many disadvantaged youth are "undermatching"—the most academically gifted among them are seldom applying to the selective colleges that their test scores and grades should be earning them entry into.[30] What we have documented with Bob, Bridget, and other youth in our study is perhaps an extreme version of undermatching: gifted adolescents not enrolling in *any* four-year institution.

At the end of his book on the power of character and grit, Paul Tough writes, "There is no anti-poverty tool we can provide for disadvantaged young people that will be more valuable than the character strengths that [young adults from his book] possess in such impressive quantities."[31] Chapter 3 shows that many of the youth in Baltimore's poorest neighborhoods have plenty of grit, often sparked by their identity projects. But for many, grit is just not enough.

Chapter 6 | "In and Out Before You Know It": The Educational and Occupational Traps of Expedited Adulthood

IN CHAPTER 5, we told the stories of two young adults, Bob and Bridget, who had their sights set on college and seemed to have the intellectual acumen to get there. But we saw their promising futures—and those of many of their peers—derailed by the social origins they had seemed destined to soar above. Instead of spending four years in college discovering who they wanted to be, these disadvantaged youth found themselves on an expedited path to adulthood, in a hurry to get out on their own and gain financial stability. As high school graduation approached they began to perceive a fork in the path ahead. One option was the most expedient— direct entry into the labor market after high school. The second was some form of postsecondary education, enrolling in either a two- or four-year college or a for-profit trade school that offered an "insta-career" that could be achieved in a year or less.

In this chapter, we explore these early career and college starts. We begin with the question: What are the labor market experiences of youth, especially those who do not go on directly to a postsecondary institution? Second, we ask: Why are youth drawn to trade schools and occupationally oriented programs offered by community colleges rather than more academically focused programs at two- or four-year schools? Even in these short-duration programs, why don't more of them persist? And why do they so often compound one failure with another try, lengthening the process of acquiring a postsecondary credential considerably and often even exceeding the four years that would have been required to gain a bachelor's degree?

First, we look at the youth who take the most expedited route and enter the labor market directly after high school, usually triggered by both the urge to get out on their own and financial necessity. Viewing college as too expensive or "not for them," these youth, mostly male, try their hand in the low-wage service and retail sectors. They aspire to traditional working-class careers in auto mechanics, construction, and carpentry, but rarely find work in those fields. Instead, if they can get work at all, they settle for jobs in the fast-food industry or in big-box stores—even after seeking help from employment centers. But they soon discover that the work does not pay nearly enough, it is rarely engaging, and most of the jobs will not help them cultivate the careers they seek. Before long, most start to consider going back to school.

Next, we spend the bulk of this chapter looking at the experiences of youth in the postsecondary education market and how they make trade-offs and decisions about where to go and what careers to pursue. Middle-class youth see higher education as a four-year plan (or more if they go to graduate school), but most low-income youth in Baltimore find that time line far too long and uncertain (and expensive); instead, they tend to make their postsecondary education decisions on the basis of how closely linked the course of study is to a concrete occupation and of how quickly they can finish school and start work. Unfortunately, as we show, this strategy ends up costing them in the long run: quick decisions to launch often entail a commitment to a trade before they have had a chance to explore the occupational paths that really fit their abilities and interests. Their quick launch triggers a series of fits and starts as they learn the hard way what they are interested in and how to navigate the confusing maze of community colleges and the exploitative traps of for-profit trade schools.

"A REAL LIFETIME JOB"

Twenty-year-old Brandon announced, "College is not for *everyone*," when we interviewed him in 2010.[1] In line with national trends, opting for the labor market rather than school was more common among the young men we spoke with than it was among their female counterparts—only 38 percent of males tried college (including trade school) in the years after high school, compared to 64 percent of females.[2] This is partly because slightly fewer males finished high school; of these high school graduates, 34 percent of the men chose work over school, while the figure was only 17 percent for women. Some were daunted by the costs, but others were intimidated by the academic demands college imposed, especially in light of their poor performance in high school. Paul, twenty-two, saw the writing on the wall by his junior year—his grades were too low. "No university is going to accept me . . . with sixties [for grades]." Elijah, twenty-one, said that he "thought about goin' to college, and [then] I thought about all the *work*, and I was like, I don't know." Ralph, twenty-one, had no interest in staying in school any longer than he had to. "I ain't want to do no college . . . no school period. Because you know, I had academic problems, I was in special education all my life."

But their lack of interest in college did not mean that they were not eager to work hard. In fact, many held tightly to the dream of having a "lifelong" working-class job, often in the automotive, construction, or carpentry trade. Elijah beamed when he told us about his "fantasy" job— to have his own automotive shop. He explained: "Like [my] fantasy, [I'd] like a big shop where, a big garage, automotive garage where you can wait for your car, you know, [with an area where] you can eat if you want, nice little, like a little buffet or something." Omar, twenty-two, worked a forklift, moving pallets around, in a Giant grocery store chain's warehouse. It was his first job out of high school, and he enjoyed working the machinery. He had been there "four years, and I'm proud of myself." He said that he would like to work there as "long as they let me stay there! . . . like it could be a career."

Nineteen-year-old Adam dropped out of high school—after his principal threatened to expel him for behavior problems—but was working toward a GED at the Youth Opportunities (YO!) center in West Baltimore. When we met him, he had seventeen out of twenty-two credits he needed to earn the GED already under his belt. Adam's dream was to have, "like, a, a real job, a lifetime job . . . health benefits and . . . a place I can retire from." Adam had his eye on construction—it had been a passion of his since he was a kid because:

> It's competitive, you got to . . . finish this by a certain time, you got to have this done, you got to have it in order. . . . You gotta make sure the street safe and no cracks in the streets. . . . That's a man job . . . everything you do in the construction field it have to be right and you have to take your time. It ain't no rushing job or no sitting back job, just sitting around and it's challenging. . . . It got to be right, everything got to be right in the construction field. It, it can't be no wrongs or no mess-ups.

But Adam's knowledge of the job did not come from experience—he had never held any work in the formal labor market, having done only odd jobs for his uncle. Instead, he had learned about construction work by watching from afar, eagerly soaking it in while sitting on the curb near construction sites in the city. "I sit back sometimes and look and see how it is, and I know from there that you got to be a patient and willing person to do construction. . . . And sometimes I ask questions, like, how you all got to do this and how you all do that, and sometimes some people will just sit down and tell me."

Brandon had been one of the lucky few who secured steady work after high school, and he hoped that the work would lead to a stable career with decent pay. Ever since his first job through YouthWorks at fifteen, work had been a priority for him—he even quit his high school's basketball team to work more hours at KFC. For him, college seemed like too much to juggle, especially because he needed to earn money. He explained: "I was thinking, well, college would be good for me, but at the same time, I still want to work and make money. I don't want to be stressing about me having time to study my schoolwork and then still work." Brandon started working full-time with his stepfather's cleaning company a month after he graduated from high school, making $9.25 an hour. Brandon was just biding his time, however, at this job. In about six months, he would be age-eligible to apply for a job with the Maryland Transit Authority, and if all went well, he would drive a bus like his grandfather did for thirty-nine years. He said that when he starts out as a bus driver, he will make $13.75, but this wage will increase to $23.75 when the job becomes full-time salaried work. Not only would driving a bus offer Brandon a stable salary and benefits, but it would also be a career that he would enjoy. "I want to do something that I love doing. And I say driving, I ain't gotta worry about my boss being on my back, 'Well, this ain't done right,' . . . I'm on my own bus, just driving."

But jobs like the ones Adam and Elijah aspired to have are few and far between. Unlike Brandon, most youth lack connections to people who can help them get these jobs. In *Labor's Love Lost*, Andrew Cherlin writes compellingly that older industrial cities such as Baltimore, once-thriving centers for blue-collar work that offered a substantial enough living to raise a family, have been gradually bleeding jobs since the 1950s.[3] In that era, young men who wanted to enter the workforce right out of high school (or even before) could do so and make a living. This was especially true for white young men, and this pattern has not changed. Recall that Karl Alexander and his colleagues find that the share of young white men in industrial and construction jobs is three times higher than the share of African American men, all else being equal.[4] And the job discrimination starts early. Studying Baltimore high schools in the 1990s, Dee Royster found that the black youth who attended vocational schools in Baltimore were shut out of the trades in which their white peers were able to land jobs, even when the two groups of young men had attended the same schools.[5]

Recent numbers continue to reflect these trends. Estimates from the American Community Survey (2008–2012) show that the unemployment rate for African American men ages sixteen to twenty-four in Baltimore was over three times as high as that for white men. When Kathryn Edin and Peter Rosenblatt sat down with Gary, then twenty-three years old, in the quiet Hamilton neighborhood of Northeast Baltimore, he described the racial bias he encountered while searching for jobs, even though he was aided in landing interviews by his "white-sounding" name. "You don't look like a [Gary]," he had been told. Yet he thought that employers did not call him back after interviews once they discovered he was African American. "They think all black males are the same," he said.

Many became demoralized when they received so few callbacks despite applying to dozens of jobs. Elijah earned a certification for automotive repair and even completed an internship at a car dealership, but when he applied at a Toyota dealer in the nearby suburbs, he never heard back. "I went to Jimmy's Toyota on Belair Road, he ain't never called me back. . . . I called him for like a whole week." Elijah was plagued with worry about whether he had done something wrong, even though he had tried to play by the rules and dress the part and felt confident in how he had answered questions: "I think I answered all the questions to my best ability, and I think I was talking well mannered. . . . Yeah, I think I was looking fine, looking all right. I ain't have no [baggy] clothes on [or anything]."

Both field experiments and correspondence studies suggest that there may be employer discrimination against African American job applicants.[6] Devah Pager finds that employers looking to fill an entry-level job are more likely to call back a white man with a felony record than a black man without a record.[7] And economists Marianne Bertrand and Sendhil Mullainathan find that applicants with "white-sounding" names are 50 percent more likely to get a callback than those with "African-American-sounding" names.[8]

As indicated earlier, in addition to the barrier of racial bias during the job search, youth often lack social ties that can connect them with jobs. Bart, twenty-one, said that he did not really know anyone who could help him find a job. "A lot of our family isn't very good [at getting jobs] themselves, like we're all pretty much poor, so—like welfare and stuff." Instead, these youth had to resort to taking the "cold call" route of dropping applications off or applying online. Adam was trying for an entry-level construction job, yet despite numerous applications, he could not get any bites—he only got calls back from McDonald's. His was not an uncommon experience: many among our youth got their first job in the fast-food sector. Like the East Harlem youth profiled by Katherine Newman in *No*

Shame in My Game, several took fast-food work when they could get it and remained hopeful that these jobs could lead to something bigger.[9] Christopher—the first male to graduate high school in his family—wanted to open his own restaurant and saw his job at Burger King as a possible route. "I didn't really care if it was a fast-food restaurant [or] whether it's a five-star restaurant. . . . That's what I was working my way up to, at Burger King, you know, wanting to own one, or to be a store manager *of* one." Martin told us, "You can make any little thing big. . . . I was working at the McDonald's, I was only cleaning the dining room, only two, three hours a day, but my mind was just bigger than just cleaning the dining room, you know, that's why after a while I was offered supervisors and manager positions. . . . Working in a McDonald's, you might own your own restaurant one day."

But despite his optimism, even Christopher struggled. To jump-start his dream of becoming a restaurateur, he envisioned completing a degree at the Baltimore International College (now Stratford University) to earn a certification in culinary arts. Even though he started his first semester there, he ended up leaving school and working at Burger King instead because his family relied on his financial contributions. But after being promoted to assistant manager, he quit after the manager refused to give him challenging work or sufficient hours, despite the fact that he had spent several years at the franchise in a variety of roles. "No, I had quit from Burger King because they didn't believe that I was strong manager [material], so they like, they give me stupid stuff to do, or they like try to push me out the door . . . so he like, 'Oh, well, you're only gonna work like two days and one hour.'"

Christopher was already looking for new jobs by the time he left. He was not picky—he searched all six of the malls in the Baltimore area and "applied for all jobs no matter what it was. My mind is trained to learn quickly . . . [but] because I wanted to be a cook, I always looked at like restaurants, or anything like the Cheesecake Factory, Outback, Friday's. But they never called me [either]." The rejections took a toll on Christopher, though many of his friends were in the same boat. "Um, I was in a lil' doubt, like, I wasn't gettin' a job. I wasn't gonna be able to help my mother. You know, I was just feeling a little down, you know."

Eventually, Christopher's perseverance paid off—while out shopping one day at the mall he dropped into a clothing store where he saw a friend at the cash register. The friend was able to hook him up with a job there. Last time we saw him he was still working at the store for $7.50 an hour, full-time. The following fall he was hoping to have enough money to return full-time to the culinary institute.

Ralph, a special education student, knew he needed some extra support once he graduated from high school and attempted to find a job. He explained: "I wasn't interview-ready. [I] was looking good with the suit and everything, but my words was all messed up."[10] Ralph explored every resource in the city he could find. First, he called the East Baltimore YO! center for help. They helped him land his first job in a suburban warehouse as a stock boy.

When he got laid off from that job, the city unemployment office helped him obtain a job as an orderly at Sinai Hospital through its apprenticeship program. Ralph enjoyed spending time in the hospital and felt important delivering shipments to the doctors. "When I was there, I had tooken a lot of boxes from UPS and FedEx up to the people, up to the surgeons that need the utensils to do surgery. Yeah, we used to go all around the hospital. . . . It was very satisfying, yeah." But that job too was temporary, which saddened Ralph. "I could have made a career out of that job," he said, even though it paid only $7.25 an hour. He returned once more to YO!, which found him an internship in construction. To prepare, Ralph was trying to address deficits in his math skills. "They getting ready to train me . . . but I got to pass the math test because it's got math in it. . . . I am very, very poor with the math . . . I am taking classes now. I got to go up there . . . every Friday . . . it's nothing but math."

Ralph hoped the internship would lead to something more stable. Meanwhile, he worked through a temp agency as a forklift operator a couple of days a week. Because he was hired through the temp agency, he was paid a fraction of what the regular employees earned. "You know, that guy could be makin' twenty dollars an hour and I [am making minimum wage]."

After a few years of trying to make it work, holding out hope in fast-food jobs, seeking support from job centers, and tapping social ties, many of our youth who went directly into the labor market found that the work did not pay nearly enough to get by. But the problem was not just the money—the work was unsatisfying, monotonous, and even dangerous at times. Devin's job at Target paid $12 an hour—because he had been there nearly three years—but he did not want to "spend my whole life there," because "counting produce is boring and tedious." Kyle was working at Smoothie King, making $6.15 an hour; when his wage was eventually bumped to $7.25 with an increase in the minimum wage, his hours were cut back, so he quit. He had been at Sears the last two years, but even after two raises—moving from the cash register to the loading dock—he was making only $7.90 an hour. The money helped toward his portion of his mother's rent—he gave her about $300 a month—but it did not leave much for anything else. Kyle wanted something more and had applied to the Baltimore City Police Department, but his application was denied.

In spite of the tedium and low pay, many youth still found value even in these menial jobs. Omar told us, "Something is better than nothing." Robert worked at a food processing plant, hanging chicken and stacking boxes in the warehouse on the Eastern Shore of Maryland. At $11 an hour, he clocked in almost 50 hours a week—not counting his one hour commute each way. While he said the pay was "good" and the hours were plenty, the work was physically grueling, with no paid vacation. Robert said he had learned to "deal with it" because the money helped him provide for his family—his primary concern. He said, "you always keep it in the back of your mind, like what would I do if I couldn't take care of my family? [To take care of them] I'll do just about anything."

Others found that legal work provided an appealing alternative to the street. Despite the pull of "easy money" that encouraged some of our youth to sell drugs for a time, many held the goal of working a formal-sector job and becoming a taxpayer. Marcus extolled the intrinsic satisfaction that comes from earning money the "slow way," asserting that "dope money" is "dirty money." He claimed that "if you work for it" rather than sell drugs, then "you're gonna feel good if you got it . . . you work hard on it and you know how to manage your own money."

In sum twenty-two of our youth opted to go right into the labor market after high school, some of them having made the realistic assessment that they were unlikely to ever attend college, and unlikely to finish if they tried. Yet their alternatives were bleak. The jobs they managed to obtain after high school were typically low-wage and rarely promised full-time work; nevertheless, with frequent shift changes, they required full-time availability. Many youth juggled multiple jobs from temp agencies that paid far less than regular employees were paid; after covering transportation costs, they rarely made enough to cover their bills. Plus, these jobs cost them their time but did not provide the dividends of a career path—the more satisfying work that so many sought.

THE NEW FORGOTTEN HALF

The Forgotten Half: Pathways to Success for America's Youth and Young Families, published in 1988, focused on the limited life chances of the roughly one-half of youth ages sixteen to twenty-four who were transitioning to adulthood with a high school diploma or less and were unlikely to ever attend college.[11] While the authors noted the potential of these young adults, describing their commitment to seeking work and a productive

Table 6.1   Degree Ever Attempted by Youth with a High School Diploma or
GED Who Ever Entered a Postsecondary Institution (N = 59)

Trade Certification	Associate's Degree	Bachelor's Degree
53%	39%	25%

Source: Authors' compilations.
Note: Includes only youth with a high school diploma or GED.

role in the American economy, they also painted a grim picture. Table after table showed bleak prospects for the non-college-bound: high rates of unemployment, lower earnings compared to a prior generation, and higher risk of poverty and single-parenthood. In some ways, the youth described in *The Forgotten Half* sound a lot like those we have been describing in this book—young people who are at significant risk but full of potential and deeply committed to work. Yet there is a key difference between the young adults coming of age in the late 1980s and low-income youth these days. Both in our study and nationwide, the majority of disadvantaged youth are now likely to enroll in college or pursue postsecondary occupational training, often at a community college or trade school.

Nearly 70 percent of the youth in our study who, by the time of last interview, had obtained a high school diploma or GED continued their education beyond high school.[12] But as table 6.1 shows, the most common pathway taken after high school was not attendance at a four-year college or even a community college, but enrollment in a for-profit trade school.[13]

Of the fifty-nine youth who tried some form of postsecondary education, over half (53 percent) enrolled at least once in a for-profit trade school, while only one-quarter ever enrolled in a four-year college.[14] And though 39 percent tried community college, almost half did so in order to pursue terminal occupational certification programs, not with the intention of transferring to a four-year school.

For-profit trade schools typically offer programs that are short—usually less than a year in duration—and prepare students to earn certifications to work in a wide range of fields. Popular programs include: automotive mechanics; certified nursing assistant; cosmetology; electrical technology; heating, ventilation, air conditioning, and refrigeration (HVAC); commercial driving; welding; medical assistant; computer networking; phlebotomy; and drywall technology. While certifications in some of these areas can also be obtained from lower-cost community colleges, such as Baltimore City Community College (BCCC)—where a number of young people pursued occupational certifications—the for-profit trade schools proved more attractive, for reasons we describe in more detail later. Adding to their allure in particular were the power of their ad-

Table 6.2   Educational Status of Youth with a High School Diploma or GED
Who Ever Entered a Postsecondary Institution, 2010 (N = 59)

	Trade Certification	Associate's Degree	Bachelor's Degree	Total
Earned a credential	10	1	1	20%
Left institution before completing credential	12	8	2	37%
Currently enrolled	10	14	14	64%

Source: Authors' compilations.
Note: Includes only youth with a high school diploma or GED.

vertisements, the shorter duration of their programs (even relative to a community college), the perceived guarantee of employment, and the packaging of coursework that offered a clear roadmap to completion.

Yet the speed and ease with which trade school certifications could be earned was no guarantee of completion. At the time of last interview, over one-third (38 percent) of the young adults who had ever enrolled in one had dropped out (similar to the percentage of all attempters who dropped out of at least one program; see table 6.2). Five youth who left some kind of postsecondary program tried again, sometimes at a community college but more often at another for-profit trade school. By 2010, only about one in five youth had earned any credential, most of those in a trade school. Our data, however, are "right censored"—64 percent of those who ever attempted any kind of postsecondary education were still enrolled when we last spoke with them—so we did not observe most youth long enough to know whether they would eventually complete a credential (table 6.2). As the stories in this chapter suggest, within just a few years after high school many experienced at least one false start at a postsecondary institution, often at the expense of time, forgone wages, and the acquisition of significant debt.[15]

As we argued in the last chapter, postsecondary pathways for youth in our study were limited by the poor academic preparation they had received in high school, along with the undertow of family trauma and neighborhood risk. But there was more to the story: the very nature of the expedited launch into adulthood made credential completion difficult. As we have shown, overcrowded living situations, family conflict, and the desire for independence accelerated these young people's perceived need to be out on their own sooner rather than later. This made attending a four-year—or even a two-year—program a luxury that these youth felt they could ill afford: they needed to start making money immediately.[16] It is the for-profit trade school that promises the quickest, most transparent connection to a career.[17] But as we will show, what starts out as a practical solution to the pressing problem of expedited adulthood often ends up being an institutional trap that actually *increases* the time needed to earn a credential and often leaves young people with a greater load of debt than that they might have taken on had they attended a public four-year university.

One of our central claims is that the very attributes that make the trade school path appear to be most efficient—a short-term narrow curriculum and a focus on a particular career—are also its downfall. To obtain a credential from a trade school, youth must *commit* before they have had time to *explore* whether the career in question actually fits with their interests and skills. As we argue in the last chapter, in the months immediately after high school graduation, our youths' situations bore little resemblance to those of their more affluent counterparts: they were not taking a gap year to work on sustainable farms, planning to study abroad at some point during their college careers, or looking to land the ideal internship that would aid them in their process of self-discovery. Yet they were not immune to the powerful message from the broader culture based in the emerging adulthood model—that the late teens and early twenties are a period of self-exploration. Despite their initial expedited launch, these youth also ended up finding it important to explore what their interests were, to see what "clicked," and to identify meaningful careers they were passionate about.[18] But for them, all of this unfolded in educational trajectories characterized by fits and starts. It is important to emphasize here that our young people's expectations were considerably more modest than those of middle-class emerging adults. Nonetheless, they sought occupations that would do more than just meet an economic need.[19]

For example, twenty-three-year-old Gary sought a geriatric nursing assistant license in part so that he could eventually care for his father (who had raised him after his parents divorced), a retired long-haul truck driver entering his seventieth year. Sherika, the vigilant older sister we met in the last chapter, aspired to a career in which you do not have to "drag yourself off to work . . . [where you're] happy [and it's] something you want to do until you retire." Terry and Chantal, whom we introduced in chapter 3, wanted careers that would allow them to give back to their communities and help other youth who struggled just as they did. Cody and Antonio both aspired to become police officers so that they could protect and improve their city.

While pursuing the educational pathways they hoped would eventually get them into meaningful careers, youth in our study moved in and out of the same low-wage labor market as their non-college-bound peers we described earlier. They too learned quickly that these jobs were non-starters: virtually no job paid enough to enable them to achieve the independence and self-sufficiency they were seeking. Nor were those jobs, except in rare circumstances, rungs on a career ladder. They were stuck between a rock and a hard place—many knew they needed postsecondary education to command a decent wage, but felt pressed to provide for themselves sooner rather than later. For this reason, their schooling was often accompanied by part- or full-time jobs. For example, Shadow had been working on and off at Burger King and KFC for several years but was also enrolled in a certified nursing assistant program. Fast-food was not what she had in mind for the long term, because "I can't live off that with a child . . . so that's not a career, that's not what I wanna be two or three years from now." Similarly, Devin had been working at Target for four years, but saw the job merely as "money in my pocket." He planned to pursue training in construction or auto mechanics at a trade school within the next year.

Four-year colleges, through a broad range of course work that allows students to experiment, offer room for young people on the cusp of adulthood to engage in a trial-and-error process of vocational discovery that is consistent with the overarching culture of the emerging adult. That culture—which our youth are not immune to—clashes sharply, however, with the structure of the for-profit school (and even many of the occupationally focused programs offered by community colleges). Committing to a program structured to prepare students for only one career before they have had an opportunity to explore other options puts youth in the position of having to do the experimenting while in the program. After enrolling in trade school, they might discover that they do not have the stomach for drawing blood—the task demanded of the phlebotomist day in and day out—or that they are not very adept with computers. Such realizations come after they have already enrolled and paid a semester or two of tuition. In college, a student only has to change her major when her interests change. Not only is that relatively easy to do in the context of a four-year education, but the courses already taken may still count toward general education requirements or electives. In trade schools and in many community college programs, false starts cannot be counted against the total course work required, since courses can rarely be transferred, not even in related fields (CNA and medical technology training, for example).

About half of the time youth who dropped out of one program had already tried another by the time we interviewed them, and more would no doubt do so over time. Other research has shown that as they move through their twenties and thirties, many young people continue to "try,

try again." Based on our data, we have reason to believe that it is the short time frame of these programs that may prompt youth to enroll without carefully considering whether the program will be a good fit with their interests and skills. For example, Taniya said, "The [medical assistant] program is only nine months, I'm still gonna be young, and I can always go back to school, it's never too late." Short time frames may also lure youth in before they have fully considered the financial obligations they will have to take on, as Jackson's story will show. The net result is that the young people in our study who attended trade schools or enrolled in oc- cupationally focused community college programs often ended up swirl- ing among multiple programs.[20] They lost time and accumulated signifi- cant debt, sometimes with no credential to show for it in the end.

"WHY WAIT YEARS TO BECOME SOMETHING?"

Our youth generally came to the end of their high school years knowing that they did not want to try for a bachelor's degree (at least not yet), but not knowing much else about how to move beyond mere "jobs" and in- stead pursue "careers." In high school, information about college was of- ten delivered in large group sessions rather than during one-on-one face time with a counselor. Typically, youth told us, any contact with counsel- ing staff was oriented toward college, not trade schools or occupationally based community college programs. Thus, they left high school having received virtually no guidance about how to traverse those landscapes. Sometimes that dearth of information was directly revealed in our inter- views, as youth turned to us for advice. Ryan, twenty-one, asked Peter Rosenblatt, "What do you think? About the steps I should be taking?"

Nyesha, sixteen, was already considering going to a trade school for cosmetology, but complained that her teachers and counselors only talked about college. In fact, the school required that students apply to at least one college in order to graduate. Ashanti, twenty, was also interested in learning about occupationally focused training, but when asked if anyone ever talked to her about these programs, she said, "No, I have done re- search on them on my own, but they [school staff] never talked to me." Interestingly, even students who attended vocational high schools said that they received little guidance on how to actually ply their trade after graduation or obtain any further certification that might be necessary for them to do so.[21]

The one piece of information that *was* widely known was that such pro- grams were not supposed to take very long. As Ashanti put it, "It's quicker, it's not a real big, big commitment as much as college is. And you can be over and done with before you know it, and that's what I need, in and out." Crystal, the young woman from East Baltimore we introduced in the last chapter, told us that her dream job was to be a lawyer, but that she had decided instead to settle for being a CNA, "because a lot of programs I can get in and you come out [with a CNA] or something quick, in like six months. So why wait years to become something when you can become something in like the course of a year?"

If not from school, where were they finding the information about what was required to enroll? Ayesha's narrative reflected what we heard from many young adults: "I just knew about trade schools because there were commercials on TV." Youth described tantalizing ads showing successful professionals working in offices, hospitals, or dental exam rooms, assisting with what looked like complicated procedures. Jayden, twenty-two, explained how the trade school he attended had caught his eye and how it put the local community college at a disadvantage in his estimation: "Yeah, the commercial [is] convincing when they show people riding in yachts and big cars . . . I ain't never see BCCC with no commercial with nobody buying a yacht!" Rico, twenty-one, had recently lost his job as a groundskeeper at Johns Hopkins Hospital and was now working as a grave digger at a cemetery in suburban White Marsh. He was considering trade school, wavering between programs in commercial truck driving and automotive mechanics. Rico admitted to Stefanie DeLuca that TV advertising was the only source of information he was drawing on as he thought about what came next in his life: "I was looking at the commercial the other day. Like, I love dirt bikes, so like I think it's called ITT Tech or something. Like you can work on dirt bikes. I was thinking about calling them. I never really like looked at [other information]. I just looked at the commercial."[22]

These ads tell young people everything they want to hear: "You can have a career in any of these trades!" and, "It's quick!" They imply that meaningful work can be had, as well as luxurious lifestyles. Despite federal laws that require for-profit schools to make information public and accessible online, our youth rarely mentioned taking the time to research additional details about the schools after their attention had been captured by these ads and their equally compelling websites. Specifically, youth who were enrolled or scheduled to enroll in a trade school almost never had a clear sense of how much the program cost, what the completion rate was, whether and what credits would transfer if they changed their mind, and how many students graduated on time from these schools. Information about the significant debt they were likely to accumulate once their financial aid was exhausted was almost completely absent; these youth assumed that the school would take care of such matters. They were usually surprised to find out that additional licensing or certifying exams were commonly required to start work after they acquired their credential, and that failing these tests would make the credential useless for starting their careers. Most surprising of all—because so many pursued training for occupations held by family and friends—youth rarely had a good sense of what the expected starting salary of a given occupation would be.

Information was also gleaned from family and friends and sometimes from employers.[23] The fact that so many of our young women had friends and relatives in relatively low-paying jobs and so few pursued other, higher-paying occupations led to a process of social reproduction: cosmetologist, CNA, and medical technician (or assistant) were the trades that most quickly came to mind for them, while, for the same reason, many of our young men leaned toward training in automotive technology or HVAC installation or repair. Dana, creator of *Dana's TV Show*, graduated from one of the best high schools in Baltimore, and teachers and parents were sure that she was destined for college. Yet she downshifted to becoming a CNA because "I would hear some of my friends that probably graduated before me say, 'I took a CNA course,' and I'm like, okay, maybe that's something I can do, I don't wanna go to college [right now], can't really afford it anyway, so that was another excuse, so I said I'll try this out." Iyeshia, twenty-two, was planning on attending a local trade school to get her CNA certificate too; she explained just how constrained (and saturated) her network was with information about just one field: "[People are doing] *nothing* but CNA stuff. Like everybody is doing something far as with the hospital. Nurse's assistant, dental [assistant], and all that. That's what mostly everybody, most my friends is doing. Like it's crazy."

Relying on social ties to spark vocational aspirations is nothing new. Indeed, we note in chapter 1 that social reproduction is an age-old process documented vividly by the work of the sociologist Paul Willis, whose book *Learning to Labor* documents why, in a previous industrial age, sons so often followed their fathers onto the factory floor rather than aspiring to college.[24] We should also note that for those in semiskilled occupations, particularly those in the medical field, Kristen Turney and her colleagues have shown that ties to others in similar occupations can be useful, as informal referrals are often the key to getting and keeping these jobs (as her analyses of the parents' job strategies in the 2003–2004 wave of our study showed).[25] But too often, lack of information in high school about the trade school route, coupled with an overreliance on flashy ads and redundant information from social ties, led youth to land in a small range of occupationally focused programs. Even if completed, a number of these careers would have placed them in corners of the semiskilled economy infamous for their instability and low pay.

"I'M STILL IN THE MIXTURE OF TRYING TO FIGURE OUT WHAT I WANT TO DO"

Here we explore in greater depth a theme we introduced earlier—that a key institutional feature of the trade school or occupationally focused community college program is the requirement that a student commit to the program before exploring alternatives. This requirement is at odds with the wider culture and its emphasis on self-discovery in the post–high school years. Ayesha, twenty, had attended a trade school program to become a medical assistant, but never finished. She said, "I wasn't focused there. It was something I was trying to fulfill, but I wasn't interested in it." Kim, also twenty, admitted that though she had enrolled in a gerontology program at BCCC, she had no idea what the word meant: "I'm gonna be honest with you, I didn't even know what it was. I just heard gerontology, oh, that sounds serious. . . . And then I found out what it was about and my final grade in the class was a B." She left the program soon afterwards and was one of the few to enroll in an academically focused associate of arts program at CCBC, then transfer to a four-year college—Coppin State—to study psychology. We heard similar stories about phlebotomy: students would enroll because it sounded impressive, with no idea that it involved blood.

Reflecting their poor academic preparation, some who enrolled in trade schools (which seldom offer remedial courses, as community colleges do—both a curse and a blessing) simply found the curriculum too difficult. Jayden, who was lured to the trade school by the depiction of a graduate driving a yacht, told us:

> Yeah, the commercial is convincing when they show people riding in yachts and big cars. But they don't tell you that these people already *went* to [a four-year] college *already*, they coming back to advance themselves [in a particular trade]. They don't let you know none of that. When I got to school and they, they just jumped into things instead of starting from ground one— they jumped into things you *supposed* to know—how am I supposed to know that? I never went to school for that! I was trying to tell them I went to a city . . . school that hardly taught you anything. I really needed my mind refreshed. I had to stay over almost every class to learn what they was talking about.

The cost of enrolling in a for-profit trade school can make the price of this trial-by-error exceptionally high. In chapter 2, we introduced Jackson—the "computer whiz" and self-published author who was driven to defy his brother's taunts and the "behavior problem" label he was given by teachers early on. In the summer after high school, he enrolled at BCCC, convinced that there was no other way to secure stable employment in the postrecessionary economy. His goal was to complete a program in computer engineering. After rushing through the placement tests—not realizing that they would determine which courses he would be allowed to take—he spent the first year enrolled in "pre-classes," remedial courses that did not count toward any certification or degree. To get by while attending school, he apprenticed at a local barber shop (an alternative means of gaining cosmetology certification in Maryland), thinking he could earn cash and have a backup trade.[26] After a year and a half at BCCC, and one semester into the two-year program, a client at the barber shop told Jackson about the programs at TESST College of Technology,[27] a for-profit school, where he could be done in less than a year. Frustrated by his slow progress at BCCC, Jackson found the information appealing. As he explained later, "[It is] a trade school, so you know, you can finish the college thing quicker . . . so I went for it."

When Jackson first got to TESST, wanting to build on what he had learned at BCCC, he enrolled in the computer-assisted design program. He soon found himself overwhelmed academically, and he did not feel like he received enough support from the instructor. He then switched to the medical assistance program, still within TESST. Shortly after starting this program, he learned that he did not have the stomach to draw blood. "Yeah, it was nerve-wrecking. I think I did it twice, but after that . . . [laughs]." In retrospect, he regretted his decision to move over to TESST because it cost him the degree at BCCC: "I should have stayed at BCCC because it wasn't as long to go." Now, after three years of attending school full-time and amassing over $14,000 in debt (tuition at TESST runs over $25,000 a year; see table 6.3), he still lacked a credential and had virtually no course work that would transfer:

> At BCCC, I couldn't transfer my credits over to TESST because that was different, a completely different program. [When I] transferred from computers to health [within TESST], I couldn't transfer any credits either. Nothing I did at TESST will transfer back to BCCC because it was in a different type of school—because it wasn't *college* college. It was a trade school, so I couldn't transfer nothing over . . . because at the trade school you just get a certification.

All this time, Jackson was accruing more debt. BCCC might have been cheap, but it was not exactly free, with tuition averaging just over $9,600 per year for a full-time student (see table 6.3), and being obliged to do a year of noncredit course work, as Jackson was, added to the burden. Still, TESST had a far heftier tuition price tag, and there were the monthly fees associated with his training materials there. When he moved from one program to another within that institution, he had to take out a second loan. "Financial aid pays some, they say about twenty-five percent, but the other you have to take out in loans. I had to take out two loans. They was about eight or six thousand. Both [of them]. So, it was a lot more expensive. So, I should've just stayed at BCCC, but being fast, wanting to hurry up and get through everything, I just went to TESST." The last time we spoke with Jackson, he had not paid on either loan and was in default, a status that would preclude his taking out more student loans.

Then, to accommodate the demanding course work at TESST, Jackson stopped working at the barber shop. But soon afterward, his girlfriend became pregnant. He began taking on hours as a security guard to save for the crib, stroller, and other items he felt he ought to provide in preparation for the birth. In the short term, this job was better than his apprenticeship at the barber shop, where he had been paid only a portion of whatever the day's take was and had lacked any benefits: "I needed a guaranteed amount to know what I'm going to have to work with, so I had left and started doing security," he explained. The security job was at a suburban shopping center only accessible by car. One day as he traversed the Baltimore streets on the way to the suburbs, he hit a manhole lacking a cover and damaged his car irreparably. Relegated to hitching rides with friends, he had trouble making it to work on time, if at all, and he was soon fired for missing too many days. This—along with his queasy stomach while drawing blood—was another reason to leave TESST: "Once I lost my job, I had to stop at TESST because I didn't want to keep paying [the fees] knowing that I had a child on the way. . . . I was focused on getting my money together for my son."

Soon after he left TESST, Jackson and his girlfriend moved to Southeast D.C. to be near his girlfriend's mother. He was unemployed for about a year, but enjoyed his time being a stay-at-home dad for his son and his girlfriend's daughter (from a previous relationship) while she supported the household by working full-time as a medical assistant. Eventually Jackson got restless at home with no money of his own and started working security jobs at night, when his girlfriend could be home with the children. But he could not find assignments that paid much more than the minimum wage. During one particular shift, he and his coworkers had to

Table 6.3   Costs and Completion and Loan Default Rates at Local Colleges and Trade Schools, 2013–2014

College or Trade School	Net Price[a]	Percentage Part-time	Two-Year Graduation Rate[b]	Four-Year Graduation Rate	Six-Year Graduation Rate	Overall Graduation Rate	Default Rate (2010)
Four-Year Schools[c]							
West Virginia University	$6,366	8%	N/A	33%	57%	57%	9.8%
University of Maryland, College Park	7,605	7	N/A	67	85	85	4.2
Coppin State University	7,677	23	N/A	4	14	14	22.5
Towson University	8,194	12	N/A	40	65	65	5.2
Salisbury University	8,595	8	N/A	47	67	67	5.3
Bowie State University	8,920	19	N/A	13	35	35	16.1
University of Maryland, Eastern Shore	10,315	10	N/A	13	32	32	23.5
Delaware State	10,762	8	N/A	18	37	37	13.6
McDaniel College (Md.)	11,215	7	N/A	62	68	68	4.5
University of Maryland, Baltimore County	11,793	15	N/A	37	65	65	5.3
Morgan State University	12,405	12	N/A	11	34	34	24.3
Frostburg State University	13,511	14	N/A	20	49	49	11.0
Johns Hopkins University	13,611	4	N/A	87	93	93	2.4
Notre Dame (Md.)	13,886	57	N/A	45	53	53	9.9
York College (Penn.)	15,123	11	N/A	37	57	58	5.1
Howard University	15,177	7	N/A	40	61	61	10.7
Stevenson University	15,649	17	N/A	42	56	56	7.0
University of Baltimore	16,235	42	N/A	23	38	38	7.8
Goucher College	18,189	2	N/A	59	68	68	3.7
Loyola University Maryland	21,629	1	N/A	79	84	84	3.0
Maryland Institute College of Art	24,911	7	N/A	67	73	73	4.9
Strayer University (Md.)	26,604	86	N/A	16	21	23[d]	15.1

Community colleges							
Garrett College	$4,937	19%	13%	29%	N/A	29%	29.2%
Community College of Baltimore County–Essex, Catonsville	5,154	67	2	12	N/A	7	13.4
Howard County Community College	8,240	63	5	15	N/A	15	12.4
Baltimore City Community College	9,639	67	1	5	N/A	5	16.6
Anne Arundel Community College	10,375	70	5	16	N/A	16	18.3
For-profit trade schools							
Fortis (Medix)–Towson	$10,565	0%	7%	56%	N/A	56%	11.3%
All State Trade School	13,185	0	42	69	N/A	70	20.4
North American Trade School	17,233	0	67 (one-year)	65 (two-year)	N/A	69	31.0
Fortis (Medix)–Baltimore	19,398	0	17	55	N/A	55	20.4
ITT–Owings Mills[e]	21,645	30	N/A	N/A	N/A	34	28.6
Lincoln Tech–Columbia	21,752	23	26	60	N/A	60	29.9
TESTT–Baltimore	25,362	0	48	56	N/A	62	33.7
TESTT–Towson	25,867	0	59	63	N/A	63	23.6

Source: Authors' compilations using United States Department of Education, National Center for Education Statistics College Navigator.

Note: N/A = Not Applicable.

[a] Net price calculated for a student-household income of $0 to $30,000.

[b] This includes completion of a one-year (if offered) or two-year degree on time.

[c] Some also offer two-year certificates.

[d] Six-year rate is 9 percent for males, 38 percent for females.

[e] ITT also offers career-oriented bachelor's degrees.

stand out in freezing rain with no raincoats. Soon after, he resolved to return to school.

Jackson then enrolled in a bartending school, paying tuition out of pocket, though he wasn't sure tending bar was what he really wanted to do: "I'm still in the mixture of trying to figure out what I want to do. [Maybe] I want to do real estate, [or] I want to own my own business," he explained. With little ones at home, however, it was hard combining work and school, and his girlfriend's mother was unwilling to ease the young family's burden as she had promised: "Her mother wasn't willing to help us out as far as getting him from day care or watching him for like an hour until his mother get home because our times conflicted."

The last time we spoke to Jackson in 2012, he was back in Baltimore. His relationship with his son's mother had ended, and he had just begun a new relationship with his boyfriend, Sean. Now twenty-four, he finally seemed to have figured out what he really wanted to do: get into the hospitality industry and eventually purchase a hotel or nightclub. He had worked security at a Marriott while in D.C., and while there had found that he had a strong interest in the hotel business. By this time he was ready to move on from the security guard jobs. He saw too much turnover, as companies brought on temp workers to replace many of their permanent employees, then cut the pay of the permanent staff from $14 or $15 per hour down to as low as $8 or $9.

Since being back in Baltimore, he had applied numerous times for hotel reception jobs, as one way to enter the business. Unfortunately, he had not landed one yet. "This has been the hardest time I had with getting a job. . . . It got so bad and stressful." Just when he thought he had gotten a chance after tentatively being offered a job at a Holiday Inn, he found out the next day that the motel had decided on an inside candidate instead. Then he applied at the Best Western at the BWI airport, where he passed the drug test and impressed the interviewer, but the background check turned up a warrant for his arrest for unpaid traffic violations—he had missed the court date. "So I had to turn myself in. . . . Oh my God it was so stressful that day." At the police station, he was informed that it would take up to two months for his record to be cleared. Exasperated, Jackson recalled thinking, "I'm just like, 'The job will be gone two months from now!'"

In the meantime, Jackson had begun working as a cashier at Chick-fil-A, hoping this would somehow get him in on the ground floor of the hospitality industry. "It's in hospitality, but it's not the part of hospitality that I'm wanna do. . . . It ought to be a big experience because . . . I've never worked in a fast-food restaurant before because the hospitality I was lookin' for was hotel—front desk." Still, he had decided that he would "work my way up from the bottom" there because the hotels were not calling back. "It's like I'm workin' a job that I'm way overqualified for, and I'm getting a little bit of income and workin' hard and stuff, and it's ridiculous," he said.

The week of our last meeting with Jackson, he had an upcoming interview at a Hyatt Regency in Washington, D.C. As a backup, he also set up an interview at a Pepsi-Cola warehouse and distribution facility in the southern suburbs between Baltimore and Washington, an area accessible by light rail. He was holding out once again for the hotel job: "Hopefully that goes right 'cause . . . they start out at $16.50, so that's the income that I'm trying [to achieve]. I'm twenty-four now, I don't want to keep goin' from job to job to job. . . . I have bills and stuff to pay and a child to take care of, so I can't be switchin' jobs and laid off and stuff like that." Jackson had not given up on college, however, telling us, "I also want to go back to school for hospitality management. That's why I was tryin' to lock them in a hospitality job. . . . There's so many [things] I want to do . . . like I wanted to open a club, I wanted to open a barbershop from state to state, I wanted to open a little mini-hotel—maybe not a motel but like a Residence Inn." For now, Jackson figured, the Chick-fil-A would have to do: "I want to try to get promoted at Chick-fil-A because the guy that hired me, which is the manager, he said he can make up to $30 . . . right now he's at $25 or $26 an hour."

"I DON'T LIKE TO FEEL LIKE I'M NOT DOING ANYTHING"

So far, we have described a landscape of postsecondary education where youth are forced to commit—often based on precious little information—before they have explored and therefore end up swirling, as Jackson had done. But others adapt to the uncertainty of their situation by intentionally hedging their bets, pursuing one path but holding on to a fail-safe plan. In fact, we heard some of this willingness to adapt in Jackson's story: he was pursuing the barber apprenticeship at the same time he was enrolled in community college.[28] Hedgers do not commit fully but start down one path provisionally while cultivating a backup plan to ensure that they make forward progress even if they encounter obstacles in pursuit of their provisional goal. There are two ways of going about this. Some intentionally invest in more than one credential—sometimes attempting to earn them simultaneously. Others select programs of very short duration, with the expectation that they will have to return to the academic marketplace repeatedly to secure the credentials necessary to stay employed. In the world of semiskilled work, this strategy actually makes a good deal of sense, as one downside of trade schools is that trades can become quickly obsolete as the technology or requirements for an occupation change. Photofinishing technology, popular in the 1970s and 1980s, is one of many examples of a trade that has simply ceased to exist (except for very high-end practitioners) over time. Hedging also makes sense when the occupations in question are among the most unstable in the labor market. Stacking up two or three credentials can keep the bills paid as job demands ebb and flow.[29]

In short, there are clear practical reasons to hedge. Yet the desire to hedge is also stoked by the process of self-discovery that is still unfolding as youth move through adolescence and into early adulthood. Veronica, only fifteen, was already hedging. She said that she would ideally like to be a doctor or a lawyer, but was leaning toward trade school in cosmetology because "I switch and switch all the time. . . . Well, I did want to be a doctor, but that take too much school time. I did want to be a lawyer, but that take too much time. I want to do hair, so that's it." Here we see downshifting mixed in with the hedging, yet it is also the case that Veronica was not sure she had hit on the right vocational goal. Similarly, Taniya, who wanted to be an RN, was hedging by enrolling in a medical assistant program at the for-profit Medix. She had not given up on her dream of becoming an RN but was hesitant to fully commit right now. In the meantime, she reasoned, she would keep adding qualifications in the medical field until she found an occupation that really suited her. "I figure, you know, when I'm done [with the medical assistant certification] I can do the CNA, GNA, and then if I'm not happy with just that, you know, it's seven weeks, and it's like the more qualifications you have under your belt the more money you make." (The last statement is not actually true. These certifications are not additive. Nor would any of the training Taniya was planning on give her any credit toward a nursing degree.)

Vicky, who loved pigeons, was enrolled in a medical assistant program at TESST—the same one Jackson quit. She was doing well in the program and loved learning about "bones" and taking blood pressure. But while walking around the building during lunch one day, she noticed a whole separate floor full of HVAC "equipment." Watching the students work with this equipment sparked an interest in pursuing a certification in heating and cooling technology: "They really be enjoying it, working on air conditioners, takin it apart, putting it back together. I like that. I wanna take something apart, put it back together, I really do." She said that she hoped to collect a few of these "careers," just to have backup: "Like after [the medical assistant externship], I might go back and try and get my CNA/GNA so I can have my nurse's assistant or whatever. Try to get a couple careers or whatever."

Bella was enrolled full-time at Frostburg State, a four-year school, but she too had a backup plan. "I'm actually studying my certification to try to become a certified pharmacist [technician], just to have something to fall back on as throughout my years of school. Just to have something extra, I mean, like it never hurts to have extra." Sheri had spent the last few years working at Wendy's and a plastics factory. She had a certificate in cosmetology but had just started a training program that would certify her in early childhood education. She hoped to run a day care center, and she thought that she would still take the recertification test necessary to keep her cosmetology license current, just in case. "Right, something that I wanna have under my belt just in case I wanna draw back on that and, you know, day care."

Just like the "try, try again" strategy Jackson employed, hedging can also have a downside. As Brooke's story will show, hedging can exact a price, in that a provisional commitment may decrease the motivation to complete any one degree. Brooke, twenty-two, had worked since she was fourteen, beginning with a job helping an aunt clean houses. Since then, she had been highly entrepreneurial about finding employment: "I've been a receptionist. I've been a prep cook. I've been a cashier. I've been a [data] encoder. . . . I've worked at those a long time." At twenty-two, she found herself unemployed for the first time since she could remember—her two small children had made it harder to find and keep work. The summer we first met her, in 2010, she had spent the coolest part of the day—the morning hours—hitting the pavement to find a job, children in tow. She went anywhere she could reach without a car, applying for jobs at supermarkets and local businesses. Her live-in boyfriend (not the father of the children) was a manager at Burger King and brought in some support, but she needed to pay her portion of the bills.

Sick of the low-wage jobs she had been stuck in since fourteen, her plan was to complete some kind of medical certification program through the Red Cross that fall: "They train for everything, GNA, CNA, Medical Donor Corps. . . . It's cheaper, and the classes are much shorter—like six months versus a year—so I thought I should do that so I can have a career." Unfortunately, she had found out about the Red Cross program a little too late to be able to save for the application fee. To bide time until the next round of Red Cross classes started and keep moving forward—to "feel like I am accomplishing something"—she enrolled at BCCC, thinking that, to use her time wisely, "I could get certified in something else that I like [until the Red Cross starts]." Having done data encoding at another job, she was attracted by BCCC's coding specialist certificate.[30] It was not the first time she had tried community college—she had attended both

BCCC and CCBC before. Brooke acknowledged experimenting with various occupations since high school, but was still struggling to find her passion:

> Off and on I have been trying to change schools to see like what I want to major in. . . . When I first started, it was just like, "Oh I want to do this." And then I would end up thinking of something else. So [my boyfriend] told me to pick something I would like to do and enjoy and just stick with it. That's why I want to do the medical recoding. 'Cause I like working in the hospitals, being behind the desk just doing that stuff.

Yet even after starting back at BCCC, Brooke felt torn. "I'm working on it [my medical billing certification], but I am really leaning towards the Red Cross . . . because everything was much cheaper and it doesn't take as long. It's six months," she said. Then, as is common among our youth who attended community college, Brooke mistakenly enrolled in several classes not actually required for the coding specialist program, owing to an error in the list of required courses that had been posted online. She explained: "They were like, 'Oh, you really didn't need to take that.' So it was like everything they had online was all screwed up. So it was messin' a lot of students up, and I was kind of like fed up with it. Yeah, it wasn't organized at all."

By the time we caught up with her a year later, in 2011, Brooke had left BCCC and enrolled instead at the for-profit American Career Institute (ACI) for medical coding, expecting to graduate in early 2012.[31] She had also picked up some hours at the Wendy's at BWI, the same restaurant where Bob used to work before he caught the eye of the manager, who gave him a better job. She had completed a year of classes at BCCC while waiting to enroll in the Red Cross program, but it turned out that the wait list for the Red Cross program was three years long. She reasoned that all had turned out for the best because "I don't like to do like the blood, the stickin.'" She believed that a career in medical billing would allow her to "help people," in a field she would enjoy, a "field that I know I would like . . . I would be doin' like insurance claims and stuff like that and billing the patients."

Brooke appreciated that all of the classes were packaged in a way that did not allow for the kind of error that had cost her time and dollars at BCCC. "Everything is on point" at ACI, she said. Brooke admitted that the cost was steep: one of the few who could actually report the price, she told us that it was $14,000. "I get a little financial aid . . . but I got two student loans, one for $4,500 and the one is for $2,500. The remainder I just pay every month with the monthly payments of $197. It's killin' me." The most appealing aspect of ACI, in Brooke's view, was the school's promise to place her with an externship with a company that might hire her full-time and its pledge to find her a job. "Yeah, so that's guaranteed. They have to help you find a job when you're finished . . . they have to. I made sure I read that in the little papers I signed."

"IT MIGHT BE TOUGH WHEN I'M GOIN' THROUGH IT, BUT I GOTTA LOOK AT THE FUTURE"

While those who "try, try again" or who "hedge" often end up pursuing postsecondary education in fits and starts, a handful of others saw their trade programs all the way through the first time, sometimes to a job in the field. But even those who completed a credential, whether at a trade school or an occupationally focused community college program, struggled after they finished because the payoffs were typically lower than they had expected. Amanda, twenty-two, received her CNA license and was working at a hospital when we talked with her in 2010. The benefits and security of that job might have been better had she been an actual hospital employee, but Amanda had been hired through a temporary agency, which took a cut of what it billed the hospital for her time. When we met her, she was pregnant with her second child, and though she worked full-time in a health care organization, she had no benefits and had to apply for Medicaid. As a temporary employee, she would not qualify for maternity leave. However, she was faced with an even bigger problem. Her live-in boyfriend and the father of her oldest child did not want another child and refused to renew the lease on their apartment unless she got an abortion. Amanda, unwilling to do so, was in a bind. "I mean, my job doesn't pay. So it's not enough where I can't afford something like this [apartment]. I don't have anywhere to go. So it will be tough."

Gary, twenty-three, was in a more secure position than Amanda. He was living with his father, a homeowner, in a working-class neighborhood in Northeast Baltimore; dedicated to the role of caretaker for the elderly man, he had no desire to move out on his own. Gary had acquired two certifications, one in high school for HVAC and a second through a program offering training as a dual GNA (geriatric nursing assistant) and CNA. Despite his diligence, Gary had struggled to stay stably employed. In his senior year of high school, Gary had been accepted at two small and moderately selective private liberal arts colleges, but he already had a part-time job as an HVAC specialist, working for a large construction company that was building some of the new million-dollar waterfront condominiums along Baltimore's Inner Harbor. Gary opted to stay with the construction company rather than enroll in college, assuming he would work his way up from within the company. He told us that he was thinking at the time, "I'd get good in this company, you know, then have a job." Eventually, he realized that the head of the company he was working for was not interested in promoting him. He was given more responsibility but never a raise, and he was not even being paid as much as some of the other employees who performed the same tasks.

> That wasn't really a good company to work for . . . because I was only getting paid about seven dollars an hour. And I at least wanted at least nine or ten, at least—I got a HVAC certification license! . . . I was just bein' [paid as] a helper, but I was doing the same thing the other people was doin'. I was laying ductwork, I was running copper pipes . . . it was kind of tough. And that made me kind of like scared from, you know, I don't know if I wanna do this anymore.

A year after leaving high school, Gary quit the job. He then spent about a year working at the Coca-Cola bottling plant, moving large heavy pallets in the warehouse. Although the job paid well—at $14 an hour—it was a "very physical, demanding job, [it was] brutal." The job required twelve-hour shifts, six days a week, leaving no time at all for a personal life. After a year Gary quit this job too, figuring that "it's not worth my health or none of that, it's not worth it at all." He held a series of warehouse jobs after that, "where they don't really care about you, you're just another number." Then, when the Great Recession hit, he could not find a job at all. During this time he made ends meet by hacking—driving an unlicensed taxi—using a vintage car he had painstakingly restored and detailed himself. On a good day he could make up to $300. Most often this happened when the elderly people in the neighborhood got their Social Security checks around the first of the month and stocked up on groceries and other essentials. But that work could be dangerous and the take unpredictable, so Gary got up early every morning to complete online job applications at the local branch of the Enoch Pratt Library. "Every day just tried to get up and just tried to do something, just tried to fill out applications somewhere. I don't even care if it was Walmart, somewhere. Every day I was goin' there and never got a call back from anybody," he said.

Finally, in 2010, Gary got a break. He learned from a former girlfriend about a competitive training program run by St. Vincent DePaul, a private nonprofit group, where they paid students to train for a CNA/GNA license. Gary was thrilled to be among the eight students in his cohort who got admitted into the program. About a month before we spoke with him, he had finished the program and was already working at a nursing home in suburban Towson, on the northern edge of the city. But even a month into the job, Gary could see that it was not a career. At $8 an hour to start, he could not earn enough to do much more than maintain his vehicle and pay for his food. He was relieved to be working and enjoyed the job, but he was already looking for ways to advance in the health care field by getting additional certifications. After getting to know others in a number of occupations at the nursing facility, Gary was starting to come up with some new ideas. He was thinking he could stick out the job for about a year before returning to school:

> I'm tryin' to figure out what I wanna do. I talked to the people that's in physical therapy, you know, how to go about, you know, goin' to school. And then I go up to the dialysis side, I talk to one of them in there, they tell me, you know, how you get in—I'm just trying to like feel my way through there, where I think I'll fit in there, you know. But I'm kind of like leaning more towards like physical therapy, 'cause I walk past, I goes in there sometimes, you know, they help them walk . . . stuff like that. . . . Yeah, I think I'd be good in that, that's something I'd be really interested in. That's like a whole different department, like I'd have to go back to school for that, yeah, 'cause they have, I think to be like an assistant you have to go for like two years. And then for physical therapy you have to go for four years.

Even though achieving his goals in this stepwise manner—first the CNA/GNA and then four years of physical therapy training—would require that he spend at least six and a half years in school, Gary did not consider going directly to college at that time, as he had at seventeen. That step had begun to feel too risky. He felt good about the larger field he had chosen—the medical field—given what he had seen on the news about hiring trends. "Yeah, on CNN . . . they said the medical field is the number-one thing that's hiring, so that's another reason why I got into it. . . . I'll just have to work out how much I'll have to pay. I mean in the long run it'll be worth it . . . it might be tough when I'm goin' through it, but I gotta look at the future."

It is striking that even just a few years out of high school, one-third of the youth who tried some kind of postsecondary schooling had already dropped out of at least one program, often to enroll again. Were they simply noncommittal, unable to see anything through? How different was Jackson from a college freshman trying to figure out what to major in? How did Jayden, who felt underprepared for technical school, compare to the premed aspirant whose dreams of becoming a doctor vanish once he realizes that organic chemistry is over his head? As with their college-going counterparts, these setbacks were usually not enough to make our youth quit. Even after four failed attempts at trade school and community college, a failed apprenticeship, and at least ten jobs, Jackson still believed that he could accomplish his dream of owning a club or hotel, a passion he had not discovered until he turned twenty-four and started working security at that Marriott.

Rather than being scatterbrained and fickle, these youth are trying to navigate the world after high school with little good information from their school counselors and limited job leads from what sociologists call "redundant ties"—social networks that can only link you to others like yourself, many of whom you already know, rather than to others in broader social circles. These youth then encounter an educational marketplace full of traps, especially the expensive trap of the for-profit trade schools, which, like occupationally focused community college programs, force students to commit to the program before they have explored enough to know what they really want and need. Even among those who persist and complete a credential, what too often awaits is demanding work that yields precious little economic payoff.

As shown by the stories told here, the low credential and degree completion rates among youth from disadvantaged origins do not necessarily reflect a lack of effort on their part. Of the fifty-nine youth who enrolled in some form of postsecondary education, thirty-eight (64 percent) were still enrolled when we spoke with them last. We really do not know how many will eventually succeed because we did not observe them long enough: it is common for students to take up to six years to complete a bachelor's degree and three years to complete an associate's degree; for those attending school part-time, it can take even longer.[32] But if these youth were anything like other low-income students around the country, eight out of ten will fail to complete the credential for which they were enrolled. The picture is not rosier for college. As Susan Dynarski shows, nationally only 41 percent of low-income students who score in the highest quartile of math ability will complete their college degree (compared to 74 percent of their high-income counterparts), and fewer than 5 percent of those scoring in the lowest math quartile will do so.[33] If these statistics are any guide, Rhiannon and Erica (who we met in chapter 2) could well be the only ones among the seventeen youth in our study who enrolled in a four-year school to finish their degrees.

YOU NEVER KNOW WHAT YOU'RE DOING WRONG

In the spring of 2015, the for-profit educational chain Corinthian College made national news when it announced that it was closing all of its campuses. The company crumbled amid lawsuits, a Securities and Exchange

Commission (SEC) inquiry, and allegations that the for-profit chain had engaged in a "broad pattern of deception in recruiting students, bogus reporting of job placement data and a strategy of combining high tuitions and debt levels with a substandard educational profit."[34] Thousands of students were left in the lurch. The complaint filed against Corinthian included material from internal documents that showcased its exploitative demographic targeting. The documents showed evidence that Corinthian preyed on students who were "isolated" or "impatient but want[ing] quick solutions," individuals with "low self-esteem," those with "few people in their lives who care about them," and those who were "stuck" and "unable to see and plan well for future."[35] In some ways, these words describe many of the youth in our study, who were already struggling against their own origins—they hardly needed another challenge.

Few were prepared for the high cost of trade school. While the majority of students received some financial aid, it was rarely enough to cover even half the cost.[36] Students also talked about having to pay money both before their classes began and during their time in school in order to "hold their place"—a practice not mentioned on the trade schools' websites. Even though Jayden never completed his computer technology program at ITT, he still owed thousands of dollars. He put the street life behind him after he had his daughter, and he had been trying to make ends meet by working at Popeye's Chicken. But he was so worried about losing even his meager earnings there that he would not open a savings account. "They're threatening me with garnishing my taxes and stuff, so a bank account right now is out of the question. But if I put my little $500 paycheck in there and they take it from me, I'm going to be sick." He wished that he had made a less expensive choice, but BCCC did not advertise the "yachts" he saw in the commercial. "When I look about it now, I should've gone to my community college. . . . Working at Popeye's makes me feel like a loser. Honestly. Like, my friends be like, 'What you working, boy?'"

Jaquan, twenty-two, had encountered financial aid trouble at a technology trade school but still hoped to get his certificate. He too found out about a popular trade school via commercials, began the program, then had to quit before he received his certificate because he had to begin paying off his loans and needed to work more to do so. When asked where he would like to be five years in the future, he said, "Hopefully by then I should at least have a certificate in something 'cause I should be already back in school, already workin', you know, so I would have a better opportunity at getting a gooder-paying job in the networking field, or any type of job, really, with that skill. And I could do a lot more than what I can right now." Jaquan was considering going back to the same trade school, but also looking at programs for different trades.

It is certainly the case that the costs and some of the practices of for-profit schools make it difficult to finish. But even if the programs were more effective, the fundamental structure, requiring one to commit before one explores, still did not work for many of our youth. It turned their enrollments into false starts, and instead of helping them get "something quick," delayed their career launches and led to more years of schooling. Would it have been better for these youth to have opted for a community college? Perhaps. It would certainly have cost less, but the tuition still added up, especially for those who had to add a year of remedial coursework.[37] Financial aid policies can also be cumbersome at community colleges, and because these youth juggled work, family, and school, they sometimes attended for a longer period of time than financial aid covered.

When Annmarie enrolled at CCBC, she discovered, like Jackson, that she would need remedial math to start her associate's degree program. "It's supposed to be a two-year college," she said, with frustration, "but I'd be there like five or six years. Then I [stopped school and] went to the temp agency and got a job at Costco [as an] overnight stocker—I had to. I have to provide for my son." Eventually, Annmarie started a computer technology program at TESST.

Whether they pursued trade schools or community colleges, we saw that students lacked the kind of information they needed to weigh the costs and benefits of their options. Even though high school counselors emphasized college, not trade school, they did not always communicate the more fine-grained information that would have allowed students to make an informed choice.[38] As we see in the following examples of Jamila, Jessica, and Chanel, youth were missing key information that might have helped them better navigate their postsecondary pathways. In the absence of such guidance about degree requirements and job prospects, young adults employed strategies that seemed to make sense to them, but ended up costing more time in the long run. Jamila, twenty, was about to start her second year at Coppin State when we first met her, and she was also working part-time as an MTA bus tracker, a job she found "boring . . . you count people on the bus . . . to see if they need more buses." Her high school had emphasized four-year college, and she was proud of her choice: "[I] wasn't like, 'Oh, I'm gonna just go to BCCC for two years and get this AA real quick,' you know? [My teachers] were like, 'You need a *bachelor's*.'" She chose Coppin State because her high school counselor had told her that its nursing program was one of the best. But shortly after enrolling, she learned that the program was "hard to get into"—she did not know that she needed to take a test to be accepted into the nursing program, and when she did, she did not pass. Jamila was crushed. "You never know what you're doing wrong until something happens, and then you be like, 'I won't do that anymore because this is what happened.'" She adapted quickly and decided to change her major to criminal justice. That way she figured she could get a better job than what she had, and perhaps become one of the MTA police she had seen at work. Soon after the bad news about the nursing admissions test, Jamila took the MTA police agility test and submitted to the background check, both of which she easily passed. Jamila still wanted to get her college degree, "just to have that piece of paper, just in case something happened," but was planning to quit Coppin if she got into the academy. She explained: "Well, the academy is a guaranteed thing, you getting paid every week, you know, that's money in your pocket. Whereas with school you go to school in the morning, in the evening you can only work a certain amount of hours. Why not take the academy?"

Jessica, twenty-three, and Chanel, twenty-one, were both successful high school students who attended local four-year colleges on almost full scholarships, Jessica at Frostburg and Chanel at Towson. But halfway through, each returned home to Baltimore because of financial issues: Jessica could no longer afford living expenses, and Chanel had to help her mother cover the bills. Both were used to being successful in high school but found college challenging. With no "advice or encouragement" from her family, first-generation college student Chanel felt unprepared. "I don't think I was really prepared for college anyway, because of the school I went to. It was like, when I got to college, it was just, like, thrown in my face so, I was like, 'Wow, I ain't used to this.'"

After leaving their four-year institutions, both women ended up taking out significant loans to attend local trade schools, Jessica for cosmetology and Chanel for a certified nursing assistant program. Both finished these programs and found employment. Jessica was working at her aunt's salon, and Chanel was caring for her uncle and another patient as a GNA. However, neither seemed completely satisfied with her chosen occupation. Chanel felt that she was underpaid and that her job was too physically demanding. She said, "I'll probably go this route, but I don't know if I wanna do this 'cause this job, it really, you can hurt yourself. A lot of people got back problems and stuff, and that's why I really don't wanna do it." Jessica "loved" her experience in cosmetology school and loved the "challenge . . . it taught me new skills." But once she got into the field, Jessica no longer saw "hair" as a lifelong career and was considering going back to school to get a degree in accounting or even try to become a dental assistant.

In addition to the lack of good options in the labor market, the institutional traps set by the for-profit schools, and the confusing community college menus, there is another structural problem that worked against the youth in our study, and against low-income youth in Baltimore more generally: the set of postsecondary schools they even consider attending is severely circumscribed. As discussed earlier, not only do these youth hail from some of the nation's most economically disadvantaged families, but they must also struggle with a severe poverty of information. As we first noted in chapter 2, hardly any had parents who had entered college, let alone obtained a degree. And with the few exceptions, like Dana and Chantal, most had attended high schools where the majority of their peers tested in the lowest quintile of the state. In other words, they were already at a loss when it came to preparing for college. Not only did their narratives reflect little understanding of the relative differences across schools in terms of quality, but they also misunderstood the differences in how much the schools would cost low-income students like themselves—what the Department of Education calculates as the "net price."[39]

Figure 6.1 shows a selection from the range of schools ever *mentioned* by the youth in our study.[40] Some of these are schools that they had simply heard about; others are schools that they said they had visited, were considering applying to, or had already applied to. There is considerable variety in the list, which ranges from Ivy League schools like Harvard all the way to for-profit trade schools. Figure 6.2, in comparison, shows the institutions ever *attended* by those who graduated from high school. The picture changes dramatically here: the range and quality of schools narrows considerably, from a wide range of selective and moderately selective four-year schools, community colleges, and trade schools to just a handful of local schools: two-year colleges (BCCC and CCBC), trade schools like TESST, local historically black colleges and universities (HBCUs) Coppin and Morgan State, and just two moderately selective four-year colleges, Frostburg and Towson.

Staying local does not have to be an educational liability, and it was a reasonable choice for the low-income youth in our study. For one, it could save the high costs of living expenses when youth move away from home, like those that led Jessica to leave Frostburg. But as table 6.3 makes clear, those choices are consequential. The table includes the array of local options for Baltimore City's graduating seniors. These include all schools attended by the youth in our study and those attended by the last four cohorts of BCPSS graduates to provide a better range of possible options for college in the area.[41]

The table shows that youth approach the transition to higher education with the following menu in mind: *for-profits*, which have high net prices, low completion rates, and high default rates; *community colleges*, which have low net prices and low completion rates; and the popular HBCUs,

Figure 6.1   Postsecondary Institutions Ever Mentioned

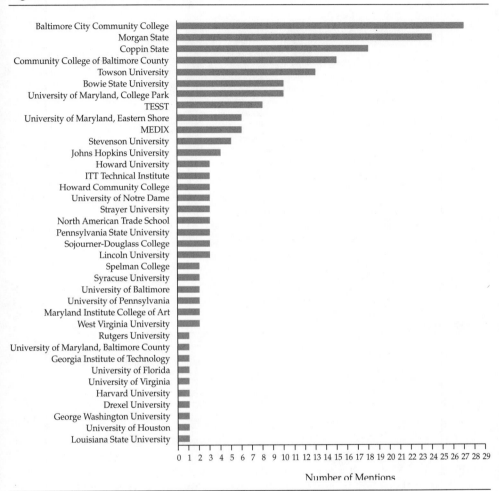

Source: Authors' compilations.

which have moderate prices but very low completion rates and moderate default rates. Yet there are a plethora of higher-quality schools nearby that these youth almost never mention, let alone attend. The net price differences between the higher-performing and low-performing schools are not as much as one might think. For example, the net price of Coppin State, at $7,677, with a six-year completion rate of only 14 percent, is virtually in-

Figure 6.2   Postsecondary Institutions Attended

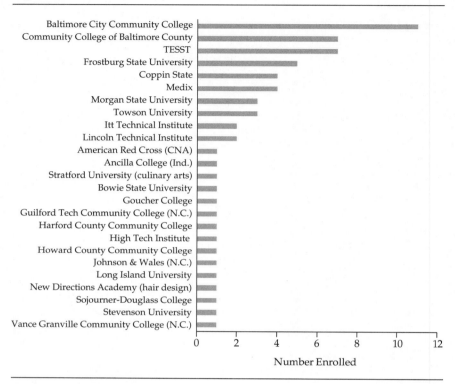

Source: Authors' compilations.

distinguishable from the University of Maryland (UMD) at College Park at $7,605, but UMD's completion rate is 85 percent. Morgan State is just a little cheaper per year than Johns Hopkins, Loyola, Notre Dame, Frostburg, and York College, but it graduates only 37 percent of its students in six years. UMD–Baltimore County, Loyola, Goucher, and Notre Dame, to name a few, all have net prices that are half as much for the first year—or less than half as much—as the trade schools. This means that the college-bound youth in our study could, in theory, afford to attend higher-performing schools, sometimes at a fraction of the costs, but they do not realize it.[42]

Of course, we cannot say whether the high school graduates in our sample could get accepted to more selective schools like the University of Maryland or Johns Hopkins, or whether they could keep up academically once there. But it seems clear that Bob, Bridget, Bella, and Chantal would have had a chance if they had tried. Moreover, we cannot really equate the one-year cost of a trade school with the four-year cost of one of the better colleges. Considering the low degree completion rates and high loan default rates at these shorter-duration programs, however, it is reasonable to ask whether the costlier but higher-quality institutions, which graduate over five times more students, are as expensive as they seem in the long run—especially considering the average returns for a bachelor's degree.[43]

We also want to be fair to local schools like Coppin State, Morgan State, UMD–Eastern Shore, and BCCC, where so many of our youth got their first college foothold. These institutions are in a tough position. They are simultaneously the catalyst for the intergenerational gains that many of Baltimore's young adults hope to achieve and the bearers of the enormous responsibility of educating low-income students from the city's most distressed schools. They are making noble attempts to help the next generation become upwardly mobile, but they have few resources and serve youth with even less. This is a difficult task, and in the next chapter we outline additional strategies for moving forward.

Chapter 7 | "If It Can Cause Some Kind of Change": Policies to Support Identity Projects and Reduce Educational and Neighborhood Inequality

THE STORIES OF these youth should make two things clear: First, many young adults born into extremely disadvantaged circumstance have tremendous potential and can flourish when their social contexts change. Second, their optimism and determination may be enough to get them to the starting gate, but are often not enough to win the race. The mechanisms of social reproduction—family disadvantage, ongoing risk in their neighborhoods, and underperforming schools—are strong. Even if youth navigate these land mines, they often encounter a stunted labor market and a postsecondary landscape full of snares. Far too many end up as pale reflections of what they could have achieved.

Yet it would be unfair to claim that what the youth in our study had accomplished so far was not meaningful. The large majority were "on track"—they were "about something," whether it was college, trade school, or employment. Perhaps more importantly, they were "not about that life"—they had beaten the streets, at least so far. But after reading the stories of Bob, Dana, and so many others who had clearly fallen short of their potential, readers might ask: On track for what? Scraping by?[1] It is true that the triumphs of these youth were not what many Americans would consider success. Yet many seemed to be doing their part. Changes in federal housing policy during their lifetimes had arguably helped, but we can only guess what these youth could have achieved if they had spent their childhoods in the resource-rich neighborhoods and stellar schools of many of their suburban peers. These stories also indict both the postsec-

ondary educational market—which seemed confusing at best and exploitative at worst—and labor market policy, as the jobs they found almost
never paid a living wage, let alone moved them into the middle class.

In this chapter, we propose a policy agenda to amplify the potential of
such youth and leverage the inner resources they already possess.

The conventional wisdom holds that our nation should focus its investments on the very young—infants, toddlers, and preschool children—as
interventions during these years seem to yield impressive returns.[2] But
our nation cannot stop investing at age five. Simulations by Isabell Sawhill
and Quentin Karpilow of the Brookings Institution remind us that what
America's young people really need are consistent investments throughout childhood and adolescence.[3]

The April 2015 Baltimore unrest drew attention to the rising number of
young people ages sixteen to twenty-four who are disconnected—neither
working nor in school.[4] More than one-fifth of America's black youth (and
one in seven young people overall) now qualify as disconnected.[5] In July
2015, Starbucks CEO Howard Schultz announced that his company, together with seventeen other major firms, had pledged to provide 100,000
jobs to disconnected youth. "While some have lost hope in this population, blaming them and their families for creating their own problems, we
believe these young people represent a significant untapped resource of
productivity and talent," Schultz and his wife Sheri wrote in a *New York
Times* op-ed article on July 13, 2015.[6] A Social Science Research Council
(SSRC) study estimates that the cost to society of disconnected youth
reached $27 billion in 2013.[7] While it requires money to *support* disadvan-
taged young people's efforts to launch, it is perhaps more expensive to
ignore them.[8]

Most youth in our study were at risk of becoming disconnected, often
for multiple reasons. Each spent his or her earliest years in some of the
most distressed public housing in the nation; these developments were
not only physically degraded but had become breeding grounds for addiction and crime. Many youth were raised in troubled families who introduced trauma into their lives. Yet when we followed these youth for more
than a decade, we found that they held many of the same aspirations as
more privileged young people across our nation. Where one might have
expected defeatism or a dismissal of society's rules, we often found optimism and a firm determination to "be about something positive." Yet, despite their dedication and perseverance, these young people continued to
live in neighborhoods with few resources and too many risks. By 2010 the
majority remained in families living below the poverty line, as do just
over one in five American young people between the ages of sixteen and
twenty-four—and fully one-third of African Americans in that age range.[9]

This chapter asks: What next? Specifically, how do we keep young people out of harm's way and help them grow up in safe, opportunity-rich neighborhoods? How do we support adolescents' quest for meaning and identity by helping more of them grab on to an identity project, ideally one rooted in a web of peer and institutional supports? How can we better scaffold these youth through the postsecondary education landscape, particularly those who feel a keen sense of urgency to take an expedited path to adulthood? Examining evidence-based practices in each area, we advocate for policies that recognize and promote the inner strength of youth from disadvantaged origins.[10]

IMPROVING ACCESS TO HIGH-OPPORTUNITY NEIGHBORHOODS

Through HOPE VI and other programs, Baltimore demolished all of its high-rise public housing as well as many low-rise units. In Baltimore, some of the dislocated were merely moved to another housing project, while others were given vouchers but little relocation assistance.[11] By definition, the high-rises themselves were contexts of highly concentrated poverty, so when families left through the HOPE VI program, they experienced, on average, a dramatic drop in neighborhood poverty.[12] However, the program was also met with bitter opposition from some community members because of the loss of hard-unit public housing (most lost units have not been replaced), the severing of local social networks, and the involuntary relocation of many families.[13] Although there was a silver lining for those youth in our study who left the projects during their childhoods because of HOPE VI, many families who left ended up in racially segregated neighborhoods that became poorer over time.[14] Few would argue that it was not a good idea to get families out of the distressed high-rises, but entirely different policies are required to help them reach higher-opportunity neighborhoods.

A growing volume of research, including ours, now validates William Julius Wilson's claim that growing up in a neighborhood of concentrated poverty will diminish the life chances of poor children. Given that this is so, policies that create racially-segregated, high-poverty neighborhoods— or trap families in them—are indefensible. There has never been a better time and better evidence, and perhaps never a stronger mandate, for doing so than now. In 2015, in the case *Texas Department of Housing and Community Affairs v. Inclusive Communities Project*, the Supreme Court upheld the disparate impacts doctrine: under that ruling, institutional practices that have discriminatory effects can be found to violate the 1968 Fair Housing Act, even if they were not intended to do so. Following this decision, HUD established a rule requiring recipients of federal funds to affirmatively further fair housing.[15] In combination, these two rules mean that affordable housing cannot be concentrated in high-poverty, segregated areas and developers and property owners must make efforts to racially and economically integrate housing in order to keep their federal funding. Such integration can be achieved by a variety of means: mobility programs, affordable housing development in opportunity-rich neighborhoods, inclusionary zoning, or other "in place" strategies that restore the economic vitality of our communities.

Mobility Programs

Despite the reduction in poverty that our youth experienced when they were young, moving from neighborhoods that were 60 percent poor to those that were just under 30 percent poor (roughly the median neighborhood poverty rate for the youth in this study in 2010) is far from what we would consider moves to real opportunity. Even for those who received the MTO voucher, the program did not produce the neighborhood and school quality gains that were anticipated. This happened for a variety of reasons: "counseling," the process through which participants were supposed to receive assistance in locating eligible units in resource-rich areas, was limited;[16] the vouchers were not easily portable across jurisdictions; and the payment standards (usually set between 40 and 50 percent of a metro area's median income) were too low to allow families to lease up in the most affluent suburbs with the best schools.[17]

A more recent housing mobility program, the Baltimore Housing Mobility Program (BHMP), has several strong programmatic advantages over MTO and has shown tremendous promise in helping families with children escape poor neighborhoods and enter better school districts—and remain in these areas for the long run. BHMP has relocated over three thousand families to high-resource suburbs since 2003. Designed as a partial remedy for a class-action desegregation lawsuit brought against HUD and the Housing Authority of Baltimore City, BHMP offers low-income black families a voucher that requires recipients to lease up in neighborhoods that are below 10 percent poor and below 30 percent African American and in which fewer than 5 percent of the residents live in subsidized housing.[18] To facilitate these moves, the program combines strong counseling (search assistance, neighborhood tours, second-move support) with innovative programmatic features, such as higher payment standards and portability.[19] Stefanie DeLuca and her team followed the first two thousand of BHMP participants, who, on average, found units located in tracts where only 8 percent of their neighbors were poor and 75 percent were white. In their children's schools, only 29 percent of their peers qualified for free or reduced-price lunch, compared to 80 percent in their old neighborhoods.[20] Up to nine years later, more than two-thirds of these families had remained in resource-rich communities, a sharp departure from the pattern in MTO.[21] DeLuca and her colleagues also saw early gains in academic achievement that were not found in MTO.[22]

Although mobility strategies have shown significant benefits for families and children, some have argued that geographically targeting vouchers may not work for all households. Recently, HUD has also experimented with another approach to increasing housing opportunity for voucher holders, using an alternative to the fair market rent (FMR) measure that it uses to determine the rent paid to landlords.[23] Public housing authorities in five cities are experimenting with a formula that would set the FMR using the median rents of "small areas"—usually zip codes. This means that the voucher would be more in line with local variations in rent prices: thus, it would be worth more in affluent areas and less in high-poverty neighborhoods than it is now. Early results from Dallas indicate that the small area fair market rent (SAFMR) experiment has been successful in moving voucher holders from the bottom fifth of neighborhood poverty to the second fifth, without any cost to the government.[24] We believe that with additional housing counseling—for both families and landlords—the SAFMR program could also go a long way in helping families reach higher-opportunity neighborhoods.

Nationwide, just over two million households currently hold some kind of housing choice voucher, yet vouchers typically have no geographic restrictions and few public housing authorities provide mobility counseling to help families identify resource-rich neighborhoods and strong schools.[25] In the absence of such counseling—even though a voucher adds roughly $7,000 to $9,000 to a family's housing budget—standard voucher holders rarely move to neighborhoods that differ appreciably from those in which poor families without any form of housing assistance reside.[26] Perhaps as a result, offering a family a voucher does not typically lead to better child outcomes.[27] In our view, housing choice vouchers are a powerful policy tool that prevents homelessness and reduces overcrowding and housing instability.[28] However, the government should not invest such a large sum to house families in communities where the streets are unsafe and the schools hamper rather than bolster kids' chances at a brighter future.

The track record on mobility programs shows that we can do better: families move to higher-resource neighborhoods if they are required, or offered support, to do so.[29] Many are likely to stay if housing counseling is ongoing and their children are benefitting.[30] However, past experience has shown that mobility interventions must be carefully designed and implemented to yield these gains in neighborhood and school quality.[31]

Affordable Housing

While mobility programs have shown significant promise, housing assistance in the United States is not an entitlement; only about one-quarter of those families who are categorically eligible for housing assistance actually receive it in some form.[32] One strategy to address the shortfall is to increase the supply of affordable housing in high-resource communities by leveraging the Low-Income Housing Tax Credit (LIHTC) program, a program that incentivizes investors and nonprofit developers to build affordable housing.[33] As in many metropolitan areas, most of the LIHTC developments in the Baltimore metropolitan area are located in the poorer and more racially-segregated areas of the city.[34] Thus, the LIHTC program may reinforce rather than reduce income and racial segregation in the region.[35] In a promising turn, the Baltimore Metropolitan Council recently convinced the State of Maryland to modify its LIHTC funding process to ensure that more units are built in high-resource areas.[36]

One example of a successful affordable housing strategy is the Ethel Lawrence Homes in Mount Laurel, New Jersey, which drew on LIHTC funds. The Ethel Lawrence Homes complex contains 140 townhomes that are exclusively for families whose income falls within 10 to 80 percent of the area's median income. Thirty years prior to its completion in 2004, a committee of low-income, mainly African American residents proposed a small affordable housing complex for this suburban community, noting how difficult it was to cover the costs of housing there. Like many suburbs, Mount Laurel was zoned in a way that best accommodated single-family homes with large yards, and the township rejected the plan. The ensuing legal fight, lasting decades, resulted in a series of court decisions. The final ruling, dubbed the "Mount Laurel Doctrine," has been used by fair housing advocates around the country to push for affordable housing in affluent communities. Like most LIHTC properties, Ethel Lawrence is mixed-income by design, unlike traditional public housing, which is limited to those with the lowest incomes.[37]

Douglas Massey and his colleagues found that despite the initial fears of white residents, crime rates continued to fall and property values rose further after the opening of Ethel Lawrence.[38] Moreover, the families there benefited too. Those moving to Ethel Lawrence (compared to those who applied for units but could not yet be accommodated owing to space requirements) experienced significantly less exposure to neighborhood disorder and violence and reductions in psychological distress.[39] In addition, parents were more likely to be economically self-sufficient, and children attended schools that were higher in quality and lower in disorder.[40]

Montgomery County, an affluent part of Maryland that encompasses several D.C. suburbs, used an innovative approach to inclusionary zoning (which requires developers to include a certain percentage of affordable units for purchase or rental) to accomplish similar aims. Thus far, the policy has led to the construction of over twelve thousand moderately priced homes. The local public housing authority has purchased a portion of these homes and leases them to families whose income qualifies them for public housing. Families in Montgomery County's scattered-site public housing program were randomly selected from a waiting list and offered public housing chosen by the housing authority staff. As a result, children in these households attended a wide range of elementary schools across the county. Heather Schwartz, a researcher at RAND, found that children who lived in public housing that was residentially assigned to the most-advantaged schools had significantly higher math scores than their counterparts in the least-advantaged schools in the county. Schwartz also showed that over a five- to seven-year period, those residing in such homes saw the gap between their test scores and those of their peers in more affluent schools drop by half in math and by one-third in reading.[41]

Place-Based Strategies

While some of the programs described have helped many poor, minority families enter high-opportunity neighborhoods and school districts, these families should not have to leave their communities to find opportunity. Instead, policymakers should help them flourish where they are. Unfortunately, we have little empirical evidence that place-based interventions generate significant gains for residents. The HOPEVI program, described in chapter 2, is one type of place-based initiative. Beyond funding the demolition of highly-distressed public housing across the country, HOPEVI was also intended to promote mixed-income neighborhoods. Studies of HOPEVI developments in many cities, including Baltimore, have shown modest positive spillover effects in the surrounding areas, such as an increase in bank lending, an increase in real estate values, and a reduction in crime.[42] However, it seems less clear how well HOPEVI helped to diversify the socioeconomic mix of these new communities, or whether the residents who moved into the new developments saw individual-level benefits.[43]

Sandtown-Winchester, the West Baltimore neighborhood of Freddie Gray and many of our youth, was the site of one of the largest comprehensive community revitalization efforts in the country in the 1990s and 2000s.[44] Over $130 million in private and public funding supported the

Sandtown-Winchester Transformation Initiative, a multifaceted intervention with participation by a wide range of community stakeholders. Housing was a key part of the initiative, with over one thousand units rehabilitated or newly built.[45]

Yet when Stefanie DeLuca and Peter Rosenblatt examined a variety of socioeconomic trends in Sandtown-Winchester, they found little evidence that it fared much better than other similarly disadvantaged neighborhoods in the city, especially in terms of children's school performance, crime, and poverty rate.[46] However, they found that while unemployment did not decrease much over the twenty-year period from 1990 to 2009, it was lower than it might have been in the absence of the intervention; also, the number of homeowners almost doubled during that period. But this increase seems to have been a double-edged sword: predatory lenders also exploited the residents during the years of the intervention. At the height of the Great Recession, Sandtown-Winchester was among the hardest hit by foreclosures of any neighborhood in the city. By 2009 fully one-third of the properties in the neighborhood lay vacant.[47]

In sum, there is not a firm case to be made that the huge investment of private philanthropy and public dollars "worked" for Sandtown-Winchester. DeLuca and Rosenblatt speculate that perhaps the redevelopment efforts were not enough to counteract the generations-long disinvestment in Baltimore neighborhoods like Sandtown-Winchester, which has been chronicled in stark detail in Antero Pietila's *Not in My Neighborhood: How Bigotry Shaped a Great American City*.[48] Compounding that possibility is the fact that for a generation the neighborhood has been virtually bereft of jobs (despite the empowerment zone designation). The lack of employment, combined with an intense police presence and what we now know to be brutal policing tactics, left Sandtown with one of the highest incarceration rates in the city of Baltimore in 2010.[49]

Sandtown-Winchester is a portrait of urban renewal gone unfulfilled, but it is difficult to identify effective place-based initiatives beyond the much-lauded Harlem Children's Zone, a $50 million per year intervention that, because of its cost and the unusual charisma of its founder, Geoffrey Canada, few believe can be replicated elsewhere.[50] First, these interventions are difficult to mount because there are many dimensions to consider. To see impact, it might be necessary to improve public safety, schools, and the quality of housing and to ensure job availability all at once. Second, it is difficult to evaluate the effects of place-based approaches.[51] As a result, most efforts have not been comprehensively assessed. Success stories are no doubt out there, but absent credible evidence, there is no guidance as to best practices. Third, perhaps the most difficult aspect of measuring impact is the high degree of residential mobility among the poor. Those who could have benefited most may have moved on to other neighborhoods, particularly if they were priced out by rising real estate values.[52]

So, as attractive as it sounds to focus investment in a neighborhood to improve the quality of life of its residents, there is a dearth of evidence-based success stories to date. What anecdotal evidence does exist suggests that initiatives that address multiple facets of the community simultaneously yet are realistic about what they can contribute are most likely to succeed. Some initiatives have had a positive impact by focusing on what they do best and identifying partners who can address other community needs. Collaborating with partners from other neighborhoods can be a way to address the extralocal factors, such as labor market challenges or low-performing schools, that limit what a strictly place-based initiative can accomplish. The reality, however, is that many communities have been so underresourced for years that it will require a huge—and strategic—influx of resources to yield significant impact.[53]

SUPPORTING THE CREATION OF IDENTITY PROJECTS

As the stories in chapter 3 show, having developed an identity project was one of the most important factors distinguishing those youth who were on track by our study's end from those who were not. Identity projects serve a powerful purpose—they keep youth off the streets, help them weather tough circumstances, and inspire the grit necessary to accomplish their goals. We also find that youth are resourceful and construct their identity projects in innovative ways. No single program would support every type of identity project we observed. We have argued that those that link young people up with like-minded peers and—better yet—with institutions (with their ready-made activities, resources, and networks) work best. Those institutions most easily within the reach are our public schools, plus youth activities sponsored by local government, such as summer jobs programs. The nonprofit sector can also play a vital role too, through programs like the boys and girls' clubs, the Police Athletic League, and job sponsorship programs.

Unfortunately, over the last decade, trends in the financing of public education have reduced funds for the very activities that might encourage identity development. As schools have focused on boosting students' scores in math and reading, arts education and extracurricular activities have been left to languish.[54] State finances felt the impact of the Great Recession in trimmed budgets for public schools. Schools in struggling districts were sometimes left without sufficient funds to cover much more than faculty and staff salaries and basic supplies, much less art faculty, speech and debate teams, musicals and plays, and athletic programs. This has particularly been the case in schools and school districts with the highest proportions of low-income students.[55]

As noted in chapter 3, Philadelphia exemplifies what happens to these so-called extras when resources for public education are cut. That school district has lost hundreds of millions of dollars in funding, especially since the economic downturn began. Music, visual arts, and theater programs have been eliminated in many Philadelphia schools, and its elementary schools are now required to have only a music teacher *or* an art teacher, not both. Tellingly, in the 2012–2013 school year, Philadelphia's High School for Creative and Performing Arts (CAPA) had insufficient funds to put on a musical production, usually the highlight of the CAPA experience each year. In this climate, schools like CAPA must raise funds from the private sector to pay for music and arts offerings. A foundation set up to benefit the Baltimore School for the Arts, the special-admission public high school mentioned in chapter 5, raises about 30 percent of its operating budget each year. Otherwise, it is likely that students could not continue to receive the specialized training for which the school is known.[56]

While these cuts affect children from all social classes, those from more affluent families often continue to participate in arts and other activities because their parents can pay for them to do so. Over the last few decades, middle-class parents have increased the amount of money they spend on children's activities to a larger degree than those less financially able, leading to a widening gap.[57] The parents of those from economically disadvantaged backgrounds are often unable to fill the gap when funding for programs in the arts, music, speech and debate, athletics, and other clubs are cut back. These youth are striving to find their passion at the same developmental stage as affluent youth, but with many fewer outlets at hand.

Activities both inside and out of school can provide a space for youth to try on different identities and see what fits best with how they view themselves, as Bob, Cody, Erica, and others found. They provide an avenue for young people to discover talents, to bolster self-esteem, and to build leadership skills. In these spaces, young adults can also find a sense of belonging and a supportive network of caring adults.[58] Such programs—particularly those that feature supportive adults—can help youth engage in school and improve their grades as well.[59] Building relationships with prosocial peers through such activities increases school attachment and academic achievement, as Bob found when he joined his middle school chess team and later found academically motivated fellow classmates in high school.

It is also possible for schools to provide the raw material for the kind of career-based identity projects within the context of a school that a number of our youth found so compelling. Career academies represent one of the more successful evidence-based programs for integrating education with a career focus. Begun in the 1970s, these learning communities of about 150 to 200 students are sited within high schools and organized around a career theme. A randomized controlled trial found significant earnings gains over the next eight years relative to a control group. These gains were concentrated among males, who earned nearly $30,000 more over this time period than their control counterparts. Although students who attended career academies were not more likely to graduate from high school or enroll in college, they were 23 percent more likely by their mid-twenties to be living in an independent household with a partner and child(ren), 13 percent more likely to be married, and 16 percent more likely to have custody of their children than those in the control group.[60] These are remarkable.

We call for a sharp reversal of the tide away from funding for the arts and other activities, both in school and out, and an increase in high-quality, career-focused learning communities such as career academies. Our contention is that it is precisely these kinds of activities that have the greatest chance of turning lives around, since—as we argued in chapter 4—much of the allure of the street lies in its role as a second-class substitute for the passions that those with an identity project are pursuing.

CHANGING THE POSTSECONDARY LANDSCAPE

In chapter 5, we argued that the youth described in this book are often on an expedited path to adulthood. The "triple threat" from neighborhood, family, and school can traumatize youth in ways that shorten their time horizons. They feel pressure to take on adult roles, and they want to get on with the business of establishing an independent household and embarking on a career sooner rather than later. This pressure, in turn, makes the idea of pursuing a four-year college degree seem like a risky gamble to take with their precious time. Information is also a problem. Only about one-quarter of these youths' parents had finished high school, and hardly any parents had an associate's or a bachelor's degree; thus, parents had a difficult time advising their children on how to proceed if they wanted to attend a four-year school. Underlying all of these dynamics was the financial squeeze: few of these parents had the resources to support their children beyond age eighteen. Indeed, many of these youth had begun to support themselves and their families in high school through part-time jobs or participation in the informal or underground economy. Though many had aspired to four-year or graduate degrees in professions like medicine or law, these pursuits ended up looking like a luxury they could not afford. Even the strong academic contenders with top grades downshifted; what we see in our data, repeatedly, is that the aspiring nurse, for example, ends up spurning college for a program that promises to earn her a certification instead and get her out working in the "health care profession" in just a few months' time.

How might policy slow the transition to adulthood so that youth can make better decisions? How do we prevent downshifting among the college-ready? Upstream approaches that address disadvantage at the family, school, and neighborhood levels present one way forward. Yet focusing only on the upstream leaves the current generation of youth behind. In the meantime, we need to find ways to support a better-informed transition so that young adults can make decisions about their postsecondary education that will result in living-wage employment without incurring unmanageable student debt. And for those who want to go directly into the workforce—as many of the young men in our study do—there need to be better avenues for building valuable skills and experience on the job, as well as connections to viable occupations.

The Path from High School to Postsecondary Education

In *The New Forgotten Half,* James Rosenbaum and his colleagues note that unlike several generations ago, the problem facing young adults is no longer college access—it is college completion.[61] There is no clear payoff for pursuing "some college," yet that is now the modal outcome for high school graduates who pursue higher education.[62] The real benefits come when youth finish a degree. In 2010 those with a bachelor's degree or higher made 74 percent more than those with a high school diploma.[63] For a cohort of students who graduated from high school in 2004, those with an associate's degree made, on average, 22 percent more by 2011 than those holding only a high school diploma, while the earnings of those who had completed a certificate program rose by 13 percent on average.[64] Given that by 2020 an estimated two-thirds of job openings will require a postsecondary degree, how can we equip young adults from disadvantaged origins to be prepared?[65]

High School   First, we must improve college and career counseling in high school so that youth can make informed choices.[66] The dominant "college-for-all" norm that prevails in many high schools encourages students to aspire to a four-year degree, but it does little to prepare them to navigate other pathways, such as direct entry into the labor market, occupationally based community college programs, or trade schools.[67] Most of the youth in our study who pursued postsecondary education chose for-profit trade schools. Many of the rest enrolled in community colleges. Even those who enrolled in a four-year college considered only a narrow range of local schools, some with very low completion rates and very high loan default rates. Yet they knew little about the schools they enrolled in. High schools must deliver information about how various postsecondary options stack up against one another—including average time to completion, costs (including the real cost to the student after financial aid), job placement rates, and average wages in the occupation. The youth in our study were almost never given this kind of information. Some who were clearly college-ready, at least in our assessment, never even considered four-year schools, while others were left vulnerable to the flashy commercials and aggressive recruitment tactics of for-profit trade schools.

Some high schools have integrated academic and occupational course work (like the career academies), and there is evidence that doing so promotes better labor market outcomes.[68] Most recently, the federal government has required that schools receiving funding under the Perkins IV Act—the primary way the federal government supports career and technical education—must implement programs of study (POS) that give students the chance to explore career options and earn industry-recognized credentials.[69] It is too soon to tell whether POS will improve postsecondary outcomes.[70]

Four-Year College Enrollment   As noted earlier, those who did enroll in four-year schools often considered only a narrow range of local universities and colleges, usually ones with high loan default rates and low degree completion rates, even though there were higher-performing colleges and universities nearby, several with lower net prices. Some have described this phenomenon as "undermatching." Not only do students who are undermatched get a less valuable credential, but, as recent evidence suggests, students are more likely to graduate when they attend the most selective institution that accepts them.[71] In an effort to reduce undermatching, MDRC has recently launched a program, Project Match, that helps students understand which four-year institutions are within their reach given their test scores and grades.[72] Though it is too early to be sure about the impact of this program, pilot studies in New York and Chicago show promise.

The College Coach Program (CCP), implemented in twelve Chicago public high schools, takes another approach by transforming the traditional duties of high school counselors; CCP performs better in rigorous evaluation than Upward Bound—a program to support college enrollment for low-income students that boosts enrollment only in trade school, not in college.[73] CCP counselors conduct outreach to encourage students to make concrete postsecondary plans, and they meet with students one-on-one and in groups to build rapport and trust. They walk through the college application process step-by-step with both students and their families. Students from schools with CCP counselors were more likely than those without these coaches to enroll in college, and they were more likely to attend a nonselective four-year college than a two-year college.[74]

Community College   Not all youth matriculate directly to a four-year school—some choose to explore postsecondary education at a community college first. Community colleges are responsible for much of the progress our nation has seen in college enrollment, especially among low-income and minority youth.[75] These institutions now enroll about four in ten (42 percent) new college students in the United States.[76] These schools provide college access for students who would probably not have enrolled at all if they had only a four-year college option.[77] However, as we showed in chapter 6, community colleges have distressingly low degree completion rates.[78] To expand opportunity, it is paramount that community colleges become gateways to four-year degrees.

Like high schools, community colleges should do more to inform students about their options and the economic payoffs to the various offerings.[79] Rosenbaum and his colleagues compared community colleges to a select group of "ideal type" accredited private occupational colleges to figure out how students could be better served at community colleges.[80] Two key features of these schools seem particularly salient for the youth in our study.

First, these model institutions took a hands-on approach to helping students make informed choices.[81] Before students decided on a course of study, they were informed of the course requirements, the job placement rates, salary expectations, and working conditions.[82] Career options that did not deliver on placement and salary were not even offered, because the payoff to the student was deemed too low to warrant the investment.

Second, these institutions typically focused on just a few programs that were carefully "packaged," ensuring that students would enroll in the right courses in the right semesters. Fewer false starts allowed students to finish more quickly. Their community college counterparts largely relied on other students to navigate course offerings and requirements on their own. Finally, the exemplary institutions prepared students for the job search, with résumé writing and interview skills workshops and job fairs. Students were guaranteed placement assistance, aided by the long-term relationships these institutions had often garnered with employers who had come to trust the schools' "products."

Another impediment to degree completion at community colleges is remedial education. The majority of new students fail college remedial exams, many after having passed high school exit exams just three months earlier.[83] Given the lackluster quality of the primary and secondary educations received by many disadvantaged youth in our nation, community colleges must make up for those deficits, but the task cannot usually be accomplished in a single semester. Like many students in the community colleges studied by Rosenbaum and his colleagues, Jackson, Annmarie, and a number of others in our study dropped out of community college because they were put in remedial math and writing courses that did not count toward their degree. To avoid this pitfall, the State of Florida administers the college placement test to high school juniors so that they can be assigned course work to address their skill gaps in their senior year.[84] New evidence from California suggests that early assessment programs such as this can significantly reduce students' need for remediation.[85]

For students who are not bachelor's-degree bound, there are other viable options at the sub-baccalaureate level. More community colleges are offering applied associate's degrees in growing fields like health care and technology. Dental assistants can earn up to $40,000 a year, and radiology technicians command close to $50,000 a year.[86] However, many of these programs are competitive, and youth who do not place well in math and writing may have a hard time gaining admission.[87] Alternatively, occupational certificates have the advantage of getting youth out into the workplace more quickly than four-year colleges, and at much less cost than for-profit trade schools charge. However, most of the certifications that our youth pursued in community college—usually as certified nursing assistants or phlebotomists—do not pay nearly as well. Many of these occupations, in fact, fail to pay a living wage.

For-Profit Trade Schools   As we've shown, a for-profit trade school was the modal option among the youth we studied. The narratives of those who enrolled in these institutions were riddled with examples of programs either not completed or, for graduates, jobs that bore little resemblance to the smiling employee in the well-crafted television ad; moreover, most left these programs with a large load of debt.[88] How can we improve these institutions so that they provide a launching pad for low-income young adults seeking a way out of poverty?

For-profit schools commanded less than 1 percent of the market in 1967, but roughly 12 percent by 2011.[89] More so than public institutions, or even private colleges and universities, for-profit institutions aggressively market their programs to prospective students. Youth like ours are often their target: in 2008 the average family income for students at for-profit colleges was just under $23,000, about half that of families of students at state colleges and universities, and only about one-third of the family incomes of those at private four-year schools.[90] A profit motive may drive these schools to deliver a high-value product, and do so efficiently,[91] but it might also motivate some to encourage students to max out on grants and loans without a full understanding of the terms involved—loans that must be repaid even if they do not complete the program.[92] Perhaps for this reason, students at for-profit institutions take out more loans (and end up paying more out of pocket) on average than students at public two- or even four-year schools.[93] Furthermore, students at for-profits—especially those in the shortest programs—have higher loan balances than students in other types of postsecondary institutions. Not surprisingly, they also have lower repayment rates and higher default rates.[94]

The practices of the "exemplar" private occupational colleges that Rosenbaum and his colleagues document in *After Admission* could go a long way in improving outcomes for youth who attend trade schools too.[95] It is critical, however, that these schools be held accountable. In 2015 the Department of Education implemented new regulations to protect students at for-profit trade schools from becoming saddled with debt they cannot repay. Known as the "gainful employment" rule, these regulations require these schools to improve their graduation and job placement rates in order to continue to receive federal student aid. According to former U.S. secretary of education Arne Duncan, "Career colleges must be a stepping stone to the middle class. But too many hard-working students find themselves buried in debt with little to show for it. That is simply unacceptable."[96] The law requires these institutions to prepare students for "gainful employment in a recognized occupation."[97] Under the new regulations, a for-profit program meets the gainful employment requirements if its graduates have annual loan payments that are less than 8 percent of their total earnings. The law does nothing to address the problem of noncompletion, yet the array of degree programs offered and the experiences of graduates may well improve under these regulations.

Work

For those who cannot earn a bachelor's degree, we must shore up the labor market. The weakening of unions, offshoring, and technological changes in skills that reward those with a college degree have dampened the prospects of unskilled and semiskilled workers.[98] Expanding the Earned Income Tax Credit (EITC) (a tax credit toward the incomes of low-wage workers, especially those with dependent children) by including non-custodial parents and those who are not yet parents is one way to make work pay, as is increasing the minimum wage. But a focus on work conditions—especially involuntary part-time employment and unpredictable hours—is an even more fundamental need. In their 2015 book *$2 a Day*, Edin and Schaefer advocate for a dramatic expansion of work opportunity for our nation's most-disadvantaged citizens and advocate for both private- and public-sector solutions.[99]

Apprenticeship programs provide another approach.[100] In 2015 the U.S. Department of Labor distributed $175 million to forty-six programs that plan to train more than thirty-four thousand new apprentices over the next five years in manufacturing, health care, information technology, and other high-growth fields. OpenTech in Los Angeles is designed to train "at-risk" youth for jobs in biotechnology and other high-growth technology fields. A consortium in Nevada will create apprenticeships in advanced manufacturing, gaming technology, and electronic cars.[101] Philadelphia Works has designed a curriculum to bolster literacy and math skills to prepare youth from underperforming schools for careers in information technology and behavioral health.[102] More innovation, along with rigorous evaluation, should be focused in this area.

CONCLUSION

The research record is clear: giving poor families of color the opportunity to live in lower-poverty neighborhoods through the demolition of distressed public housing, the use of mobility programs, or the expansion of the supply of affordable units in middle-income suburbs can make a world of difference. Since the *Brown v. Board of Education* decision, rendered in 1954, our nation has avowed that separate is not equal.

But racial and economic segregation does more than just prevent families from access to the geography of opportunity. It also breeds an even more insidious psychology than "out of sight, out of mind"—it leaves people of all incomes vulnerable to poor sources of information about those who are at a different place on the income spectrum or a different racial group than they are. Daniel Kahneman, the Nobel Prize–winning psychologist and author of *Thinking Fast and Slow*, has identified different thinking. The brain's default is to think fast—what Kahneman calls "System I" thinking. System I is "hopelessly bad at the kind of statistical thinking often required for good decisions, it jumps wildly to conclusions and it's subject to a fantastic suite of irrational biases and interference effects," writes Galen Strawman, who reviewed the book for *The Guardian*.[103]

System I thinking suffers from what Kahneman calls "denominator neglect." In Kahneman's words: "If your attention is drawn to the winning marbles, you do not assess the number of non-winning marbles with the same care."[104] System I also falls prey to what Kahneman and his longtime collaborator Amos Tversky call the "availability heuristic," a mental short-cut people take when judging the probability of events, drawing on what examples most easily come to mind.[105] "Availability" can be influenced by the emotional power of examples—ones that are especially lurid or inspiring. Taken together, denominator neglect and the availability heuristic can lead to "gross exaggeration of minor threats, sometimes with important consequences," writes Kahneman.[106]

So what does this have to do with segregation? Building on Kahneman, it is reasonable to expect that affluent folk who lack meaningful personal contact with low-income minority youth may be more likely to render judgments based on poor sources of information. The shocking story on TV or in print has more play if we cannot easily draw on counterexamples from our experience. Meanwhile, what is "available" to middle-class Americans is fed by what has become a veritable industry seemingly devoted to presenting low-income black children in the city as alien. Most of the time, when poor African American youth are portrayed on TV, in movies, in news stories, and even in some ethnographic accounts, they are not portrayed as "our kids," to draw again on Robert Putnam's terminology. Instead, they are depicted as "risky" kids whose lives and perspectives are so different from our own that we cannot imagine sending our children to the same school with them, much less choosing to live on the same block.[107] These outliers command our attention, and we fail to attend to all of the other cases that do not fit the pattern.

We drew a sample of youth from the poorest neighborhoods of Baltimore and followed them over time. Most of the communities they had resided in were geographically isolated from the eyes of those in the middle and upper classes, for whom it is easy to forget about those who struggle in poverty or overgeneralize about how different "they" are from "us." Yet our study revealed not how aberrant but, poignantly, how ordinary most of these young people were, even down to Ron and Whitney, two teens who sold drugs.

Ultimately, however, we believe that what research can accomplish is only a start. Americans have to see disadvantage for themselves, in their own backyard. Unfortunately, as income inequality has grown, so too has our propensity to live, work, worship, and socialize separately. In 2009 one-third of American families lived in either the poorest neighborhoods or the most affluent neighborhoods—those on opposite extremes of the continuum. This was twice the proportion of families who lived on the extreme ends of the distribution in 1970, and the trend indicates that we are witnessing a growth in geographic segregation by income that mirrors the growth in income inequality. In fact, the income inequality of a given metropolitan area is highly correlated with how separated the rich and the poor are in that area.[108] This seemingly inexorable trend makes it even more imperative that we prioritize policy tools to push back. We feel there is real power in this idea that, as Kahneman argues, firsthand experiences are more "available" for making decisions than things we think only happen to others.

We hope that this book has made the clear case that we cannot afford to squander the potential of the young people who hail from America's most-disadvantaged communities. Unfortunately, many Americans see policy as a zero-sum game. They think that if someone else's kids are getting SNAP, a housing subsidy, or a subsidized summer job, their kids are losing. But here we have argued that if "those kids" do not become "our kids," everybody loses. Many of "those kids" are an essential part of our lives—when a doctor orders important lab tests, they are the ones taking your blood. They are preparing your fast-food meals at the airport while you rush to catch a plane. They are tending to your elderly and sick family members at retirement communities and in hospitals.

We have the power to help these youth achieve their modest goals and even more. And we know enough about what works to proceed. Writing on MTO and other proven interventions on June 3, 2015, *New York Times* columnist Thomas Edsall wrote:

> The modest but genuine success of the most fully conceived programs of this nature [like MTO] suggests that a disadvantaged class marked by test scores at the bottom of the ability distribution is not inevitable. Instead, the question of what to do becomes a political issue about the distribution of resources—both private and public—and, above all, about the will of the electorate.[109]

On April 27, 2015, Americans were riveted to their TVs as people looted and burned a CVS, robbed liquor stores, and set cars ablaze. Before the unrest, the image of Baltimore that came most easily to mind for many were the TV serials *The Wire, The Corner,* or the multipart National Geographic special report "Baltimore Is the U.S. Heroin Capital," broadcast in August 2014, with similar coverage in dozens of other leading news outlets.[110] Middle-class Americans who are less and less likely to live near and interact with those who are poor see these slivers of life in Baltimore and think of the city and the people who live there—even the young people—as a lost cause—or worse, as threats. These images are far from representative. Yet if Kahneman's research is any guide, few of us question the source of our information—we do not think about the empirical reality of "base rates" and we practice "denominator neglect." If the story is vivid, coherent, and easy to believe, we assume it is the norm.

Antonio, the proud security guard we introduced in chapter 2, told us that he hoped sharing his story would go far beyond our interview and effect real change. The last time we spoke, he said: "I want you to understand that this isn't [just] about the life of [Antonio]. This is about the life of young, black people . . . a lot of young black people. . . . Whatever you all are trying to do, if it can grow and get a message out there, if it can cause some kind of change, that would be wonderful."

Kahneman also tells us that offering people statistics that disagree with their preexisting beliefs does little to change their beliefs—they do not tend to apply that information. Instead, stories are what they remember, and draw on, when deciding what to think and how to act. If this is true, perhaps the story that Antonio shared, along with the stories of 149 other Baltimore youth, will have the power to help bridge the divide between the two Americas.

Appendix A | Study History and Methodology

THE ORIGINS OF MOVING TO OPPORTUNITY

In the early 1990s, many public housing projects had become war zones in American cities. By then, nearly everyone had concurred with the historian Arnold Hirsch's charge that federal housing policy had merely remade the ghetto and that many of these housing projects were incubators for the social ills they sought to alleviate.[1] In few places was this truer than in Baltimore. As we noted in chapter 2, a significant portion of the city's neighborhoods with poverty rates of 40 percent or more were dominated by public housing almost entirely populated by African Americans, including four clusters of high-rise towers. While some within these developments created supportive networks of relatives and friends, life was also fraught with fear and trauma, according to those in our study. The deteriorating physical conditions of the buildings added additional stress and risk.

The U.S. Department of Housing and Urban Development and local housing authorities implemented a variety of policies to reduce concentrated poverty, including the demolition of the worst public housing stock while "vouchering out" at least a portion of those who were displaced (the rest were assigned to other public housing) and the rehabilitation of other complexes. The HOPE VI program funded much of the demolition and subsequent redevelopment of public housing. As a consequence, most of the projects that the youth in our sample originally hailed from are no longer standing.

Around the same time that HUD was implementing HOPE VI, another approach to reducing concentrated poverty emerged, one with roots that went all the way back to the remedy from a Supreme Court case brought on behalf of a Chicago Housing Authority (CHA) tenant, Dorothy Gau-

202

treaux, in the 1960s. Her lawyers had argued that by placing practically all public housing in heavily black neighborhoods, the CHA had denied African Americans the opportunity to enter white neighborhoods via subsidized housing. This had served to segregate low-income African Americans in the city's worst neighborhoods, in violation of the Equal Protection Clause of the Fourteenth Amendment and the Civil Rights Act. In 1976 the Supreme Court ruled that HUD could be required to provide a Section 8 voucher–based remedy that could be metropolitan in scope.[2] Part of that remedy was the Gautreaux program, which would move thousands of black Chicago public housing residents and applicants out of the projects and into the private market through a special voucher—one that could only be used to lease up in a neighborhood that met strict race criteria: no more than 30 percent African American. The program proved so popular that when CHA announced that applications were being received, traffic was shut down in Chicago's Loop owing to the press of CHA tenants who wanted to get in line.[3]

James Rosenbaum decided to study some of the participating families to see how the program affected their lives. In his eyes, it was an incredible opportunity to learn about the impact that neighborhoods could have on the lives of families and children. But the Gautreaux Program, as it came to be known, was not a random assignment experiment—it was a legal remedy not designed with research in mind.[4] However, Rosenbaum soon learned that there was quite a lot of variation in the kinds of neighborhoods to which Gautreaux families moved. Some found units within "revitalized" areas of the city, while others moved to the mostly white suburbs. In both cases, families would leave the projects, but the city and suburban locales to which they moved were quite different in a number of other ways. Not only were the suburbs generally whiter, but they typically had better schools, safer streets, and additional amenities.[5] Rosenbaum and his colleagues (who later included Stefanie DeLuca) used a quasi-experimental approach to examine whether the suburban movers benefited over and above those who remained in the city.[6]

By 1992, *Newsweek, 60 Minutes, Good Morning America,* and even *The Phil Donahue Show* were applauding the "stunning" results from the Gautreaux Program. The *New York Times* went so far as to call it "a modest variation on the Underground Railroad."[7] Rosenbaum's research had shown that children who moved through Gautreaux to the suburbs of Chicago were four times more likely to graduate from high school and twice as likely to attend college compared with their peers who remained in the city.[8] Parents also got more education, were more likely to hold jobs, and earned more. And so, when policymakers sought a solution for the problems spawned by the concentration of poverty and racial segregation that had been fueled by the construction of public housing across the nation, they looked to Gautreaux.

At the urging of one of the civil rights attorneys who litigated the Gautreaux case, Alex Polikoff, HUD launched an ambitious housing mobility demonstration in five cities that replicated some aspects of Gautreaux. This time the program's architects decided to impose a "gold standard" experimental design, randomly assigning applicants to experimental and control groups. Beyond the experimental design, MTO would differ in one other key way from the Gautreaux Program: instead of requiring families to lease up in a neighborhood that fit certain racial criteria, MTO's rules would require that families lease up in a neighborhood that was less than 10 percent poor. Families living in what were deemed "highly distressed" public housing developments in Baltimore, Boston, Chicago, New York, and Los Angeles were offered the chance to sign up for MTO.

In all five cities, families flocked to the program, just as they had in the case of Gautreaux in Chicago. In Baltimore, the parents of the 150 fifteen- to twenty-four-year-olds whose stories we have featured here were among the more than 600 families who signed up for the program and met the criteria for inclusion. Once vetted for eligibility, families were randomly assigned to a control group, an experimental group, and a group of families who received a voucher exactly like those given out by housing authorities all over the country (with no geographic restrictions), called the "Section 8" voucher group. Those in the experimental group had to move to a neighborhood where fewer than 10 percent of the residents were living below the poverty line and remain there for at least a year or forfeit their voucher.

In 2002 a team of economists conducted an interim impact evaluation— a survey of 4,248 participant households. As outlined in chapter 2, after comparing the outcomes of the experimentals relative to the controls, the results were both disappointing and puzzling. Given the results of the Gautreaux Program, policymakers and social scientists had anticipated that more of the adults in the experimental group would be employed and that children and adolescents would be doing better in school. None of these results materialized.[9] Moreover, there were no a priori reasons to expect gender differences in the impact of the experiment on children, yet it turned out that girls in the experimental group were benefiting much more, in terms of improved mental health and reduced risk behaviors, than boys. In fact, some analyses suggested that boys in the experimental group were engaging in more risk behaviors than those in the control group.[10] There were also significant positive effects—mothers enjoyed gains in mental health on par with standard antidepressant therapies and treatments, and they were much less likely to be obese.[11] Still, the results of the MTO experiment were not what its architects had hoped.

In 2002 Kathryn Edin was approached by Jeffrey Kling, then an economist at Princeton and a driving force behind the Moving to Opportunity interim survey, about the possibility of conducting in-depth qualitative interviews with a subsample of survey respondents from the MTO interim evaluation. The survey team had underspent their budget, so Kling wished to redeploy funds awarded by the Russell Sage Foundation to better understand the surprising results of the interim evaluation by gathering qualitative data from participants, and the foundation had agreed.

Kling believed in the value of qualitative research. He, together with the Harvard economists Lawrence Katz and Jeffrey Liebman, two of his collaborators on the MTO study, had conducted and published a small qualitative study in advance of the interim survey, a rare move for three economists.[12] It was this research, with families who were part of the MTO demonstration in Boston, that had convinced Kling and his collaborators to add measures of physical and mental health to the interim survey—outcomes neither they nor HUD, which oversaw and facilitated their work, had considered including before. The decision proved prescient—lower rates of obesity and better mental health were the only significant gains for those in the experimental group identified in the interim study.

MTOQ5: 2003–2004

MTOQ5—our shorthand for the first wave of our Moving to Opportunity qualitative study, conducted six to ten years after random assignment—was launched in 2003 and led by Edin, Kling, and Greg Duncan, another of Kling's co–principal investigators and a colleague of Edin's at Northwestern University. Edin, Duncan, and Kling specifically designed MTOQ5 to identify mechanisms that might explain the lack of results on educational achievement and economic self-sufficiency, along with the surprising results of benefits for girls and detriments for boys. They decided to deploy the study in two of the five MTO cities, Baltimore and Chicago, because these cities showed the greatest contrast between the poverty rate in the origin neighborhoods and the neighborhoods where households moved through MTO.[13]

Edin and Duncan ran the Chicago portion of the study with the assistance of several talented graduate students and professional staff. Kling supervised the Baltimore portion of the study, recruiting two new PhDs to join the study as postdoctoral fellows at Princeton, Susan Clampet-Lundquist and Rebecca Joyce Kissane. Stefanie DeLuca, then a new assistant professor at Johns Hopkins, and Annette Waters, who had just completed her PhD in sociology at the University of Maryland, also joined the Baltimore team. Alessandra Del Conte Dickovick, who held a master's degree in public policy from the Woodrow Wilson School at Princeton, coordinated the logistics of the research team in Baltimore and helped conduct interviews and school observations. We launched the study in July 2003 and remained in the field for a year.[14]

In each city, research participants were recruited from a random, stratified subsample of households who had participated in MTO. On the recommendation of Duncan, an expert in child development, the team restricted their sample to households of parents with children at two different developmental periods—middle childhood (eight to thirteen) and adolescence (fourteen to nineteen).[15] As already noted, MTO had three treatment arms—a control group, an experimental group, and a group that received a standard Section 8 voucher with no geographical restrictions. Because the researchers were primarily interested in the contrast between control group members and experimental households that had received the special MTO voucher, which could only be used to lease up in a neighborhood that was less than 10 percent poor, they selected fewer households from the Section 8 group than from the others.

In the Baltimore site—the focus of this volume—the team drew a sample of 149 households and ended up interviewing 124 parents (a response rate of 80 percent), plus 15 primary caregivers (added when a parent lost custody of the focal child or died).[16] In ten cases, we interviewed two adults connected to the same child. We engaged in one or more in-depth conversations with each parent or caregiver, asking them about their own life experiences and their children's as well—and specifically the child who had been designated a focal child (between ages eight and thirteen) or a focal youth (between ages fourteen and nineteen). Parents were asked to describe these children's daily routines, any struggles or risk behaviors, their friends, their school performance, and so on. We also conducted in-depth interviews with 83 of the adolescents from the 112 sampled, a response rate of 74 percent.[17]

With both the adults and the youth, interviews were conducted in a private place to ensure confidentiality and to facilitate rapport. Parents and youth were asked to choose a convenient time and a comfortable place for the interview, and most chose their homes.[18] After they left each interview, interviewers tape-recorded their answers to a series of questions that addressed the neighborhood and home environment, described the respondent, and summarized the key points of the interview. In addition, they filled out a template (see appendix B) that detailed parent employment and education and children's schooling and behavior. Our conversations with adults usually ran more than two hours, with a handful lasting four to five hours. Sometimes we had to come back a second time to complete the interview. Interviews with adolescents were typically shorter, with few exceeding two hours. Parents and youth were often interviewed at the same time in separate locations in the home. All participants were compensated for their time.

Given the surprising absence of academic achievement differences in the interim survey, the MTOQ5 team had a strong interest in understanding the younger children's experiences in school. Although we did not interview the focal children (the eight- to thirteen-year-olds), we observed nearly eighty classrooms of a subsample of forty in a reading or math class and interviewed one of each child's teachers (a math or language arts teacher). Most of Baltimore's MTO youth had remained within the Baltimore City Public Schools (BCPSS), even many of those whose parents had originally moved to the suburbs.[19] BCPSS granted us permission to conduct research in the schools.[20] Some of our observational data appear in this book, as fifteen of those we observed in the 2003 wave were also interviewed in 2010 during a second wave of in-depth interviews.

After analyzing these interviews and observations, we, along with other colleagues who worked on the project—Greg Duncan, Jeffrey Kling, Rebecca Kissane, and Kristin Turney—wrote a number of academic papers offering answers to various mysteries in the survey results.[21] We found that living in low-poverty neighborhoods did not provide a helpful boost to employment for adults, as their more affluent neighbors were not good sources for the kinds of entry-level jobs they were seeking, mostly in retail and health care. Moving away from the city also added transportation barriers to work.[22] As for the disappointing academic achievement results, we found that most parents kept their children in the same struggling school districts that they had been in before the experiment began, sometimes even the same schools, owing to fears that changing schools would be disruptive.[23] Thus, MTO had little impact on school quality on average.[24] The gender differences were due, in part, to the ease with which female teens fit into their new neighborhood environments and their adherence to daily routines that kept them closer to supervising adults or out of risky neighborhood situations altogether. Boys, on the other hand, were often the target of unwarranted attention by the police as their dress and behavior marked them as outsiders. They also lost access to crucial male role models, especially maternal uncles.[25]

THE 2006 PILOT STUDY FOR MTOQ10

Two years after we had completed the 2003–2004 interviews, the William T. Grant Foundation awarded us a small grant to conduct a pilot wave of interviews in Baltimore in preparation for the 2010 wave, where we planned to observe youth at an older stage—during the transition to adulthood. DeLuca, Clampet-Lundquist, and graduate students from the University of Pennsylvania and Temple University conducted interviews with sixteen parents and twelve older adolescents who had participated in MTOQ5. In these interviews, they piloted the questions about the transition to adulthood that we then deployed in MTOQ10. Because we focused on youth who had been zero to ten at the time of random assignment in 2010, only two of the youth who were interviewed in 2006 also ended up in the MTOQ10 sample, along with the siblings of another three youth.

MTOQ10: 2010

With additional funding from the William T. Grant Foundation, the authors of this volume launched MTOQ10 in July 2010 along with: University of Pennsylvania postdoctoral researcher Melody Boyd; project manager Gretchen Wright; a team of graduate students drawn from Harvard (Megan Holland, Carly Knight, Eva Rosen, Tracy Shollenberger, Jacqueline Hwang, and Queenie Zhu), St. Joseph's University (Bridget Davis), and Johns Hopkins (Peter Rosenblatt, Barbara Condliffe, and Siri Warkentien); two Johns Hopkins undergraduates (Kathryn Mercogliano and Tanya Lukasik); and one high school student (Marisa Edin-Nelson).[26] As was true in the 2003–2004 wave, our interviews followed closely on the heels of the second survey wave, the MTO final evaluation, led by Jens Ludwig and Larry Katz and completed in 2009. This time we drew a stratified random sample of 200 youth from the survey who had been ages zero to ten at random assignment and were fifteen to twenty-four in 2010 (see table A1). We oversampled older youth—ages nineteen to twenty-four—and youth in the experimental group whose parents had "complied" (moved using their voucher). We interviewed 150 of these youth, a response rate of 75 percent (see table A2).

To examine whether the youth we did not interview differed from those who participated, we cross-walked the data from our sample with data from the MTO final evaluation survey, in which these youth had participated in 2009. We observed no differences between the respondents and nonrespondents in terms of gender, employment (as measured in the previous week), delinquent or risky behaviors, age, or the poverty rate of

Table A1   MTOQ10 Sample

	Age Fifteen to Eighteen		Age Nineteen to Twenty-Four		
	F	M	F	M	Total
Experimental compliers	15	15	29	29	88
Experimental noncompliers	7	7	14	14	42
Controls	11	11	24	24	70
Total	33	33	67	67	200

Source: MTOQ10 Qualitative Study.

Table A2   MTOQ10 Respondents

	Age Fifteen to Eighteen		Age Nineteen to Twenty-Four		
	Female	Male	Female	Male	Total
Experimental compliers	11	10	20	25	66
Experimental noncompliers	5	6	11	9	31
Controls	9	6	18	20	53
Total	25	22	49	54	150

Source: MTOQ10 Qualitative Study

their current neighborhood. Respondents in our study were slightly more likely to report that a member of their household had been victimized in the past six months than were those in the survey, and female nonrespondents were somewhat more likely to have gotten pregnant. The differences were not statistically significant in either case.

In 2010 our research team was largely female and white, though it also included one white male, one African American female, one Puerto Rican female, and two women of Asian descent. All interviewers had significant prior experience working with disadvantaged populations, either as researchers or volunteers or through programs in disadvantaged communities and schools such as Teach for America. Per our agreement with HUD, which oversaw our efforts, each researcher was given contact information for only five respondents at a time. All identifying information was kept in a locked cabinet inside a locked office, as required by the Homewood Institutional Review Board at Johns Hopkins University. As an extra precaution, we obtained a Certificate of Confidentiality from the National Institutes of Health (NIH), which offers legal protection in cases where prosecutors might try to subpoena research files. All names used in any publication, as well as the names of other individuals mentioned in interviews, plus all K-12 schools, retail stores, or other places of employment, have been changed.[27]

Recontacting youth a year after the survey team had found them was not always easy, particularly given the high rate of residential mobility among the households in the survey. First, we sent a letter to their 2009 addresses, asking the youth to call if they were interested in participating and noting that they would receive a $50 compensation. We soon received a flurry of calls. We called those who did not respond using the phone numbers given in 2009. When neither of these methods worked, we visited the 2009 address and knocked on the door. If no one answered, sometimes we were able to get information from neighbors about whether the family still lived there and, if not, where they might be living now.[28] If that failed, we got in touch with the two or three people they had listed as contacts when completing the survey—parents, siblings, grandmothers, aunts, and uncles—and searched for them online via Lexis-Nexis.

In the 2010 wave, we were less focused on understanding results from the survey and concentrated instead on explaining variation in young people's trajectories as they moved into adulthood. We explored five domains: education, employment, family formation, risk behaviors, and mental and physical health. Our primary goal was to explore a critical point in the life course—the transition to adulthood—for young people from very disadvantaged origins, a demographic group that the research on the subject had largely ignored.

To ensure that we gathered consistent information from each youth, interview conversations covered a predetermined set of topics. However, as had been true in the earlier interview wave, the phrasing of the questions was broad and open-ended. We drew out the details we were seeking in the course of the conversations through skillful probing, not usually via direct queries, such as those used in surveys. Right from the start, we needed to signal to these youth that our interaction would be very different from the MTO survey, which was still fresh in many participants' minds. To this end, we began each conversation in 2010 with the question: "Tell me the story of your life." As each youth's narrative unfolded, we would follow his or her lead, exploring each of the five domains of interest as they arose in the conversation rather than following a prescribed order.

As a result, our interactions with these youth resembled free-flowing exchanges more than short questions and answers elicited from a structured guide. Whenever possible, we would ask youth to give us specific examples when they made general statements. For example, if a respondent told us that her neighborhood was not safe, we might say, "Describe what happened the last time you felt unsafe in the neighborhood," instructing her to "tell me the whole story from start to finish" or to "tell me more about that." Following the advice of the sociologist Howard S. Becker (Edin's qualitative methods teacher at Northwestern), we trained interviewers to phrase questions in a particular way.[29] Rather than ask questions beginning with *why* (for example, "Why did you decide to go to community college rather than a four-year school?"), which invites general statements and justifications, we asked questions beginning with *how* ("Tell me the whole story of how you ended up at community college"), which elicits stories of process in which experiences, thoughts, and actions are usually described in sequential order. Sequential order can be very useful in the analysis phase as researchers try to assess whether it is plausible that one event might be the cause of another, or how one event or action relates to the next. Furthermore, to elicit as much narrative as possible, we trained interviewers to avoid phrasing their questions in ways that they could be answered with a single word (such as "yes" or "no"). For example, rather than ask, "Do you like school?" an interviewer might say, "Tell me how you feel about school," or, "What is the best thing about your school? Tell me more about that," following up with, "Now how about the worst thing?"

In the 2010 wave, interviews typically lasted from ninety minutes to three hours and were also conducted at a place and time of participants' choosing—usually at the young person's home. As in earlier rounds, with their permission, interviews were recorded and transcribed verbatim, with an ID number but no name attached to the file. Interviewers again completed detailed field notes using a proscribed template (see appendix B) after each interview. Both interviews and field notes were then uploaded into Atlas.ti, a qualitative analysis software program, for coding and analysis. In consultation with the principal investigators (Edin, Clampet-Lundquist, and DeLuca), postdoctoral researcher Melody Boyd developed a codebook based on the questions in the interview guide and on themes that emerged inductively from open-ended questions. For example, deductive codes included SCHOOL ACTIVITIES or TRAINING PROGRAM. Inductive codes included TURNING POINT or HOPELESS-NESS. Team members met at least weekly to resolve queries about specific cases and maintain consistency in how codes were being applied. Boyd recoded one-third of the interviews at random to ensure that codes were being applied correctly.

In general, the codes used at this initial stage were fairly broad, incorporating all of the text that related to that specific theme, regardless of what question the text was in response to or whether the text was also included in other codes. But a second stage of coding was required as well.

This was the process we engaged in for the analyses in this book and for papers using these interview data. For this secondary coding, we took the text captured in a given code or group of codes and systematically looked for patterns in the data.

THE IDENTITY PROJECT ANALYSIS

Some of our analysis for the identity project was inspired by the findings from a book chapter titled "I Do Me: Young Black Men and the Struggle to Resist the Streets" by Peter Rosenblatt, Kathy Edin, and Queenie Zhu. Analyzing a subsample of the males interviewed for MTOQ10, they found that many young men talked about drawing a "bright line" between what they were about and what they saw in the streets around them.[30] This concept resonated with what we were seeing in the sample as a whole, and we set out to test whether the pattern held for young women as well, how it developed, and how it worked. Our next step was to search for evidence of identity projects in a systematic way across the sample. We examined codes such as FUTURE PLANS, JOB MEANING, IMPORTANT ADULTS, ADULTHOOD, and TURNING POINTS for each respondent. We then created an analysis template with themes emerging from the codes such as "What Does She/He Want to Be About," "Survival Strategies," and "Key People Who Made a Difference" to fill in information from these data.

With three graduate students, we analyzed the data after completing the templates. We looked for activities, interests, hobbies, passions, institutional relationships, and key adults who seemed to matter to youth in such a way as to keep them motivated and to stay on track. We noted how youth described what they were passionate about ("Wanna see my birds?"), what they were known for ("I'm really into school"), and how they saw themselves ("I'm a working man"). We then explored whether these identities were connected to concrete activities, peer groups, and institutions; when they developed; and how they operated in the lives of each youth (we detail this in chapter 3).

HOW WE USED DATA FROM MTOQ5, THE 2006 PILOT STUDY, AND MTOQ10

As noted in chapter 1, one particularly rich feature of the data is that there is significant overlap in interviews and observations among family members across waves. Although this does not constitute a panel study, there is enough overlap across waves to allow for some intergenerational and longitudinal analysis. This allowed us to incorporate data from some of the parents and siblings of our youth. We also drew on the school observations and teacher interviews conducted in 2003–2004 in some cases.

THE ETHNOGRAPHIC STUDY: 2012–2013

In 2012 we launched the ethnographic phase of the study, identifying twenty youth for follow-up who represented the range of outcomes we had observed in the 2010 interviews. Some had been high fliers in high school, and others were floundering after dropping out or getting caught up in the street. A team of graduate students from Johns Hopkins University (those previously mentioned plus Phil Garboden, Anna Rhodes, and Elizabeth Talbert) followed these youth for about a year. This portion of the study was directed by postdoctoral researcher Jennifer Darrah. Darrah's team began by conducting a follow-up interview tailored to a youth's individual situation (as gleaned from previous interviews). The team then arranged for at least one "hang-out." These informal interactions at a place and time of the youths' choosing occurred at their home, at the mall, at a restaurant, or the park; on a drive around the neighborhood or during a visit to an ice cream shop; and, in one case, on a paddleboat ride in the Inner Harbor. In some cases, we also accompanied the youth to important events, such as a court hearing, an eviction, or a move into a first apartment. As noted in chapter 1, the frequency and length of these interactions varied according to the willingness and availability of the youth. All of these youth completed the interview plus at least one informal interaction. In eleven cases we met the goal of completing at least one additional unstructured observation, and in seven cases we exceeded that goal, with multiple informal interactions.

THE QUANTITATIVE ANALYSES

Since the study began in 2003, our efforts have benefited from a close relationship with those at HUD who oversaw the MTO demonstration and the economists who designed and implemented the interim and final evaluation surveys, particularly Jeffrey Kling and Greg Duncan, who have coauthored several of the key articles that have emerged from our larger body of work. For this book, HUD granted access to our youths' survey responses (we provided justification for each item requested). Our various publications have drawn on the data in a number of ways, but in this book we have mainly relied on items that describe the census tracts that youth reported residing in between random assignment and 2009.[31] We have used the data both descriptively, as part of the case studies embedded in our narrative, and analytically to measure each youth's exposure to concentrated poverty or to a low-poverty or majority-white community. All of the maps and some of the tables in chapter 2 are based on these data, for example, along with several of the tables in other chapters.

Because our sample is rather large, at least for a qualitative study, and was selected through stratified random sampling (see tables A1 and A2), we felt it would be useful to conduct rudimentary quantitative analyses. Whenever possible, we deployed this technique as a check on the face validity of claims we were making based on our qualitative analysis. For example, in chapter 3 we conducted logistic regression analyses to determine whether having a DIY identity project or an institutionally supported identity project seemed to matter more for predicting whether she was "on track." In chapter 4, we conducted simple logistic regressions to examine whether there was at least suggestive evidence for the relationship between the presence or absence of an identity project and having been "ever in the street," controlling for age and sex. This analysis bolstered our claim that identity projects might be protective and was significant at the 0.05 level, despite the small sample size. However, when we looked to see whether there was similar evidence that having experienced trauma in the family of origin or years-long exposure to neighborhoods more than 30 percent poor would inhibit youths' ability to form an identity project, holding constant age and sex, we found no significant relationship, though exposure to trauma and poverty were related to the probability of being "ever in the street" at a 0.10 level, as we showed in chapter 4.

TEAM RESEARCH

One hallmark of qualitative research—perhaps especially ethnography—is that it is often carried out by a lone researcher who conducts not only all fieldwork but the analysis as well. In contrast, this book reflects a group effort. Over the course of the ten years we were in the field—between 2003 and 2013—over forty individuals were involved, including graduate students, undergraduates, postdoctoral researchers, professional staff, and faculty collaborators (see the acknowledgments). Together we recruited participants, conducted interviews, and wrote field notes; logged, transcribed, de-identified, coded, and analyzed data; and wrote and edited papers. We also shared chapters of this book for feedback from others on the team, some of whom knew certain aspects of the data better than we did.

Teamwork was woven into all aspects of the project. For example, we often interviewed in pairs. This was done in part for safety reasons, but also because it was easier for one person to drive while the other navigated, called a youth to let him know we were on our way, or began writing the field notes on the return trip home. The primary reason for interviewing in pairs, however, was that it improved the quality of the data. We have all watched each other conduct interviews and given feedback on how it could have been done better or what was missed. We debriefed as a team on a weekly (sometimes daily) basis, talking about the week's interviews, what we noticed, what surprised us, and what patterns we were observing. For instance, was there something in the interview guide that needed updating because of recent events? Did the team understand the terminology that youth used when describing their sexual or romantic relationships?

An additional advantage to team research is that it is much harder to make a mistake when others—who read and comment on your work—have all been in the same neighborhoods, interviewed others from the same family, and read the same transcripts. Often during the course of writing this book we have been challenged by colleagues who questioned whether a given conclusion is warranted. That kind of feedback sent us back to the drawing board more than a few times.

THE TOOL OF THE IN-DEPTH INTERVIEW

Though this project blends data from surveys, in-depth interviews, and ethnography, the primary tool our study deployed was the in-depth interview. At their best, in-depth interviews can be transcendent. As one person listens intently, without judgment, and another tells her story, everything else can seem to fall away—the sirens outside, the family member who might wander into the kitchen unaware that there is an interview going on, the soft buzzing of a phone set to vibrate mode. In that moment, the interviewer—an outsider—receives a profound gift: an often intense and not infrequently emotional rendition of another person's experiences and worldviews. These narratives reveal some aspects of objective reality, to be sure, but they also capture youths' subjective assessments of what they have been through, how they have come to terms with it, how they made decisions in the face of tough trade-offs, how they negotiated uncertainty, obstacles, and opportunities, and what meaning they have taken from their experiences. Patience, empathy, active listening techniques—such as maintaining eye contact and leaning in—and humor are all vital as an interviewer works to craft the conversational space that allows for what we have come to call the "holy moment"—that instant in the interview when an interviewer and her respondent feel a deep connection and, often, trust. Not all interviews contain such moments, but many do. Ultimately, connections of this depth can only occur when there is profound respect for the research participant and the story he tells. The power relations that govern social life—where the one with the PhD, the white skin, and the middle-class income holds all the cards—must be turned upside down in the interaction as much as possible. The researcher cannot succeed unless she becomes the student and places the respondent in the role of teacher.

In general, conducting fieldwork requires one to maintain a learning stance at all times. When spending time with a young person in his home or out and about in his neighborhood, the researcher experiences first-hand some of what he must deal with each day: the smell emanating from a backed-up sewer that Marcus's mother's landlord hasn't bothered to fix, despite the fact that the basement now has several inches of offal on the floor; the lovely apartment Chantal has moved to with her partner Lisa and their son, with the balcony that lets her keep a watchful eye as he plays outdoors; the daily household traffic in Vicky's home, with a noisy chorus of opening and closing doors. We learn about the deep generosity that low-income people often extend to one another—sacrifices that are sometimes hard for us to imagine making ourselves. We discover the myriad imaginative ways devised by some young people to survive traumatic childhoods and dangerous streets. Identity projects, for example, emerged as a strong theme in many narratives, though we had not anticipated this ahead of time. The technique of asking broad, open-ended questions and then probing for the more specific information as respondents tell their stories has the added advantage of inviting such unanticipated themes to bubble up. Despite our training and command of the existing research, we do not always—or even usually—know the range of possible answers to interview questions or all of the possible ways in which social factors affect the life events we are interested in. The in-depth interview allows us to truly be students of the worlds of the people we talk to.

This study was an attempt to understand the role of context—family, neighborhood, and school—and agency in the lives of young people with highly disadvantaged origins. We have explored the topic using a method that allows us to ask not just *whether* (a question sometimes best left to our colleagues analyzing the MTO survey) but *how* family, neighborhood, and school context matter. The utility of our approach, however, is not merely to document in more detail the mechanics of our research participants' outer worlds. Rather, the in-depth interview allows youth to reveal their inner world—how they see things, what they feel they are "about," how they have made sense of their past and envision their future. Myriad quantitative studies have documented the associations between structural characteristics and the life outcomes of young people living in poverty.

Fewer have explored the inner worlds of youth from disadvantaged origins, or how youths' inner worlds influence how they adapt to their circumstances with varying degrees of agency and aspiration.

By accepting our invitation to "tell me the story of your life"—that very first interview question—we allowed youth to author their stories in their own words, from their own perspective. Yet stories are not merely retellings: as any skilled therapist knows, it is sometimes only in the act of recounting a story that someone gains new insight about her life. As the 2010 conversation with Antonio drew to a close, he confided that the experience had been "like therapy a little bit. . . . You know, I'm sitting here thinking like, 'Yeah, [I] put a lot of things in perspective, I put a lot of things into perspective for myself just talking about it and looking back.'"

IS TALK CHEAP? INTERVIEWS VERSUS ETHNOGRAPHY

Qualitative interview studies also have limitations. Colin Jerolmack and Shamus Khan go so far as to argue that those who conduct in-depth interviews are often guilty of the "attitudinal fallacy," wherein researchers take what respondents say at face value as indicative of their actions. They write: "From interviews alone, we cannot know what actually happens in interaction, but only what people think about situations and how they feel about them."[32] They warn that if researchers do not observe subjects in the midst of social interaction, where that meaning is negotiated, they are left to rely on "socially decontextualized" information. Jerolmack and Kahn argue that ethnography—naturalistic observations of behaviors and interactions—is superior to the in-depth interview method because it avoids this pitfall.[33]

Our response is "both/and." We believe that both methods have advantages and liabilities, but that they are highly complementary and should be combined when possible. Taking participants' statements simply at face value is certainly a mistake; the dangers of the attitudinal fallacy are real. Yet we need not throw the baby out with the bathwater; surely even Jerolmack and Khan would concede that it is silly to claim that humans lack the capacity to describe their thoughts and actions, as well as their interactions, with some meaningful degree of accuracy. Indeed, most human conversations rest on this premise.

The interview techniques we describe earlier in this appendix (some adapted from Howard S. Becker, but others we have stumbled upon on our own) are specifically designed to ensure that the narrative gleaned comes closer to objective reality than it otherwise might. Techniques such as employing "how" and not "why" phrasing when posing a question, pressing for specific detailed examples, and repeatedly encouraging respondents to tell us "the whole story from start to finish" so that incidents are arrayed in sequential order can all help in-depth interviewers avoid the pitfalls outlined by Jerolmack and Kahn. We call our approach "narrative interviewing." The narrative interview rarely employs direct questions about attitudes or meaning-making at all. Instead, as we work to elicit detailed examples of specific events, expressions of attitudes and meanings emerge naturally in the course of rich conversation, tied to recollections of specific events (thus contextualizing them to some degree). Fieldworkers have long held that information that emerges spontaneously, not merely in response to a direct question, has a higher degree of validity.[34]

In-depth interviews are also a way to get around a very thorny problem for ethnographers: many things cannot be directly observed by a researcher, at least not if the researcher follows ethical standards set by institutional review boards. For example, though we have not chosen to focus in this volume on the extensive data we gleaned about our youths' sexual and romantic lives, sex is an example of an interaction that cannot usually be directly observed; nor can the pillow talk that might lead to a decision about whether or not to use contraception.[35] Yet there is no question that data about such matters are valuable, even vital, for researchers to glean.

A second difficult problem for the ethnographer is that not all research participants are available and willing to be observed in the course of their daily routines. Given the frequency with which ethnographers have written about men hanging out at a particular street corner, diner, or takeout restaurant (for example, *Streetcorner Society, A Place on the Corner, Tally's Corner, Slim's Table*), it is probably the case that the method has underrepresented their peers, who instead prefer to spend their leisure at home with their families or hanging out at the library reading books.[36] Of course, no study is perfectly representative, yet by employing standard sampling techniques that allow one to calculate a response rate, and by comparing the demographic characteristics of those sampled to the larger population one is generalizing to, as we have done here, we can at least know something about who is not represented in our study.

Representativeness is usually not attempted by ethnographers because the depth of the observations they employ often restricts their focus to a few individuals, a narrow range of activities, or a single venue. This is why Sudhir Venkatesh focused on the power brokers of the Robert Taylor Homes—the gang leader and tenant council head in *American Project*.[37] Alice Goffman's recounting of the experiences of a few young men whose lives were lived "on the run" allowed limited time to focus on the women in their lives or on the law-abiding members of the community.[38] This is not a criticism; indeed, we applaud the rich tapestry such portraits of the inner city create. But are they typical? As a complement, a systematic, in-depth interview study that follows—to the degree possible—standard sampling procedures to, at the very least, ensure heterogeneity or, at best, representativeness can offer a wider lens on diverse individuals in the community. It should be said that some ethnographies at least partially accomplish this aim, such as Mary Pattillo's classic *Black Picket Fences* and her more recent book, *Black on the Block*.[39] Such an approach can be even more effective if the sample is prospective (rather than sampling on the dependent variable), as we argued in chapter 3.

Even if Jerolmack and Khan's claim—that in-depth interviewers can learn "only what people think about situations and how they feel about them"—is partly true, it does not mean that such data should be dismissed. Indeed, this is precisely part of what makes the in-depth interview method so valuable: its ability to reveal inner worlds. Observations alone offer no direct conduit into people's inner lives, their perceptions, or the meaning-making that is going on beyond overheard conversations. Thus, ethnographers may be in danger of what we have come to call the "observational fallacy," which occurs when researchers *infer* meaning (sometimes based on their own experience) or other aspects of their research participants' inner worlds through observation alone. Imagine that we had merely observed Bob with his Goth garb and chains, listening to the controversial hip-hop duo Insane Clown Posse. We might have taken his dress and musical taste as expressions of rebellion against mainstream society. Yet for Bob, his clothing and music were actually a means to broadcast his opposition to the street. They were meant to be a symbol that he was "not about that," but "about something else."

In the end, it is not productive to argue for the superiority of one method over another. These methods are complementary, not opposed. We advocate both, whenever possible. Yet one need not mount a yearlong ethnographic component, as we have done, to make observations. In reality, in-depth interviewers who conduct their work out in the community and in people's homes are awash in observational data all the time, though they may not collect it systematically, code it, and analyze it. We recommend that in-depth interviewers take careful field notes (rather than relying solely on transcribed interviews) each time they conduct an interview. For an example, see the field note template we used in the 2010 wave of this study, included in appendix B.

Field notes can capture observation of neighborhood interactions, family routines, ad hoc conversations before and after the tape recorder is turned on, and dozens of other valuable bits of information. For example, when we interviewed Alicia the first time, we noted that the apartment was dark because filthy pillowcases had been tacked over the windows for privacy. When asked, she said that she worried that if others could see that someone was home, they might shoot at that person through the window because her brother, presently in jail, was involved in a gang. We also noted that there was little furniture on the main floor of the unit—only a twin mattress on the floor, a soiled couch they had found in the trash, a kitchen table missing a leg, and a single chair. And despite the fact that Alicia had brought her baby home from the hospital just a few weeks before, there was no formula in the home—nor much food of any kind. This was how we learned that there was no cash income of any kind coming into the household, nor had there been for quite some time. Throughout the interview an elderly man was nodding off on the couch, and about halfway through a young boy clad in pajama bottoms emerged from an upstairs room and came downstairs; he settled on the mattress on the floor, which was covered by a worn Bugs Bunny fitted sheet. Both relatives, neither on the lease, were staying there because they had no place else to go at the moment. Via observations like these, recorded in our field notes, we caught a glimpse of how fluid these youths' households often were.

OUR ETHNOGRAPHY

We chose to weave ethnography into our study for two reasons. First, we sought a "validity check" for our interview data, just as Jerolmack and Khan advise. Second, our respondents' lives were quickly unfolding, making it very difficult to accurately guess how things would turn out. To this end, we selected four to five youth who exemplified each of the different paths into adulthood (direct entry into the labor market, in college or trade school, or neither working nor in school), much in the way that Annette Lareau chose her research participants for *Unequal Childhoods*. Moving beyond the interview setting and watching youth navigate and negotiate their outer worlds involved everything from stopping by a greasy spoon with a teenage boy to accompanying a would-be mother to the prenatal clinic for a ultrasound, waiting in line at the welfare office with an economically desperate parent, meeting Whitney at court for a child custody hearing, hanging out in the courtyard of one of the low-rise projects that still dominate much of the city's east and west sides, traveling to a suburban comic book store to watch Bob play a few rounds of cards, and helping him move into an apartment with Cassie, a real milestone.

The ethnography revealed myriad ways in which not all hopes were fully realized. Bridget had resolved at age fifteen to avoid pregnancy until she had a college diploma. Not only did the U.S. Army usurp the place that Harvard had held in her plans, but the summer before she left for basic training in North Carolina, she and Damon conceived a child, foiling even those plans. Keala's "perfect" boyfriend, who made $35,000 a year installing HVAC equipment, was eventually arrested for armed robbery. Yet other youth had taken a surprisingly positive turn. Ron, for example, was back in school after having resolved to go straight once he became a dad. Similarly, Crystal's story exceeded expectations. In fourth grade, Crystal was diagnosed with ADHD; her teacher characterized her as a "bully" and "a very challenged student"—something we observed in her reading and math classrooms, when we saw her hit several other students and slam her books noisily at several points. Yet when we saw Crystal for the last time in 2012, she had graduated from high school and begun work at a driving school. Each of these revelations tempered and honed our claims.

Ethnography added complexity to our understanding of the difficulties some youth encountered during the journey toward adulthood. For example, hanging out with Alicia multiple times in 2012 showed us how challenging it can be to secure stable housing and the "price" that quest can sometimes exact. Alicia's mother, Debbie, had passed away in 2011 while in the process of being evicted by the housing authority for nonpayment of rent. After her death, her adult daughter and son (now out of jail) were not allowed to remain in the apartment in Latrobe Homes. To cope, the now-homeless Alicia had placed Taneesha, her two-year-old daughter, with an aunt who lived illegally with her boyfriend and his cousin in another unit in Latrobe. Alicia cycled between the apartments of several male "friends"—usually a different friend each night—and only visited her daughter in the afternoons after her welfare-to-work training program was completed.

Over the course of several more hang-outs, Alicia revealed more about her relationships with these men and with others she met online. She reveled in showing Jennifer Darrah the often steamy online postings from these men and the back-and-forth messages she exchanged with several of them, revealing the delicate dance she maintained to have a place to sleep each night. While at a restaurant in the Inner Harbor, Alicia and Darrah got so caught up in viewing the postings that Darrah inadvertently let her meter expire and her car was towed. Darrah, who was eight and a half months pregnant at the time, was grateful that Alicia took command of the situation: she showed Darrah how to get to the tow yard and advised her to bring cash to get her car out of the impound—credit cards were not accepted.

The last time Darrah saw Alicia, she had found a tiny room in a rooming house to rent. It was not suitable for children, but it was affordable for her now that she had begun receiving modest benefits from the Temporary Assistance for Needy Families (TANF) program. It also offered her greater autonomy than the couch-surfing she had engaged in for over a year. The catch was that it was on the west side of the city, quite far by public transportation from where Taneesha was now living with Alicia's godmother. Now Alicia was able to see her daughter only a couple of times a month.

Even considering the richness of these ethnographic interactions, we felt that the interviews were more deeply informative. The "strange situation" of sitting down together and inviting a young person to tell you the story of her life can induce that holy moment—a kind of connection that youth sometimes commented on, often noting that it was a rare experience for them. When telling their stories, many of the youth were deeply reflective. As they described themselves in contrast to, and in connection with, the people who surrounded them and the contexts in which they worked, learned, and lived, some even began to write their future story. Terry reflected at the end of his interview, "Nobody sits down and asks me these kind of questions, you know what I mean? You helpin' me now understand myself."

Telling one's story and being empathetically heard may also have therapeutic power. As the psychologist Dan McAdams writes, "Simply writing or performing a story about oneself can prove to be an experience of healing and growth."[40] Whitney ruminated on what it felt like to tell her story: "Now I'm gonna be thinking about [changing my life] because now I know all that stuff I did in the past and I still ain't do nothing. Now I know I gotta do something 'cause I done talked about it. [I got] just a new attitude, so I might go over here [to get my GED] and go ahead and finish whatever I can do. . . . You all got me thinking about it." If Whitney's experience was widespread—and we have reason to believe that it was because of the many similar accounts in our data—inviting a respondent to tell her life story may even be a modest way to give back.

Appendix B | MTOQ5 General Description Worksheet and MTOQ10 Field Note Template

MTOQ5 GENERAL DESCRIPTION WORKSHEET

General Description Worksheet
MTO Adult Pilot

*Case ID:*_____   *Pseudonym:*_____
Coder initials: ____   *Interviewer initials:* ____
                                Date of interview: _____

Interview running time: _____

1. Respondent's Age: ____

2. Location: (circle the most appropriate)
   Baltimore: west   east   south   northeast   northwest
   Suburbs
   Outside Baltimore metropolitan area

3. Indicate whether respondent is employed: ☐Yes   ☐No
   Briefly describe respondent's current job and employment history. Include current employer, job title and salary, if applicable. Include any

training received and experiences with work, commuting, managers, and attitudes about work. How did respondent locate this job? If respondent is unemployed, please note for how long and describe recent job search efforts.

4. Briefly describe respondent's completed education, training and job skills.

5. Briefly describe the respondent's housing situation, including history and current apartment, and thoughts on the neighborhood.

6. Children:

	Age	Sex	School
Focal Child			
Focal Youth			

CHILD# _____

7. Focal child: Briefly discuss how focal child is doing in school, hobbies, activities and any health or behavior concerns. Also note father's involvement, and the role of peers and friends in child's life. How does parent feel the move has affected the child?

8. Focal Youth. Briefly discuss how focal child is doing in school, hobbies, activities and any health or behavior concerns. Also note father's involvement, and the role of peers and friends in child's life. How does parent feel the move has affected the child?

9. Summarize the composition and location of respondent's family and social networks, specifically with regard to job networks, social capital and opportunity structures. Also include frequency of interactions and exchanges behavior.

10. Summarize findings of the status ladder and respondent's assessment of his/her standing in the community.

11. Health and depression. Summarize any notable health conditions, attitudes, or practices both past and present.

12. Summarize any key issues or unique circumstances, such as notable family situation or household composition, reasons for moving, and respondent's attitude during the interview:

Numeric Codes

—For an explanation of each code, see the General Codes section at the beginning of the codebook.

—On the line marked "pg.", enter the page number in the transcript where the information can be found.

—If a field is not filled, enter 98 if question was not answered and 99 if question does not apply.

AGE: _____   pg. _____

LRESN: _____   pg. _____

JOB TITLE: _____   EARNINGS: _____ (hourly or yearly)

CURASSTN (*underline all that apply*):   pg. _____

Public Aid	child care subsidies	Disability
Food Stamps	Social Security	formal child support
Medicaid/CHIP/ Medicare	Survivor benefits	other
	heating assistance	none
WIC		

MTOQ10 FIELD NOTE TEMPLATE

Date: _____
Time and duration of interview: _____
Interviewer(s): _____
Study ID: _____

Interview Context

Where did you conduct the interview?

Describe the home [size, condition, location, cleanliness, style].

Describe the neighborhood [condition, activities, people].

Who was present during the interview (other than yourself and respondent)?

Were there any unusual distractions and/or noises?

Was there any information obtained when the tape recorder wasn't on?

Describe the respondent's disposition during the interview [interaction, appearance, attitude].

Household

What is the respondent's sex, age, race, and marital status?

Who lives in the household?

Ages of spouse/partner and children

Employment

What is the respondent's job history and current job (if any)?

Describe the primary ways the respondent learned about and acquired jobs, as well as any job training they have (if any).

Education

What is the respondent's educational attainment?

Describe how many schools the respondent attended and where these schools were located, as well as future plans (if any) for further education.

Family and Friends

Describe the respondent's current partner situation. If they have children, describe their level of involvement with their children.

Describe the respondent's primary peer networks and how and where they connected with these peers.

Risk Behaviors

Describe the respondent's history of risk behaviors, as well as the risk behaviors of their parents and peers.

Mental Health

Describe the respondent's overall mental health.

Other

Describe any other issues that make this case notable.

Second Interview

Would you suggest we conduct a follow-up interview with the respondent? Why?

What unanswered questions do you have about this respondent?

Was there anything that seemed contradictory about their answers?

Was there anything you felt they were not forthcoming about?

Was there anything that, in retrospect, you would like clarified?

Notes |

PREFACE: "BALTIMORE CITY, YOU'RE BREAKING MY HEART"

1. Ta-Nehisi Coates, "The Case for Reparations," *The Atlantic,* June 2014; Luke Broadwater, "Wells Fargo Agrees to Pay $175M Settlement in Pricing Discrimination Suit," *Baltimore Sun,* July 12, 2012; Pietila 2010.
2. Ian Tuttle, "Lack of 'Investment' Is Not the Problem in Baltimore," *National Review,* April 29, 2015; Michael Tanner, "Poverty, Despair, and Big Government," *National Review,* April 29, 2015; Tierney Sneed, "Conservatives Make Baltimore Riots a Case for Welfare Reform," *U.S. News & World Report,* May 1, 2015.
3. David Brooks, "The Nature of Poverty," *New York Times,* May 1, 2015.
4. David Brooks, "The Cost of Relativism," *New York Times,* March 10, 2015.
5. Tracey Halvorsen, "Baltimore City, You're Breaking My Heart" (This Is Why People Leave)," February 7, 2014, retrieved from: https://medium.com/p/1873a505ce2a (accessed December 7, 2015).
6. Tim Barnett, "Baltimore City, You're Not Breaking My Heart (I'm Not Leaving)," 2014, retrieved from: https://medium.com/@wearyourtruth/baltimore-city-youre-not-breaking-my-heart-3e8ac15cf037 (accessed December 7, 2015).
7. Halvorsen, "Baltimore City, You're Breaking My Heart."
8. Chetty et al. 2014.
9. "Port of Baltimore Sets Container Record in August," *Baltimore Sun,* October 15, 2015.
10. Sheryl Gay Stolberg, "Fragile Baltimore Struggles to Heal After Deadly Police Encounter," *New York Times,* October 20, 2015.
11. Harrington 1962. Two recent examples of Harrington's legacy include Sasha Abramsky's (2013) *The American Way of Poverty: How the Other Half Still Lives* and Kathryn Edin and Luke Schaefer's (2015) *$2 a Day: Living on Almost Nothing in America.*

ACKNOWLEDGMENTS

1. Russell Sage #9500861.
2. William T. Grant Foundation Major Grant #553399.
3. William T. Grant Foundation Faculty Scholars Award #9031.
4. Spencer Foundation #2009000042; Century Foundation Non-Resident Fellows Program 2011–2014.

CHAPTER 1: "DIFFERENT PRIVILEGES THAT DIFFERENT PEOPLE INHERIT": SOCIAL REPRODUCTION AND THE TRANSITION TO ADULTHOOD

1. Corak 2013.
2. Pew Charitable Trusts 2012; Reeves 2013.
3. Alexander, Entwisle, and Olson 2014.
4. J. Rosen 2014.
5. Alexander, Entwisle, and Olson 2014.
6. Coates, "The Case for Reparations"; Sampson 2012; Sharkey 2013.
7. Another 5 percent of parents obtained a GED.
8. A third group received vouchers that did not come with a stipulation that they live in any particular kind of neighborhood. We interviewed parents and youth in this group in 2003–2004 but not in 2010.
9. See Coates (2015) for his description of navigating his way through West Baltimore; see also Harding 2010.
10. Erikson 1963. More recently, Tim Clydesdale (2015) has argued that finding a "vocation" can motivate college students to persevere and help them navigate their early career choices more purposefully.
11. The names of all youth, parents, teachers, and siblings have been changed to preserve confidentiality, as have elementary, middle, and high schools. All places of employment have been changed in the specific, but kept within employment sector to preserve context. For example, if a youth worked at McDonald's, we have changed it to another fast food place such as Wendy's. In all but a few cases (those requested by HUD to ensure confidentiality), names of neighborhoods reflect where youth lived.
12. Arnett 2004.
13. See MacLeod 1987 for another example of disadvantaged youth falling short of their aspirations.
14. Hoxby and Avery 2013.
15. Becker 1991.
16. Mayer 1997.

17. Reardon 2011; Duncan and Murnane 2011; Kaushal, Magnuson, and Waldfogel 2011; Magnuson and Waldfogel 2008.
18. Reardon and Yun 2001; Reardon et al. 2011; Mickelson and Nkomo 2012; Warkentien 2015; Hanushek, Kain and Rivkin 2009
19. Wilson 1987, 1996, 2009. See also Mayer and Jencks 1989 and Sampson, Morenoff, and Gannon-Rowley 2002.
20. Chetty et al. 2014; Chetty, Hendren, and Katz 2015.
21. Wilson 1987.
22. Bourdieu 1977; Bourdieu and Passeron 1977.
23. Bernstein 1975. Shirley Brice-Heath (1983) also draws on intensive fieldwork to demonstrate that linguistic cultural capital differs greatly between black and white students, and between rural students and those raised in town.
24. Willis 1977.
25. Lareau 2003.
26. Prudence Carter (2003) distinguishes between dominant and nondominant cultural capital in her study of adolescents. Dominant cultural capital aligns with mainstream middle-class language patterns, clothing, and other interests.
27. In many ways, our findings are most closely aligned with those of Jay MacLeod, whose 1987 ethnographic work presents a challenge to deterministic and cultural views. MacLeod followed two groups of low-income youth that shared the same social location but had, he found, radically different orientations and aspirations. One group, nearly all white, exhibited an outlook that resembled that of Willis's respondents, while another, all black, held middleclass aspirations, including going to college. The irony in MacLeod's account is that despite this sharp difference in outlook, the latter group ended up faring more poorly than the former, largely owing to the structural barriers faced by blacks but not by whites.
28. Sharkey 2013, 92.
29. Sharkey 2010; Sharkey and Elwert 2011; see also Sampson, Sharkey, and Raudenbush 2008; Wodtke, Harding, and Elwert 2011.

CHAPTER 2: "MORE PEOPLE THAT HAVE STUFF TO LIVE FOR HERE": NEIGHBORHOOD CHANGE AND INTERGENERATIONAL ATTAINMENT

1. Putnam 2015a.
2. Michael A. Fletcher, "Disrepair Breeds Danger at Flag House Courts," *Baltimore Sun*, May 9, 1993.
3. Michael A. Fletcher, "Once Respectable Flag House Project Enmeshed in Nightmare of Violence," *Baltimore Sun*, May 10, 1993.

4. Williams 2005.
5. M. Dion Thompson, "Public Housing Tenants Promised Relief by the City," *Baltimore Sun*, March 27, 2002; Baltimore Housing, "HABC [Housing Authority of Baltimore City]—Over 75 Years of Rich History," retrieved from: http://www.baltimorehousing.org/75th_timeline (accessed December 7, 2015).
6. Barbara Samuels, "The 1968 Riots and the History of Public Housing Segregation in Baltimore," ACLU of Maryland, April 4, 2008, retrieved from: http://www.prrac.org/pdf/riots_and_rebirth.pdf (accessed December 7, 2015).
7. Joan Jacobson and Robert Hilson Jr., "High-Rise Dream of the '50s Becomes a Nightmare of the '90s: Lafayette Courts Judged Costly Failure," *Baltimore Sun*, February 9, 1992.
8. Edward Gunts, "Layfayette Courts Building on Hopes," *Baltimore Sun*, August 18, 1995.
9. Michael Anft, "Half Staff: Facing the End at Flag House Courts, the City's Last High-Rise Project," *Baltimore City Paper*, December 22, 1999; Laurie Willis, "Goodbye to a Place That Many Called Home," *Baltimore Sun*, February 11, 2001.
10. Bauman 1987.
11. Schwartz 2006.
12. Hirsch 1983; Massey and Denton 1993.
13. Wilson 1987.
14. Epp 1998; Popkin et al. 2004; Schwartz 2006.
15. Wilson 1996.
16. Briggs, Popkin, and Goering 2010; Goering and Feins 2003; Goering, Feins, and Richardson 2002.
17. Kling, Liebman, and Katz 2007; Kling et al. 2004; Kling, Ludwig, and Katz 2005; Orr et al. 2003.
18. Sanbonmatsu et al. 2011; Ludwig et al. 2013; Ludwig et al. 2011.
19. Jay Matthews, "Neighborhoods' Effects on Grades Challenged," *Washington Post*, August 14, 2007; Thomas Edsall, "Does Moving Poor People Work?" *New York Times*, September 16, 2014; see also Goetz and Chapple 2010; Imbroscio 2008, 2012.
20. One of the hallmarks of MTO was that it was designed as a randomized experiment and, as such, would remove concerns about the selection bias that is ever-present in neighborhood effects research. For example, to measure whether growing up in a poor neighborhood affects the odds of an adolescent graduating from high school, one needs to "control away" the influences of parents, which includes anything about their parents that led them to choose that neighborhood. Despite the desire to remove selection bias from MTO through random assignment, there were still several stages at which selection came into play. Across the five cities fewer than half of those in the

experimental group used their voucher to move (Baltimore had the highest "compliance" rate of using the voucher, at 58 percent); thus, there was selection in who was able to use the voucher to secure housing in a low-poverty neighborhood. In addition, the type of nonpoor neighborhood that the household head chose to move into was significantly related to individual characteristics of the adult. Finally, subsequent moves could also have been related to family level characteristics; see Clampet-Lundquist and Massey 2008; see also Sampson 2008.

21. DeLuca and Rosenblatt 2010; Briggs et al. 2008; Sanbonmatsu et al. 2006.

22. Clampet-Lundquist and Massey 2008; Rosenblatt and DeLuca 2012.

23. As several scholars have noted, MTO families returned to higher poverty neighborhoods in the years following their first move. This occurred because of problems with landlords, issues with their vouchers, and difficulty finding affordable housing in opportunity neighborhoods during subsequent moves (Rosenblatt and DeLuca 2012; Edin, DeLuca, and Owens 2012; Briggs, Popkin, and Goering 2010; Briggs, Comey, Weismann 2010).

24. Edin, DeLuca, and Owens 2012.

25. Chicago also experienced a dramatic transformation in its public housing stock during this time period. In addition, welfare reform, an expansion of the Earned Income Tax Credit (EITC), and the economic boom of the 1990s may have reduced the employment differences observed between the control and experimental groups.

26. HOPE VI was originally designed to address the needs reported by the National Commission on Severely Distressed Public Housing, which found that 6 percent of public housing was in dire condition and responsible for "almost unimaginable distress to a segment of this Nation's most valuable resource, its people" (U.S. Department of Housing and Urban Development 1992, xiv). Thus, the primary goal was to demolish or rehabilitate these housing units and integrate the developments into the neighborhoods more seamlessly (Epp 1998). Over time, however, this mission was modified and local housing authorities began to use HOPE VI as a tool for broader neighborhood transformation, leveraging private investment with public funds. Ultimately, this created a situation where many HOPE VI–redeveloped public housing complexes near gentrifying neighborhoods became mixed-income, appealing to renters and homeowners who could afford market-rate prices (Rosenblatt 2011; Turbov and Piper 2005). Families who were originally residents of the public housing were displaced. They could use a housing choice voucher to move to private housing, or they could move to a unit in another public housing complex, if it was available. On average, they ended up in less-poor neighborhoods, but many mourned the loss of their former communities (Clampet-Lundquist 2004; Popkin et al. 2004; Goetz 2013).

27. Goetz 2011.

28. Jacobson 2007. Peter Rosenblatt (2011, 132) finds that "by the year 2000, the city had reduced its family public housing stock by almost half, to 6,854 units from a high of 12,016 in 1981." There is discrepancy in the numbers because the analyses cover different years, and Rosenblatt includes only family units.
29. Jacobson 2007.
30. Author's calculations. While households received a housing voucher if their complex was being demolished (or they were being moved to a different complex, depending on what was available), vouchers are not as permanent a segment of the affordable housing stock as "hard" public housing units. People can lose eligibility for their vouchers or be unable to find housing units and lease-up with them. Also, the number of vouchers depends on federal funding, which can be variable.
31. Rosenblatt 2011; see also Kingsley et al. 2004; Turbov and Piper 2005; Zielenbach 2003. Some researchers have pointed out that the positive gains in the neighborhood as measured by indicators such as poverty, employment, and housing value are a result of most of the original residents being permanently displaced; see Goetz and Chapple (2010) for a critique of deconcentration policies.
32. Kneebone, Nadeau, and Berube 2011, appendix B; American Community Survey (ACS), 2008–2012.
33. Kneebone, Nadeau, and Berube 2011, appendix B; ACS 2008–2012. In addition, Ann Owens (2014) and Yana Kucheva (2013) show that, on average, the loss of subsidized housing units nationwide often does not result in declines in poverty rates. Baltimore may be an exception because of market forces spurring development and the heavy reliance on HOPE VI and other demolition.
34. Kneebone, Nadeau, and Berube 2011, appendix B; ACS 2008–2012.
35. Deirdre Bloome and Ann Owens (2015) have found that children who grow up in communities with more hard-unit subsidized housing are not as economically mobile as those who grew up with less of this type of housing, even when holding other neighborhood characteristics constant. This is true only in areas that are highly segregated by race and income, suggesting that the negative effects of concentrated disadvantage are exacerbated by highly concentrated subsidized housing.
36. Forty-nine percent of the experimental compliers in the qualitative study were in 0 to 20 percent poor neighborhoods in 2010; for controls this number was 35.8 percent. Thirty-five percent of experimentals and 38 percent of controls lived in 20 to 30 percent poor neighborhoods. Neighborhoods that were 30 percent poor or higher were home to 16.7 percent of the experimental group and 26.4 percent of the controls.
37. Six youth were living out of state in 2010—two in North Carolina and one each in Indiana, South Carolina, Texas, and Washington, D.C. We also geocoded the poverty rate of these addresses in 2010.

38. We are grateful to Ann Owens for doing these analyses.

39. Similar comparisons are not available for the other four cities. However, when we look at the Baltimore control group compared to the pooled average poverty rates for all five cities in the final evaluation report, the drop is steeper than for the five cities combined. The drop in poverty for the control group is 49 percent in Baltimore and 41 percent for all five cities combined. There are also larger declines in poverty for the experimental group in Baltimore, at 56 percent, compared to 48 percent for all five cities. This may be due in part to the fact that Baltimore saw a much larger drop in concentrated poverty than the other MTO cities over the 2000–2010 period.

40. DeLuca et al. 2010; Ellen and Turner 1997; Sampson 2012; Sampson, Sharkey, and Raudenbush 2008; Sampson et al. 2002; Sharkey 2010; Wodkte et al. 2011.

41. Chetty, Hendren, and Katz 2015.

42. Our findings concur with the high school completion rates found for recent cohorts of Baltimore City public school students (Connolly et al. 2014; Durham and Olson 2013), as well as with national trends showing gains in both high school completion and college entry among low-income youth and youth of color; see National Center for Education Statistics, "Digest of Education Statistics: Table 302.20: Percentage of Recent High School Completers Enrolled in 2- and 4-Year Colleges, by Race/Ethnicity: 1960 Through 2013," retrieved from: https://nces.ed.gov/programs/digest/d14/tables/dt14_302 .20.asp?current=yesEDFacts/Consolidated%20State%20Performance%20 Report,%20SY%202012%E2%80%9313 (accessed December 7, 2015).

43. Twenty parents pursued some kind of postsecondary education. Of the twelve who earned a credential, one completed a bachelor's degree (after an associate's degree), one completed an associate's degree, nine completed a trade certificate, and one completed a credential but did not report what it was. Eight began but did not finish programs; of these, two were bachelor's degree programs, two were associate's degree programs, two were trade school or occupational programs, and two others were unclear.

44. Data from the U.S. census shows that Baltimore City's educational attainment rates increased during this period as well. In 1990, 21.3 percent of sixteen- to nineteen-year-olds in Baltimore had dropped out of high school, and 15.5 percent of adults age twenty-five or older had earned a bachelor's degree or more. By 2010 only 8.8 percent of the city's youth had dropped out of high school, and 25.2 percent of the adults in the city had a bachelor's degree or more (authors' own calculations from the 1990 and 2010 censuses).

45. However, the gap between the Baltimore youth and their counterparts nationally is still quite large. When looking at the parents of a nationally representative sample of youth who were ages twelve to sixteen in 1997—from distribution of the National Longitudinal Survey of Youth: 1997 (Bureau of Labor Statistics 2013)—we see that the highest credential completed among the parents of the youth in the survey were as follows: less than a high school

diploma, 13.8 percent; high school diploma, 30.6 percent; some college, 26.5 percent; and a college degree or more, 29.1 percent. For youth nationally the numbers were: less than high school diploma, 8.1 percent; high school diploma or GED, 53.8 percent; some college, 7.7 percent; college degree or more, 30.4 percent. (Estimates for parental education were weighted using sampwgtccr1. Estimates for the youth educational attainment when they were 26–30 years old were weighted using wgtcumcase15.) We thank Siri Warkentien for her assistance with these analyses.

46. This term, "in the street," emerged from our interviews, and it is also discussed in-depth by the sociologist Elijah Anderson, particularly in his book *Code of the Street* (1999).

47. Goering et al. 1999. In another study, Julia Burdick-Will and her colleagues (2011) compared the Baltimore and Chicago MTO households to housing choice voucher recipients in Chicago. They found that the MTO households were similar on indicators of concentrated disadvantage, such as the percentage on welfare, the percentage employed, and the tract poverty rate where households lived—with one exception: the MTO households started off in neighborhoods with poverty rates that were eight percentage points higher.

48. Coleman 1990.

49. As we describe in Appendix A, we interviewed 15 primary caregivers in addition to 124 parents.

50. We refer to the former as "mainstream" influences because they conform to the current social norms associated with positive outcomes, such as adult economic self-sufficiency.

51. Wilson 1987.

52. Research on people addicted to narcotics has found that they have often experienced family stress and trauma in their childhood and adolescence (Baer and Corrado 1974; Conners et al. 2004; Craig and Brown 1975; Hanlon et al. 2005; McCarthy and Anglin 1990). Almost half of the parents in the Baltimore MTO sample reported that in their own childhoods they had experienced significant trauma—ranging from abuse at the hands of their parents or partners to witnessing the deaths of family members or sexual assault. Parental substance use can combine with past trauma and poverty to have serious consequences for children's well-being and eventual social mobility (Conners et al. 2004; Suchman and Luthar 2000).

53. Significant mental health benefits are documented in Ludwig et al. (2013). Moreover, morbid obesity was significantly reduced for adults in the experimental group (Ludwig et al. 2011). Stress is related to both morbid obesity and diminished parenting capacity.

54. Turney, Kissane, and Edin 2012.

55. While Peaches was already eager to improve her prospects by attending community college, she told us that her move "motivated me to get more" because she saw how her neighbors lived, and she noted that most of them

worked and were "doing something positive." Eventually, she earned an associate's degree and landed a job at a hospital where she was making double the wages she had at the laundromat she had been employed at while living in the project. By the time of the 2003 interview, after a promotion, she was making $38,000 a year, with benefits.

56. Lareau 2003.

57. Chetty et al. 2014; Sampson, Sharkey, and Raudenbush 2008; Sharkey and Faber 2014.

58. Burdick-Will et al. 2011; Sharkey et al. 2012.

59. John Fritze and Doug Donovan, "Fact Check: O'Malley Lays Claim to an Ambitious Record in Md.," *Baltimore Sun,* April 18, 2015; for a critique of crime statistics during Martin O'Malley's tenure as mayor, see Bill Keller, "David Simon on Baltimore's Anguish: Freddie Gray, the Drug War, and the Decline of 'Real Policing,'" The Marshall Project, April 29, 2015, retrieved from: https://www.themarshallproject.org/2015/04/29/david-simon-on-baltimore-s-anguish (accessed August 19, 2015).

60. We drew the sibling comparisons mentioned here from interviews with children who had been somewhat older at random assignment in 2003–2004 and just happened to have siblings who fell into the 2010 random draw as well.

61. In 1995 the entire nation was reeling from high violent crime, but the national rate was 685 per 100,000 compared to Baltimore's 3,018. In 2010 that rate had dropped by over half in Baltimore, to 1,500, and to 405 in the nation. So even after the drop, Baltimore's rate was still 370 percent higher than the nation's. Federal Bureau of Investigation, "Uniform Crime Reporting Statistics Data Tool," U.S. Department of Justice, retrieved from: www.ucrdatatool.gov/Search/Crime/Local/RunCrimeJurisbyJuris.cfm and www.ucrdatatool.gov/Search/Crime/State/RunCrimeStatebyState.cfm (accessed October 23, 2015).

62. One of the side effects of heroin use can be itchy skin.

63. Rainwater 1970.

64. Hirsch 1983; Ginger Thompson, "Getting Rid of High-Rise Projects?" *Baltimore Sun,* December 2, 1990.

65. Chetty, Hendren, and Katz 2015.

CHAPTER 3: "FOLLOWING MY PASSION": HOW IDENTITY PROJECTS HELP YOUTH BEAT THE STREET AND STAY ON TRACK

1. Terry was able to graduate from West Glen High School.

2. Matthew Desmond (2012) talks about similar "disposable ties" among the urban poor.

3. Looking back, however, Terry believed that lack of support from home had diminished his academic aspirations and emotional development. He told us,

"I didn't feel like I was ever provided that [home] environment where I could really focus on being a great student . . . and it kind of killed my motivation." It was especially painful for Terry to observe the wide gulf between what he experienced as a child and what he saw afforded to other youth at his school during the year he spent in affluent Columbia. "I'd say somewhere between 70 and 75 percent of the kids [there] go to college, at least for two years . . . like, the environment that they come up in is conducive for them to grow up and go through the proper transition from teenage years to young adulthood to college grad. . . . I didn't have any of that."

4. Nancy Deutsch (2008) also notes the redemption theme for "Lorenzo" in the boys and girls' club she studied. The after-school setting gave some youth a chance to give back and help others avoid the pitfalls they had encountered.

5. Edin and Kefalas 2005; Edin and Nelson 2013.

6. In the interim impacts evaluation, Larry Orr and his colleagues (2003) report findings using both self-reported measures of arrest (ages fifteen to nineteen) and administrative data. In exhibit 5.3, the control mean for the self-reported "ever arrested" measure is 0.22 and the administrative records measure is 0.31—a difference of about nine points in the fraction of youth ever arrested. About 29 percent of the youth in our study reported ever being arrested, a number somewhere in between. If we use arrest as a proxy, however, the administrative data suggest that there could be an underreport of street activities. We have no administrative equivalent with which to test the "ever in the street" reported fraction. Therefore, an upper-bound estimate for the percentage of the youth in our study who were ever involved in any illegal activities could be as high as 27 percent. Either way, the findings suggest that being on track would still be the modal status. In appendix A, we share our strategies for mitigating against these sources of bias.

7. Elijah Anderson (1990, 1999) has also used the term "the street" to describe a set of expectations and a "code" of interacting with others in public.

8. Of the six youth who were in the street when we last saw them, two were in high school (Ron and Blake), and one (Malik) was taking classes to become a licensed nurse-practitioner. Three others were disconnected—neither formally working nor in school (Justin and David) or in prison (Chase).

9. We also considered school quality, though as it turned out, there was not enough variability in the quality of the schools these youth attended to produce any result.

10. Erik Erikson argued that identity development is a crisis that youth must resolve on the pathway to becoming fully actualized adults. During this process, youth assess what they are about, in comparison to others and their surroundings. This identity-making starts in late adolescence and early adulthood, the stage of development when youth have the cognitive skills necessary to construct identities (Erikson 1963; Habermas and Bluck 2000). Youth use autobiographical reasoning to knit together the events in their

lives in a way that expresses who they are or are trying to be. Their autobiographical reasoning is nested within a particular sociocultural context, since their meaning-making is "learned through social interactions" (Habermas and Bluck, 2000, 753). But making an identity is also very much about looking forward; as Erikson (1968, 310) put it, identity "links the actuality of a living past with that of a promising future." We argue that having an identity project is not quite the same as resolving Erikson's "crisis" between diffusion and identity. It is a precursor to the stage that Erikson described, a critical intermediate step that imbues the investment of everyday activities with a new sense of meaning (McAdams 2006). For the low-income youth we spoke with, the identity project was part of the process that allowed them to avoid the streets so that they could make it to the next step of development (resolving Erikson's identity crisis) and figure out what their adult roles might be (see also Hartner 1999).

11. See Harre (2007). Our conception of an identity project is slightly different from Nikki Harre's: ours emphasizes concrete activities as well as sources of meaning and identity. Also, Harre's outcome of interest is community engagement and activism, while our focus is on resisting the streets and building a bridge to a brighter future. Another related concept comes from the recent work of Timothy Clydesdale (2015), who finds that youth who participate in vocation-focused activities are often better able to persevere in college and craft a more purposeful route into adulthood, especially with regard to early career choice.

12. Deutsch (2008, 102) finds that youth in a boys and girls' club use the "construction of the other as an oppositional mirror" of what they do not want to be. This image functions as a motivator for them "against which they can define their own sense of self."

13. See Harre (2007) for the connection between identity projects and community service or activism.

14. Both Terry and Chantal offered what might be called a "survival script" in the retelling of their life stories. Their survival scripts were similar to the "redemption scripts" that Shadd Maruna (2001) documented in his research with men who had served time in prison. The essential components include telling a narrative about the past, describing transformative events along the way, and projecting one's actions into the future. For the redemption script as well as the survival script, this future typically includes a pledge from the individual to make positive change for others and society. Similarly, Dan McAdam's (2006) work on generativity in adulthood has demonstrated that self-defining life stories, or "personal myths," are common among highly generative people.

15. See Waterman (1993) for a discussion of "finding something to do or someone to be."

16. Margaret Spencer, Suzanne Fegley, and Vinay Harpalani (2003) discuss how

the identity development of African American youth in low-income neighborhoods can serve as a coping method that protects against the racism and structural neglect to which they are exposed. Laura DeHaan and Shelley MacDermid (1996) also find that, though growing up poor limits identity development, an identity serves as a protective buffer against a stressful environment for those who are able to establish one.

17. These identity projects stand in contrast to the literature regarding other poor and working-class youth, who may come to adopt an oppositional identity (see, for example, Willis 1977; MacLeod 1987). Some of our youth did adopt oppositional "street" identities for a time, as chapter 4 shows. However, as Daphna Oyserman and Hazel Markus (1990a, 1990b) theorize, delinquency may be the product of youth figuring out their "possible selves." Engaging in delinquency may represent a lifestyle that is rebellious and thrilling—one way to imagine one's future self. At the same time, youth balance this possible self with consideration of other possible selves that reflect positive goals. Youth learn which strategies are necessary to attain this positive self, and in so doing, they avoid strategies that would promote the negative self.

18. Margaret Somers encourages social scientists to view narratives as ontological rather than representational. She argues that "stories guide action" and that, similar to Habermas and Bluck (2000), "people make sense of what has happened and is happening to them by attempting to assemble or in some way to integrate these happenings within one or more narratives" (Somers 1994, 614). This meaning-making and action does not occur in a vacuum. Instead, Somers states, "people are guided to act in certain ways, and not others, on the basis of the projections, expectations, and memories derived from a multiplicity but ultimately limited repertoire of available social, public, and cultural narratives" (614). By connecting narrative to identity, we can connect being to action.

19. For five youth in the sample, it was unclear whether they had an identity project. We measured outcomes only for those no longer in high school, but several of the high school youth had adopted identity projects as well.

20. Based on his fieldwork with youth in Boston, David Harding (2010) finds, as we did in chapter 2, that there are many competing cultural models in high-poverty neighborhoods, providing what he calls "cultural heterogeneity." Harding does not discuss which model is the most common—rather, he argues that they are all available and all receive, to some extent, some level of social support. However, from the narratives of our youth, it is clear that the street was the most visible of all the paths available in the Baltimore neighborhoods. Even if it was the path least taken by the young adults in our study, it nonetheless had to be navigated and contended with by all of them.

21. Harding (2010) argues that the competing cultural models become problematic when there is less information about the relative costs and benefits of the

many options, making it hard for youth to choose a path, and even harder to commit to it. However, in this conceptualization there is no discussion of meaning or identity and the kinds of experiences that might inspire youth to stick to their educational and professional goals or to choose one path over another. Part of what we argue here is that the identity project plays this vital role by protecting and motivating young adults, helping them steer clear of the streets and neighborhood and school peers who threaten to derail their plans, while also giving them something more meaningful to be about.

22. Duckworth et al. 2007, 1087–88.
23. Tough 2012.
24. Duckworth et al. 2007.
25. Educators4Excellence, "The Game-Changing Factors and People Lifting School Performance in Los Angeles," retrieved from: http://www.educators 4excellence.org/latruegrit (accessed December 7, 2015). However, Duckworth recently cautioned researchers not to go as far as attaching high-stakes outcomes to measurements of grit; see Anya Kamenetz, "A Key Researcher Says 'Grit' Isn't Ready for High-Stakes Measures," NPR, May 13, 2015, retrieved from: http://www.npr.org/sections/ed/2015/05/13/405891613/a-key -researcher-says-grit-isnt-ready-for-high-stakes-measures (accessed December 7, 2015).
26. Lipset 1996.
27. Kishiyama et al. 2009; Lawson et al. 2013.
28. Marguerite Del Giudice, "Grit Trumps Talent and IQ: A Story Every Parent (and Educator) Should Read," National Geographic, October 14, 2014.
29. Charles Belfoure, "In Baltimore, Public Housing Comes Full Circle," New York Times, March 19, 2000; Dan Thanh Dang, "Good, Bad Memories Tumble Down as Lexington Terrace High-Rises Implode," Baltimore Sun, July 28, 1996.
30. DeLuca, Garboden, and Rosenblatt 2013; DeLuca, Wood, and Rosenblatt 2011.
31. Despite her love for animals and the skills she had developed in caring for them, Vicky never wanted to pursue a career in the veterinarian field, "I don't wanna be a vet 'cause I don't wanna never put a dog to sleep," she said.
32. See Larson 2011.
33. Bob was not alone—a number of other youth identified themselves as distinct by their taste in unconventional music. Twenty-two-year-old Ed was a fan of punk rock and anime, and seventeen-year-old Megan enjoyed rock music as a way to distinguish herself, even though her cousins made fun of her. Twenty-one-year-old Jacob was proud of the fact that he stood out among his peers for liking country music and rock, an interest he shared with his mother.
34. See Arnett (1996) for a study of white youth who find their identities by participating in the "metalhead" culture of thrash, "death," and heavy metal music, complete with its own style of hair and clothing.

35. Research on resilient youth also emphasizes the importance of adults, mentors, teachers, and coaches (Deutsch 2008; Hauser et al. 1985; Rutter 1979). Anderson (1990) cites the significance of the "old heads" among the adults in young people's lives who act as "guidance counselor and moral cheerleader."

36. Several longitudinal studies have shown a positive relationship between participation in youth activities and positive outcomes such as fewer problem behaviors, staying in school, and global positive adjustment. See, for example, Eccles and Barber 1999; Eccles and Templeton 2002; Hanson, Larson, and Dworkin 2003.

37. The way Antonio and Cody viewed their badges was part of what Anderson (1990) calls the "campaign of respectability."

38. George Akerlof and Rachel Kranton (2000) also argue that identity has a profound effect on behaviors, including those that are important for economic outcomes.

39. Readers may wonder whether adopting an identity project is highly correlated with family background—potentially rendering the relationships we report here spurious—or simply mechanisms through which family background advantages manifest themselves. We find that this is not the case. Those youth with an identity project were not significantly more likely to have a primary parent or guardian who graduated from high school. There was a difference in parental college or trade school attendance, though the numbers are very small (only twenty parents had ever enrolled in college or trade school). According to the youth whose parents attempted college, eleven had an identity project, seven did not, and in two cases it was unclear from the data whether or not they did. For youth who had some family trauma, a parent with drug or alcohol addiction, or a parent incarcerated, about half still found an identity project.

40. This distinction between a subculture group like Bob's and an institutional connection like Cody's may be akin to what William Bielby (2003) found with white teenagers in the 1950s who became involved with the new rock-and-roll scene and youth who were involved in organized sports in high school.

41. We ran a logistic regression predicting "on track" with type of identity project (DIY/Peer or Institutional with the reference group of youth with no identity project), controlling for age, gender, and neighborhood poverty. We found that while both types of identity project significantly predicted being on track after high school, the institutionally supported identity projects, even after controls, had an odds ratio that was twice as large as that from the DIY/Peer identity projects combined. It is possible that part of the advantage of institutional identity projects is that they provide what Xavier de Souza Briggs (1997, 1998) calls "bridging" social capital—the kind of connection that helps you "get ahead," not just "get by." Research by James Rosenbaum and his colleagues (1999) shows that high school students get higher-quality

and better-paying jobs when they find work through institutional connections, like teachers or job centers, than when they find work through their
networks of family members and friends.

42. As symbolic interactionists (like Charles Cooley) have argued, one's identity
has social reality only if it is supported by interactions that sustain it; otherwise, it has no subjective power. Cooley's (1902) "looking-glass self" suggests
that our identity lies in what is reflected back to us by significant others.

43. This is in line with Anderson's (1990) concept of the "campaign for respectability" among youth in Philadelphia.

44. There are exceptions—for Jayden, the uniform was embarrassing and the job
was not an identity project. It is also true that while a uniform can signal distinction and belonging in one way, it does not necessarily protect an individual from danger in his neighborhood.

45. In appendix A, we describe how we identified and categorized the identity
projects for youth in our study.

46. For four youth, we could not narrow down the timing from our data.

47. We thank Monica Bell for this important insight.

48. We are grateful to Monica Bell for making this incredibly important point.

49. Putnam 2015a.

50. Boyd, Martin, and Edin 2015.

51. It is worth speculating about the role of increasing economic segregation in
this regard. As communities become more economically segregated, social
networks within communities may become less able to link youth to institutions that can provide ladders out of poverty.

52. Fang 2013; Hopkins 2015. The Afterschool Alliance released a report in 2014
that examined after-school opportunities and participation across the country. It found differences in participation and access by income: low-income
families had higher rates of participation but also cited greater unmet de-
mand for after-school programs, with cost and transportation as barriers.

53. Parsad and Spiegelman 2012.

54. Anna Phillips, "Even Before Layoffs, Schools Lost 135 Arts Teachers," *New
York Times,* June 9, 2011.

55. Kornrich and Furstenberg 2013.

56. Weigand et al. 2015; see also Teen Empowerment at http://www.teen
empowerment.org/, UTEC (Breaking Barriers to Youth Success) at https://
www.utec-lowell.org/, and The Brotherhood/Sister Sol (Bro/Sis) at http://
brotherhood-sistersol.org/ (all accessed December 7, 2015).

57. In part, the identity project is about who you want to be, but it is also about
who you do not want to end up like. Clearly, the youth in this chapter were
strategic about their neighborhood and school environments, avoiding those
peers who threatened their professional or academic success. Nikki Jones
(2009) finds similar strategies among young women in Philadelphia. Some

survived violent and risky neighborhoods by practicing "situational avoid-ance" and "relational isolation": they confined themselves to the home, re-stricting activity outside and avoiding close friendships. Taking a cue from Albert Bandura's (1997) influential research on "imposed" and "selected" environments, Patrick Sharkey (2006) also argues that adolescents can choose which aspects of neighborhood life help them pursue their goals and avoid those likely to expose them to violence—something he calls "street efficacy."

58. MacLeod 1987.

CHAPTER 4: "YOU NEVER KNOW WHAT'S HAPPENING—THIS IS BALTIMORE": THE VULNERABILITY OF YOUTH WITHOUT AN IDENTITY PROJECT

1. DeLuca 2007; DeLuca and Rosenblatt 2010.
2. When we ran a logistic regression model predicting illegal activities, we found that, even controlling for age, gender, and neighborhood poverty over time, those with an identity project were only 15 percent as likely as those without an identity project to engage in illegal activities (see table A4.1).
3. Readers may wonder whether the motivation to commit crime is not merely economic. Indeed, our youths' accounts may sometimes lead one to believe this is so. Matthew, twenty-one, told us, "I didn't have no money at the time, so I just stealing cars." While an economic explanation is tempting, especially considering the restricted labor market options for youth with a high school diploma or less in a discriminatory labor market, it cannot explain the hetero-geneity among our youth in this regard. All had experienced poverty. Nearly all continued to struggle economically. Yet only a few got caught up, and only a handful for any significant period of time.
4. Chung, Little, and Steinberg 2005; Uggen and Wakefield 2005.
5. See Edin and Nelson (2013) on the role of fatherhood in the lives of low-income men.
6. One of our fieldworkers, Anna Westin, wrote a dissertation on how youth in our study experience and cope with stress, and how stress is related to their risky behaviors (Westin 2014).
7. The role of schools in facilitating the development of identity projects varies considerably across youth, even though most schools were still poor-performing ones. The high schools that had career-focused academies or were college prep seemed to be the most helpful for identity projects. It was less clear what might have been helpful in the middle schools.
8. Sara Neufeld, "All City Schools to Get Water Coolers," *Baltimore Sun*, November 8, 2007.
9. Erica Green, "Students Call on City Leaders to Pass Bottle Tax," *Baltimore Sun*, February 23, 2012.

10. For high school rankings, see SchoolDigger, "Baltimore City Public Schools," retrieved from: http://www.schooldigger.com/go/MD/schools/0009000236/school.aspx (accessed December 7, 2015).

11. Liz Bowie, "City School Board Votes to Split Off Part of Lake Clifton/Eastern High," *Baltimore Sun*, May 14, 2003.

12. These terms are also used by Elijah Anderson (1990, 1999) in his ethnography of low-income communities in Washington, D.C., and Philadelphia.

13. Criminologists typically find that a minority of male youth are responsible for the majority of offenses (Wolfgang 1983). We find this in our data as well: only 18 percent of our youth were involved in illegal activities, and only 3 percent had used a gun to threaten or harm. A study of youth living in Baltimore's public housing in the early 1990s found that 9 percent of nine- to fifteen-year-olds (younger than our youth) were involved in selling drugs (Li et al. 1996).

14. As in other cities, guns are a lethal part of Baltimore's street scene. Many youth were intimately familiar with gun violence in their neighborhoods, and for some experiences of violence were even closer to home: they reported family or friends who had been shot, as we noted in chapter 2. A few responded to this environment by having a gun themselves. Thirteen youth admitted having a gun (in one case it was a BB gun) but not using it. Typically, they discussed having it either on them or at their house for protection. Five youth—all in the "ever in the street" category—described using a gun to threaten or shoot someone, though no one claimed that they had seriously injured a person with a gun.

15. By the late 1990s, when MTO began, more than two-thirds of Baltimore's students were eligible for free or reduced lunch, relative to less than one-third of Maryland's public school students as a whole. Yet despite the increased need, Baltimore's per-pupil expenditure was just $300 more per student, compared to the state average. Not surprisingly, given the lack of resources, Baltimore City public school students score the lowest on academic achievement in reading and math compared to other school districts in Maryland (Casserly, Jepson, and Lewis 2000).

16. Quercia and Galster 1997.

17. We used six years as a threshold because it increased the chances that even the youngest children would have had the opportunity to be directly exposed to the neighborhood, through outdoor play and as they traveled to and from school. We also reasoned that the one-quarter of the sample who had less than a year's exposure would have had very little opportunity to be affected by the neighborhood, given the fact that all youth were very young at random assignment.

18. Farrington 1986; Heimer and De Coster 1999; Hirschi and Gottfredson 1983; Huizinga, Miller, and Conduct Problems Prevention Research Group 2013; Lauritsen, Heimer, and Lynch 2009; Sweeten, Piquero, and Steinberg 2013.

19. Cauffman and Steinberg 2012.
20. Mears, Ploeger, and Warr 1998; Zimmerman and Messner 2010.
21. Sampson and Laub 1992, 1995; Toby 1957.
22. Parental incarceration was not significant, probably because it was generally the father who was in prison and the youth only rarely had a father in the home; substance abuse, on the other hand, more often involved the custodial parent (see tables A4.3 and A4.4).
23. This variable was constructed through self-reports of schools attended at the final survey and through parental reports from the interim survey. The school ranking was weighted by duration spent at the school. See also DeLuca and Rosenblatt 2010; Sanbonmatsu et al. 2006.
24. Katz 1988.
25. Estimates from U.S. Census Bureau 2000.
26. In Prudence Carter's (2003) terms, Whitney displayed nondominant cultural capital, which served her well inside the neighborhood but presented her in a detrimental light when used outside the neighborhood in mainstream society. As Patricia Fernández Kelly (1994, 101) writes in an ethnographic account of another young woman who hailed from Murphy Homes: "What is wrought as an empowering symbol in an insular milieu becomes a signal that bars access to resources in the larger society."
27. Eventually, Whitney did meet the demands of the child welfare agency and obtain custody of the child.
28. John and Terrence, along with Ron's older peers, taught Ron a certain style of masculinity that James Peterson (2009) refers to as a "corner-boy masculinity."
29. Sara Neufeld, "Cuts 'Devastating' to Local Schools," *Baltimore Sun,* January 23, 2009.
30. In Paul Willis's (1977) seminal ethnographic study *Learning to Labor,* he described how young working-class males defined manual labor work as more "masculine" than "mental" work. Although Willis was discussing manual labor jobs, not selling drugs, much of his description is relevant to working on the corner: "Manual labor is suffused with masculine qualities. . . . The brutality of the working situation is partially re-interpreted into a heroic exercise of manly confrontation with the task" (Willis 1977, 150). Seen from this perspective, selling drugs on the corner may provide a better fit with an appropriately masculine activity as opposed to a "bus stop" job.
31. Anderson 1999; Wilson 1996.
32. Anderson 1999; Jones 2009. Ta-Nehisi Coates (2015, 22) mentions a similar feeling that he had as he was growing up in West Baltimore: "The streets transform every ordinary day into a series of trick questions."
33. See Harding 2010.
34. Peter Reuter and his colleagues (1990) found that men could make more

money selling drugs in Washington, D.C., than in a low-wage job. Adolescents told them that they started selling drugs for economic gain rather than to fuel their own habit, as older drug dealers were more apt to do. Jeremy Arkes (2011) suggests that drug selling among youth increases when the economy goes into a downturn. But in their analysis of a gang's accounting books, Steven Levitt and Sudhir Venkatesh (2000) argue that there are other motivations—such as the promise of future economic gain—that factor into why someone sells illegal drugs, since those at the lowest levels, the street dealers, make an amount at or below minimum wage. Kathryn Edin and Laura Lein (1997) find similarly small gains for drug dealing.

35.   Clampet-Lundquist (2013) finds that males from the 2003–2004 MTO study expressed similar desires to assist with household expenses.

36.   We looked through the archives of the *Baltimore Sun* to confirm Marcus's horrific story but could not do so. However, we take the youth's accounts at face value; although we could not corroborate the event, we include it here because it stands out in Marcus's memory as a searing and life-changing experience for him.

37.   We concur with Peter Rosenblatt and his colleagues (2015) "that it would be a mistake to conclude, as David Harding has claimed, that 'it is inaccurate to conceptualize the cultural context of the poorest neighborhoods as fundamentally different from that of other neighborhoods' (2011, 336). Despite evidence of exposure to 'mainstream' or 'middle-class' orientations and goals among our youth, the norms of 'the street' clearly exert an influence on these young men's lives, whether they embrace them or not (see also Anderson 1999)."

38.   Laub and Sampson 2006; Maruna 2001; Sampson and Laub 1995.

39.   Anderson 1999.

CHAPTER 5: "IT'S KIND OF LIKE CRABS IN A BUCKET": HOW FAMILY AND NEIGHBORHOOD DISADVANTAGE HINDER THE TRANSITION TO ADULTHOOD

1.   Victor Fiorillo, "Q&A: MacArthur Genius Award Winner Angela Duckworth," *Philadelphia*, September 26, 2013.

2.   National Merit Scholarship Corporation, "National Achievement Scholarship Program: History," retrieved from: http://www.nationalmerit.org/nasp.php (accessed December 7, 2015).

3.   Alexander, Entwisle, and Olson 2014.

4.   Our concept of "downshifting" is similar to Harding's (2010) description of "model shifting." Harding argues that cultural heterogeneity creates a wider array of acceptable options for youth to consider at the brink of adulthood

and that the competing models make it difficult to commit to any one pathway. Harding (2010, 158) also finds, as we have, that in high-poverty neighborhoods adolescents are vulnerable to "setbacks" that may push them "off track." As an adaptive strategy, youth then "model shift," perhaps choosing a GED, for instance, over high school graduation. Our concept of "downshifting" is similar in that we observed youth taking routes that were less likely to lead to a college degree. However, our concept is different in that the downshift happens not necessarily because youth are presented with a wider array of acceptable routes, but because the routes they choose expedite their transition and enable them to take a quicker path to independence in response to the challenging family, neighborhood, and personal circumstances common in high-poverty neighborhoods.

5. Settersten and Ray 2010; U.S. Census Bureau, "Figure MS-2: Median Age at First Marriage: 1890 to Present," calculated from Decennial Censuses, 1890 to 1940, and Current Population Survey (CPS), Annual Social and Economic Supplements, 1947 to 2014, retrieved from: http://www.census.gov/hhes/families/files/graphics/MS-2.pdf (accessed December 7, 2015).

6. Estimates for 1970 and 2013 are from the Centers for Disease Control and Prevention (CDC), "FastStats: Birth and Natality," retrieved from: http://www.cdc.gov/nchs/fastats/births.htm (last updated July 20, 2015); and from Mathews and Hamilton 2009.

7. Arnett 2000. James Cote (2000) also writes about the longer road to adulthood, describing it as less of a demographic phenomenon and more of a "psychological" one.

8. For sociological and demographic trends in the shift to delayed adulthood, see Buchmann 1989; Hareven 1994; Rindfuss 1991; Settersten, Furstenberg, and Rumbaut 2005.

9. The number of young adults ages eighteen to thirty-four who lived at home with their parents doubled between 1960 and 2007 (from 8 million to 19 million), going from 22 to 28 percent (Settersten and Ray 2010).

10. For a rebuttal, see Settersten and Ray 2010; see also "Room for Debate: Is It Smart to Delay Adulthood?" *New York Times,* December 25, 2014; Catherine Rampell, "A Generation of Slackers? Not So Much," *New York Times,* May 28, 2011; Jean Chatzky, "How to Avoid Raising a Slacker Millennial," *Fortune,* June 19, 2014; Pew Research Center 2014; Joel Stein, "Millennials: The Me Me Me Generation," *Time,* May 20, 2013.

11. Settersten and Ray 2010.

12. The British social scientist John Bynner (2005) also finds a widening gap between "accelerated routes" to adulthood for disadvantaged young adults and emerging routes traveled at a more leisurely pace by their advantaged counterparts among two British coming-of-age cohorts. See also Carr and Kefalas (2010) for their study on young adults from rural Iowa.

13. Osgood et al. 2005.

14. The British sociologists Andy Furlong and Fred Cartmel (1997) remarked on the "epistemological fallacy of late modernity"; Anthony Giddens (1991) famously wrote on "ontological insecurity"; and the German scholar Ulrich Beck (1992), in *Riskogesellschaft* (*The Risk Society*), described the shift in risk over the life course from the collective to the individual.

15. The East Harlem youth Katherine Newman (1999) writes about also use the phrases "crabs in a bucket" and "crab down syndrome" to refer to detrimental social ties in their families and communities (pp. 92–93).

16. Our approach—both the longitudinal in-depth interviews with youth and their family members and the follow-up ethnographic study—allowed us to observe these processes unfold over time. For example, we interviewed Bob in 2004, 2006, and 2010 and met with him six additional times in 2012. We also interviewed his mother, Teresa, in 2004. We interviewed Bridget's mother, Naomi, and her brother, Carl, in 2004, and we interviewed Bridget for the first time in 2010. During that interaction, we met Naomi again, as well as her husband, Paul, and both of Bridget's sisters. Then, in 2012, we visited Bridget multiple times and came into contact with each of these individuals again in the course of these interactions, plus an aunt and several cousins. Our fieldwork gave us purchase on more than just the youths' perspective—parents and siblings (and sometimes teachers) provided other vantage points.

17. Bob's applications were sent to relatively low-performing schools. With the exception of Howard, the other three—University of Staten Island, Coppin State, and Morgan State—do not graduate even half of their students within four years.

18. Although this chapter focuses on the impact of family, school, and neighborhood contexts on the transition into adulthood for the youth in our study, it is important to recall how the larger structural context shaped their families' circumstances in the first place. As we discussed in chapter 2, the trauma (and addiction) that parents suffered, after years in neighborhoods marked by concentrated poverty and violence, was part of what made the pull of the "crabs in a bucket" so strong. As we and others (Briggs, Comey, and Weismann 2010; Rosenblatt and DeLuca 2012) argue, many MTO families continued to churn through poor and dangerous neighborhoods in the years after MTO, in large part because of the severe housing segregation that has historically plagued Baltimore and the shortage of affordable housing in safer neighborhoods.

19. One form of adaptation to failure is taking on "a status which differs from the one he has lost or failed to gain but which provides at least a something or a somebody for him to become" (Goffman 1952, 457). A person can also "sour" on the once-desired role, no longer giving it any value in public (459). A related strategy is "hedging"—making "sure that he is not completely

committed [to the desired status] . . . keeping two irons in the fire and the more delicate practice of maintaining a joking or unserious relationship to one's involvement. All of these strategies give the mark an out; in case of failure, he can act as if the self that has failed is not one that is important to him" (460).

20. See Settersten, Furstenberg, and Rumbaut 2005.

21. The anthropologist Linda Burton's (2007) work points to the accelerated role transitions and adult responsibilities put on children and adolescents in poor households. We certainly have many examples of what Burton calls "adultification" among the youth in our study.

22. Charette et al. 2015.

23. In fact, overdose is now the leading cause of non-elderly death in the state of Maryland (TFAH/RWJF 2015).

24. BNIA 2013.

25. Witnessing one's peers die violently and young may affect an individual's own sense of mortality. One of the possible effects of post-traumatic stress disorder (PTSD), evidenced by some children and teenagers living in violent environments, is a lack of a future orientation (Garbarino 1995; Kazdin et al. 1983). If you believe that you are not likely to live past early adulthood, this belief can shape your decisions with regard to jobs, family formation, and higher education (Garbarino 1995).

26. Harding 2010.

27. Ibid., 67, 147.

28. As MacLeod (1987) noted in his study of poor youth in the 1980s, the African American youth in his study look at their parents' generation and see that they have far more opportunities in comparison. They also perceive that they can return to school at any time later, and many hold the aspiration to do so for many years.

29. We cannot know for sure whether setting the bar low for success is an act of "satisficing," or adaptation, on the part of youth or a script they employ to cope with the gap between their aspirations and their leveled reality. In some ways, we all justify less optimal outcomes by telling ourselves that "it could have been worse." We thank Monica Bell for this insight.

30. Hoxby and Avery 2013.

31. Tough 2012, 195.

CHAPTER 6: "IN AND OUT BEFORE YOU KNOW IT": THE EDUCATIONAL AND OCCUPATIONAL TRAPS OF EXPEDITED ADULTHOOD

1. See Bozick and DeLuca 2011 for work on the reasons some youth do not attend college.

2. DiPrete and Buchmann 2013.
3. Cherlin 2014.
4. Alexander, Entwisle, and Olson 2014.
5. Royster 2003.
6. Most recently, an experiment found that a college degree does not erase this bias. African American applicants with a college degree and skills identical to those of white applicants received 14 percent fewer requests for interviews (Nunley et al. 2014). This bias may be even stronger against males than females (Gibbs and Bankhead 2000; Wilson 1996).
7. Pager 2003.
8. Bertrand and Mullainathan 2004.
9. Newman 1999.
10. Ralph's mother, Niecy, who we spoke to in 2003, had quit drugs after leaving the Murphy Homes and become an avid church member. But while Ralph benefited from her new lease on life, he suffered cognitive damage from her in utero drug use, which she believed was why he struggled with school and his special education classes.
11. Youth and America's Future 1988.
12. The college enrollment rates in our sample are close to those observed for recent cohorts of graduates of Baltimore's public high schools. Numbers for the Baltimore City Public Schools (BCPSS) show college enrollment rates within twelve months of graduating of close to 50 percent for graduating cohorts between 2007 and 2012 (48.3 percent in 2008; 55.1 percent in 2009; 52.6 percent in 2010; 51.8 percent in 2011; and 50.6 percent in 2012). The percentage enrolling within sixteen to twenty-four months after graduation is slightly higher, going up to 60.8 percent for the twenty-four-month rate in 2009. Although the proportion is slightly lower than that for our sample, the BCPSS rates do not include students enrolling in for-profit schools or trade schools. If they did, we expect that they would be much closer to ours. We are grateful to Jeffrey Grigg and Curt Cronister at Johns Hopkins for compiling these data.
13. Between 2000 and 2009, for-profit institutions increased the share of full-time students they enrolled from 4 to 11 percent (Baum and Payea 2011). Certificate-conferring institutions with programs of less than two years make up 15 percent of all for-profits, and the vast majority of certificates conferred are in occupationally oriented fields (Horn, Li, and Weko 2009; Randwin and Matthews 2013). Low-income youth are overrepresented in for-profit institutions: 19 percent of poor first-year students attend a for-profit institution, compared to only 5 percent of nonpoor first-year students (IHEP 2011). More African American and Hispanic students also begin their postsecondary educations in for-profit institutions than in public or private two- or four-year institutions (IHEP 2011).
14. These numbers are not mutually exclusive, as some youth transferred be-

tween institutions. Five youth entered both a trade school and a community college, while three entered a trade school and a four-year college. Although community colleges are sometimes thought of as stepping-stones to try out college before enrolling in a four-year school, only one four-year entrant in our study, Kim, mentioned later, started her education at a community college first.

15. See Deil-Amen and Rosenbaum 2002.

16. See Deil-Amen and DeLuca 2010; Goyette 2008; Holland and DeLuca 2015; Kerckhoff 2002; Rosenbaum 2001, 2011.

17. A few youth told us that they were turned off by the four-year college route when they looked at college catalogs and saw majors listed, but not trades, which they viewed as more closely linked to future occupations.

18. Arnett 2000, 155. It is important to note here that one of the distinctive aspects of emerging adulthood (or modernity more generally) is that career exploration happens not only after high school but well into college and beyond. This contrasts with earlier periods, when many young adults learned a trade in high school (through vocational education) or entered working-class jobs after graduation that would last a lifetime. As Cherlin (2014) notes, these jobs have all but disappeared.

19. Jennifer Silva (2013) finds a related pattern in her research on working-class youth, who, amid economic uncertainty and job instability, searched for sources of dignity but were often left to create this meaning by crafting stories of their personal struggle against their pasts.

20. Goldrick-Rab 2006.

21. Of the 150 youth in our study, 24 were currently enrolled, or had been enrolled in the past, a high school with a career academy or vocational program. The five career-oriented high schools in Baltimore City were seen as very desirable, as they provided a clearer sense of purpose for youth who were eager for structure and meaning. Delmont, nineteen, picked his school "because it was a trade school and they had carpentry that I was really interested in, and I got accepted." Similarly, for Leona, seventeen, a vocational school was preferable to her neighborhood school because it had trades, and she figured that once she was there, "someone like a counselor [could] come in and to like we sit down and we actually determine different career paths that I can choose. . . . You know how like in high school you get trades and stuff, yeah, that's what I wanted to do." Rico, twenty-one, regretted not having attended a trade school and wished that there had been some occupational programs at his school. He said, "Maybe like an auto mechanic shop, a wood shop, something. Something I just could have learned something in. . . . Everybody always say like what trade they took. What trade you took? I can't tell them I took one . . . I never had a trade." As currently structured, these programs served one very important purpose—giving youth an identity

project to help them stay the course in high school. However, the high school vocational experiences of the youth we followed rarely led to concrete jobs after graduation (with the exception of Gary, described in this chapter).

22. North American Trade Schools lists a program in "Dirt Bike Mechanic School," more formally known as the "Motorcycle and Power Equipment Technology Program." See http://www.natradeschools.edu/dirt-bike -mechanic-school (accessed August 16, 2015).

23. Rosenbaum et al. 1999.

24. Willis 1977.

25. Turney et al. 2006.

26. Department of Labor, Licensing and Regulation, Division of Occupational and Professional Licensing, State of Maryland, "Apply for License—Maryland Board of Barbers," retrieved from: http://www.dllr.state.md.us/license /barbers/barbersapply.shtml (accessed December 4, 2015).

27. The acronym TESST is never spelled out in any advertising materials.

28. What we refer to as "hedging" is similar to Harding's (2010) concept of "simultaneity," in that it describes the consequences for youth who make decisions about school or work in the context of poor information or weak noise-to-signal ratios. But while simultaneity focuses on holding more than one competing cultural model, hedging (as well as the "try, try again" pathway) is more squarely focused on the adaptive strategies that youth employ to increase their chances of completing a credential.

29. As Richard Settersten and Barbara Ray (2010) ask, "How does a young person make it in a 'do it yourself economy'?"

30. Baltimore City Community College offers not only an associate's degree that allows students to take credits toward a bachelor's degree but also more than two dozen applied associate's degree programs and another two dozen certification and licensing programs.

31. ACI eventually closed, without notice, within a year of Brooke's anticipated completion. One day students showed up to class only to find the doors locked and the school shut down for good. See Gigi Barnett, "Columbia Trade School Shuts Down Without Telling Students, Faculty," CBS Baltimore, January 10, 2013, retrieved from: http://baltimore.cbslocal.com /2013/01/10/columbia-trade-school-shuts-down-without-telling-students -faculty/ (accessed December 7, 2015).

32. Adelman 2006.

33. Susan Dynarski, "For the Poor, the Graduation Gap Is Even Wider Than the Enrollment Gap," *New York Times,* June 2, 2015; see also Bailey and Dynarski 2011.

34. Mark Huelsman, "Betrayers of the Dream: How Sleazy For-Profit Colleges Disproportionately Targeted Black Students." *The American Prospect,* July 12, 2015.

35. *Consumer Financial Protection Bureau, Plaintiff, v. Corinthian Colleges, Inc.,* "Complaint for Permanent Injunction and Other Relief," Case 14-7194, U.S. District Court, Northern District of Illinois Eastern Division, retrieved from: http://files.consumerfinance.gov/f/201409_cfpb_complaint_corinthian.pdf (accessed December 7, 2015); Stephanie Armour and Alan Zibel, "For-Profit College Probe Expands," *Wall Street Journal,* January 13, 2014.

36. Baum, Ma, and Payea 2010; Levesque et al. 2008; Wei and Horn 2013; see also Goldrick-Rab 2016.

37. Putnam 2015b.

38. There were a few exceptions in our study. Megan, Leona, Sherika, Candace, and others like them had a better understanding of the requirements to get into college and what was needed to put them on their chosen career paths. Candace wanted to be a lawyer and knew that she was at a disadvantage at CCBC, but she also knew that if she delayed college, she might never go. "I'm going to college because I don't want to *wait* . . . [and] well, college is always *better* than trade school. So I always wanted to do better, I want to go to college! . . . I wish I could go to a better college than CCBC, but like a university. And I would work my hardest." Yet, she was still on her own when it came to learning these details. When asked how she learned about the field of law, she explained: "I don't know, [I] read. Internet. Google. I like, I recently Googled 'law' because I want to be a lawyer, but I want it to really show what kind of lawyer I want to be because there's lots of lawyers you can be."

39. U.S. Department of Education, IES, NCES, "College Navigator: Find the Right College for You," retrieved from: https://nces.ed.gov/collegenavigator/ (accessed December 7, 2015).

40. The full list of schools ever mentioned includes: Baltimore City Community College, Morgan State University, Coppin State University, Community College of Baltimore County, Towson State University, Bowie State University, University of Maryland College Park, TESST, University of Maryland Eastern Shore, Medix, Stevenson University, Johns Hopkins University, Howard University, ITT, Howard County Community College, Notre Dame of Maryland University, Strayer University, North American Trade School, Pennsylvania State University, Sojourner-Douglass College, Lincoln University, Anne Arundel County Community College, Spelman College, Syracuse University, Delaware State University, Cheyney University, University of Baltimore, University of Pennsylvania, Maryland Institute College of Art, Art Institute of New York City, West Virginia University, North American Trade School, Clark University, Morehouse University, Rutgers University, University of Maryland Baltimore County, William Jessup University, Berea College, Northern Virginia Community College, Massachusetts Institute of Technology, University of Georgia, York College, Florida State University, University

of Virginia, Harvard University, Salisbury University, Fairfield, Goucher College, Fairmount State University, Livingstone College, Drexel University, Loyola College, Fashion Institute of Design and Merchandising, University of Tampa, University of Chicago, Everest College, George Washington University, Baltimore Studio of Hair Design, Chesapeake College, University of Miami, Oregon State University, Texas State University, University of Houston, Sam Houston State University, Prairie View A&M University, Louisiana State University, University of South Carolina, University of California Los Angeles.

41. The data on postsecondary institutions attended by recent graduates from the Baltimore City Public Schools was provided by Durham and Olson (2013).

42. See Hoxby and Avery 2013 and Roderick, Coca, and Nagaoka 2011 for more on such "undermatching" among low-income youth.

43. Autor 2014.

CHAPTER 7: "IF IT CAN CAUSE SOME KIND OF CHANGE": POLICIES TO SUPPORT IDENTITY PROJECTS AND REDUCE EDUCATIONAL AND NEIGHBORHOOD INEQUALITY

1. We owe this observation to Monica Bell.

2. In 2015, New York mayor Bill DeBlasio promised to extend access to pre-K to every four-year-old in New York City. See Office of the Mayor of New York City 2014; see also Heckman and Masterov 2007.

3. Sawhill and Karpilow 2014.

4. McCarthy 2015; Open Society Institute-Baltimore 2015; Orlando Patterson, "The Real Problem with America's Inner Cities," *New York Times,* May 9, 2015.

5. Lewis and Burd-Sharps 2015.

6. Howard Schultz and Sheri Schultz, "Connecting Young People with Jobs," *New York Times,* July 13, 2015. President Obama made disconnected youth a focus of his administration in 2010, when he established the White House Council on Community Solutions; see Corporation for National and Community Service, "White House Council for Community Solutions: Q&A with Judith Rodin," retrieved from: http://www.serve.gov/?q=blog-category/white-house-council-community-solutions (accessed on July 29, 2015).

7. Lewis and Burd-Sharps 2015. The costs of ignoring disconnected youth can be measured in terms of youth-focused expenditures on incarceration, Supplementary Security Income (SSI), and other public benefits.

8. One study from 2007 estimated that the costs of childhood poverty in the

United States could conservatively be estimated at $500 billion a year, or 3.8 percent of the nation's GDP. This includes costs due to lower productivity and earnings, increased health problems, and higher levels of crime (Holzer et al. 2007).

9. From U.S. Census Bureau, Current Population Survey (CPS), Annual Social and Economic Supplement (ASEC), "2013 Poverty Table of Contents," retrieved from: http://www.census.gov/hhes/www/cpstables/032014/pov/pov34_100.htm (accessed December 7, 2015).

10. Deutsch et al. 2015.

11. Barbara Samuels, managing attorney at Fair Housing for American Civil Liberties Union of Maryland, personal communication with the authors, October 12, 2015.

12. Rosenblatt 2011.

13. Goetz and Chapple 2010.

14. Popkin et al. 2004; Rosenblatt 2011.

15. Adam Liptak, "Justices Back Broad Interpretation of Housing Law," *New York Times*, June 25, 2015.

16. There were significant barriers and weaknesses in the implementation of the MTO counseling, which is probably one reason that so many MTO families neither leased up at all nor moved to the kinds of communities that policymakers had hoped for. For example, the nonprofit groups in each of the cities disagreed about what kinds of services would be required to implement successful moves to low-poverty neighborhoods, and neither HUD nor Congress had budgeted for these resources, leaving the agencies in each of the sites with the responsibility of raising the matching funds necessary to do the job (Briggs, Popkin, and Goering 2010). There was also considerable variation in the management abilities of the housing authorities and the capacity of the nonprofit partners to provide these counseling services, which resulted in large differences in lease-up rates across the sites. As Xavier de Souza Briggs and his colleagues note, "The non-profit partners in MTO struggled with large workloads, staff turnover, and limited funding and other resources." See also Feins, McInnis, and Popkin 1997.

17. In addition, because there is no source of income protection for renters in Maryland, landlords could and did refuse to lease to voucher holders. The Public Justice Center in Baltimore contacted forty-two apartment complexes located in areas of adjacent Baltimore County that had few voucher holders. In thirty-four of the forty-two complexes—amounting to twelve thousand total units—property managers reported that they did not accept vouchers. Some of the same owners, however, did accept vouchers in complexes located in predominantly African American or lower-income neighborhoods (Barbara Samuels, personal communication with the authors, March 5, 2012).

18. In 1995, public housing residents sued the Department of Housing and Ur-

ban Development (HUD) and the Housing Authority of Baltimore City (HABC) for failure to desegregate Baltimore's public housing and to provide affordable housing in integrated, non-poor neighborhoods across the metropolitan region (Thompson et al. v. HUD et al., #95-309-D. MD). The court ruled that HUD (but not HABC) was liable for violating fair housing laws, due to a long history of discrimination in the siting of public housing in Baltimore that confined low-income African Americans to the inner city. The partial-consent decree called for demolition and redevelopment of Baltimore's high rise public housing sites, development of scattered site housing in a range of neighborhoods across Baltimore city and the region, and the provision of 1,988 housing vouchers, which would provide rental assistance to individuals who had lived in, or been on the waiting list for, subsidized housing in the city prior to 2002. The final case settlement in November of 2012 included the provision of an additional 2,400 vouchers and additional funding to support mobility counseling for new and current voucher holders. See NAACP Legal Defense and Educational Fund, retrieved from: http://www.naacpldf.org/case-issue/thompson-v-hud (accessed on January 26th 2016).

19. Those in the BHMP are offered housing and financial counseling during and after relocation, as well as workshops on budgeting, credit repair, and other household management strategies. The organization administering BHMP also recruits landlords in eligible tracts throughout the metropolitan area. In BHMP, exception payment standards are provided, so that families can rent units priced up to 130 percent of the area fair market rent (FMR), which is a critically important modification. The program vouchers are also fully portable—they can be used in any county without administrative hassle—and security deposit assistance is provided by the Abell Foundation to facilitate first moves. Voucher users must remain in such a neighborhood for a year and then were free to use the voucher without geographic restrictions.

20. The origin neighborhoods of families in BMP were, on average, 30 percent poor and 81 percent African American (DeLuca and Rosenblatt 2015).

21. DeLuca and Rosenblatt 2015; DeLuca, Garboden, and Rhodes 2016.

22. DeLuca, Garboden, and Rhodes 2016. However, Julia Burdick-Will and her colleagues (2011) did find test score improvements in the Baltimore and Chicago MTO sites.

23. With wide variations in rental costs across a city and its suburbs, families can get far more "bang" for their voucher "buck" in cities relative to suburbs (Edin, DeLuca, and Owens 2012; Wood 2014). Thus, a voucher used in affluent suburban Catonsville would be worth more than a voucher used in Sandtown-Winchester; see Binyamin Appelbaum, "Vouchers Help Families Move Far from Public Housing," *New York Times,* July 7, 2015.

24. Collinson and Ganong 2014.

25. Finkel et al. 2015. Brian Jacob and his colleagues (2015) have found that those who use the voucher typically do so in neighborhoods that are no less poor than households with similar incomes but no voucher. In MTO, for example, a third treatment arm was the provision of a "regular" housing choice voucher, one with no geographic restrictions. Families in that group spent not even a single month on average in a neighborhood that was less than 10 percent poor. See also Edin, DeLuca, and Owens, 2012.

26. DeLuca, Garboden, and Rosenblatt 2013; Ellen et al. 2015; McClure 2008, 2010; Metzger 2014; Newman and Schnare 1997; Sard and Rice 2014.

27. Jacob, Kapustin, and Ludwig 2015; Horn, Ellen, and Schwartz 2014.

28. Wood, Turnham, and Mills 2008; see also Gubits et al. 2015 for recent work showing that vouchers can improve family and child well-being for homeless households.

29. DeLuca and Rosenbaum 2003; DeLuca and Rosenblatt 2015; Julian and McCain 2009; Schwartz 2010.

30. Darrah and DeLuca 2014; DeLuca and Rosenbaum 2003; DeLuca and Rosenblatt 2015.

31. Boyd et al. 2010; Briggs, Popkin, and Goering 2010; Briggs and Turner 2006; DeLuca et al. 2010; Edin, DeLuca, and Owens 2012.

32. Sard and Rice 2014.

33. Created in 1986, the LIHTC had helped finance the construction of 2.6 million rental units as of 2013. Developers can apply to receive the tax credits from the state and apply them when they build or rehabilitate rental complexes in which a certain percentage of units are reserved for low-income renters.

34. Ellen et al. 2015; Horn and O'Regan 2011. On average, units funded by the LIHTC are located in tracts that are less poor than other types of subsidized housing, but more poor than the average tract in the metropolitan area.

35. A recent study by the Opportunity Collaborative of the Baltimore Metropolitan Council (2015) showed that those communities throughout Baltimore and its surrounding counties that scored in the bottom two quintiles in terms of "opportunity" held 60 percent of the metropolitan area's subsidized units, whereas the two top quintiles contained only 20 percent of the units.

36. Dan Rodricks and Connor Graham, "Fair Housing" (interview with Dan Pontious, housing policy coordinator for the Opportunity Collaborative of the Baltimore Metropolitan Council), *Midday with Dan Rodricks*, WYPR, July 8, 2015, retrieved from: http://wypr.org/post/fair-housing (accessed December 7, 2015).

37. Massey et al. 2013.

38. Massey et al. 2013; see also Ronald Smothers, "Decades Later, Town Considers Housing Plan for the Poor," *New York Times*, March 3, 1997, and "Low-Income Houses and a Suburb's Fears," *New York Times*, April 5, 1997.

39. Massey and his colleagues (2013) used propensity score models to compare

people who had applied and gotten into the Ethel Lawrence Homes with people who had applied but not yet gotten in.

40. Ibid.
41. Schwartz 2010; Schwartz et al. 2012.
42. Kingsley et al. 2004; Rosenblatt 2011; Tach 2015; Zielenbach 2003. Susan Popkin and her colleagues (2004) at the Urban Institute have conducted pioneering work on the families who were displaced from HOPE VI, which can be found in a number of reports at www.urban.org. For highlights of findings from the program's first decade, see Popkin et al. (2004).
43. Chaskin and Joseph 2013; Joseph and Chaskin 2010; Tach 2009; Kleit 2005.
44. Edelman 2003; Goetz 1996.
45. Brown, Butler, and Hamilton 2001. Joan Walsh, "Baltimore's Shame Is America's Shame: How Job Flight and Police Brutality Spelled Doom for Freddie Gray's Neighborhood," Salon, April 28, 2015, retrieved from: http://www.salon.com/2015/04/28/freddie_gray%E2%80%99s_neighborhood_why_sandtown_winchester_remains_hopeless/ (accessed on June 22, 2015).
46. Rosenblatt and DeLuca (2015) use propensity score models to test whether the trends in Sandtown-Winchester look different from trends in other similar neighborhoods in the city.
47. DeLuca and Rosenblatt 2013.
48. DeLuca and Rosenblatt 2013; Pietila 2010.
49. Justice Policy Institute and Prison Policy Initiative 2015.
50. Using a regression discontinuity design, Will Dobbie and Roland Fryer (2009) find that the impact of the Promise Academies, the school-based portion of the Harlem Children's Zone program, yielded gains large enough to erase the black-white test score gap.
51. Measuring the yield from place-based initiatives is difficult, as there is no ideal "control group" with which to compare (Galster et al. 2004).
52. Theodos, Coulton, and Turner 2012.
53. Kubisch 2005.
54. Fang 2013; Hopkins 2015.
55. Parsad and Spiegelman 2012.
56. Hopkins 2015.
57. Kornrich and Furstenberg 2013.
58. Deutsch 2008; Eccles et al. 2003; Hartmann, Good, and Edmunds 2011.
59. Charmaraman and Hall 2011; Deutsch et al. 2015; Eccles et al. 2003; Peck et al. 2008; Hynes, Greene, and Constance 2012.
60. Bloom 2010; Kemple and Willner 2008.
61. Rosenbaum et al. 2015. Both entering and completing college are strongly related to family income (Bailey and Dynarski 2011). Raj Chetty, Nathaniel Hendren, and their colleagues (2014) have shown that for children born between 1980 and 1982, just under one-third whose families ranked in the tenth

percentile of income attended college by the time they were twenty-one, compared to nearly 90 percent of those in the ninetieth percentile of income.

62. Carnevale, Rose, and Cheah 2011; Grubb 2002; Rosenbaum et al. 2015.

63. Carnevale, Hanson, and Gulish 2013. See also Autor 2014.

64. Rosenbaum et al. 2015. Note that these estimates controlled for student socioeconomic background, race, gender, and test scores.

65. Carnevale, Hanson, and Gulish 2013.

66. Counseling can play an important role—recent research has found that occupational uncertainty or ambiguity can reduce youths' educational outcomes and occupational attainment and stability; see Morgan et al. 2012; Morgan et al. 2013; Sabates, Harris, and Staff 2011; Staff et al. 2010.

67. Deil-Amen and DeLuca 2010; Goyette 2008; Kerckhoff 2002; Rosenbaum 2001, 2011; Rosenbaum and Rosenbaum 2013.

68. Plank, DeLuca, and Estacion 2008; Rosenbaum et al. 2015; Stern et al. 1997; U.S. Department of Education 2013.

69. U.S. Department of Education, "Programs," retrieved from: http://www2 .ed.gov/programs/rigorousprogramsofstudy/index.html (last modified August 12, 2010).

70. Perkins Collaborative Resource Network, "Programs of Study," retrieved from: cte.ed.gov/initiatives/promoting-rigorous-programs-of-study-rpos -project (accessed January 19, 2016).

71. Hoxby and Avery 2013; Bowen and Bok 2002; Roderick, Coca, and Nagaoka 2011; Alon and Tienda 2005; Westlund 2015.

72. MDRC, "The College Match Program: Agenda, Scope, and Goals," retrieved from: http://www.mdrc.org/project/college-match-program#agenda-scope -goals (accessed December 7, 2015).

73. The Upward Bound program has been rigorously evaluated, with mixed results; see Seftor, Mamun, and Schirm 2009.

74. Rosenbaum et al. 2015; Stephan and Rosenbaum 2013.

75. Enrollment has increased fivefold in public two-year colleges over the past forty years; see Rosenbaum, Deil-Amen, and Person 2009.

76. Knapp, Kelly-Reid, and Ginder 2012, table 1; Juszkiewicz 2014. However, there was a drop in community college enrollment between 2012 and 2013 (Juszkiewicz 2014).

77. Rosenbaum, Deil-Amen, and Person 2009; Goldrick-Rab et al. 2009.

78. Knapp, Kelly-Reid, and Ginder 2012, 1; Goldrick-Rab 2010.

79. In a study of 84,000 community college students in Florida, Diana Furchtgott-Roth and her colleagues (2009) found that those who concentrated in a health care field, in computer science, or in engineering saw earnings returns seven years after leaving school that were significantly higher than earnings returns in fields such as communications, human services, and performing arts. These researchers also noted an information deficit among low-income students, who failed to recognize that different fields yielded different returns.

80. Rosenbaum, Deil-Amen, and Person 2009; Rosenbaum, Redline, and Stephan 2007.

81. See also Furchtgott-Roth, Jacobson, and Mokher 2009; Carnevale, Hanson, and Gulish 2013.

82. The Georgetown Center on Education and the Workforce argues for providing students with information about the costs, completion rates, and post-completion employment rates for institutions that they are considering. For most states, these data are available, but not in a user-friendly format (Carnevale, Hanson, and Gulish 2013). We spent time navigating the websites of all the sub-baccalaureate schools the youth in our study attended and observed this firsthand. We found that the websites for BCCC and some of the for-profit trade schools would list course requirements and credit totals for some programs and certificates, but not for others; see, for example, Baltimore City Community College, "Degree Programs and Certificates," retrieved from: http://www.bccc.edu/programs (accessed August 19, 2015). Most of the information on completion and placement rates was hidden in PDF form in links that were not clearly labeled.

83. Deil-Amen and Rosenbaum 2002; Goldrick-Rab 2010.

84. Mokher et al. 2013.

85. Howell, Kurlaender, and Grodsky 2010. Experts also recommend accelerated remedial programs (which require students who came closer to passing entrance tests to do less remedial coursework), learning communities (cohorts of students working together on assignments), early registration (so that students do not miss key requirements), and tutoring, but there is less systematic evidence on these interventions (Goldrick-Rab 2010; Goldrick-Rab et al. 2009; CCSE 2013). Washington State's community colleges have tried to address completion concerns another way. All thirty-four community and technical colleges in the state have the Integrated Basic Education and Skills Training (I-Best) program, which provides training in a range of high-demand workforce trades. I-BEST courses are taught by both a career-technical education (CTE) instructor and a basic skills instructor, with supplemental instruction available outside the classroom for those students who need it (Wachen et al. 2012). This approach avoids the need to require remedial skills classes that do not count toward a degree. In fact, even GED completion can be blended with I-BEST training (Bloom 2010). Because these programs are highly structured, students do not have to navigate complex course offerings and requirements (Wachen et al. 2012). Unfortunately, though participation in I-BEST did increase the probability of earning a certificate or degree, there was no impact on labor market performance, possibly because the evaluation took place during the Great Recession (Zeidenberg, Cho, and Jenkins 2010; Wachen et al. 2012).

86. U.S. Department of Labor, Bureau of Labor Statistics (BLS), "Occupational Employment Statistics: Occupational Employment and Wages, May 2014, 31-

9091 Dental Assistants," retrieved from: http://www.bls.gov/oes/current /oes319091.htm (last modified March 25, 2015); U.S. Department of Labor, BLS, "Occupational Employment Statistics: Occupational Employment and Wages, May 2014, 29-2034 Radiologic Technologists," retrieved from: http://www.bls.gov/oes/current/oes292034.htm (accessed December 7, 2015).

87. Deil-Amen and DeLuca 2010.
88. Holland and DeLuca 2015.
89. Tierney 2011.
90. Austin 2012.
91. See Vedder 2012.
92. Tierney 2011.
93. Horn and Paslov 2014.
94. This relationship holds true even after taking into account differences in student body composition, course provision, and institutional practices (Belfield 2011).
95. Rosenbaum, Deil-Amen, and Person 2009.
96. U.S. Department of Education, "Obama Administration Announces Final Rules to Protect Students from Poor-Performing Career College Programs," October 30, 2014, retrieved from: http://www.ed.gov/news/press-releases /obama-administration-announces-final-rules-protect-students-poor -performing-care (accessed December 7, 2015).
97. Ibid.
98. Autor 2014.
99. Edin and Schaefer 2015.
100. Reed et al. 2012.
101. U.S. Department of Labor, "American Apprenticeship Grants," retrieved from: http://www.dol.gov/apprenticeship/grants.htm (accessed December 7, 2015).
102. Barr 2015.
103. Galen Strawman, "*Thinking, Fast and Slow* by Daniel Kahneman" (review), *The Guardian*, December 13, 2011.
104. Kahneman 2011, 311.
105. Tversky and Kahneman 1973, 1974.
106. Kahneman 2011, 144.
107. "The Problem We All Live With," *This American Life*, July 31, 2015, retrieved from: http://www.thisamericanlife.org/radio-archives/episode/562/the -problem-we-all-live-with (accessed December 7, 2015).
108. Bischoff and Reardon 2014; Reardon and Bischoff 2011.
109. Thomas Edsall, "How Do We Get More People to Have Good Lives?" *New York Times*, June 3, 2015.
110. Carter M. Yang, "Baltimore is the U.S. Heroin Capital," ABC News, March

14, 2015, retrieved from: http://abcnews.go.com/US/story?id=92699 (accessed July 29, 2015).

APPENDIX A: STUDY HISTORY AND METHODOLOGY

1. Hirsch 1983; see also Thompson 1990.
2. Polikoff 2006.
3. Ibid.
4. Families were put on a wait list, and when their number came up a housing counselor gave them the option of taking the most recent apartment on the list, one that the real estate staff had located.
5. The ongoing legacy of institutional racism tends to ensure that predominantly white areas have more resources, including public amenities, relative to predominantly African American areas (Massey and Denton 1993; Pattillo-McCoy 1999; Sampson 2012; Sharkey 2013).
6. The Gautreaux team consisted of James Rosenbaum, Stefanie DeLuca, Greg Duncan, Micere Keels and Ruby Mendenhall.
7. Polikoff 2006, 251.
8. Kaufman et al. 1991.
9. Kling, Liebman, and Katz 2007; Kling et al. 2004; Orr et al. 2003.
10. Kling, Ludwig, and Katz 2005; Orr et al. 2003.
11. Orr et al. 2003.
12. Kling, Liebman, and Katz 2005.
13. Another team of qualitative researchers, led by Xavier de Souza Briggs, Susan Popkin, and John Goering, conducted parallel work in the other three cities between 2003 and 2005, as has been described in their award-winning book *Moving To Opportunity: The Story of an American Experiment to Fight Ghetto Poverty.*
14. The study was supported by the Russell Sage Foundation and by the Center for Health and Wellbeing and the Center for Research on Child Wellbeing at Princeton University.
15. The three household types were as follows: as of July 2003, households with only children eight to thirteen years old and no fourteen- to nineteen-year-olds; households with only children fourteen to nineteen years old; and households with children both eight to thirteen years old and fourteen to nineteen years old. In households with more than one child in a given age group, we identified a "focal child" or "focal youth" at random. In households with children in both age groups, two children—one child and one youth—were identified.
16. The response rate is calculated for the adult interviewees only, not the pri-

mary caregivers. Ten of these primary caregiver interviews supplemented a parent interview, and five replaced parent interviews.

17. In addition to the typical barriers to response, such as being hard to find, the response rate for youth was affected by death (one of our respondents was killed in the course of our study) and foster care placement. We did not interview any youth who lived in out-of-home placement.

18. One interview was conducted with a youth in prison.

19. DeLuca and Rosenblatt 2010; Sanbonmatsu et al. 2006.

20. We were unable to obtain permission to conduct research from the Baltimore County Public Schools, where children whose families remained in the suburbs usually attended school.

21. See DeLuca et al. 2012 for a summary of the mixed-methods papers.

22. Turney et al. 2006.

23. Rosenblatt and DeLuca 2012; Briggs, Popkin, and Goering 2010.

24. DeLuca and Rosenblatt 2010.

25. Clampet-Lundquist et al. 2011.

26. Melody Boyd, then a postdoctoral fellow from the Population Studies Center at the University of Pennsylvania, also assisted with the training and much of the early logistics of the data collection.

27. Very large employers, such as Johns Hopkins University, are referred to by name, as the size of their labor force minimizes the risk that employees who participated in our study could be identified.

28. At no time did we share that the family had been a part of the Moving To Opportunity demonstration or had a housing subsidy. Instead, we identified ourselves to neighbors as "researchers for a study on Baltimore's neighborhoods."

29. Becker 1998.

30. Rosenblatt, Edin, and Zhu 2015.

31. All maps in the book were developed using ArcGIS, drawing on decennial census data for 1990 and 2000. To get reliable, tract-level estimates for 2010, we used the five-year estimates from 2008 to 2012 from the American Community Survey. For tracts with populations less than fifty, we set the percentage of individuals living below poverty to "missing."

32. Jerolmack and Khan 2014, 184.

33. Ibid., 181, 195.

34. Becker 1998.

35. See Edin et al. 2015 for more details on how the youth in our study approached romantic relationships, contraception, and having children.

36. Anderson 1978; Duneier 1992; Liebow 1967; Whyte 1943.

37. Venkatesh 2002.

38. Goffman 2014.

39. Pattillo-McCoy 1999; Pattillo 2007.

40. McAdams 1993, 32.

References |

Abramsky, Sasha. 2013. *The American Way of Poverty: How the Other Half Still Lives.* New York: Nation Books.

Adelman, Clifford. 2006. *The Toolbox Revisited: Paths to Degree Completion from High School Through College.* Washington: U.S. Department of Education (February). Retrieved from: http://www2.ed.gov/rschstat/research/pubs/toolboxrevisit/toolbox.pdf (accessed January 13, 2016).

Afterschool Alliance. 2014. "America After 3PM: New Summer Data." Retrieved from: http://www.afterschoolalliance.org/documents/AA3PM-2014/AA3PM_National_Report.pdf (accessed January 13, 2016).

Akerlof, George A., and Rachel E. Kranton. 2000. "Economics and Identity." *The Quarterly Journal of Economics* 115: 715–53.

Alexander, Karl, Doris Entwisle, and Linda Olson. 2014. *The Long Shadow: Family Background, Disadvantaged Urban Youth, and the Transition to Adulthood.* New York: Russell Sage Foundation.

Alon, Sigal, and Marta Tienda. 2005. "Assessing the 'Mismatch' Hypothesis: Differences in College Graduation Rates by Institutional Selectivity." *Sociology of Education* 78(4): 294–315.

Anderson, Elijah. 1978. *A Place on the Corner.* Chicago: University of Chicago Press.

———. 1990. *Streetwise: Race, Class, and Change in an Urban Community.* Chicago: University of Chicago Press.

———. 1999. *Code of the Street: Decency, Violence, and the Moral Life of the Inner City.* New York: Norton.

Arkes, Jeremy. 2011. "Recessions and the Participation of Youth in the Selling and Use of Illicit Drugs." *International Journal of Drug Policy* 22(5): 335–40.

Arnett, Jeffrey. 1996. *Metalheads: Heavy Metal Music and Adolescent Alienation.* Boulder, Colo.: Westview Press.

———. 2000. "Emerging Adulthood: A Theory of Development from the Late Teens Through the Twenties." *American Psychologist* 55(5): 469–80.

———. 2004. *Emerging Adulthood: The Winding Road from the Late Teens Through the Twenties.* New York: Oxford University Press.

265

Austin, Algernon. 2012. "For-Profit Colleges Have the Poorest Students and Richest Leaders." Working Economics Blog, Economic Policy Institute (August 8). Retrieved from: http://www.epi.org/blog/profit-colleges-poorest-students-richest/ (accessed May 25, 2015).

Autor, David H. 2014. "Skills, Education, and the Rise of Earnings Inequality Among the 'Other 99 Percent.'" *Science* 344(6186): 843–51.

Baer, Daniel, and James J. Corrado. 1974. "Heroin Addicts' Relationships with Parents During Childhood and Early Adolescent Years." *Journal of General Psychology* 124(1): 99–103.

Bailey, Martha J., and Susan M. Dynarski. 2011. "Inequality in Postsecondary Education." In *Whither Opportunity? Rising Inequality, Schools, and Children's Life Chances,* edited by Greg J. Duncan and Richard J. Murnane. New York: Russell Sage Foundation.

Baltimore Metropolitan Council. 2015. "Opportunity Collaborative: Baltimore Regional Plan for Sustainable Development." Baltimore: Baltimore Metropolitan Council (June). Retrieved from: http://www.opportunitycollaborative.org/assets/RPSD_Final_June_2015.pdf?ae56d8 (accessed July 9, 2015).

Baltimore Neighborhood Indicators Alliance (BNIA). 2013. "Life Expectancy." Baltimore: BNIA. Retrieved from: http://bniajfi.org/indicator/Children%20and%20Family%20Health/ (accessed August 18, 2015).

Bandura, Albert. 1997. *Self-Efficacy: The Exercise of Control.* New York: W. H. Freeman/Times Books/Henry Holt & Co.

Barr, Sarah. 2015. "Federal Apprenticeship Grants Include Youth-Focused Programs." *Youth Today,* September 10. Retrieved from: http://youthtoday.org/2015/09/federal-apprenticeship-grants-include-youth-focused-programs/ (accessed October 4, 2015).

Baum, Sandy, Jennifer Ma, and Kathleen Payea. 2010. "Education Pays, 2010: The Benefits of Higher Education for Individuals and Society" (policy brief). College Board Advocacy and Policy Center, Trends in Higher Education Series. Retrieved from: https://trends.collegeboard.org/sites/default/files/education-pays-2010-full-report.pdf (accessed January 13, 2016).

Baum, Sandy, and Kathleen Payea. 2011. "Trends in for-Profit Postsecondary Education: Enrollment, Prices, Student Aid, and Outcomes" (policy brief). College Board Advocacy and Policy Center, Trends in Higher Education Series. Retrieved from: https://trends.collegeboard.org/sites/default/files/trends-2011-for-profit-postsecondary-ed-outcomes-brief.pdf (accessed January 13, 2016).

Bauman, John F. 1987. *Public Housing, Race, and Renewal: Urban Planning in Philadelphia, 1920–1974.* Philadelphia: Temple University Press.

Beck, Ulrich. 1992. *Risk Society: Towards a New Modernity.* London: Sage Publications Ltd.

Becker, Gary. 1991. *A Treatise on the Family.* Cambridge, Mass.: Harvard University Press.

Becker, Howard S. 1998. *Tricks of the Trade: How to Think About Your Research While You're Doing It.* Chicago: University of Chicago Press.

Belfield, Clive R. 2011. "Student Loans and Repayment Rates: The Role of For-Profit Colleges." *Research in Higher Education* 54(1): 1–29.

Bernstein, Basil. 1975. *Class, Codes, and Control: Theoretical Studies Towards a Sociology of Language.* New York: Schocken Books.

Bertrand, Marianne, and Sendhil Mullainathan. 2004. "Are Emily and Greg More Employable Than Lakisha and Jamal? A Field Experiment on Labor Market Discrimination." *American Economic Review* 94(4): 992–1013.

Bielby, William T. 2003. "Rock in a Hard Place: Grassroots Cultural Production in the Post-Elvis Era." *American Sociological Review* 69(February): 1–13.

Bischoff, Kendra, and Sean F. Reardon. 2014. "Residential Segregation by Income, 1970–2009." In *Diversity and Disparities: America Enters a New Century,* edited by John Logan. New York: Russell Sage Foundation.

Bloom, Dan. 2010. "Programs and Policies to Assist High School Dropouts in the Transition to Adulthood." *The Future of Children* 20(1): 89–108.

Bloome, Deirdre, and Ann Owens. 2015. "Assisted Housing and Intergenerational Income Transmission: Exploring the Geography of Unequal Opportunity." Paper presented to the annual meeting of the Population Association of America, San Diego, Calif. (April–May 2).

Bourdieu, Pierre. 1977. *Outline of a Theory of Practice.* Cambridge: Cambridge University Press.

Bourdieu, Pierre, and Jean-Claude Passeron. 1977. *Reproduction in Education, Society, and Culture.* London: Sage Publications.

Bowen, William G., and Derek Bok. 2002. *The Shape of the River: Long Term Consequences of Considering Race in College and University Admissions.* Princeton: Princeton University Press.

Boyd, Melody L., Kathryn Edin, Susan Clampet-Lundquist, and Greg J. Duncan. 2010. "The Durability of Gains from the Gautreaux Two Residential Mobility Programs: A Qualitative Analysis of Who Stays and Who Moves from Low-Poverty Neighborhoods." *Housing Policy Debate* 20(1): 119–46.

Boyd, Melody L., Jason Martin, and Kathryn Edin. 2015. "Youth Civic Engagement: The Role of Neighborhood Deinstitutionalization." Unpublished paper. The State University of New York, College of Brockport.

Bozick, Robert, and Stefanie DeLuca. 2011. "Not Making the Transition to College: School, Work, and Opportunities in the Lives of American Youth." *Social Science Research* 40(4): 1249–62.

Brice-Heath, Shirley. 1983. *Ways with Words: Language, Life, and Work in Communities and Classrooms.* Cambridge: Cambridge University Press.

Briggs, Xavier de Souza. 1997. "Moving Up Versus Moving Out: Neighborhood Effects in Housing Mobility Programs." *Housing Policy Debate* 8(1): 195–234.

———. 1998. "Brown Kids in White Suburbs: Housing Mobility and the Many Faces of Social Capital." *Housing Policy Debate* 9(1): 177–221.

Briggs, Xavier de Souza, Jennifer Comey, and Gretchen Weismann. 2010. "Struggling to Stay Out of High-Poverty Neighborhoods: Housing Choice and Locations in Moving to Opportunity's First Decade." *Housing Policy Debate* 20(3): 383–427.

Briggs, Xavier de Souza, Kadija S. Ferryman, Susan J. Popkin, and María Rendón. 2008. "Why Did the Moving to Opportunity Experiment Not Get Young People into Better Schools?" *Housing Policy Debate* 19(1): 53–91.

Briggs, Xavier de Souza, Susan J. Popkin, and John Goering. 2010. *Moving To Opportunity: The Story of an American Experiment to Fight Ghetto Poverty*. New York: Oxford University Press.

Briggs, Xavier de Souza, and Margery Austin Turner. 2006. "Assisted Housing Mobility and the Success of Low-Income Minority Families: Lessons for Policy, Practice, and Future Research." *Northwestern Journal of Law and Social Policy* 25: 25–61.

Brown, Prudence, Benjamin Butler, and Ralph Hamilton. 2001. *The Sandtown-Winchester Neighborhood Transformation Initiative: Lessons Learned About Community Building and Implementation*. Baltimore: The Annie E. Casey Foundation and the Enterprise Foundation.

Buchmann, Marlis. 1989. "The Life Course in Modern Society: Social Construction and Individual Organization." In *The Script of Life in Modern Society: Entry into Adulthood in a Changing World*, edited by Marlis Buchmann. Chicago: University of Chicago Press.

Burdick-Will, Julia, Jens Ludwig, Stephen W. Raudenbush, Robert J. Sampson, Lisa Sanbonmatsu, and Patrick Sharkey. 2011. "Converging Evidence for Neighborhood Effects on Children's Test Scores: An Experimental, Quasi-Experimental, and Observational Comparison." In *Whither Opportunity? Rising Inequality, Schools, and Children's Life Chances*, edited by Greg J. Duncan and Richard J. Murnane. New York: Russell Sage Foundation.

Bureau of Labor Statistics, U.S. Department of Labor. 2013. *National Longitudinal Survey of Youth 1997 Cohort, 1997–2014 (Rounds 1–16)*. Columbus, Ohio: Center for Human Resource Research, The Ohio State University.

Burton, Linda. 2007. "Childhood Adultification in Economically Disadvantaged Families: A Conceptual Model." *Family Relations* 56(4): 329–45.

Bynner, John. 2005. "Rethinking the Youth Phase of the Life-Course: The Case for Emerging Adulthood." *Journal of Youth Studies* 8(4): 367–84.

Carnevale, Anthony P., Andrew R. Hanson, and Artem Gulish. 2013. *Failure to Launch: Structural Shift and the New Lost Generation*. Washington, D.C.: Georgetown University, Georgetown Public Policy Institute, Center on Education and the Workforce (September). Retrieved from: https://cew.georgetown.edu/wp-content/uploads/2014/11/FTL_FullReport.pdf (accessed May 23, 2015).

Carnevale, Anthony P., Stephen J. Rose, and Ban Cheah. 2011. *The College Payoff: Education, Occupations, Lifetime Earnings*. Washington, D.C.: Georgetown University Center on Education and the Workforce.

Carr, Patrick J., and Maria J. Kefalas. 2010. *Hollowing out the Middle: The Rural Brain Drain and What It Means for America.* Boston: Beacon Press.

Carter, Prudence. 2003. "'Black' Cultural Capital, Status Positioning, and Schooling Conflicts for Low-Income African-American Youth." *Social Problems* 50(1): 136–55.

Casserly, Michael, Jack Jepson, and Sharon Lewis. 2000. *Adequate Financing of Urban Schools: An Analysis of Funding of the Baltimore City Public Schools.* Washington, D.C.: Council of the Great City Schools.

Cauffman, Elizabeth, and Laurence Steinberg. 2012. "Emerging Findings from Research on Adolescent Development and Juvenile Justice." *Victims and Offenders* 7(4): 428–49.

Center for Community College Student Engagement. 2013. "A Matter of Degrees: Engaging Practices, Engaging Students (High-Impact Practices for Community College Student Engagement)." Austin, TX: The University of Texas at Austin, Community College Leadership Program.

Charette, Allison, Chris Herbert, Andrew Jakabovics, Ellen Tracy Marya, and Daniel T. McCue. 2015. *Projecting Trends in Severely Cost-Burdened Renters: 2015–2025.* Joint Center for Housing Studies, Harvard University.

Charmaraman, Linda, and Georgia Hall. 2011. "School Dropout Prevention: What Arts-Based Community and Out-of-School-Time Programs Can Contribute." *New Directions for Youth Development* (Supplement 1): 9–27.

Chaskin, Robert, and Mark Joseph. 2013. "'Positive' Gentrification, Social Control, and the 'Right to the City' in Mixed-Income Communities: Uses and Exceptions of Space and Place." *International Journal of Urban and Regional Research* 37(2): 480–502.

Cherlin, Andrew. 2014. *Labor's Love Lost: The Rise and Fall of the Working-Class Family in America.* New York: Russell Sage Foundation.

Chetty, Raj, and Nathaniel Hendren. 2015. "The Impacts of Neighborhoods on Intergenerational Mobility: Childhood Exposure Effects and County-Level Estimates." Unpublished paper. Harvard University and National Bureau of Economic Research, Cambridge, Mass.

Chetty, Raj, Nathaniel Hendren, and Lawrence F. Katz. 2015. "The Effects of Exposure to Better Neighborhoods on Children: New Evidence from the Moving To Opportunity Experiment." Working Paper 21156. Cambridge, Mass.: National Bureau of Economic Research.

Chetty, Raj, Nathaniel Hendren, Patrick Kline, and Emmanuel Saez. 2014. "Where Is the Land of Opportunity? The Geography of Intergenerational Mobility in the United States." Working Paper 19843. Cambridge, Mass.: National Bureau of Economic Research.

Chung, He Len, Michelle Little, and Laurence Steinberg. 2005. "The Transition to Adulthood for Adolescents in the Juvenile Justice System: A Developmental Perspective." In *On Your Own Without a Net: The Transition to Adulthood for Vul-*

nerable Populations, edited by D. Wayne Osgood, E. Michael Foster, Constance Flanagan, and Gretchen R. Ruth. Chicago: University of Chicago Press.

Clampet-Lundquist, Susan. 2004. "Moving Over or Moving Up? Short-Term Gains and Losses for Relocated HOPE VI Families." *Cityscape* 7(1): 57–80.

———. 2013. "Baltimore Teens and Work: Gendered Opportunities in Disadvantaged Neighborhoods." *Journal of Adolescent Research* 28(1): 122–49.

Clampet-Lundquist, Susan, Kathryn Edin, Jeffrey Kling, and Greg Duncan. 2011. "Moving Teenagers Out of High-Risk Neighborhoods: How Girls Fare Better Than Boys." *American Journal of Sociology* 116(4): 1154–89.

Clampet-Lundquist, Susan, and Douglas S. Massey. 2008. "Neighborhood Effects on Economic Self-sufficiency: A Reconsideration of the Moving To Opportunity Experiment." *American Journal of Sociology* 114(1): 107–43.

Clydesdale, Timothy Thomas. 2015. *The Purposeful Graduate: Why Colleges Must Talk to Students About Vocation.* Chicago: University of Chicago Press.

Coates, Ta-Nehisi. 2015. *Between the World and Me.* New York: Spiegel & Grau.

Coleman, James S. 1990. *Foundations of Social Theory.* Cambridge, Mass.: Belknap of Harvard University Press.

Collinson, Robert, and Peter Ganong. 2014. "Incidence of Voucher Generosity." Working paper, Harvard University.

Conners, Nicola A., Robert H. Bradley, Leanne Whiteside Mansell, Jeffrey Y. Liu, Tracy J. Roberts, Ken Burgdorf, and James M. Herrell. 2004. "Children of Mothers with Serious Substance Abuse Problems: An Accumulation of Risks." *American Journal of Drug and Alcohol Abuse* 30(1): 85–100.

Connolly, Faith, Linda S. Olson, Rachel E. Durham, and Stephen Plank. 2014. *Indicators of College Readiness: A Comparison of High School and College Measures.* Baltimore: Baltimore Education Research Consortium.

Cooley, Charles H. 1902. *Human Nature and the Social Order.* New York: Scribner's.

Corak, Miles. 2013. "Income Inequality, Equality of Opportunity, and Intergenerational Mobility." *Journal of Economic Perspectives* 27(3): 79–102.

Cote, James. 2000. *Arrested Adulthood: The Changing Nature of Maturity and Identity.* New York: New York University Press.

Craig, Starlett, and Barry S. Brown. 1975. "Comparisons of Youthful Heroin Users and Nonusers from One Urban Community." *International Journal of Addiction* 10(1): 53–64.

Darrah, Jennifer, and Stefanie DeLuca. 2014. "'Living Here Changed My Whole Perspective': How Escaping Inner City Poverty Shapes Neighborhood and Housing Choice." *Journal of Policy Analysis and Management* 33(2): 350–84.

DeHaan, Laura, and Shelley MacDermid. 1996. *Identity and Poverty: Defining a Sense of Self Among Urban Adolescents.* New York: Garland.

Deil-Amen, Regina, and Stefanie DeLuca. 2010. "The Underserved Third: How Our Educational Structures Populate an Educational Underclass." *Journal of Education for Students Placed at Risk* 15(1–2): 27–50.

Deil-Amen, Regina, and James E. Rosenbaum. 2002. "The Unintended Consequences of Stigma-Free Remediation." *Sociology of Education* 75(3): 249–68.

DeLuca, Stefanie. 2007. "All Over the Map: Explaining Educational Outcomes of
the Moving To Opportunity Program." *Education Next* 7(4): 28–36.

DeLuca, Stefanie, Greg Duncan, Ruby Mendenhall and Micere Keels. 2010. "Gautreaux Mothers and Their Children: An Update." *Housing Policy Debate* 20(1):
7–25.

———. 2012. "The Notable and the Null: Using Mixed Methods to Understand the
Diverse Impacts of Residential Mobility Programs." In *Neighborhood Effects Research: New Perspectives*, edited by Maarten Van Ham, David Manley, Nick Bailey, Ludi Simpson, and Duncan Maclennan. Dordrecht: Springer.

DeLuca, Stefanie, Philip Garboden, and Anna Rhodes. 2016. *The Power of Place:
How Housing Policy Can Boost Educational Opportunity.* A Report to the Abell
Foundation. Baltimore: Abell Foundation.

DeLuca, Stefanie, Philip Garboden, and Peter Rosenblatt. 2013. "Segregating Shelter: How Housing Policies Shape the Residential Locations of Low-Income Minority Families." *Annals of the American Academy of Political and Social Science*
647(1): 268–99.

DeLuca, Stefanie, and James E. Rosenbaum. 2003. "If Low Income Blacks Are
Given a Chance to Live in White Neighborhoods, Will They Stay? Examining
Mobility Patterns in a Quasi-Experimental Program with Administrative Data."
Housing Policy Debate 14(2): 305–46.

DeLuca, Stefanie, and Peter Rosenblatt. 2010. "Does Moving to Better Neighborhoods Lead to Better Schooling Opportunities? Parental School Choice in an
Experimental Housing Voucher Program." *Teachers College Record* 112(5): 1443–
91.

———. 2013. "Sandtown-Winchester: Baltimore's Daring Experiment in Urban
Renewal: 20 Years Later, What Are the Lessons Learned?" *The Abell Report* 26(8):
1–12. Retrieved from: http://www.prrac.org/pdf/Abell_Sandtown_Report
.pdf (accessed January 13, 2016).

———. 2015. "Walking Away from *The Wire:* Housing Mobility and Neighborhood
Opportunity in Baltimore." Unpublished paper. Loyola University Chicago
and Johns Hopkins University, Baltimore.

DeLuca, Stefanie, Holly Wood, and Peter Rosenblatt. 2011. "Why Poor People
Move (and Where They Go): Residential Mobility, Selection, and Stratification."
Paper presented to the annual meeting of the American Sociological Associa-
tion, Las Vegas (August 20–23).

Desmond, Matthew. 2012. "Disposable Ties and the Urban Poor." *American Journal
of Sociology* 117(5): 1295–1335.

Deutsch, Nancy L. 2008. *Pride in the Project: Teens Building Identities in Urban Contexts.* New York: New York University Press.

Deutsch, Nancy L., Dale A. Blyth, Janet Kelley, Patrick H. Tolan, and Richard M. Lerner. 2015. "Let's Talk After School: The Promises and Challenges of Positive Youth Development for After-School Research, Policy, and Practice." Working paper, The University of Virginia.

DiPrete, Thomas A., and Claudia Buchmann. 2013. *The Rise of Women: The Growing Gender Gap in Education and What It Means for American Schools.* New York: Russell Sage Foundation.

Dobbie, Will, and Roland G. Fryer Jr. 2009. "Are High Quality Schools Enough to Close the Achievement Gap? Evidence from a Social Experiment in Harlem." Working Paper 15473. Cambridge, Mass.: National Bureau of Economic Research.

Duckworth, Angela, Christopher Peterson, Michael Matthews, and Dennis Kelly. 2007. "Grit: Perseverance and Passion for Long-Term Goals." *Journal of Personality and Social Psychology* 92(6): 1087–1101.

Duncan, Greg J., and Richard J. Murnane, eds. 2011. *Whither Opportunity? Rising Inequality, Schools, and Children's Life Chances.* New York: Russell Sage Foundation.

Duneier, Mitchell. 1992. *Slim's Table: Race, Respectability, and Masculinity.* Chicago: University of Chicago Press.

Durham, Rachel E., and Linda S. Olson. 2013. *College Enrollment and Degree Completion of Baltimore City Graduates Through the Class of 2012.* Baltimore: Baltimore Education Research Consortium.

Eccles, Jacquelynne S., and Bonnie L. Barber. 1999. "Student Council, Volunteering, Basketball, or Marching Band: What Kind of Extracurricular Involvement Matters?" *Journal of Adolescent Research* 14(1): 10–43.

Eccles, Jacquelynne S., Bonnie L. Barber, Margaret Stone, and James Hunt. 2003. "Extracurricular Activities and Adolescent Development." *Journal of Social Issues* 59(4): 865–89.

Eccles, Jacquelynne S., and Janice Templeton. 2002. "Extracurricular and Other After-School Activities for Youth." *Review of Research in Education* 26: 113–80.

Edelman, Peter. 2003. *Searching for America's Heart: RFK and The Renewal of Hope.* Washington, D.C.: Georgetown University Press.

Edin, Kathryn, Monica C. Bell, Holly Michelle Wood, and Geniece Crawford. 2015. "Trust but Verify: How Disadvantaged Youth Understand the Price of Parenthood." Unpublished paper. Johns Hopkins University, Harvard University, and Yale University.

Edin, Kathryn, Stefanie DeLuca, and Ann Owens. 2012. "Constrained Compliance: Solving the Puzzle of MTO's Lease-Up Rates and Why Mobility Matters." *Cityscape: A Journal of Policy Development and Research* 14(2): 181–94.

Edin, Kathryn, and Maria Kefalas. 2005. *Promises I Can Keep: Why Poor Women Put Motherhood Before Marriage.* Berkeley: University of California Press.

Edin, Kathryn, and Laura Lein. 1997. *Making Ends Meet: How Single Mothers Survive Welfare and Low-Wage Work.* New York: Russell Sage Foundation.

Edin, Kathryn, and Timothy Nelson. 2013. *Doing the Best I Can: Fatherhood in the Inner City.* Berkeley: University of California Press.

Edin, Kathryn J., and H. Luke Schaefer. 2015. *$2 a Day: Living on Almost Nothing in America.* Boston: Houghton Mifflin Harcourt.

Ellen, Ingrid Gould, Keren Horn, Yiwen Kuai, Roman Pazuniak, and Michael David Williams. 2015. *Effect of QAP Incentives on the Location of LIHTC Properties.* Washington: U.S. Department of Housing and Urban Development, Office of Policy Development and Research (April 7). Retrieved from: http://www.huduser.org/portal//publications/pdf/QAP_incentive_mdrt.pdf (accessed April 7, 2015).

Ellen, Ingrid Gould, and Margery A. Turner. 1997. "Does Neighborhood Matter? Assessing Recent Evidence." *Housing Policy Debate* 8(4): 833–64.

Epp, Gayle. 1998. "Emerging Strategies for Revitalizing Public Housing Communities." In *New Directions in Urban Public Housing,* edited by David P. Varady, Wolfgang F. Preiser, and Francis P. Russell. New Brunswick, N.J.: Rutgers University, Center for Urban Policy Research.

Erikson, Erik H. 1963. *Childhood and Society.* New York: Norton.

———. 1968. *Identity, Youth, and Crisis.* New York: Norton.

———. 1980. *Identity and the Life Cycle.* New York: Norton. (Originally published in 1959.)

Fang, Marina. 2013. "Public Schools Slash Arts Education and Turn to Private Funding." Think Progress, August 5. Retrieved from: http://thinkprogress.org/education/2013/08/05/2412381/public-schools-slash-arts-education-relying-more-on-private-arts-funding/ (accessed June 18, 2015).

Farrington, David P. 1986. "Age and Crime." In *Crime and Justice: An Annual Review of Research,* edited by Michael Tonry and Norval Morris. Chicago: University of Chicago Press.

Feins, Judith D., Debra McInnis, and Susan J. Popkin. 1997. *Counseling in the Moving to Opportunity Program.* Report HC-5953. Washington: U.S. Department of Housing and Urban Development.

Fernández Kelly, Patricia. 1994. "Towanda's Triumph: Social and Cultural Capital in the Transition to Adulthood in the Urban Ghetto." *International Journal of Urban and Regional Research* 18(1): 88–111.

Finkel, Meryl, Jennifer Turnham, Larry Buron, Melissa Vandawalker, Bulbul Kaul, Kevin Hathaway, and Chris Kubacki. 2015. *Housing Choice Voucher Program Administrative Fee Study: Final Report.* Washington: U.S. Department of Housing and Urban Development (August). Retrieved from: http://www.huduser.org/portal/publications/pdf/AdminFeeStudy_2015.pdf (accessed June 25, 2015).

Furchtgott-Roth, Diana, Louis Jacobson, and Christine Mokher. 2009. *Strengthening*

Community Colleges' Influence on Economic Mobility. Washington, D.C.: Pew Trusts Economic Mobility Project (October). Retrieved from: http://www.pewtrusts.org/~/media/legacy/uploadedfiles/wwwpewtrustsorg/reports/economic_mobility/EMPCOLLEGESv10pdf.pdf (accessed May 20, 2015).

Furlong, Andy, and Fred Cartmel. 1997. *Young People and Social Change: Individualization and Risk in Late Modernity.* Berkshire: Open University Press.

Galster, George, Kenneth Temkin, Chris Walker, and Noah Sawyer. 2004. "Measuring the Impacts of Community Development Initiatives: A New Application of the Adjusted Interrupted Time-Series Method." *Evaluation Review* 23(6): 502–38.

Garbarino, James. 1995. "The American War Zone: What Children Can Tell Us About Living with Violence." *Journal of Developmental and Behavioral Pediatrics* 16(6): 391–451.

Gibbs, Jewelle Taylor, and Teiahsha Bankhead. 2000. "Joblessness and Hopelessness: The Case of African American Youth in South Central Los Angeles." *Journal of Ethnic and Cultural Diversity in Social Work* 9(1–2): 1–20.

Giddens, Anthony. 1991. *Modernity and Self-identity: Self and Society in the Late Modern Age.* Stanford, Calif.: Stanford University Press.

Goering, John, and Judith Feins, eds. 2003. *Choosing a Better Life? Evaluating the Moving To Opportunity Social Experiment.* Washington, D.C.: Urban Institute Press.

Goering, John, Judith F. Feins, and Todd M. Richardson. 2002. "A Cross-Site Analysis of Initial Moving To Opportunity Demonstration Results." *Journal of Housing Research* 13(1): 1–30.

Goering, John, Joan Kraft, Judith Feins, Debra McInnis, Mary J. Holin, and Huda Elhassan. 1999. *Moving To Opportunity for Fair Housing Demonstration Program: Current Status and Initial Findings.* Washington, D.C.: U.S. Department of Housing and Urban Development, Office of Policy Development and Research.

Goetz, Edward G. 1996. "Sandtown-Winchester, Baltimore: Housing as Community Development." In *Housing and Urban Development in the U.S.: Learning from Failure and Success,* edited by Willem van Vliet. Thousand Oaks, Calif.: Sage Publications.

———. 2011. "Where Have All the Towers Gone? The Dismantling of Public Housing in U.S. Cities." *Journal of Urban Affairs* 33(3): 267–87.

———. 2013. "Too Good to Be True? The Variable and Contingent Benefits of Displacement and Relocation Among Low-Income Public Housing Residents." *Housing Studies* 23(2): 235–52.

Goetz, Edward G., and Karen Chapple. 2010. "'You Gotta Move': Advancing the Debate on the Record of Dispersal." *Housing Policy Debate* 20(2): 1–28.

Goffman, Alice. 2014. *On the Run: Fugitive Life in an American City.* Chicago: University of Chicago Press.

Goffman, Erving. 1952. "On Cooling the Mark Out: Some Aspects of Adaptation to Failure." *Psychiatry* 15(4): 451–63.

Goldrick-Rab, Sara. 2006. "Following Their Every Move: An Investigation of Social-Class Differences in College Pathways." *Sociology of Education* 79(1): 67–79.

———. 2010. "Challenges and Opportunities for Improving Community College Student Success." *Review of Educational Research* 80(3): 437–69.

———. 2016. *Paying the Price: College Costs, Financial Aid, and the Betrayal of the American Dream*. Chicago: University of Chicago Press.

Goldrick-Rab, Sara, Douglas N. Harris, Christopher Mazzeo, and Gregory Kienzl. 2009. *Transforming America's Community Colleges: A Federal Policy Proposal to Expand Opportunity and Promote Economic Prosperity*. Washington, D.C.: Brookings Institution Metropolitan Policy Program.

Goyette, Kimberly A. 2008. "College for Some to College for All: Social Background, Occupational Expectations, and Educational Expectations over Time." *Social Science Research* 37(2): 461–84.

Grubb, W. Norton. 2002. "Learning and Earning in the Middle, Part I: National Studies of Pre-baccalaureate Education." *Economics of Education Review* 21(4): 299–321.

Gubits, Daniel, Marybeth Shinn, Stephen Bell, Michelle Wood, Sam Dastrup, Claudia D. Solari, Scott R. Brown, Steven Brown, Lauren Dunton, Winston Lin, Debi McInnis, Jason Rodriguez, Galen Savidge, Brooke E. Spellman, and Abt Associates, Inc. 2015. *Family Options Study: Short-Term Impacts of Housing and Services Interventions for Homeless Families*. Washington: U.S. Department of Housing and Urban Development, Office of Policy Development and Research.

Habermas, Tilmann, and Susan Bluck. 2000. "Getting a Life: The Emergence of the Life Story in Adolescence." *Psychological Bulletin* 126(5): 748–69.

Hanlon, Thomas E., Kevin E. O'Grady, Terry Bennett-Sears, and Jason M. Callaman. 2005. "Incarcerated Drug-Abusing Mothers: Their Characteristics and Vulnerability." *American Journal of Drug and Alcohol Abuse* 31(1): 59–77.

Hannerz, Ulf. 1969. *Soulside: Inquiries into Ghetto Culture and Community*. New York: Columbia University Press.

Hanson, David M., Reed W. Larson, and Jodi B. Dworkin. 2003. "What Adolescents Learn in Organized Youth Activities: A Survey of Self-Reported Developmental Experiences." *Journal of Research on Adolescence* 13(1): 25–55.

Hanushek, Eric A., John F. Kain, and Steven G. Rivkin. 2009. "New Evidence About *Brown v. Board of Education*: The Complex Effects of School Racial Composition on Achievement." *Journal of Labor Economics* 27(3): 349–83.

Harding, David. 2010. *Living the Drama: Community, Conflict, and Culture Among Inner-City Boys*. Chicago: University of Chicago Press.

———. 2011. "Rethinking the Cultural Context of Schooling Decisions in Disadvantaged Neighborhoods: From Deviant Subculture to Cultural Heterogeneity." *Sociology of Education* 84(4): 322–39.

Hareven, Tamara K. 1994. "Aging and Generational Relationships: A Historical and Life Course Perspective." *Annual Review of Sociology* 20: 437–61.

Harre, Nikki. 2007. "Community Service or Activism as an Identity Project for Youth." *Journal of Community Psychology* 35(6): 711–24.

Harrington, Michael. 1962. *The Other America: Poverty in the United States.* New York: Macmillan.

Hartmann, Tracey, Deborah Good, and Kimberly Edmunds. 2011. "Keeping High-Risk Youth on Track to Graduation through Out-of-school Time Supports." *Afterschool Matters* 14(Fall): 20–29.

Hartner, Susan. 1999. *The Construction of the Self: A Developmental Perspective.* New York: Guilford Press.

Hauser, Stuart T., Mary Anne B. Vierya, Alan M. Jacobson, and Donald Wertlieb. 1985. "Vulnerability and Resilience in Adolescents: Views from the Family." *Journal of Adolescence* 5(1): 81–100.

Heckman, James J., and Dimitriy V. Masterov. 2007. "The Productivity Argument for Investing in Young Children." *Review of Agricultural Economics* 29(3): 446–93.

Heimer, Karen, and Stacy De Coster. 1999. "The Gendering of Violent Delinquency." *Criminology* 37(2): 277–312.

Hirsch, Arnold, R. 1983. *The Making of the Second Ghetto: Race and Housing in Chicago 1940 to 1960.* New York: Cambridge University Press.

Hirschi, Travis, and Michael Gottfredson. 1983. "Age and the Explanation of Crime." *American Journal of Sociology* 89(3): 552–84.

Holland, Megan, and Stefanie DeLuca. 2015. "I Never Had a Trade": Low-Income African American Youth and the Costly Search for Careers in Sub-baccalaureate Programs." Unpublished paper. State University of New York at Buffalo and Johns Hopkins University, Baltimore.

Holzer, Harry, Diane Whitemore Schanzenbach, Greg J. Duncan, and Jens Ludwig. 2007. *The Economic Costs of Poverty in the United States: Subsequent Effects of Children Growing Up Poor.* Washington, D.C.: Center for American Progress (January 24). Retrieved from: https://www.americanprogress.org/wp-content/uploads/issues/2007/01/pdf/poverty_report.pdf (accessed January 13, 2016).

Hopkins, Marc. 2015. "Uphill Battle to Educate Young Artists." *Art Business News,* March 25. Retrieved from: http://artbusinessnews.com/2015/03/the-uphill-battle-to-educate-young-artists/ (accessed June 22, 2015).

Horn, Keren Mertens, Ingrid Gould Ellen, and Amy Ellen Schwartz. 2014. "Do Housing Choice Voucher Holders Live Near Good Schools?" *Journal of Housing Economics* 23(1): 28–40.

Horn, Keren Mertens, and Katherine M. O'Regan. 2011. *The Low Income Housing Tax Credit and Racial Segregation.* New York: NYU Furman Center.

Horn, Laura, Xiaojie Li, and Thomas Weko. 2009. "Changes in Postsecondary Awards Below the Bachelor's Degree, 1997 to 2007." NCES 2010-167. Washington: U.S. Department of Education, IES, NCES. Retrieved from: http://nces.ed.gov/pubs2010/2010167.pdf (accessed January 16, 2016).

Horn, Laura, and Jonathan Paslov. 2014. "Out-of-Pocket Net Price for College."

NCES 2014-902. *Data Point* (April). Washington: U.S. Department of Education, NCES. Retrieved from: http://files.eric.ed.gov/fulltext/ED544790.pdf (accessed May 25, 2015).

Howell, Jessica S., Michal Kurlaender, and Eric Grodsky. 2010. "Postsecondary Preparation and Remediation: Examining the Effect of the Early Assessment Program at California State University." *Journal of Policy Analysis and Management* 29(4): 726–48.

Hoxby, Caroline, and Christopher Avery. 2013. "The Missing 'One-Offs': The Hidden Supply of High-Achieving Low-Income Students." *Brookings Papers on Economic Activity* (Spring). Retrieved from: http://www.brookings.edu/~/media/Projects/BPEA/Spring-2013/2013a_hoxby.pdf?la=en (accessed August 3, 2015).

Huizinga, David, Shari Miller, and Conduct Problems Prevention Research Group. 2013. *Developmental Sequences of Girls' Delinquent Behavior*. Washington: U.S. Department of Justice, Office of Justice Programs, Office of Juvenile Justice and Delinquency Prevention (December). Retrieved from: http://www.ojjdp.gov/pubs/238276.pdf (accessed July 18, 2015).

Hynes, Kathryn, Kaylin Greene, and Nicole Constance. 2012. "Helping Youth Prepare for Careers: What Can Out-of-School-Time Programs Do?" *Afterschool Matters* 16(Fall): 21–30.

Imbroscio, David. 2008. "[U]nited and Actuated by Some Common Impulse of Passion: Challenging the Dispersal Consensus in American Housing Policy Research." *Journal of Urban Affairs* 30(2): 111–30.

———. 2012. "Beyond Mobility: The Limits of Liberal Urban Policy." *Journal of Urban Affairs* 34(1): 1–20.

Institute for Higher Education Policy (IHEP). 2011. "Portraits: Initial College Attendance of Low-Income Young Adults." Washington, D.C.: IHEP (June). Retrieved from: http://www.ihep.org/sites/default/files/uploads/docs/pubs/portraits-low-income_young_adults_attendance_brief_final_june_2011.pdf (accessed January 13, 2016).

Jacob, Brian A., Max Kapustin, and Jens Ludwig. 2015. "The Impact of Housing Assistance on Child Outcomes: Evidence from a Randomized Housing Lottery." *Quarterly Journal of Economics* 130(1): 465–506.

Jacobson, Joan. 2007. "The Dismantling of Baltimore's Public Housing: Housing Authority Cutting 2,400 Homes for the Poor from Its Depleted Inventory: A 15-Year Trend Shows a Decrease of 42 Percent in Occupied Units." Baltimore: Abell Foundation (update of report first published September 30, 2007). Retrieved from: http://www.abell.org/sites/default/files/publications/Housing.update.1007.pdf (accessed August 19, 2015).

James, William. 1890. *Principles of Psychology*. New York: H. Holt.

Jerolmack, Colin, and Shamus Khan. 2014. "Talk Is Cheap." *Sociological Methods and Research* 43(2): 178–209.

Jones, Nikki. 2009. *Between Good and Ghetto: African-American Girls and Inner-City Violence*. New Brunswick, N.J.: Rutgers University Press.

Joseph, Mark, and Robert Chaskin. 2010. "Life in a Mixed-Income Development: Resident Perceptions at Two Developments in Chicago." *Urban Studies* 47(11): 2347–66.

Julian, Elizabeth K., and Demetria L. McCain. 2009. "Housing Mobility: A Civil Right." In *The Integration Debate: Competing Futures for American Cities*, edited by Gregory Squires and Chester Hartman. New York: Routledge.

Justice Policy Institute and Prison Policy Initiative. 2015. "The Right Investment? Corrections Spending in Baltimore City." Washington, D.C., and Easthampton, Mass.: Justice Policy Institute and Prison Policy Initiative (February). Retrieved from: http://www.justicepolicy.org/uploads/justicepolicy/documents/right investment_design_2.23.15_final.pdf (accessed May 28, 2015).

Juszkiewicz, Jolanta. 2014. *Recent National Community College Enrollment and Award Completion Data*. Washington, D.C.: American Association of Community Colleges (January). Retrieved from: http://www.aacc.nche.edu/Publications/Re ports/Documents/Enrollment_AwardData.pdf (accessed January 19, 2016).

Kahneman, Daniel. 2011. *Thinking, Fast and Slow*. New York: Farrar, Straus and Giroux.

Katz, Jack. 1988. *Seductions of Crime: Moral and Sensual Attractions in Doing Evil*. New York: Basic Books.

Kaufman, Julie E., Susan J. Popkin, James E. Rosenbaum, and Jennifer Rusin. 1991. "Social Integration of Low-Income Black Adults in Middle-Class White Suburbs." *Social Problems* 38(4): 448–61.

Kaushal, Neeraj, Katherine Magnuson, and Jane Waldfogel. 2011. "How Is Family Income Related to Investments in Children's Learning?" In *Whither Opportunity? Rising Inequality, Schools, and Children's Life Chances*, edited by Greg J. Duncan and Richard J. Murnane. New York: Russell Sage Foundation.

Kazdin, Alan E., Nancy H. French, Alan S. Unis, Karen Esveldt-Dawson, and Rosanna B. Sherick. 1983. "Hopelessness, Depression, and Suicidal Intent Among Psychiatrically Disturbed Inpatient Children." *Journal of Consulting and Clinical Psychology* 51(4): 504–10.

Kemple, James J., with Cynthia J. Willner. 2008. *Career Academies: Long-Term Impacts on Labor Market Outcomes, Educational Attainment, and Transitions to Adulthood*. New York: MDRC.

Kerckhoff, Alan C. 2002. "The Transition from School to Work." In *The Changing Adolescent Experience: Societal Trends and the Transition to Adulthood*, edited by Jeylan T. Mortimer and Reed W. Larson. Cambridge: Cambridge University Press.

Kingsley, G. Thomas, Martin D. Abravanel, Mary Cunningham, Jeremy Gustafson, Arthur J. Naparstek, and Margery Austin Turner. 2004. *Lessons from HOPE VI for the Future of Public Housing*. Washington, D.C.: Urban Institute.

Kishiyama, Mark M., Thomas W. Boyce, Amy M. Jimenez, Lee M. Perry, and Robert T. Knight. 2009. "Socioeconomic Disparities Affect Prefrontal Function in Children." *Journal of Cognitive Neuroscience* 21(6): 1106–15.

Kleit, Rachel. 2005. "HOPE VI New Communities: Neighborhood Relationships in Mixed-Income Housing." *Environment and Planning A* 37(8): 1413–41.

Kling, Jeffrey R., Jeffrey B. Liebman, and Lawrence F. Katz. 2005. "Bullets Don't Got No Name: Consequences of Fear in the Ghetto." In *Discovering Successful Pathways in Children's Development: Mixed Methods in the Study of Childhood and Family Life,* edited by Thomas S. Weisner. Chicago: University of Chicago Press.

———. 2007. "Experimental Analysis of Neighborhood Effects." *Econometrica* 75(1): 83–119.

Kling, Jeffrey R., Jeffrey B. Liebman, Lawrence F. Katz, and Lisa Sanbonmatsu. 2004. "Moving To Opportunity and Tranquility: Neighborhood Effects on Adult Economic Self-sufficiency and Health from a Randomized Housing Voucher Experiment." Working Paper 481. Princeton, N.J.: Princeton University, Department of Economics, Industrial Relations Section.

Kling, Jeffrey R., Jens Ludwig, and Lawrence F. Katz. 2005. "Neighborhood Effects on Crime for Female and Male Youth: Evidence from a Randomized Housing Voucher Experiment." *Quarterly Journal of Economics* 120(1): 87–130.

Knapp, Laura G., Janice E. Kelly-Reid, and Scott A. Ginder. 2012. "Enrollment in Postsecondary Institutions, Fall 2010; Financial Statistics, Fiscal Year 2010; and Graduation Rates, Selected Cohorts, 2002–07." NCES 2012-280. Washington: U.S. Department of Education, IES, NCES (March). Retrieved from: http://nces.ed.gov/pubs2012/2012280.pdf (accessed January 13, 2016).

Kneebone, Elizabeth, Carey Nadeau, and Alan Berube. 2011. "The Re-emergence of Concentrated Poverty: Metropolitan Trends in the 2000s." Washington, D.C.: Brookings Institution, Metropolitan Policy Program (November). Retrieved from: http://www.brookings.edu/~/media/research/files/papers/2011/11/03-poverty-kneebone-nadeau-berube/1103_poverty_kneebone_nadeau_berube.pdf (accessed August 19, 2015).

Kornrich, Sabino, and Frank Furstenberg. 2013. "Investing in Children: Changes in Parental Spending on Children, 1972–2007." *Demography* 50(1): 1–23.

Kubisch, Anne C. 2005. "Comprehensive Community Building Initiatives—Ten Years Later: What We Have Learned About the Principles Guiding the Work." *New Directions for Youth Development* 106(Summer): 17–26.

Kucheva, Yana Andreeva. 2013. "Subsidized Housing and the Concentration of Poverty, 1977–2008: A Comparison of Eight U.S. Metropolitan Areas." *City and Community* 12(2): 113–33.

Lareau, Annette. 2003. *Unequal Childhoods: Class, Race, and Family Life.* Berkeley: University of California Press.

Larson, Reed W. 2011. "Positive Development in a Disorderly World." *Research on Adolescence* 21(2): 317–34.

Laub, John H., and Robert J. Sampson. 2006. *Shared Beginnings, Divergent Lives: Delinquent Boys to Age 70.* Cambridge, Mass.: Harvard University Press.

Lauritsen, Janet L., Karen Heimer, and James P. Lynch. 2009. "Trends in the Gender Gap in Violent Offending: New Evidence from the National Crime Victimization Surveys." *Criminology* 47(2): 361–99.

Lawson, Gwendolyn M., Jeffrey T. Duda, Brian B. Avants, Jue Wu, and Martha J. Farah. 2013. "Associations Between Children's Socioeconomic Status and Prefrontal Cortical Thickness." *Developmental Science* 16(5): 641–52.

Levitt, Steven D., and Sudhir A. Venkatesh. 2000. "An Economic Analysis of a Drug-Selling Gang's Finances." *Quarterly Journal of Economics* 115(3): 755–89.

Levesque, Karen, Jennifer Laird, Elisabeth Hensley, Susan P. Choy, Emily Forrest Cataldi, and Lisa Hudson. 2008. *Career and Technical Education in the United States: 1990–2005*. Statistical Analysis Report, NCES 2008-035. Washington: U.S. Department of Education, Institute for Educational Sciences.

Lewis, Kristen, and Sarah Burd-Sharps. 2015. "Zeroing in on Place and Race: Youth Disconnection in America's Cities." Measure of America Project. Brooklyn, N.Y.: Social Science Research Council (June 10). Retrieved from: http://ssrc-static.s3.amazonaws.com/wp-content/uploads/2015/06/MOA-Zeroing-In-Final.pdf (accessed June 22, 2015).

Li, Xiaoming, Bonita Stanton, M. M. Stanton, and Susan Fiegelman. 1996. "Persistence of Drug-Trafficked Behaviors and Intentions Among Urban African-American Early Adolescents." *Journal of Early Adolescence* 16(4): 469–87.

Liebow, Elliot. 1967. *Tally's Corner: A Study of Negro Streetcorner Men*. Boston: Little, Brown.

Lipset, Seymour M. 1996. *American Exceptionalism: A Double-Edged Sword*. New York: Norton.

Ludwig, Jens, Greg J. Duncan, Lisa A. Gennetian, Lawrence F. Katz, Ronald C. Kessler, Jeffrey R. Kling, and Lisa Sanbonmatsu. 2013. "Long-Term Neighborhood Effects on Low-Income Families: Evidence from Moving To Opportunity." Working Paper 18772. Cambridge, Mass.: National Bureau of Economic Research.

Ludwig, Jens, Lisa Sanbonmatsu, Lisa Gennetian, Emma Adam, Greg J. Duncan, Lawrence F. Katz, Ronald C. Kessler, Jeffrey R. Kling, Stacy Tessler Lindau, Robert C. Whitaker, and Thomas W. McDade. 2011. "Neighborhoods, Obesity, and Diabetes: A Randomized Social Experiment." *New England Journal of Medicine* 365(16): 1509–19.

MacLeod, Jay. 1987. *Ain't No Makin' It: Leveled Aspirations in a Low-Income Neighborhood*. Boulder, Colo.: Westview Press.

Magnuson, Katherine, and Jane Waldfogel, eds. 2008. *Steady Gains and Stalled Progress: Inequality and the Black-White Test Score Gap*. New York: Russell Sage Foundation.

Maruna, Shadd. 2001. *Making Good: How Ex-convicts Reform and Rebuild Their Lives*. Washington, D.C.: American Psychological Association.

Massey, Douglas, Len Albright, Rebecca Casciano, Elizabeth Derickson, and David Kinsey. 2013. *Climbing Mount Laurel: The Struggle for Affordable Housing and Social Mobility in an American Suburb.* Princeton, N.J.: Princeton University Press.

Massey, Douglas, and Nancy Denton. 1993. *American Apartheid: Segregation and the Making of the Underclass.* Cambridge, Mass.: Harvard University Press.

Mathews, T. J., and Brady E. Hamilton. 2009. "Delayed Childbearing: More Women Are Having Their First Child Later in Life." National Center for Health Statistics (NCHS) Data Brief 21 (August). Retrieved from: http://www.cdc.gov/nchs/data/databriefs/db21.pdf (accessed August 6, 2015).

Mayer, Susan. 1997. *What Money Can't Buy: Family Income and Children's Life Chances.* Cambridge, Mass.: Harvard University Press.

Mayer, Susan, and Christopher Jencks. 1989. "Growing Up in Poor Neighborhoods: How Much Does it Matter?" *Science* 243: 1441–45.

McAdams, Dan P. 1993. *The Stories We Live By: Personal Myths and the Making of the Self.* New York: Guilford Press.

———. 2006. "The Redemptive Self: Generativity and the Stories Americans Live By." *Research in Human Development* 3(2, 3): 81–100.

McCarthy, Patrick. 2015. "Foundation President's Statement on Freddie Gray Death." Baltimore: Annie E. Casey Foundation (April 28). Retrieved from: http://www.aecf.org/blog/foundation-presidents-statement-on-freddie-gray-death/ (accessed July 29, 2015).

McCarthy, William J., and M. Douglas Anglin. 1990. "Narcotic Addicts: Effect of Family and Parental Risk Factors on Timing of Emancipation, Drug Use Onset, Pre-addiction Incarcerations, and Educational Achievement." *Journal of Drug Issues* 20(l): 99–123.

McClure, Kirk. 2008. "Deconcentrating Poverty with Housing Programs." *Journal of the American Planning Association* 74(1):90–99.

———. 2010. "The Prospects for Guiding Housing Choice Voucher Households to High Opportunity Neighborhoods. *Cityscape* 12(3): 101–22.

Mears, Daniel P., Matthew Ploeger, and Mark Warr. 1998. "Explaining the Gender Gap in Delinquency: Peer Influence and Moral Evaluations of Behavior." *Journal of Research in Crime and Delinquency* 35(3): 251–66.

Metzger, Molly W. 2014. "The Reconcentration of Poverty: Patterns of Housing Voucher Use, 2000–2008." *Housing Policy Debate* 24(3): 544–67.

Mickelson, Roslyn M. and Mokubung Nkomo. 2012. "Integrated Schooling, Life Course Outcomes, and Social Cohesion in Multiethnic Democratic Societies." *Review of Research in Education* 36: 197–238.

Mokher, Christine, Louis Jacobson, James Rosenbaum, and Robert LaLonde. 2013. *Assessment of the Florida College and Career Readiness Initiative: Year 1 Report.* Arlington, Va.: CNA Corporation (November 6). Retrieved from: http://files.eric.ed.gov/fulltext/ED555555.pdf (accessed January 13, 2016).

Morgan, Stephen L., Theodore S. Leenman, Jennifer J. Todd, and Kim A. Weeden.

2012. "Occupational Plans, Beliefs About Educational Requirements, and Patterns of College Entry." *Sociology of Education* 86(3): 197–217.

———. 2013. "Stutter-Step Models of Performance in School." *Social Forces* 91(4): 1451–74.

Newman, Katherine S. 1999. *No Shame in My Game: The Working Poor in the Inner City.* New York: Knopf and Russell Sage Foundation.

Newman, Sandra J., and Ann B. Schnare. 1997. "And a Suitable Living Environment . . . : The Failure of Housing Programs to Deliver on Neighborhood Quality." *Housing Policy Debate* 8(4): 703–42.

Nunley, John M., Adam Pugh, Nicholas Romero, and Richard A. Seals Jr. 2014. "An Examination of Racial Discrimination in the Labor Market for Recent College Graduates: Estimates from the Field." Working Paper auwp2014-06. Auburn, Ala.: Auburn University, Department of Economics.

Office of the Mayor of New York City. 2014. "Ready to Launch: New York City's Implementation Plan for Free, High-Quality, Full-Day, Universal Pre-Kindergarten." New York: Office of the Mayor of New York City, Office of Management and Budget, Department of Education, Administration for Children's Services (January). Retrieved from: http://www1.nyc.gov/assets/home/downloads/pdf/reports/2014/Ready-to-Launch-NYCs-Implementation-Plan-for-Free-High-Quality-Full-Day-Universal-Pre-Kindergarten.pdf (accessed July 29, 2015).

Open Society Institute–Baltimore. 2015. "Statement by OSI-Baltimore in Response to the Killing of Freddie Gray." Baltimore: OSI-Baltimore (April 28). Retrieved from: http://www.audaciousideas.org/2015/04/statement-by-osi-baltimore-in-response-to-the-killing-of-freddie-gray/ (accessed July 29, 2015).

Orr, Larry, Judith D. Feins, Robin Jacob, Erik Beecroft, Lisa Sanbonmatsu, Lawrence F. Katz, Jeffrey B. Liebman, and Jeffrey R. Kling. 2003. "Moving To Opportunity: Interim Impacts Evaluation." Washington: U.S. Department of Housing and Urban Development.

Osgood, D. Wayne, E. Michael Foster, Constance Flanagan, and Gretchen R. Ruth, eds. 2005. *On Your Own Without a Net: The Transition to Adulthood for Vulnerable Populations.* Chicago: University of Chicago Press.

Owens, Ann. 2014. "Assisted Housing and Neighborhood Poverty Dynamics, 1977–2008." *Urban Affairs Review.* Published online December 14, 2014, doi:10.1177/1078087414562007.

Oyserman, Daphna, and Hazel Markus. 1990a. "Possible Selves and Delinquency." *Journal of Personality and Social Psychology* 59(1): 111–25.

———. 1990b. "Possible Selves in Balance: Implications for Delinquency." *Journal of Social Issues* 46(2): 141–57.

Pager, Devah. 2003. "The Mark of a Criminal Record." *American Journal of Sociology* 108(5): 937–75.

Parsad, Basmat, and Maura Spiegelman. 2012. "Arts Education in Public Elementary and Secondary Schools: 1999–2000 and 2009–2010 (NCES 2012-014)." Washington: U.S. Department of Education, IES, NCES. Retrieved from: http:// nces.ed.gov/pubs2012/2012014rev.pdf (accessed June 18, 2015).

Pattillo, Mary. 2007. *Black on the Block: The Politics of Race and Class in the City*. Chicago: University of Chicago Press.

Pattillo-McCoy, Mary. 1999. *Black Picket Fences: Privilege and Peril Among the Black Middle Class*. Chicago: University of Chicago Press.

Peck, Stephen C., Robert W. Roeser, Nicole Zarrett, and Jacquelynne S. Eccles. 2008. "Exploring the Roles of Extracurricular Activity Quantity and Quality in the Educational Resilience of Vulnerable Adolescents: Variable and Pattern-Centered Approaches." *Journal of Social Issues* 64(1): 135–55.

Peterson, James Braxton. 2009. "Corner-Boy Masculinity: Intersections of Inner-City Manhood." In *The Wire: Urban Decay and American Television*, edited by Tiffany Potter and C. W. Marshall. New York: Continuum International Publishing Group.

Pew Charitable Trusts. 2012. *Pursuing the American Dream: Economic Mobility Across Generations*. Washington, D.C.: Pew Charitable Trusts, Economic Mobility Project (July 9). Retrieved from: http://www.pewtrusts.org/en/research-and -analysis/reports/0001/01/01/pursuing-the-american-dream (accessed October 28, 2015).

Pew Research Center. 2014. "Millennials in Adulthood: Detached from Institutions, Networked with Friends." March 7. Retrieved from: http://www.pew socialtrends.org/2014/03/07/millennials-in-adulthood/ (accessed August 18, 2015).

Pietila, Antero. 2010. *Not in My Neighborhood: How Bigotry Shaped a Great American City*. Chicago: Ivan R. Dee.

Plank, Stephen B., Stefanie DeLuca, and Angela Estacion. 2008. "High School Dropout and the Role of Career and Technical Education: A Survival Analysis of Surviving High School." *Sociology of Education* 81(4): 345–70.

Polikoff, Alexander. 2006. *Waiting for Gautreaux: A Story of Segregation, Housing, and the Black Ghetto*. Evanston, Ill.: Northwestern University Press.

Popkin, Susan J., Bruce Katz, Mary K. Cunningham, Karen Brown, Jeremy Gustafson, and Margery A. Turner. 2004. "A Decade of HOPE VI: Research Findings and Policy Challenges." Washington, D.C.: Urban Institute.

Putnam, Robert D. 2015a. *Our Kids: The American Dream in Crisis*. New York: Simon & Schuster.

———. 2015b. "Workforce Training and the American Dream." Washington, D.C.: Thomas B. Fordham Institute (May 20). Retrieved from: http://edexcellence .net/articles/workforce-training-and-the-american-dream (accessed August 19, 2015). Excerpt from Robert D. Putnam, *Our Kids: The American Dream in Crisis* (New York: Simon & Schuster, 2015).

Quercia, Roberto G., and George C. Galster. 1997. "Threshold Effects and the Ex-

pected Benefits of Attracting Middle-Income Households to the Central Cities."
Housing Policy Debate 8(2): 409–36.

Radwin, David, and Morgan Matthews. 2013. *Characteristics of Certificate Completers with Their Time to Certificate and Labor Market Outcomes.* NCES 2013-157. Washington: U.S. Department of Education, Institute for Educational Sciences.

Rainwater, Lee. 1970. *Behind Ghetto Walls: Life in a Federal Slum.* Chicago: Aldine.

Reardon, Sean F. 2011. "The Widening Academic Achievement Gap Between the Rich and the Poor: New Evidence and Possible Explanations." In *Whither Opportunity? Rising Inequality, Schools, and Children's Life Chances,* edited by Greg J. Duncan and Richard J. Murnane. New York: Russell Sage Foundation.

Reardon, Sean F., and Kendra Bischoff. 2011. "Income Inequality and Income Segregation." *American Journal of Sociology* 116(4): 1092–1153.

Reardon, Sean F., Elena Tej Grewal, Demetra Kalogrides, and Erica Greenberg. 2011. "Brown Fades: The End of Court-Ordered School Desegregation and the Resegregation of American Public Schools." *Journal of Policy Analysis and Management* 31(4): 876–904.

Reardon, Sean F., and John T. Yun. 2001. "Suburban Racial Change and Suburban School Segregation, 1987–95." *Sociology of Education* 74(2): 79–101.

Reed, Debbie, Albert Yung-Hsu Liu, Rebecca Kleinman, Annalisa Mastri, David Reed, Samina Sattar, and Jessica Ziegler. 2012. *An Effectiveness Assessment and Cost-Benefit Analysis of Registered Apprenticeship in Ten States.* Oakland, Calif.: Mathematica Policy Research.

Reeves, Richard V. 2013. "The Other American Dream: Social Mobility, Race, and Opportunity." Washington, D.C.: Brookings Institution (August 28). Retrieved from: http://www.brookings.edu/blogs/social-mobility-memos/posts/2013/08/28-social-mobility-race-opportunity-reeves (accessed October 28, 2015).

Reuter, Peter, Robert MacCoun, and Patrick Murphy. 1990. *Money from Crime: A Study of the Economics of Drug Dealing in Washington, D.C.* Santa Monica, Calif.: RAND Corporation.

Rindfuss, Ronald. 1991. "The Young Adult Years: Diversity, Structural Change, and Fertility." *Demography* 28(4): 493–512.

Roderick, Melissa, Vanessa Coca, and Jenny Nagaoka. 2011. "Potholes on the Road to College: High School Effects in Shaping Urban Students' Participation in College Application, Four-Year College Enrollment, and College Match." *Sociology of Education* 84(3): 178–211.

Rosen, Jill. 2014. "Study: Children's Life Trajectories Largely Determined by Family They Are Born Into." The Hub, *Johns Hopkins Magazine,* June 2. Retrieved from: http://hub.jhu.edu/2014/06/02/karl-alexander-long-shadow-research (accessed January 13, 2016).

Rosenbaum, James E. 2001. *Beyond College for All: Career Paths for the Forgotten Half.* New York: Russell Sage Foundation.

———. 2011. "The Complexities of College for All Beyond Fairy-Tale Dreams." *Sociology of Education* 84(2): 113–17.

Rosenbaum, James, Caitlin Ahearn, Kelly Becker, and Janet Rosenbaum. 2015. "The New Forgotten Half and Research Directions to Support Them." William T. Grant Foundation Inequality Paper. New York: William T. Grant Foundation (January). Retrieved from: https://www.luminafoundation.org/files/resources/the-new-forgotten-half-and-research-directions-to-support-them.pdf (accessed January 19, 2016).

Rosenbaum, James E., Regina Deil-Amen, and Ann E. Person. 2009. *After Admission: From College Access to College Success.* New York: Russell Sage Foundation.

Rosenbaum, James E., Stefanie DeLuca, Shazia R. Miller, and Kevin Roy. 1999. "Pathways into Work: Short- and Long-Term Effects of Personal and Institutional Ties." *Sociology of Education* 72(3): 179–96.

Rosenbaum, James E., Julie Redline, and Jennifer Stephan. 2007. "Community College: The Unfinished Revolution." *Issues in Science and Technology* 23(4). Retrieved from: http://issues.org/23-4/rosenbaum/ (accessed December 7, 2015).

Rosenbaum, James E., and Janet Rosenbaum. 2013. "Beyond BA Blinders: Lessons from Occupational Colleges and Certificate Programs for Non-traditional Students." *Journal of Economic Perspectives* 27(2): 153–72.

Rosenblatt, Peter. 2011. "The Renaissance Comes to the Projects: Public Housing, Urban Redevelopment, and Racial Inequality in Baltimore." PhD dissertation, Johns Hopkins University.

Rosenblatt, Peter, and Stefanie DeLuca. 2012. "'We Don't Live Outside, We Live in Here': Neighborhoods and Residential Mobility Decisions Among Low-Income Families." *City and Community* 11(3): 254–84.

Rosenblatt, Peter, and Stefanie DeLuca. 2015. "What Happened in Sandtown-Winchester? Understanding the Impacts of a Comprehensive Community Initiative." *Urban Affairs Review.* Published online December 16, 2015, doi: 10.1177/1078087415617852.

Rosenblatt, Peter, Kathryn Edin, and Queenie Zhu. 2015. "I Do Me: Young Black Men and the Struggle to Resist the Streets." In *The Cultural Matrix: Understanding Black Youth,* edited by Orlando Patterson and Ethan Fosse. Cambridge, Mass.: Harvard University Press.

Royster, Deirdre A. 2003. *The Invisible Hand: How White Networks Exclude Black Men from Blue-Collar Jobs.* Berkeley: University of California Press.

Rutter, Michael. 1979. "Protective Factors in Children's Responses to Stress and Disadvantage." In *Primary Prevention of Psychopathology: Social Competence in Children,* vol. 3, edited by Martha Whalen Kent and Jon E. Rolf. Hanover, N.H.: University Press of New England.

Sabates, Ricardo, Angel L. Harris, and Jeremy Staff. 2011. "Ambition Gone Awry: The Long Term Socioeconomic Consequences of Misaligned and Uncertain Ambitions in Adolescence." *Social Science Quarterly* 92(4): 959–77.

Sampson, Robert J. 2008. "Moving to Inequality: Neighborhood Effects and Experiments Meet Social Structure." *American Journal of Sociology* 114(1): 189–231.

———. 2012. *Great American City: Chicago and the Enduring Neighborhood Effect*. Chicago: University of Chicago Press.

Sampson, Robert J., and John H. Laub. 1992. "Crime and Deviance in the Life Course." *Annual Review of Sociology* 18: 63–84.

———. 1995. *Crime in the Making: Pathways and Turning Points Through Life*. Cambridge, Mass.: Harvard University Press.

Sampson, Robert J., Jeffrey Morenoff, and Thomas Gannon-Rowley. 2002. "Assessing 'Neighborhood Effects': Social Processes and New Directions in Research." *Annual Review of Sociology* 28: 443–78.

Sampson, Robert J., Patrick Sharkey, and Stephen Raudenbush. 2008. "Durable Effects of Concentrated Disadvantage on Verbal Ability Among African-American Children." *Proceedings of the National Academy of Sciences* 105(3): 845–52.

Samuels, Barbara, ACLU of Maryland. 2008. "The 1968 Riots and the History of Public Housing Segregation in Baltimore." Presentation at University of Baltimore symposium "Baltimore 68: Riots and Rebirth." Baltimore (April 4, 2008). Retrieved from: http://www.prrac.org/pdf/riots_and_rebirth.pdf (accessed August 19, 2015).

Sanbonmatsu, Lisa, Jeffrey Kling, Greg Duncan, and Jeanne Brooks-Gunn. 2006. "Neighborhoods and Academic Achievement: Results from the Moving To Opportunity Experiment." *Journal of Human Resources* 41(4): 649–91.

Sanbonmatsu, Lisa, Jens Ludwig, Lawrence F. Katz, Lisa A. Gennetian, Greg J. Duncan, Ronald C. Kessler, Emma Adam, Thomas W. McDade, and Stacy Tessler Lindau. 2011. "Moving To Opportunity for Fair Housing Demonstration Program: Final Impacts Evaluation." Washington: U.S. Department of Housing and Urban Development, Office of Policy Development and Research.

Sard, Barbara, and Douglas Rice. 2014. *Creating Opportunity for Children: How Housing Location Can Make a Difference*. Washington, D.C.: Center on Budget and Policy Priorities.

Sawhill, Isabel V., and Quentin Karpilow. 2014. "How Much Could We Improve Children's Life Chances by Intervening Early and Often?" Center on Children and Families Brief 54. Washington, D.C.: Brookings Institution (July 8). Retrieved from: http://www.brookings.edu/research/papers/2014/07/improve-child-life-chances-interventions-sawhill (accessed July 29, 2015).

Schwartz, Alex. 2006. *Housing Policy in the United States*. New York: Routledge.

Schwartz, Heather. 2010. *Housing Policy Is School Policy: Economically Integrative Housing Promotes Academic Success in Montgomery County, Maryland*. Century Foundation Report. New York: Century Foundation (October 15). Retrieved from: http://www.tcf.org/assets/downloads/tcf-Schwartz.pdf (accessed January 13, 2016).

Schwartz, Heather L., Liisa Ecola, Kristin J. Leuschner, and Aaron Kofner. 2012. *Is Inclusionary Zoning Inclusionary? A Guide for Practitioners*. Santa Monica, Calif: RAND Corporation.

Seftor, Neil S., Arif Mamun, and Allen Schirm. 2009. *The Impacts of Regular Upward Bound on Postsecondary Outcomes 7–9 Years After Scheduled High School Graduation: Final Report.* Princeton, N.J.: Mathematica Policy Research, Inc. (January). Retrieved from: http://www.mathematica-mpr.com/~/media/publications /PDFs/upwardboundoutcomes.pdf (accessed July 29, 2014).

Settersten, Richard A., Jr., Frank F. Furstenberg Jr., and Rubén G. Rumbaut. 2005. *On the Frontier of Adulthood: Theory, Research, and Public Policy.* Chicago: University of Chicago Press.

Settersten, Richard, and Barbara E. Ray. 2010. *Not Quite Adults: Why 20-Somethings Are Choosing a Slower Path to Adulthood, and Why It's Good for Everyone.* New York: Bantam Books.

Sharkey, Patrick T. 2006. "Navigating Dangerous Streets: The Sources and Consequences of Street Efficacy." *American Sociological Review* 71(5): 826–46.

———. 2010. "The Acute Effect of Local Homicides on Children's Cognitive Performance." *Proceedings of the National Academy of Sciences* 107(26): 11733–38.

———. 2013. *Stuck in Place: Urban Neighborhoods and the End of Progress Toward Racial Equality.* Chicago: University of Chicago Press.

Sharkey, Patrick, and Felix Elwert. 2011. "The Legacy of Disadvantage: Multigenerational Neighborhood Effects on Cognitive Ability." *American Journal of Sociology* 116(6): 1934–81.

Sharkey, Patrick T., and Jacob W. Faber. 2014. "Where, When, Why, and for Whom Do Residential Contexts Matter? Moving Away from the Dichotomous Understanding of Neighborhood Effects." *Annual Review of Sociology* 40: 559–79.

Sharkey, Patrick T., Nicole Tirado-Strayer, Andrew V. Papachristos, and C. Cybele Raver. 2012. "The Effect of Local Violence on Children's Attention and Impulse Control." *American Journal of Public Health* 102(12): 2287–93.

Silva, Jennifer. 2013. *Coming Up Short: Working-Class Adulthood in an Age of Uncertainty.* New York: Oxford University Press.

Somers, Margaret R. 1994. "The Narrative Constitution of Identity: A Relational and Network Approach." *Theory and Society* 23(5): 605-49.

Spencer, Margaret Beale, Suzanne G. Fegley, and Vinay Harpalani. 2003. "A Theoretical and Empirical Examination of Identity as Coping: Linking Coping Resources to the Self Processes of African American Youth." *Applied Developmental Science* 7(3): 181–88.

Staff, Jeremy, Angel Harris, Ricardo Sabates, and Laine Briddell. 2010. "Uncertainty in Early Occupational Aspirations: Role Exploration or Aimlessness?" *Social Forces* 89(2): 659–83.

Stephan, Jennifer L., and James E. Rosenbaum. 2013. "Can High Schools Reduce College Enrollment Gaps with a New Counseling Model?" *Educational Evaluation and Policy Analysis* 35(2): 200–219.

Stern, David, Neal Finkelstein, Miguel Urquiola, and Helen Cagampang. 1997. "What Difference Does It Make if School and Work are Connected? Evidence on Cooperative Education in the United States." *Economics of Education Review* 16(3): 213–29.

Suchman, Nancy E., and Suniya S. Luthar. 2000. "Maternal Addiction, Child Maladjustment, and Socio-demographic Risks: Implications for Parenting Behaviors." *Addiction* 95(9): 1417–28.

Sweeten, Gary, Alex R. Piquero, and Laurence Steinberg. 2013. "Age and the Explanation of Crime, Revisited." *Journal of Youth and Adolescence* 42(6): 921–38.

Tach, Laura. 2009. "More Than Bricks and Mortar: Neighborhood Frames, Social Processes, and the Mixed-Income Redevelopment of a Public Housing Project." *City and Community* 8(3): 269–99.

Theodos, Brett, Claudia Coulton, and Margery Turner. 2012. "Residential Mobility and Neighborhood Change: Real Neighborhoods Under the Microscope." *Cityscape* 14(3): 55–90.

Thompson, Ginger. 1990. "Getting Rid of High-Rise Projects?" *The Baltimore Sun*, December 2, 1990.

Tierney, William G. 2011. "Too Big to Fail: The Role of For-Profit Colleges and Universities in American Higher Education." *Change: The Magazine of Higher Learning* 43(6): 27–32.

Toby, Jackson. 1957. "Social Disorganization and Stake in Conformity: Complementary Factors in the Predatory Behavior of Hoodlums." *Journal of Criminal Law and Criminology* 48(1): 12–17.

Tough, Paul. 2012. *How Children Succeed: Grit, Curiosity, and the Hidden Power of Character*. New York: Houghton Mifflin Harcourt.

Trust for America's Health (TFAH) and Robert Wood Johnson Foundation (RWJF). 2015. *The Facts Hurt: A State-by-State Injury Prevention Policy Report*. Washington, D.C.: TFAH (June). Retrieved from: http://healthyamericans.org/reports/injuryprevention15/ (accessed January 13, 2016).

Turbov, Mindy, and Valerie Piper. 2005. *HOPE VI and Mixed-Finance Redevelopments: A Catalyst for Neighborhood Renewal*. Washington, D.C.: Brookings Institution, Metropolitan Policy Program (September). Retrieved from: http://www.brookings.edu/~/media/research/files/reports/2005/9/metropolitanpolicy-piper/20050913_hopevi.pdf (accessed June 21, 2015).

Turney, Kristin, Susan Clampet-Lundquist, Kathryn Edin, Jeffrey Kling, and Greg Duncan. 2006. "Neighborhood Effects on Barriers to Employment: Results from a Randomized Housing Mobility Experiment in Baltimore." In *Brookings-Wharton Papers on Urban Affairs*, edited by Gary Burtless and Janet Rothenberg Pack. Washington, D.C.: Brookings Institution Press.

Turney, Kristin, Rebecca Kissane, and Kathryn Edin. 2012. "After Moving To Opportunity: How Moving to a Low-Poverty Neighborhood Improves Mental Health Among African-American Women." *Society and Mental Health* 3(1): 1–21.

Tversky, Amos, and Daniel Kahneman. 1973. "Availability: A Heuristic for Judging Frequency and Probability." *Cognitive Psychology* 5(2): 677–95.

————. 1974. "Judgments Under Uncertainty: Heuristics and Biases." *Science*, new series 185 (4157): 1124–31.

Uggen, Christopher, and Sara Wakefield. 2005. "Young Adults Reentering the Community from the Criminal Justice System: The Challenge of Becoming an Adult." In *On Your Own Without a Net: The Transition to Adulthood for Vulnerable Populations*, edited by D. Wayne Osgood, E. Michael Foster, Constance Flanagan, and Gretchen R. Ruth. Chicago: University of Chicago Press.

U.S. Census Bureau. 2005–2009. *American Community Survey (ACS)*. Washington: U.S. Department of Commerce, U.S. Census Bureau. Retrieved from: http://www2.census.gov/ (accessed January 27, 2016).

U.S. Census Bureau. 2008–2012. *American Community Survey (ACS)*. Washington: U.S. Department of Commerce, U.S. Census Bureau. Retrieved from: http://www2.census.gov/ (accessed January 27, 2016).

U.S. Department of Education, Office of Planning, Evaluation and Policy Development, Policy and Program Studies Service. 2013. *National Assessment of Career and Technical Education: Interim Report*. Washington: U.S. Department of Education.

U.S. Department of Housing and Urban Development (HUD). 1992. *The Final Report of the National Commission on Severely Distressed Public Housing*. Washington: HUD (August). Retrieved from: https://portal.hud.gov/hudportal/documents/huddoc?id=DOC_9836.pdf (accessed August 20, 2015).

Vedder, Richard. 2012. "In Praise of Profit." *Contexts* 11(4): 19–20.

Venkatesh, Sudhir. 2002. *American Project: The Rise and Fall of a Modern Ghetto*. Cambridge, Mass.: Harvard University Press.

Wachen, John, Davis Jenkins, Clive Belfield, and Michelle Van Noy. 2012. *Contextualized College Transition Strategies for Adult Basic Skills Students: Learning from Washington State's I-BEST Program Model*. New York: Columbia University, Teachers College, Community College Research Center (December). Retrieved from: http://ccrc.tc.columbia.edu/media/k2/attachments/i-best-program-final-phase-report.pdf (accessed May 24, 2015).

Warkentien, Siri. 2015. "Racial School Segregation and the Transition to College." PhD dissertation, Johns Hopkins University Department of Sociology.

Waterman, Alan S. 1993. "Finding Something to Do or Someone to Be." In *Discussions on Ego Identity*, edited by Jane Kroger. Mahwah, N.J.: Erlbaum.

Wei, Christina Chang, and Laura Horn. 2013. "Federal Student Loan Debt Burden of Noncompleters. Stats in Brief (NCES 2013-155)." *National Center for Education Statistics*. Washington: Institute of Education Sciences, U.S. Department of Education.

Weigand, Andrew, Michelle Manno, Sengsouvanh Leshnick, Louisa Treskon, Christian Geckeler, Heather Lewis-Charp, Castle Sinicrope, Mika Clark, and Brandon Nicholson. 2015. "Adapting to Local Context: Findings from the YouthBuild Evaluation Implementation Study." New York: MDRC (February).

Retrieved from: http://www.mdrc.org/sites/default/files/Adapting_to _Local_Context.pdf (accessed December 8, 2015).

Westin, Anna. 2014. "Youth Adjustment in the Context of Neighborhood Disadvantage: A Focus on Stress, Coping, and Mental Health." PhD dissertation, University of Maryland Baltimore County.

Westlund, Erik. 2015. "The Origins and Implications of Postsecondary Academic Mismatch." PhD dissertation, Johns Hopkins University.

Whyte, William Foote. 1943. *Streetcorner Society: The Social Structure of an Italian Slum.* Chicago: University of Chicago Press.

Williams, Rhonda Y. 2005. *The Politics of Public Housing: Black Women's Struggles Against Urban Inequality.* New York: Oxford University Press.

Willis, Paul. 1977. *Learning to Labor: How Working-Class Kids Get Working-Class Jobs.* New York: Columbia University Press.

Wilson, William Julius. 1987. *The Truly Disadvantaged.* Chicago: University of Chicago Press.

———. 1996. *When Work Disappears.* New York: Alfred A. Knopf.

———. 2009. *More Than Just Race: Being Black and Poor in the Inner City.* New York: Norton.

Wodtke, Geoffrey, David J. Harding, and Felix Elwert. 2011. "Neighborhood Effects in Temporal Perspective: The Impact of Long-Term Exposure to Concentrated Disadvantage on High School Graduation." *American Sociological Review* 76(5): 713–36.

Wolfgang, Marvin. 1983. "Delinquency in Two Birth Cohorts." *The American Behavioral Scientist* 27(1): 75–86.

Wood, Holly. 2014. "When Only a House Makes a Home: How Home Selection Matters in the Residential Mobility Decisions of Lower-Income, Inner-City African American Families." *Social Service Review* 88(2): 264–94.

Wood, Michelle, Jennifer Turnham, and Gregory Mills. 2008. "Housing Affordability and Family Well-Being: Results from the Housing Voucher Evaluation." *Housing Policy Debate* 19(2): 367–412.

Youth and America's Future: William T. Grant Foundation Commission on Work, Family, and Citizenship. 1988. *The Forgotten Half: Pathways to Success for America's Youth and Young Families: Final Report.* Washington, D.C.: William T. Grant Foundation Commission on Work, Family, and Citizenship (November). Retrieved from: http://www.aypf.org/wp-content/uploads/2014/12/The-Forgotten-Half-Optimized.pdf (accessed January 13, 2016).

Zeidenberg, Matthew, Sung-Woo Cho, and Davis Jenkins. 2010. "Washington State's Integrated Basic Education and Skills Training Program (I-BEST): New Evidence of Effectiveness." Working Paper 20. New York: Columbia University, Teachers College, Community College Research Center (September). Retrieved from: http://ccrc.tc.columbia.edu/media/k2/attachments/i-best-evidence -effectiveness.pdf (accessed May 24, 2012).

Zielenbach, Sean. 2003. "Assessing Economic Change in HOPE VI Neighborhoods." *Housing Policy Debate* 14(4): 621–55.

Zimmerman, Gregory M., and Steven F. Messner. 2010. "Neighborhood Context and the Gender Gap in Adolescent Violent Crime." *American Sociological Review* 75(6): 958–80.

Index |

Boldface numbers refer to figures and tables.

293